Roman Alcester Series

Volume 2

ROMAN ALCESTER:
DEFENCES AND DEFENDED AREA

GATEWAY SUPERMARKET AND GAS HOUSE LANE

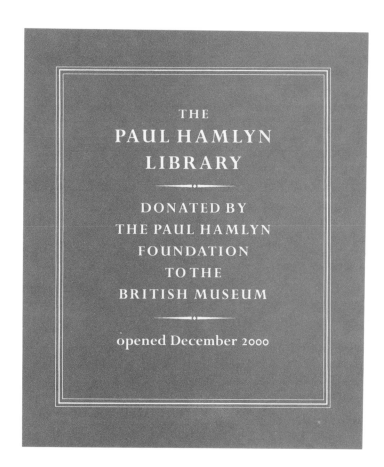

Roman Alcester Series

Volume 2

ROMAN ALCESTER: DEFENCES AND DEFENDED AREA

GATEWAY SUPERMARKET AND GAS HOUSE LANE

edited by Stephen Cracknell

with contributions by
Denise Allen, Justine Bayley,
Matthew Canti, Jeremy Evans, John Evans, Rowan Ferguson,
James Greig, Cathy Groves, Julie Hamilton, Glenys Lloyd-Morgan,
Gerry McDonnell, Beverley Meddens, Lisa Moffett, Graham
Morgan, Quita Mould, Christine Osborne, Stephanie Ratkai,
W A Seaby, Ann Stirland, Harold Smith, Vanessa Straker,
Margaret (Bulmer) Ward, and Lorraine Webb

CBA Research Report 106
Council for British Archaeology
1996

Published 1996 by the Council for British Archaeology
Bowes Morrell House, 111 Walmgate, York YO1 2UA

British Library Cataloguing in Publication Data
A catalogue for this book is available from the British Library

ISSN 0141 7819

ISBN 1 872414 77 X

Typeset from authors' disks by Archetype, Stow-on-the-Wold
<http://ourworld.compuserve.com/homepages/Archetype>

Printed by Thornton & Pearson (Printers) Ltd, Bradford

Front cover Excavation of timber piles from under the town wall
Back cover Reconstruction model showing the Gateway supermarket site as it might have appeared at the beginning
of Phase II, from the north. The granary is being demolished to make way for the town wall

Contents

List of illustrations vii

List of tables ix

List of plates xii

List of microfiche xiii

Acknowledgements xiv

Summary xv

Introduction 1

Gateway supermarket site 4

    Method of investigation 4

    Summary of the stratigraphy 6

    Finds: summary table 18

    Samian ware *by Margaret (Bulmer) Ward* 19

    Roman pottery *by Rowan Ferguson* 20

    Medieval pottery *by Stephanie Ratkai* 31

    Building materials 33

    Metalwork 33

        Copper alloy and lead *by Glenys Lloyd-Morgan* 33

        Iron *by Quita Mould* 33

        Coins *by W A Seaby* 34

        Copper alloy working debris *by Justine Bayley* 34

    Bone 34

        Human bone *by Ann Stirland* 34

        Animal bone *by Julie Hamilton* 34

    Ecological remains 35

        Charred plant remains *by Lisa Moffett* 35

        Snails *by Beverley Meddens* 35

        Waterlogged plant remains *by James Greig* 35

        Soil analysis *by Matthew Canti* 35

    Other finds 36

        Glass and shale *by Denise Allen* 36

    Radiocarbon dating 36

    Discussion 36

Gas House Lane site 42

    Method of investigation 42

    Summary of the stratigraphy 43

    Finds: summary table 58

    Roman pottery *by Jeremy Evans with the samian by Margaret (Bulmer) Ward* 58

    Post-Roman pottery *by Stephanie Ratkai* 97

    Building materials 99

        Stone building materials *by Lorraine Webb* 100

        Ceramic and stone tile *by Lorraine Webb* 100

        Mortar and plaster *by Graham Morgan* 100

        Burnt daub *by Lorraine Webb* 102

    Metalwork 102

        Copper alloy *by Glenys Lloyd-Morgan* 102

        Lead objects *by Glenys Lloyd-Morgan* 104

        Iron objects *Quita Mould* 104

        Iron slag *by Gerry McDonnell* 109

        Coins: summary list *by W A Seaby* 109

    Bone 109

        Worked bone *by Glenys Lloyd-Morgan* 109

        Human bone *by Christine Osborne* 111

        Animal bone *by Julie Hamilton* 111

    Ecological remains 112

        Charred plant remains *by Lisa Moffett* 112

        Plant remains from trench A *by James Greig* 114

    Other finds 115

        Roman glass *by Denise Allen* 115

        Stone objects *by Lorraine Webb with contributions by John Crossling* 119

    Radiocarbon dating 120

    Discussion 120

Defences and defended area 125

    Introduction 125

    Davis Collection and other unpublished pottery from the defended area of the town
    by Jeremy Evans 125

    Ceramic evidence for the occupation of the defended area *by Jeremy Evans* 126

    Animal bone *by Julie Hamilton* 126

    Discussion *by Stephen Cracknell* 127

Bibliography 141

Index 149

List of illustrations

Gateway supermarket site

1   Location of the excavations and topography of the Roman town. 1: Mahany's site M. 2: Tomlinson's Tibbet's Close site. 3: Nos 9 and 11 Meeting Lane. 4: Taylor's Malt Mill Lane site. 5: Bear Inn. 6: Mahany's site K. 7: Bulls Head Yard Phase 1. 8: Bulls Head Yard Phase 2. 9: Market site. 10: Coulters Garage. 11: Midland Bank. 12: Royal Oak Passage. 13: Lamb's Gas House Lane watching brief. 14: Booth's Malt Mill Lane site. 15: Cracknell's Tibbet's Close (AL 12). 16: 27 High Street. 17: Rectory Garden 1991. 18: Baptist chapel. 19: No 1 Meeting Lane/38 Henley St. 20: Old Police Station, Henley St. (AL18, Gateway supermarket site; AL23, Gas House Lane site.)

2   Location of the Gateway supermarket site areas A–E, boreholes, and adjacent archaeological work at Bull's Head Yard (Phases 1 and 2) (7 & 8), the Market site (9), Coulters Garage (10), the Midland Bank (11), and on the Moorfield Marsh (14)

3   Height of gravel river terrace and extent of peat and early clay deposits in the vicinity of the Gateway supermarket site

4   NW side of area B: composite section showing Phase A bank at NE end

5   Remains of Phase A bank at NE end of area B and contemporary deposits. For safety reasons only the central part of the trench was dug full depth

6   The substantial stone building and contemporary remains at the end of Phase I in areas C, D, E and Coulters Garage area 7 (excluding Phase I/II remains). (Area 7 plan courtesy of Paul Booth)

7   North west side of the central baulk across area D: NE–SW section showing Phase IIa rampart (left), construction and demolition layers of town wall (centre) and Phase I stone building and subsequent layers (right)

8   The surviving traces of the construction of the Phase IIa town wall and the Phase IIb bastion, and other contexts dating to the end of Phase IIb. Areas C, D, E.

9   SE side of area E: section showing robber trench of town wall (left) and layers through which it cut

10   Roman pottery, nos 1–18

11   Roman pottery, nos 19–27

12   Medieval pottery

13   Copper alloy and iron finds

14   Pollen diagram

Gas House Lane

15   Details of site layout

16   Subdivision of the site into phases with approximate equivalences and dates

17   Key to plans and sections

18   Main structural features on trenches B, C, 7(n), and 7(s). **A: early to mid-3rd century** – first defences on trench 7(s), Building A (Phase C12), Building D (Phase C22). **B: mid-3rd century** – Building B (Phase C13), Building E (Phase C23), and possibly Building F (Phases C32–3). **C: mid- to late 3rd century** – Building C (Phase C14), posthole and slot on trench B (Phase C24), and possibly Building F (Phases C32–3). **D: late 3rd century** – post settings on trench 7(n) (Phase C15)

19   Trench B, early features: Period A and Phase C21

20   Trench B, Phase C22, building D, with earlier layers in S

21   Trench B, Phase C23, building E, with Phase C24 features hatched, and earlier layers still visible in SW

22   Trench 7(n), Phase C12, building A

23   Trench 7(n), Phase C13, building B

24   Trench 7(n), Phase C14, building C

25   Trench 7(n), Phase C15

26   Trench C, south end, showing features of various phases: Phase C32, building F, posthole (2111) and clay floor (2112); Phase C33, building F beam slot (2093); Phase C33, ?more traces of building C, 2081, 2082, 2083, 2097, 2098, 2110, with the E edge of trench 7(n) Phase C14 shown for comparison (see also fig 24)

27   Section showing the SW side of trench A with the 4th century defences at the S end

28   Section showing the western end of the NW side of trench B

29   Section showing the SW side of trench 7(s) including the first town defences

30   Section showing the SW side of trench 7(n)

31   Section showing the SW side of trench C, south end

32   Form type series for fabrics B.11–C.15

33   Form type series for fabrics F.21–G.44

34   Form type series for fabrics M.22–M.43

35   Form type series for fabrics O.22–O.24

36   Form type series for fabrics O.24–O.27

37   Form type series for fabrics O.29–O.55

38   Form type series for fabrics O.81–R.37

39   Form type series for fabrics R.41–W.15

40   Histogram of major fabric proportions for 3rd-century phases from trench B (by sherd nos)

41   Histogram of major fabric proportions for 3rd-century phases from trench C (by sherd nos)

42   Histogram of major fabric proportions for 3rd-century phases from trench 7(n) (by sherd nos)

43   Histogram of major fabric proportions for later 4th-century phases from the site, arranged from earliest to latest (by sherd nos)

44   Samian

45   Histogram showing distribution of samian per decade, from all phases; maximum 691 vessels against date of manufacture

46   Function figures for Neatham, Chichester, and *Verulamium*, after Millett (1979) and Millett and Graham (1986)

47   Common finds by phase from Gas House Lane (numbers of bones are derived from site lists and are counted on a different basis to the numbers given in the bone report). The vertical logarithmic scale indicates the number of examples of a particular material divided by the number of pottery sherds from the same phase.

48   Common finds ratios by period from Segontium, North Wales

49   Ceramic small finds and graffiti

50   Map showing principal sources of fabrics at Alcester in the late 4th century by fabric weight (trench 5, Period D). Greywares are attributed to south-west England and South-Western Brown Slipped Ware to the vicinity of Wycombe.

51   Map showing principal sources of fabrics at Alcester in the early 3rd century (figures taken from Phase C13 by fabric weight). Severn Valley wares are attributed to lower Severn Valley and greywares to Tiddington area arbitrarily.

52   Medieval pottery

53   Ceramic and stone tile

54   Burnt daub

55   Copper alloy objects

56   Iron objects

57   Worked bone objects

58   Roman glass

59   Stone objects

Defences and defended area

60   Section showing the SW side of Mahany's site K XIV

List of tables

Text

Gateway supermarket site

1   Dates of archaeological phases at the Gateway supermarket site
2   Summary table of all finds excavated at the Gateway supermarket site
3   Summary of samian forms and fabrics from all contexts
4   Area B. Number of sherds of each fabric in Phase C contexts
5   Areas A, C, D, and E. Number of sherds in each fabric in Roman and post-Roman contexts.
6   Proportions of different fabric groups present at sites in Alcester
7   Area B. Minimum number of vessels in each fabric
8   Areas A, C, D, and E. Minimum number of vessels in each fabric
9   Vessel proportions on excavated sites in Alcester (in percentages)
10 Stratified iron finds from area B
11 Stratified iron finds from areas C, D, and E
12 Summary table of all finds excavated

Gas House Lane

13 Cirencester coarsewares (after Keeley 1986)
14 Frequencies of BB1 forms in period C
15 Bar Hill BB1 forms compared with Gas House Lane Period C
16 Functional analysis of BB1 forms from stratified Roman deposits at Gas House Lane
17 Functional analysis of vessels in fabric C.11
18 Summary of samian forms and fabrics from all contexts (maximum numbers)
19 Average sherd weight of Central Gaulish samian by phase
20 Proportions of Oxfordshire, Nene Valley, and South-Western Brown Slipped wares by phase
21 Functional analysis of Nene Valley ware (F52) from Gas House Lane
22 Functional analysis of Oxfordshire colour-coated ware F51 (excluding *mortaria* M71)
23 Functional analysis of Nene Valley wares (F52) and South-Western Brown Slipped ware (F59) from selected 4th-century groups
24 Relative proportions of finewares from various later 4th-century groups in the south-west
25 Vessels represented in Malvernian ware, fabric G44
26 Functional analysis of Severn Valley wares from Gas House Lane
27 Functional analysis of vessels in oxidized fabric O81
28 Functional analysis of Gas House Lane pottery by minimum number of rims per context
29 Functional analysis of Gas House Lane pottery by percentage of rim (RE)
30 Comparative functional analyses from Silchester, Ilchester, and Cirencester
31 Incidence of sooting and limescale (?) by fabric
32 Gas House Lane: proportions of pottery finewares and glass compared with the total quantity of pottery and glass combined
33 Proportion of finewares from various Roman sites in southern England
34 Iron objects
35 Total list of plants represented by charred and ?chemically preserved remains
36 Stray finds of building materials perhaps indicating well-appointed buildings nearby
37 Proportions of South, Central, and East Gaulish samian and total numbers of sherds from various Alcester sites with over 50 samian sherds

Defences and defended area

38 Alcester High Street Builder's Yard fabric proportions
39 Occurrence of forms in the High Street Builder's Yard group
40 Function figures for Alcester High Street Builder's Yard
41 Excavations on the defences
42 Excavations within the defended area

Microfiche

Gateway supermarket site

M1   Typical soil section, boreholes A–L
M2   Typical soil section, boreholes M–U
M3   Numbers of sherds found in boreholes
M4   Proportions of different medieval pottery fabrics
M5   Weight and thickness of ceramic tile
M6   Weight of ceramic tile from each area
M7   Weight and thickness of limestone tile
M8   Weight and thickness of sandstone tile
M9   Mortar analysis
M10   Coins
M11   Animal bone. Fragment numbers and minimum numbers of individuals. Area B, Phases A and B
M12   Animal bone. Fragment numbers and minimum numbers of individuals. Areas A, C, D and E, Phases I, IIa, and IIb
M13   Charred plant remains from area B
M14   Charred plant remains from areas D and E
M15   Snail species from the soil sample
M16   Wood species from the copper alloy working deposit (805)
M17   Seeds and molluscs from the 130cm sample
M18   Pollen and spores not included in the pollen diagram (fig 14)
M19   Radiocarbon dates from the timber piles below the wall and bastion

Gas House Lane

M20   Cross-joins between phases at Gas House Lane
M21   Major fabric groups recovered in sieved sample (no of sherds)
M22   Percentages of fabrics occurring by phase
M23   Description of fabrics occurring at Gas House Lane
M24   Occurrence of form types by phase in stratified Roman deposits
M25   Fabric concordance of old fabric numbers with new fabric codes
M26   Summary of samian forms and fabrics from Period C (general) (maximum numbers)
M27   Summary of samian forms and fabrics from Phase C12 (maximum numbers)
M28   Summary of samian forms and fabrics from Phase C13 (maximum numbers)
M29   Summary of samian forms and fabrics from Phase C14 (maximum numbers)
M30   Summary of samian forms and fabrics from Phase C15 (maximum numbers)
M31   Summary of samian forms and fabrics from Phase C21 (maximum numbers)
M32   Summary of samian forms and fabrics from Phase C22 (maximum numbers)
M33   Summary of samian forms and fabrics from Phase C23 (maximum numbers)
M34   Summary of samian forms and fabrics from Phase C31 (maximum numbers)
M35   Summary of samian forms and fabrics from Phase C32 (maximum numbers)
M36   Summary of samian forms and fabrics from Phase C33 (maximum numbers)
M37   Summary of samian forms and fabrics from Phases D and D2 (maximum numbers)
M38   Summary of samian forms and fabrics from Periods E and unstratified (maximum numbers)
M39   Numbers of post-Roman sherds in each fabric and trench
M40   Number of ceramic tile types in each fabric (except unidentifiable fragments)
M41   Number of ceramic and stone tile types in each phase (excludes unidentifiable fragments)
M42   Number of ceramic tile fragments in each fabric and phase (excludes identified types: for these see tables M40 and M41)
M43   Particle size and solubility of mortar/plaster samples
M44   Burnt daub
M45   Quantities of slag recovered
M46   Coins
M47   Fragment numbers, skeletal elements and MNIs of mammal bone, Period C
M48   Fragment numbers, skeletal elements and MNIs of mammal bone, Period D
M49   Fragment numbers and MNIs of birds at Gas House Lane
M50   Fragment numbers in samples (Period C)
M51   Fragment numbers, skeletal elements and MNIs of mammal bone in the tanning pit (2001/1)
M52   Cattle epiphyseal fusion data, Periods C and D

M53   Cattle mandible wear stage data (Grant 1982), Periods C and D
M54   Cattle horn core stage data (Armitage 1982), Periods C and D
M55   Sheep epiphysial fusion data, Periods C and D
M56   Sheep mandible wear stage data (Grant 1982), Periods C and D
M57   Sheep mandible wear data (Payne 1973), Periods C and D
M58   Pig epiphyseal fusion data, Periods C and D
M59   Pig mandible wear stage date (Grant 1982), Periods C and D
M60   Selected cattle measurements (mm unless otherwise indicated) (von den Driesch 1976), Periods C and D
M61   Selected sheep measurements (mm unless otherwise indicated) (von den Driesch 1976), Periods C and D
M62   Roman and post-Roman charred and chemically preserved plants: detailed listing

List of plates

Gateway supermarket site

1   Detail of section across Phase A bank at NE end of area B. (See section fig 4). Looking NW. Scale 2m

2   Trenches cutting through Phase A bank and deeper deposits outside it at NE end of area B. (See section in fig 4). Looking W. Scale 2m

3   North corner of the substantial Phase I stone building, demolished at the beginning of Phase II. The corner was subsequently robbed during Phase III. Area D. Looking S. Scale 2m

4   Section across centre of area D. Showing Phase IIa rampart (left), wall foundation trench (centre), and Phase I stone building (right). (See fig 7). Looking SE. Scale 2m

5   Surviving tops of timber piles in centre of area D belonging to Phase IIa town wall foundation. Looking E. Scale 1m

6   Traces of timber lacing in Phase IIa town wall foundation at the SE end of area D. Looking E. Scale 2m

7   Horizontal squared timber (469) slot trench in Phase IIa town wall foundation as first seen in trench II, area D. Note the voids where vertical timbers once stood and the void of the horizontal timber continuing under the baulk. Looking NW. Scale 0.5m

8   Rubble and voids in the fill of the Phase IIb construction trench for the tower. Area E. Looking W. Scale 1m

9   Reconstruction model showing the southern part of the Gateway supermarket site as it might have appeared at the beginning of Phase II, from the north. The granary is being demolished to make way for the town wall

Gas House Lane

10   Trench 7(s), south-west side, Period B, showing the first town defences: with the rampart at top centre and possible ditch deposits in the foreground (see fig 29). Looking W. Horizontal scales 2m; vertical scale 1m

11   Trench 7(s), south-west side, Period B, detail of the first town rampart (see fig 29). Looking SW. Scale 2m

12   Trench 7(n), Period C. Showing Phase C12 building A slot (7210) and stake holes (see fig 22, and Phase C13 building B (see fig 23). Looking SE. Scales 2m

13   Trench B, Phase C23, building E (see fig 21). (The modern pig burial just to the S of the building had not been excavated at the time of the photograph.) Looking NW. Scales 2m

14   Trench C, south end, Phases C32, C33 (see fig 26). Beam slot of building F at lower left; rubble spreads, perhaps associated with building C in centre. Looking NW. Scales 2m

15   Trench A, S end, Period D. Showing the 4th-century rampart which backed the town wall. Timber piles associated with the wall were later recovered from the very SW corner of the trench (top left in photo). The dark staining above the tail of the rampart is modern chemical contamination. Looking SW. Horizontal scales 2m; vertical scale 1m

16   Trench C, north end, Period E. Late medieval stone-lined pit. Looking S. Horizontal scale 0.5m, vertical scale 1m

17   Trench C, north end, Period E. Late medieval drying kiln with partially excavated flue. Looking SW. Scale 0.5m

List of microfiche

Gateway supermarket M1:A2

    Stratigraphic description of the excavated areas M1:A2

    Watching brief M1:B14

    Boreholes. M1:B14

    Pottery from the boreholes M1:C3

    Medieval pottery M1:C3

    Dendrochronology. M1:C7

    Building materials M1:C8

    Metalwork. M1:C13

    Bone. M1:D5

    Ecological remains M1:D11

    Other finds M1:E8

    Radiocarbon dating. M1:E8

Gas House Lane M1:E9

    List of main periods M1:E9

    Method of excavation M1:E9

    Details of the stratigraphy and structures M1:E12

    List of site contexts. M1:G14

    Roman pottery M2:C6

    Post-Roman pottery M3:C5

    Building materials M3:C12

    Metalwork. M3:D9

    Bone. M3:F7

    Ecological remains M4:A4

Acknowledgements

Gateway supermarket site

I would like to thank Gateway Foodmarkets for allowing us to excavate the site and for financing an exhibition of the discoveries which went on show in the finished supermarket. The model of the granary and the town wall shown in plate 9 was made by Zette Braithwaite for the exhibition. English Heritage, the Manpower Services Commission Community Programme Scheme, and Warwickshire Museum financed the excavation and publication work. English Heritage also funded the radiocarbon dating. Helen Maclagan provided support and assistance and read drafts of the report. I would also like to thank Paul Booth for comments on this report. The drawings are by Justin Jones and Chris Smith. Lastly, I am grateful to my site supervisor Ian Greig and all those who worked on the site or in the office.

The Sheffield Dendrochronological Laboratory is funded by English Heritage.

Gas House Lane

The work was financed by Tom Pettifer (Contractors) Ltd, Stratford-on-Avon District Council, and English Heritage. The programme was organized by Warwickshire Museum, with the final stages of the post-excavation process being completed by Archetype Archaeological Services of Stow-on-the-Wold.

The iron objects were radiographed by Glynis Edwards and the minerally preserved organic remains were identified by Jacqui Watson, both at the Ancient Monuments Laboratory, English Heritage. Conservation was by Barbara Clayton.

Lorraine Webb would like to thank Stephanie Ratkai and Jeremy Evans for their assistance with her reports. Jeremy Evans would wish to thank Nick Cooper, Jane Evans and Victoria Buteux for discussions and comparisons of fabric types and Severn Valley forms and Malcolm Lyne and Stephanie Ratkai for several useful discussions. Lisa Moffett is grateful to Phillipa Tomlinson for identifying tree buds and gorse leaves. The bulk of the pottery drawings are the work of Nina and Robin Dallaway. The samian drawings, the site plans and some of the pottery drawings are the work of Steve Rigby.

Summary

This report brings together all the known information on Roman Alcester's defences and defended area. In recent years several excavations have revealed new data although these parts of the town are still not as well known as the extramural area to the south. The excavations in the late 1980s at the Gateway supermarket site and in 1988–9 at Gas House Lane are reported in detail. Where the printed text is amplified in the microfiche the location is indicated at the start of each section, eg [M1:A10]. The text was completed in December 1992.

Gateway supermarket site

Excavations in 1985–6 at the Gateway supermarket site investigated the town's defences in a series of area excavations, trenches, and boreholes. Two defensive lines were revealed. The first defences consisted of a timber-revetted clay-and-gravel rampart surviving to a maximum height of 0.65m. In front of the rampart the ground sloped away into the marsh but there was no formal ditch. The defences are thought to date to about AD 200 on the basis of excavations elsewhere but no useful dating evidence was recovered from this site. They enclosed an area of about 8ha.

The large stone 'granary' dated by Booth to c AD 300 (Booth 1985) was partly re-excavated. This building lay well outside the first defences which by this time were probably derelict. The building was demolished to make way for a second phase of the defences: a stone wall on a new alignment, dating to late in the 4th century.

A total length of 17m of the wall was excavated revealing foundations made up of timber piling and stone supporting a timber lattice on which the wall itself would have been built. None of the superstructure survived. There was no ditch. The dating evidence for the wall suggests a *terminus post quem* of AD 364.

An external tower was also located. Although the construction techniques were similar to those used for the wall, it was clear that it was added to an already existing structure and dendrochronology suggests that the tower was probably built seven years later than the wall. The circuit now enclosed an area of about 9.3ha.

The finds, which are summarized in table 2, included the detritus of copper alloy working, charred remains of beetroot and hemlock, a coin hoard dating to the late 4th century, and timbers from below the town wall.

Gas House Lane

Excavations at Gas House Lane in 1989 revealed further traces of the defences and also buildings within the defended area. Apart from possible traces of agricultural or horticultural activity, there appears to have been little activity before the construction of the first, earthwork, defences around AD 200. This date is based largely on an assessment of the earliest finds on the site and is not derived directly from the defences themselves.

Several timber and timber-and-stone buildings can be dated to the 3rd century and two building plots on slightly different alignments have been recognized. Modern truncation had removed the early 4th-century deposits on part of the site. Activity intensified in the late 4th century with the building of the town wall but only a small part of the wall was visible in the corner of one of the trenches. A medieval drying kiln and a possible tanning pit were also found. The drying kiln has now been reconstructed on a nearby site.

The finds are summarized in table 12. The large collection of Roman pottery from the site is one of the most significant assemblages from the town. It is presented as a type series with detailed discussion of implications for the dating of the site and of the pottery supply to the town. Other finds include charred asparagus seeds (confirming evidence from Tibbet's Close), relics of antler working, and another coin hoard of a similar date to the one from the Gateway supermarket site.

Defences and defended area

There have now been thirteen investigations of the town's defences since they were first identified in the mid-1960s and a similar number of sites have been dug within the defended area. Most sites have been small but, in addition to the two reported here, there were two others of significant size: Mahany's site M (Mahany 1994) and Cracknell's Tibbet's Close site (Cracknell 1985a).

It now seems increasingly likely that, when the decision was taken to defend the town, the most defensible area, rather than the most populous area, was selected. The new defences, probably dating to about AD 200, were protected by a river on their north and east sides and protected by a marsh on the west side and – to a lesser extent – on the south side. They enclosed an area of about 8ha, which was largely undeveloped; the total area of the town (including the new 'addition') was up to 35ha. This analysis seems to imply that, in Alcester's case at least, defensive considerations outweighed matters of civic pride in the selection of the area for protection.

Development of the defended area was rapid but not to the detriment of the rest of the town and large buildings, including a possible granary, were erected in the unprotected zone. The variety of buildings in the defended zone appears to mirror the range from the extramural area. By the middle of the 4th century the marshes to the west of the town were drying out and when the stone wall was built the circuit was extended to the south and west to include an extra 1.3ha. There has not been a great deal of work in the area between the two defensive lines but at present it appears that this area was not developed. The date of the later defences – provisionally after AD 364 – would make Alcester one of the last towns in Britain to be walled. This may reflect its distance from any external threat but a second factor may be important: although it was in the territory of the Dobunni, the town was almost on the edge of the *civitas* and in the late Roman period Alcester may have become a local administrative centre of some kind. The decision to renew the defences in stone and add an external tower should be seen in this context.

Finally, three future research areas are suggested. Firstly, the development of the defended area from about AD 200 can provide significant information on the dating of artefacts at about that time and also about residuality in general. Secondly, evidence from the defended area broadly confirms the trading connections with the Severn Valley basin noted in earlier volumes on Alcester and further investigations are warranted. Thirdly, Alcester's western cemetery should have a high priority in any archaeological strategy for the town. The publication of the 'Alcester series' by the CBA has revealed the broad outlines of the urban structure leaving the disposal of the dead as the one major lacuna in our knowledge.

Übersicht

Dieser Bericht ist eine Zusammenfassung aller anerkannten Informationen über die Verteidigung und über das verteidigte Gebiet der römischen Stadt Alcester. In den letzten Jahren resultierten eine Anzahl von Ausgrabungen in neue Daten, obwohl dieser Teil der Stadt noch nicht so gut bekannt ist als das südlich gelegene Gebiet außerhalb der Mauer. In diesem Bericht werden die in der letzten Hälfte der 80ger Jahre am Supermarkt Gateway und die 1988–89 in der Gas House Lane stattgefundenen Ausgrabungen in allen Einzelheiten beschrieben. Wo der gedruckte Text im Microfische verstärkt ist, ist der Ort dieser Ausgrabungen nach jedem Abschnitt angegeben, wie z. B. [M1:A10] Der Text wurde Dezember 1992 fertiggestellt.

Das Gelände am Supermarkt Gateway

Bei einer Serie von Flächen-, Gräben- und Bohrlöchergrabungen wurden 1985–86 am Gelände des Supermarktes Gateway die Abwehrmaßnahmen der Stadt untersucht. Dabei fand man zwei Abwehrlinien. Die ersten waren Schutzwalle, die mit Lehm, Holz und Kiesel ausgekleidet waren und die, bei einer Maximalgröße von 0, 65 m, erhalten geblieben sind. Vor dem Schutzwall fiel der Boden in einen Sumpf ab; es gab keinen formellen Graben. Aufgrund anderswo durchgeführter Ausgrabungen, nimmt man an, daß man diese Verteidigungslinien um 200 AD datieren kann. Jedoch wurden auf diesem Gelände keine brauchbaren Datierungshinweise gefunden.

Der große, aus Stein gebaute 'Getreidespeicher' wurde von Booth (1985) circa um 300 AD datiert und wurde teilweise wieder ausgegraben. Dieses Gebäude lag weit außerhalb der ersten Befestigung und war um diese Zeit wahrscheinlich aufgegeben. Es wurde demoliert, um einer neuen Phase Abwehrmaßnahmen den Weg freizugeben: einer Steinmauer mit neuem Alignement, die bis spät in das 4. Jahrhundert datiert.

Bei der Ausgrabung eines insgesamt 17m langen Abschnitts der Mauer wurde festgestellt, daß das Fundament aus Holzstapeln und Steinen gebaut war und das wiederum ein Holzgitter stützte, auf dem die Mauer selbst gebaut worden wäre. Keine der Superstrukturen sind überliefert worden. Es gab auch keinen Graben. Der Datierungsbeweis läßt annehmen, daß diese Mauer aus *terminus post quem* 364 AD stammt.

Einen äußeren Turm hat man auch ausfindig gemacht und obwohl die Baumethode der der Mauer ähnelt, ist man sich bewußt, daß dieser äußere Turm an eine schon existierende Struktur angebaut war. Die Dendrochonomie läßt annehmen, daß der Turm wahrscheinlich 7 Jahre später als die Mauer gebaut wurde. Dieser Kreis umzirkelte nun einen 9.3 ha große Fläche.

Die in der Tabelle 2 zusammengefaßten Funde beinhalten kupferlegierten Detribus, verkohlte rote

Rüben- und Schierlingsreste, einen Münzenvorrat, der bis spät in das 4. Jahrhundert zurückdatiert werden kann, und Holz vom Fundament der Stadtmauer.

Gas House Lane

1989, bei den Ausgrabungen am Gelände der Gas House Lane, wurden weitere Spuren der Befestigung und dazugehörende Gebäude in der verteidigten Fläche entdeckt. Bis auf die Spuren der Landwirtschaft- und Gartenbautätigkeit, scheint es um 200 AD vor dem Bau des ersten Schanzwerks und Befestigung wenig Aktivitäten gegeben zu haben. Dies begründet sich größtenteils auf die Einschätzung des Datums der auf dem Gelände ausgegrabenen Funde und stammt nicht direkt von den Abwehrmaterialien selbst.

Eine Anzahl von Holz- und Holzsteinbauten können bis in das 3. Jahrhundert zurückdatiert werden und zwei sich auf einem klein bißchen abgerückten Alignement befindende Grundstücke sind anerkannt worden. Moderne Beschneidungsmethoden hatten die Ablagerungen des frühen 4. Jahrhunderts auf einer Seite des Geländes entfernt. Mit dem Bau der Stadtmauer im spätem 4. Jahrhundert begann auch ein regeres Leben. Es war aber nur ein kleines Stück der Mauer von der Ecke einer der Gräben sichtbar. Ein mittelalterlicher Trockenofen und eine Gerbereigrube wurden auch gefunden. Der Trockenofen wurde auf einem in der Nähe gelegenen Gelände rekonstruiert.

Die Funde sind auf der Tabelle 12 zusammengefaßt. Die große Sammlung der auf diesem Gelände gefundenen römischen Tonscherben ist eine der bedeutensten Amblagen aus dieser Stadt. Es wird als eine Art Serie mit ausführlichen Diskussionen über Implikationen hinsichtlich der Datierung des Geländes und der Töpferwaren-Versorgung der Stadt dargestellt. Andere Funde bestehen aus verkohlten Spargelsamen, die das Beweismaterial aus Tibbet's Close bestätigen, Geweihverarbeitungen – Relikte und noch einen Münzenschatz ähnlicher Datierung wie dieser am Gelände des Supermarkts Gateway.

Abwehrmaßnahmen und das verteidigte Gebiet

Seitdem die Stadtabwehrmaßnahmen in der Mitte der 60er Jahre des 20. Jahrhunderts zuerst identifiziert wurden, gab es bis jetzt 13 Untersuchungen. Eine ähnliche Zahl von Geländen wurde innerhalb des verteidigten Gebietes ausgegraben. Die meisten Gelände waren klein. Zusätzlich zu den beiden in diesem Band beschriebenen Geländern, gab es noch zwei, die von bedeutender Größe waren: das noch zu erscheinende Gelände Mahany M (Mahany 1994) und Cracknells Tibbet's Close (Cracknell 1985a).

Es wird immer glaubwürdiger, daß, wenn die Entscheidung getroffen wurde die Stadt zu verteidigen, nicht das einwohnerstärkste Gebiet zur Verteidigung bestimmt wurde sondern das Gebiet, das am fähigsten war, die Stadt zu verteidigen. Die neuen Abwehreinrichtungen, die wahrscheinlich bis zurück um 200 AD datiert werden können, wurden durch einen Fluß auf der nördlichen und östlichen Seite und durch einen Sumpf an der westlichen und – im geringeren Maße – der südlichen Seite geschützt. Sie umringten ein ungefähr 8 ha langes Gebiet, welche zum Großteil unterentwickelt war. Die Gesamtfläche der Stadt (einschließlich der neuen 'Zugabe') betrug bis zu 35 ha. Diese Analyse scheint anzuzeigen, daß zu mindest im Falle der Stadt Alcester die Verteidigungs-überlegungen bei der Auswahl, des Schutzgebietes den Vorrang über den Burgerstolz hatten.

Die Entwicklung der verteidigten Gebiete war schnell. Trotzdem geschah diese nicht zum Schaden der restlichen Stadt und große Gebäude, einschließlich eines möglichen Getreidespeichers, wurden in der ungeschützten Zone errichtet. Die Vielfaltigkeit der Gebäude in der verteidigten Zone wiederspiegelt die der außerhalb der Mauer errichteten Bauten. Um die Mitte des 4. Jahrhunderts trockneten die Sümpfe westlich der Stadt aus und, als die Steinmauer gebaut wurde, wurde dabei der Umkreis südlich und westlich davon erweitert, um einem zusätzlichen 1,3 ha großen Gebiet Platz zu machen. Keine große Anzahl von Arbeiten wurde zwischen den beiden Verteidigungslinien unternommen. Es scheint zur Zeit, als ob dieses Gebiet nicht entwickelt wurde. Das Datum der letzteren Verteidigungslinie – vorläufig nach 364 AD – würde Alcester zu einer der letzten der Städte in Britannien machen, die mit einer Mauer umgeben war. Das könnte den Mangel jeglicher äußerlichen Drohung reflektieren aber auch ein zweiter Faktor könnte von Bedeutung gewesen sein: Obwohl Alcester ein Territorium der Dobunni war, war die Stadt fast am Rande der *civitas* und in der späten römischen Periode könnte die Stadt eine Art regionales Verwaltungszentrum geworden sein. Die Entscheidung die Verteidigungslinien aus Stein zu erneuern und einen außerhalb gelegenen Turm dazuzubauen, muß in diesem Kontext gesehen werden.

Schließlich werden drei weitere Forschungsgebiete vorgeschlagen. Erstens, die Untersuchung der Entwicklung des verteidigten Gebietes um 200 AD. Sie kann wichtige Informationen über die Datierung der Artifakten um diese Zeit herum und generell über den Überrest geben. Zweitens, Beweismaterialien des verteidigten Gebietes allgemein bestätigen die Handelsverbindungen mit dem Becken des 'Severn Valley', die in früheren Bänden über Alcester erwähnt worden sind, und weitere Untersuchungen sind deshalb gerechtfertigt. Drittens, der westliche Friedhof in Alcester sollte in allen archäologischen Strategien der Stadt vorrängig behandelt werden. Mit der Publikation der 'Alcester Serie' sind die breiten Umrisse der städtichen Strukturen bekannt geworden, bleibt nur noch die bedeutende Lakuna in unserem Wissen zu füllen: Die Beseitigung der Toten.

Sommaire

Ce rapport réunit toutes les informations connues à ce jour sur les fortifications d'Alcester à l'époque romaine et sur la zone qu'elles protégeaient. Ces dernières années, plusieurs fouilles ont révélé de nouvelles informations mais ces parties de la ville ne sont toujours pas aussi bien connues que la zone extra-muros au sud. Ce rapport présente en détail les résultats des fouilles menées au site du supermarché Gateway à la fin des années 80 et à Gas House Lane en 1988–9. Lorsque le texte imprimé est amplifié sur microfiche, l'emplacement est indiqué au commencement de chaque section, par exemple [M1:A10]. La rédaction du texte fut complétée en 1992.

Site du supermarché Gateway

Les fouilles menées en 1985–6 sur le site du supermarché Gateway avaient examiné les fortifications de la ville à travers une série de fouilles dans la zone en question, de tranchées et de trous de sonde. Elles révélèrent deux lignes de fortifications. Les premières consistaient en un rempart en argile et gravier revêtu de bois dont les vestiges atteignaient une hauteur maximale de 0,65m. Devant le rempart, le terrain descendait en pente jusqu'au marécage mais il n'y avait pas de fossé bien déterminé. Sur la base de fouilles dans d'autres endroits, on pense que les fortifications remontaient à environ 200 mais on n'a pas découvert d'indices de datation utiles sur ce site. Elles entouraient une superficie d'environ 8 hectares.

On a refait des fouilles partielles du grand 'grenier' en pierre que Booth avait daté à environ 300 (Booth 1985). Ce bâtiment était bien à l'extérieur des premières fortifications qui, à l'époque, étaient probablement abandonnées. Le bâtiment fut démoli pour faire place à une seconde phase des fortifications: un mur en pierre établi sur un nouvel alignement et remontant à la fin du 4ème siècle.

Des fouilles furent effectuées sur une longueur totale de 17 mètres du mur et révélèrent des fondations constituées de supports en bois et en pierre soutenant un treillis en bois sur lequel aurait été construit le mur lui-même. Il ne restait rien de la superstructure. Il n'y avait pas de fossé. Les indices de datation du mur suggèrent un *terminus post quem* de 364.

On découvrit également une tour extérieure. Les techniques de construction étaient similaires aux techniques utilisées pour le mur mais il est toutefois clair que la tour fut ajoutée à une structure déjà existante et la dendrochronologie suggère qu'elle fut probablement construite sept ans après le mur.

L'enceinte renfermait alors une zone d'environ 9,3 ha.

Les découvertes, résumées dans la table 2, comprenaient des détritus de fabrication d'objets en alliage de cuivre, des restes carbonisés de betterave et de ciguë, un trésor de pièces remontant à la fin du 4ème siècle et du bois provenant d'en dessous du mur de la ville.

Gas House Lane

Les fouilles effectuées à Gas House Lane en 1989 révélèrent d'autres traces des fortifications ainsi que des bâtiments à l'intérieur de la zone protégée. Hormis de possibles indices d'activités agricoles ou horticoles, il semble qu'il n'y ait guère eu d'activités avant la construction des premières fortifications (terrassement) vers 200. Cette date est basée essentiellement sur une évaluation des découvertes les plus anciennes sur le site et n'est pas dérivée directement des fortifications elles-mêmes. On peut dater plusieurs bâtiments en bois et en bois-et-pierre au 3ème siècle et on peut reconnaître deux terrains à bâtir alignés de manière légèrement différente. Des perturbations modernes avaient enlevé les gisements du début du 4ème siècle dans une partie du site. Les activités s'intensifièrent vers la fin du 4ème siècle avec la construction du mur de la ville mais une petite partie du mur seulement était visible dans le coin d'une des tranchées. On découvrit également un four de séchage médiéval et une fosse de tannage possible. Le four de séchage a actuellement été reconstruit près du site.

On trouvera le résumé des découvertes dans la table 12. La grande collection de céramique romaine du site est l'un des assemblages les plus significatifs de la ville. Elle est présentée comme une série de types et est accompagnée d'une discussion détaillée sur ses conséquences par rapport à la datation du site et de la fourniture de céramique à la ville. Les autres découvertes comprennent des graines d'asperge carbonisées (confirmant les indices de Tibbet's Close), des vestiges de travail des andouillers et un autre trésor de pièces de date similaire à celui du site du supermarché Gateway.

Fortifications et zone protégée

A ce jour, il y a eu treize études des fortifications de la ville depuis leur première identification au milieu des années 60 et on a effectué des fouilles dans un nombre similaire de sites à l'intérieur de la zone protégée. La plupart étaient de petits sites mais, outre les deux sites dont il est question ici, il y en avait deux autres de bonne taille: le site M de Mahany (Mahany 1994) et le site de Tibbet's Close de Cracknell (Cracknell 1985a).

A l'heure actuelle, il semble de plus en plus probable que, quand on prit la décision de défendre la ville, on choisit la zone la plus facile à défendre plutôt que la zone la plus peuplée. Les nouvelles fortifications, qui remontaient probablement à l'an 200 environ, étaient protégées par une rivière au nord et à l'est, et protégées par un marécage à l'ouest et, à un moindre degré, au sud. Elles comprenaient une zone d'environ 8 ha, qui était essentiellement non développée; la superficie totale de la ville (y compris la nouvelle 'addition') était de 35 ha. Cette analyse semble sous-entendre que, an moins dans le cas d'Alcester, c'était la défense qui l'emportait sur la fierté civique quand on choisissait la zone à protéger.

La zone protégée se développa rapidement, mais non pas au détriment du reste de la ville, et de grands bâtiments, y compris un grenier possible, furent édifiés dans la zone non protégée. La diversité des bâtiments de la zone protégée semble refléter l'ensemble des bâtiments de la zone extra muros. Les marécages à l'ouest de la ville commencèrent à s'assécher avant le milieu du 4ème siècle et, lors de la construction du mur, l'enceinte fut agrandie au sud et à l'ouest et renferma 1,3 ha supplémentaire. Il n'y a guère eu de fouilles dans la zone comprise entre les deux lignes de fortifications mais il semble pour le moment que cette zone n'était pas développée. La date des fortifications ultérieures, fixée pour le moment après l'an 364, ferait de Alcester une des dernières villes qu'on ait fortifiées en Grande-Bretagne. Ceci reflète peut-être son éloignement de toute menace extérieure mais un second facteur peut également avoir de l'importance: bien que la ville fut au sein due territoire des Dobunni, elle était presque en marge de la *civitas* et, à la fin de la période romaine, Alcester était peut-être une sorte de centre administratif local. C'est dans ce contexte qu'on doit considérer la décision de reconstruire les fortifications en pierre et d'ajouter une tour extérieure.

Finalement, on suggère trois zones de recherches pour l'avenir. Premièrement, le développement de la zone protégée à partir d'environ 200 pourrait fournir d'importantes informations concernant la datation des objets façonnés à cette date approximative ainsi que sur la durée de vie des objets façonnés et sur les modèles de gisement en général. Deuxièmement, les éléments découverts dans la zone protégée confirment généralement les rapports commerciaux avec le bassin de la vallée de la Severn mentionnés dans les volumes précédents sur Alcester et des recherches ultérieures sont justifiées. Troisièmement, le cimetière occidental d'Alcester devrait avoir la priorité au sein de toute stratégie archéologique pour la ville. La publication de la 'série d'Alcester' a révélé les grandes lignes de la structure urbaine mais les informations relatives aux sépultures font encore défaut et c'est là une grande lacune.

Introduction

Roman Alcester was a small town in the *civitas* of the Dobunni. It lay at the junction of Ryknild Street and the 'Salt Way' (which ran from Droitwich to Ettington and beyond) and was near to the crossing of the River Alne. The settlement was roughly equidistant from three *civitas* capitals, *Corinium*, *Viriconium*, and *Ratae*. There is no significant evidence of a pre-Roman settlement and it has been suggested that the origins of the town may be connected with an early Roman fort (Booth and Cracknell 1986, 7; Booth, Chadderton, and Evans, forthcoming). The town prospered and was important enough to be defended, at first probably by earthworks, later by a stone wall. However, there is only very limited evidence that the settlement survived the Roman occupation and it was not until the 12th century that it again emerged as a town.

Modern Alcester, once again a small town, is situated 30km to the south of Birmingham (fig 1; NGR 090575). It has expanded considerably in the last 30 years, initially taking in areas of hitherto undisturbed Roman remains, but lately the expansion has been more restricted and archaeological factors have played a larger part in the planning process. With the advent of developer funding, the pace of archaeological destruction has been further reduced and significant information is now beginning to emerge from developer-funded sites, complementing that available from earlier excavations.

This report deals largely with the defences and defended area and describes the results of two excavations, the Gateway supermarket site and the Gas House Lane site, which were directed by the author in the late 1980s. The printed part of the publication contains summaries of the main discoveries and finds, and discussion of areas of general interest. The microfiche contains the supporting data and other information, directed mainly at specialist workers. The figures and plates are all reproduced in the printed section; tables are divided between print (tables 1–42) and microfiche (tables M1–M62).

Geological background

Broadly speaking, the geology that underlies the Roman town is divisible into four main units. The parts of the town near to the river, the area known as the Moorfield, and the area adjacent to Spittle Brook (close to the line of Ryknild Street) lie on Quaternary alluvium. The central part of the town lies on the river terrace. To its west is Arden Sandstone, patchy in places. Mercian Mudstone lies beyond and also to the east.

Excavations on the Gateway supermarket site encountered the river terrace as the lowest deposit. Widespread clay and peat deposits were revealed on top of the river terrace and the nature of these layers is discussed in the report.

At Gas House Lane the lowest visible geological component was Mercian Mudstone. On some parts of the site this was overlain by river terrace gravels; alluvium was present at the southern end of the site.

Archaeological background

A considerable amount of archaeological information has been unearthed since Bernard Davis first started digging in Alcester in the 1920s and several sites are relevant to the discussions here (fig 1). By and large the work to 1985 was concentrated on the southern, extramural part of the town but six excavations and three watching briefs looked at the town defences. The excavations were all on a small or very small scale and publication has been very limited. This work suggested that the northern one-fifth of the town was defended by an earth bank from perhaps about AD 200, and that the defences were strengthened by the construction of a wall in the 4th century. On the east side of the town the earth bank and stone wall may have been on the same alignment. On the west side, however, the discovery of timber-piled foundations outside the putative line of the earthworks indicated that a larger area was enclosed. The reason for this was not known. On the basis of this work it seemed highly likely that the defences would be encountered on the Gateway supermarket site. In addition, investigations to the SW of the site, at Coulters Garage in 1978–9, had recorded traces of an important stone building, one end of which was now threatened with destruction (Booth 1985). The Coulters Garage site also produced organic deposits which suggested that part of the area had been a marsh in the Iron Age and was still uninhabitable during the Roman occupation. This was the archaeological background to the Gateway supermarket excavations.

Although the Gateway dig established many details of the defences including the provision of external towers, it did not provide definitive dating evidence. Nor did it add significantly to the information about the nature of the area being defended.

In the 1980s there were two watching briefs (at Malt Mill Lane (unpublished), and at 27 High Street (Cracknell 1985b)) and one small-scale excavation within the defences (at Tibbet's Close, Cracknell 1985a). These observations confirmed the existence

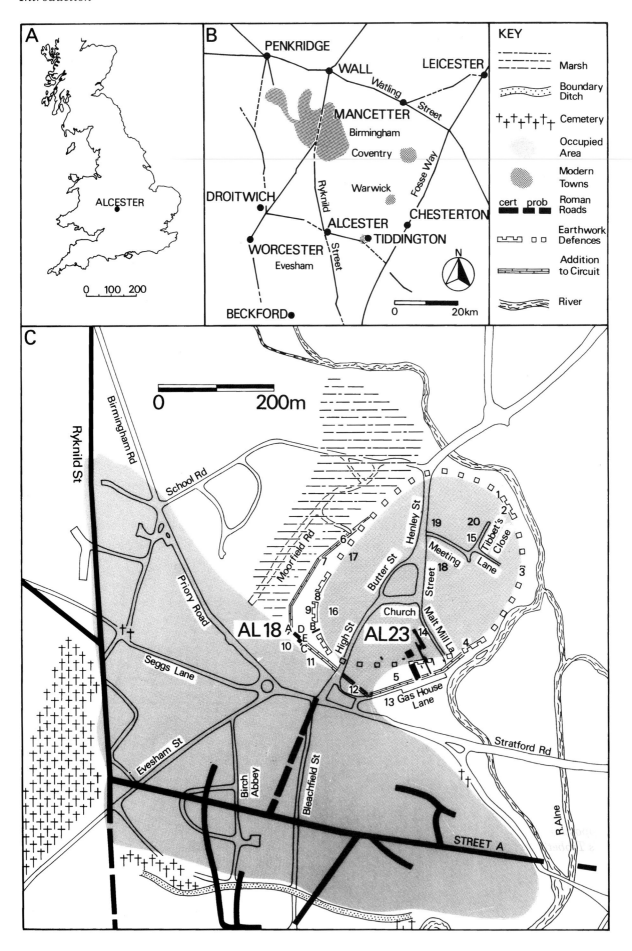

of intramural settlement including stone buildings but were limited in scope. Previous chance finds suggested that some of the better appointed buildings should lie in the defended area. The Gas House Lane excavations offered the opportunity to look at both the defences and the area within them.

The specific site-related objectives of the two excavations are discussed in the introductions to the sites themselves.

Figure 1 (opposite)   Location of the excavations and topography of the Roman town. 1: Mahany's site M. 2: Tomlinson's Tibbet's Close site. 3: Nos 9 and 11 Meeting Lane. 4: Taylor's Malt Mill Lane site. 5: Bear Inn. 6: Mahany's site K. 7: Bull's Head Yard Phase 1. 8: Bulls Head Yard Phase 2. 9: Market site. 10: Coulters Garage. 11: Midland Bank. 12: Royal Oak Passage. 13: Lamb's Gas House Lane watching brief. 14: Booth's Malt Mill Lane site. 15: Cracknell's Tibbet's Close (AL 12). 16: 27 High Street. 17: Rectory Garden 1991. 18: Baptist chapel. 19: No 1 Meeting Lane/38 Henley St. 20: Old Police Station, Henley St. (AL18, Gateway supermarket site; AL23, Gas House Lane site.)

Gateway supermarket site

This section describes the archaeological work, principally an examination of the town defences (see figs 1, 2; NGR 08805735), which took place between November 1985 and March 1986 in advance of the building of the supermarket. The excavation and publication were financed by English Heritage, Warwickshire County Council, and the Manpower Services Commission. The site archive and finds will be deposited in the Warwickshire Museum under the site code AL18.

The objectives of the work on the supermarket site were defined as:

1 To examine the nature and development of the town defences
2 To complete the plan of the Coulters Garage stone building (and its possible timber predecessor) and resolve the questions of its function and official status
3 To examine the relationship of these buildings to the defences and the relationship of both to the environmentally rich marsh deposits
4 To look for other signs of Roman and post-Roman occupation, particularly those relating to the establishment of the medieval town.

Method of investigation

The nature of the development imposed some constraints on the archaeological research. Only the south-western two-thirds of the site was available for excavation as the remainder was in use until immediately prior to the development (figs 1, 2). The potential cost of reinstatement at the western end of the site, where the supermarket was due to be built, prohibited extensive trial trenching there. However, it was expected that this end of the site would not contain much in the way of archaeological features as it was known to have been marshy or wet until modern drainage relieved the situation. In consequence, work there was limited to the drilling of a series of boreholes. The eastern end of the site was to be stripped by the developers (removing, in places, over 1.5m of soil) for a car park. As our excavations would not cause any great structural problems there were fewer constraints on the archaeological work there.

Three lines of boreholes were drilled. The first line consisted of 21 holes (A–U) at 1m intervals, aligned E–W across the expected line of the 4th-century stone wall. The wall was not located for reasons which became apparent at a later stage during the excavations. A longer line of five more widely spaced holes (V–Z) was drilled more or less parallel to the first set to investigate the depth of the alluvial deposits in this area. A third line of four holes (AA–DD) was drilled at the south-west end of area B. Aligned NE–SW, it was located so as to investigate the possibility that a river channel ran through this part of the site.

During the trial season of about two months, three trenches were excavated. The first trial trench, area A, measuring 6m NNE–SSW × 2m, was laid out near to area 7 of the Coulters Garage excavation to establish how far the remains extended in a westwards direction. In particular it was hoped that the trench would pick up the continuation of a short segment of wall identified in the watching brief at Coulters Garage. It was thought that this wall might be part of a second substantial stone building, almost parallel to the first. As it turned out, area A produced evidence of late Roman stone rubble overlaying a deep clay deposit similar to that found in Coulters Garage area 7. Excavation of part of this clay by JCB uncovered a burial. These results suggested that the archaeological potential of this area was relatively low.

Area B was laid out across what was thought to be the line of the earthwork defences. The trench measured 20m NE–SW by 4m. A bank was located at the NE end of the trench but, because of the danger to the stability of nearby buildings, we were unable to excavate a section across its full width. Outside the bank was a wet and muddy area which was excavated to a depth of 2.7m below ground surface before work was abandoned for safety reasons. Work on the lowest part of the area was restricted to a trench 2m wide at the SW end of the trench as the sides of the excavation had to be stepped in to prevent them from collapsing. It would have been possible either to shore this trench or to make it wider in order to continue the work but as the lower deposits were not threatened by development it was thought that the limited resources of the excavation would be better used elsewhere.

Area C measured 4m NNE–SSW × 2m. This trial trench was dug in the southernmost corner of the site in order to try to find more remains of the fragmentary structures identified during the Coulters

Figure 2 (opposite) Location of the Gateway supermarket site areas A–E, boreholes, and adjacent archaeological work at Bull's Head Yard (Phases 1 and 2) (7 & 8), the Market site (9), Coulters Garage (10), the Midland Bank (11), and on the Moorfield Marsh (14)

4

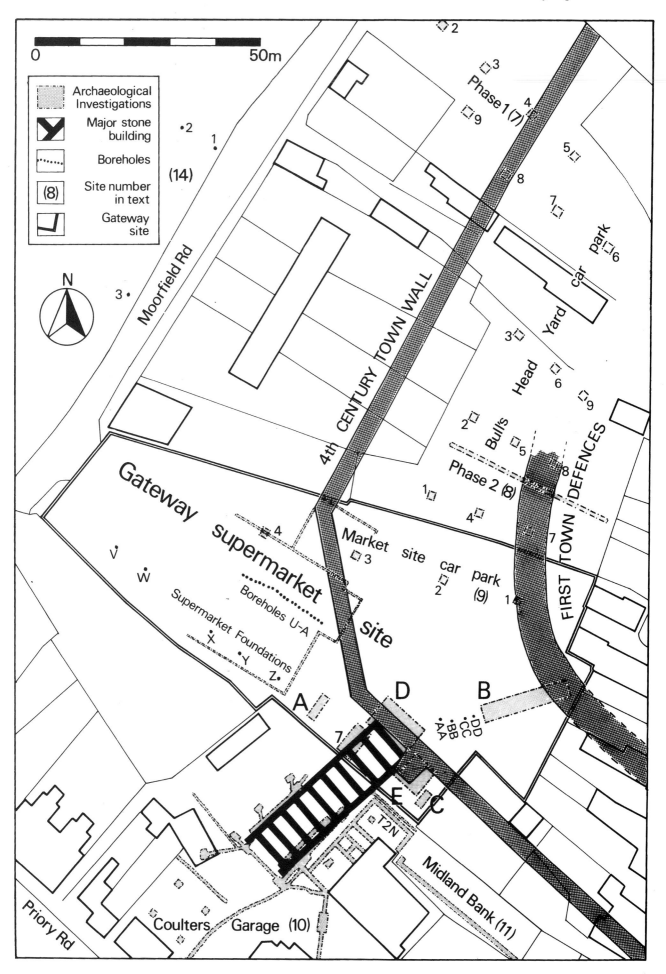

Table 1 Dates of archaeological phases at the Gateway supermarket site

Area B	Areas A, C, D, E	Date
Phase A construction and use of earthwork defences		AD 150–250?
Phase B disuse of earth defences	Phase I Large stone building	AD 300–*tpq* 364
Phase B	Phase IIa Building of town wall	*tpq* AD 364
Phase B	Phase IIb Building of bastion	*tpq* AD 371?
Phase C post-Roman activity	Phase III Robbing of wall and bastion	post-Roman/?part 13thC
Phase C	Phase IV Medieval and post-medieval activity	Medieval and later

Garage work to the east of the large stone structure. The discovery of a series of mortar floors and a post-and-slot wall confirmed the potential of this area of the site. This trench was not excavated down to the undisturbed substratum as it was apparent that the remains would be better understood in the context of a larger excavation.

On the basis of the trial excavations it was clear that the area of greatest archaeological potential was in the southern corner of the site, between Coulters Garage area 7 and area C, and perhaps extending a few metres to the north. An area of 400sq m was stripped and a line of stone rubble which appeared to indicate the north end of the stone building was noted. Area D was laid out to incorporate it.

Area D measured 11m NW–SE × 7.2m. Its size was restricted by the need to cover it with a polyspan to enable work to continue through the frosts of January and February. Further cleaning revealed that the south-western three-quarters of area D was strewn with rubble and that the north-eastern part contained a compact clay deposit. Two trenches (I and II) were dug across the clay deposits and one of them then extended across the rubble (fig 6). It was only at this stage that it became apparent that the rubble was the fill of a robber trench 4.1m wide. Only when a significant part of the robber trench had been excavated was it seen that it indicated the line of the town wall and that the clay deposit was a supporting rampart. Work continued with the excavation of the end wall of the substantial stone building first seen in Coulters Garage area 7 and the removal of the fills of the town wall robber trench. The fills of the construction trench for the town wall were investigated by means of a 2.4m wide trench cut through them at right angles, effectively continuing trench II downwards. Waterlogged timber piles were recovered from the bottom of the construction trench.

Area E was sited between area D and the trial trench, area C. The intention was to trace the line of the town wall, to pick up the SE wall of the stone building, and to continue the excavation of the mortar floors and other structures first identified on area C. Only a month could be allowed for the work on this area and this severely restricted the size of the site which measured 6m NE–SW × 6.8m, with two small extensions. The work revealed that much of the SE wall of the stone building had been destroyed by the building of an external tower in front of the town wall. The robber trench of the tower was excavated, but apart from in small areas the construction fills were not tackled by hand. About fifteen of the waterlogged timber piles which had supported the tower were recovered for dating purposes by a Hy-mac. The southern corner of the site, which was not damaged by the defences, was excavated down to the top of the extensive clay deposit which had also been seen on the other sites. Samples were taken from the boreholes, the rampart in area B, the clay make-up on area A, and elsewhere and their soil morphology and botanical remains were analysed.

Observation of the digging of the foundation trenches for the supermarket and the site clearance for the car park revealed more of the town wall and some of the line of the earlier earthwork defences. (See [M1:B14].)

Summary of the stratigraphy
(figs 3–9, plates 1–9)

[M1:A2] The remains in area B were divided into three phases (A, B, C). They were stratigraphically unrelated to the remains in areas A, C, D and E which were divided into four phases (I–IV). The *approximate* dates of the phases are given in table 1. Details of the stratigraphy can be found in the microfiche; context numbers are only included in the printed section where they clarify the description of a particular feature. Those in **bold** appear on plans; those in *italic* appear on sections.

The whole of the site was underlain by river terrace gravel which was seen in the contractor's test pits, on areas A and D, and in the boreholes (fig 3). The contours of the gravel indicate that the site was on

Figure 3 (opposite) Height of gravel river terrace and extent of peat and early clay deposits in the vicinity of the Gateway supermarket site

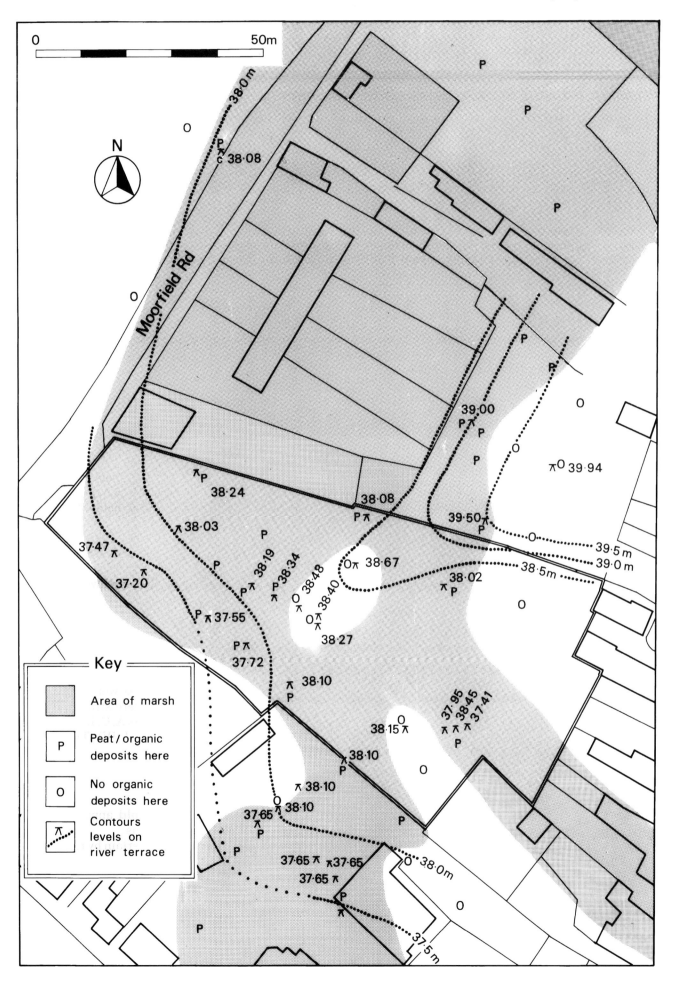

Key

Area of marsh

P Peat / organic deposits here

O No organic deposits here

↗ Contours levels on river terrace

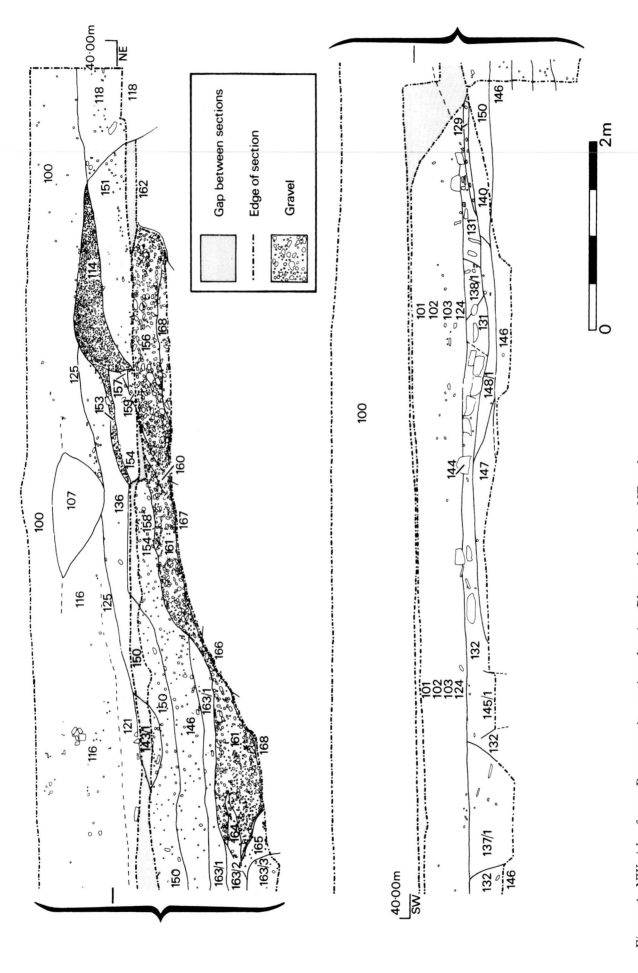

Figure 4   NW side of area B: composite section showing Phase A bank at NE end

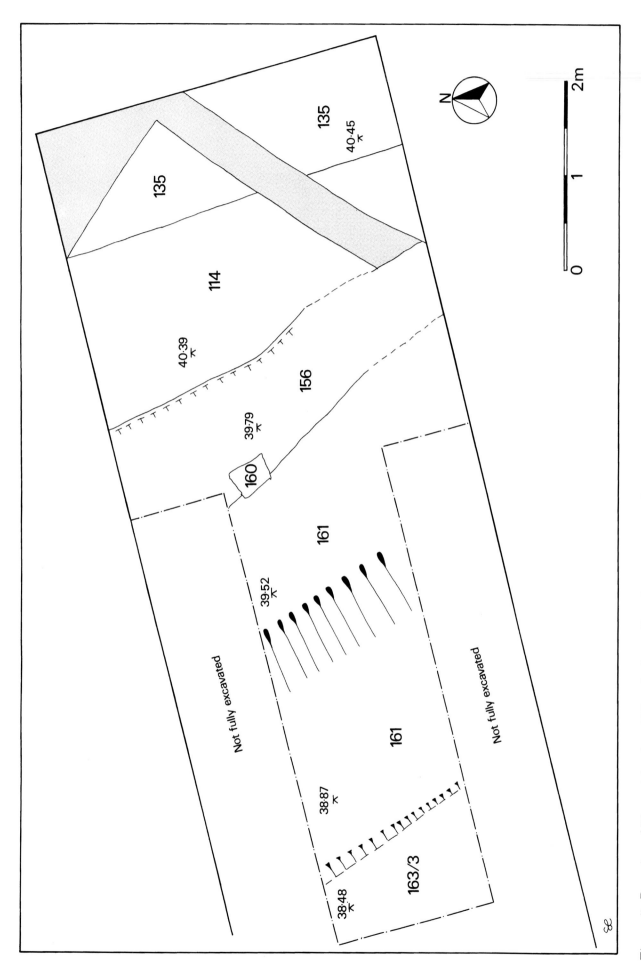

Figure 5   Remains of Phase A bank at NE end of area B and contemporary deposits. For safety reasons only the central part of the trench was dug full depth

9

Plate 1   Detail of section across Phase A bank at NE end of area B. (See section fig 4). Looking NW. Scale 2m

the corner of the gravel 'island' on which the town centre now stands.

At the west end of the site the gravel was overlaid by layers containing peat or other preserved organic material interleaved to a greater or lesser extent with layers of clay. The cumulative thickness of these layers varied between 0.4m and 0.9m.

On the eastern part of the site, except in borehole

Plate 2   Trenches cutting through Phase A bank and deeper deposits outside it at NE end of area B. (See section in fig 4). Looking W. Scale 2m

CC, peat was absent. The layers directly above the river terrace were composed of clean clay. Where measurable the layer was c 0.7m thick.

Two clay layers at the bottom of area B (*163/3*, *165*) may have been natural or artificial (figs 4, 5).

Area B contained what were probably the earliest archaeological remains (Phase A) although there was no direct dating evidence (see 'Discussion'). A heterogeneous clay layer (*168*) and a series of clay and gravel deposits (**156**, **160, 161**, *164*, *167*) were dumped at the NE end of the trench and a clay and gravel bank (**114, 135**, *151*) built on top of them (fig 5, plates 1–2). The presence of a near-vertical face on the SW side of the bank suggested a timber revetment of some kind had supported the soil. The opposite face of the bank lay outside the area of excavation. The natural lie of the land and the pre-bank make-up dump combined to create a slope in front of the bank but it was not clear if this slope had been deliberately cut back to form a ditch.

At some later time (Phase B) the defences fell into disuse and the façade was either removed or decayed. Initially, as the bank collapsed the layers (*157–9*) accumulated against its vertical face. After a while the erosion of the rampart slowed down and dumping began to occur. An unexplained band of gravel (*152*), lying parallel to the bank edge, in front of it, and

Plate 3 North corner of the substantial Phase I stone building, demolished at the beginning of Phase II. The corner was subsequently robbed during Phase III. Area D. Looking S. Scale 2m

Plate 4 Section across centre of area D. Showing Phase IIa rampart (left), wall foundation trench (centre), and Phase I stone building (right). (See fig 7). Looking SE. Scale 2m

separated from it by 700mm was deposited at this time.

During the period when these earthwork defences were decaying building started some 30m to the SW (Phase I on areas A, D, and E: figs 6, 7, plates 3, 4). Initially an extensive dump of clay was deposited. A skeleton was found within the clay but its stratigraphic position was uncertain (see 'Discussion').

The clay dump was cut by the foundations of the NE end of a large stone building. Part of this structure had previously been located in excavations at Coulters Garage, and it has been interpreted as a granary (Booth 1985). There were no apparent floor levels. The overall width of the structure was confirmed to be 11.5m.

The construction trench of the town wall had cut through the area immediately to the NE of the end of the building, removing the Phase I layers, but sealed under the compact revetment bank on the opposite side of the wall were two layers of loose soil (fig 7: *473*, *452*) probably deposited during Phase I.

To the east of the stone building, on areas C and E there were several other less substantial Phase I structures and there were also a few layers of clay loam, rubble, and some small holes which might have been associated with these buildings (Phase I) or with the actual construction of the wall (Phase II).

The construction of the town wall (at the beginning of Phase IIa) must have involved the wholesale clearance of any structures in its path or immediately outside it to the SW (figs 7, 8, plates 5–9). The granary was demolished and its walls robbed.

The foundation trench of the town wall which ran SE–NW through areas E and D and then turned northwards, was 3.3m wide at the bottom and 4.1m wide at the top. It was 1.2m deep. Oak piles, originally about 2m long, had been driven into the gravel subsoil at the bottom of the trench. One, rejected because it was too thin, was dumped at the

edge of the trench. The waterlogged conditions ensured that much of the wood survived intact. (See [M1:C7] for dendrochronology.) First limestone blocks (*619*), then gravel (*618*) and then clay (*456*) were packed between the piles. A small part of the N side of the trench had collapsed into the trench before it was backfilled. The clay was overlaid by timber lacing, now only visible as beam slots. There were three, parallel, horizontal, longitudinal beams and, on top, one transverse beam, though if a longer length of trench had been uncovered more transverse beams would probably have been visible. In one place at least there was a significant gap (600mm) between the end of one longitudinal timber and the start of its continuation. The spaces between the beams were packed with stone and a peculiar sandy loam – possibly decayed mortar – as well as fragments of solid mortar of various compositions (see 'Mortar' report) (*471*) . Clays or clay loams with gravel and sandstone (*554*) lay against the SW side of the foundation trench but it was not clear if they were deliberate fill or collapse of the sides. Apart from sandstone fragments in the robber trench there was no trace of the wall itself. On the NE side of the trench there were the remains of a revetment bank of very compact clay and gravel (*425*, *426*, *449–52*).

A few years after the wall had been built an external tower or bastion was added (figs 8, 9, plate 8, Phase IIb). The method of construction was the same as that for the town wall. However, the two construction trenches were separated by a small wedge of ?natural clay (844) and alder was used for the timber piling under the tower whilst oak was used for the wall, indicating that the two structures were not contemporary. The construction trench for the tower was slightly trapezoidal with the side against the wall measuring 6.2m and the opposite, parallel side measuring 5.4m. The trench projected 5.4m from the wall. The ends of the timber lacing (again recognized as beam slots) projected beyond the vertical edge of the construction trench and were

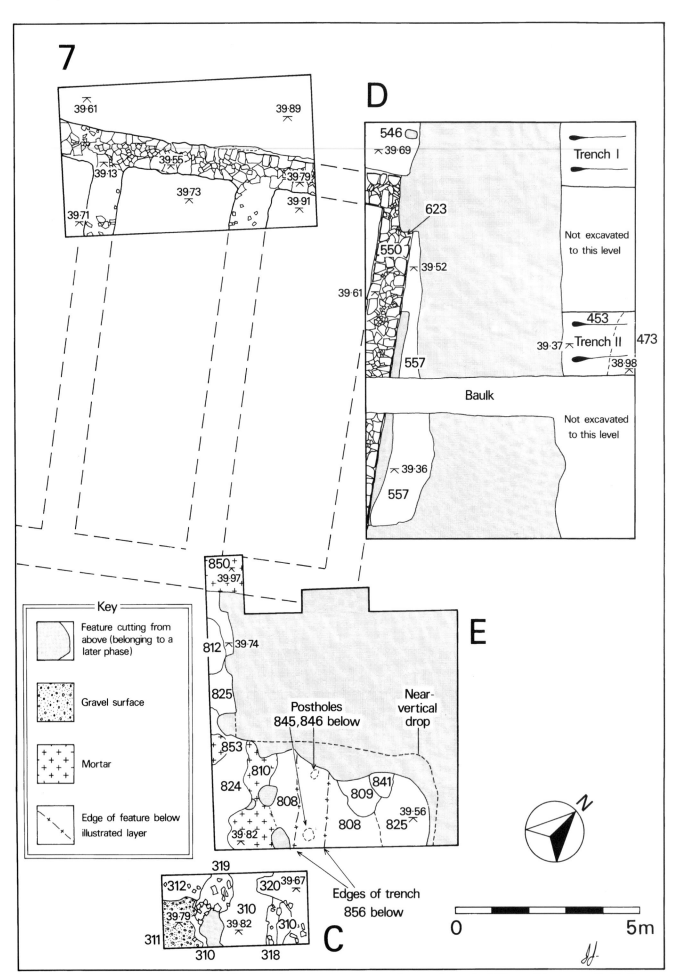

Figure 6 The substantial stone building and contemporary remains at the end of Phase I in areas C, D, E and Coulters Garage area 7 (excluding Phase I/II remains). (Area 7 plan courtesy of Paul Booth)

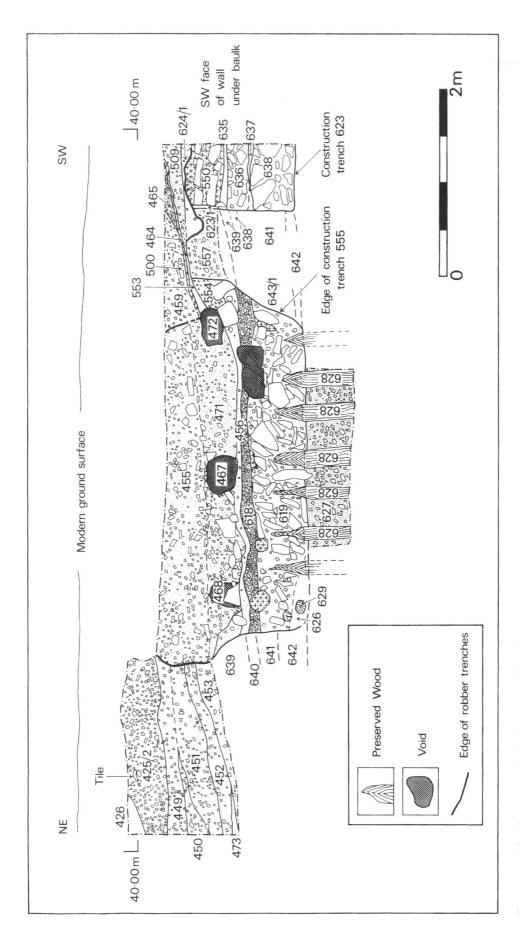

Figure 7 North west side of the central baulk across area D: NE–SW section showing Phase IIa rampart (left), construction and demolition layers of town wall (centre) and Phase I stone building and subsequent layers (right)

13

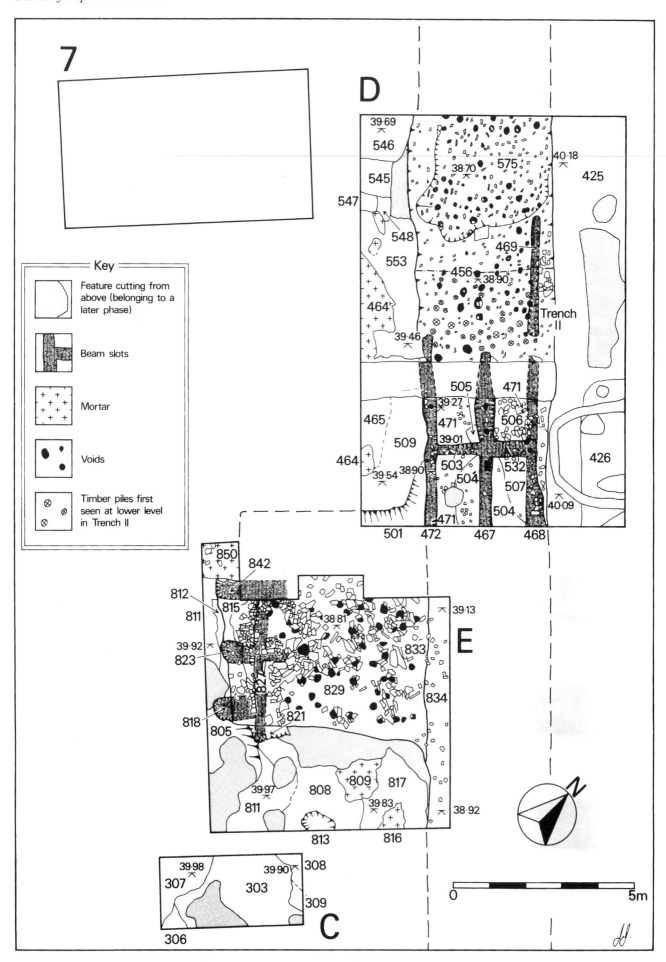

Figure 8 The surviving traces of the construction of the Phase IIa town wall and the Phase IIb bastion, and other contexts dating to the end of Phase IIb. Areas C, D, E.

Plate 5   Surviving tops of timber piles in centre of area D belonging to Phase IIa town wall foundation. Looking E. Scale 1m

Plate 6   Traces of timber lacing in Phase IIa town wall foundation at the SE end of area D. Looking E. Scale 2m

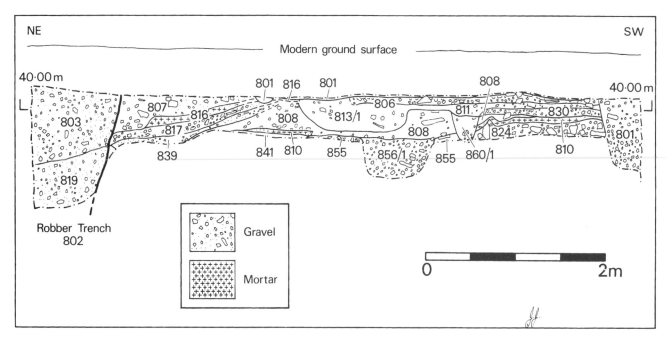

Figure 9 SE side of area E: section showing robber trench of town wall (left) and layers through which it cut

supported on the surrounding clay. Three timbers were aligned at right angles to the wall (and a fourth should have lain in the unexcavated part of the tower). On top of these beams, and parallel to the wall, was another timber which also rested on the surrounding clay. There were no signs of other beams parallel to the wall but they may have existed

nonetheless. The spaces between the beams at the SW edge of the construction trench were packed with stone and ?crushed mortar as in the wall trench.

There were several layers and features which appeared to be later than the construction fills of the tower but earlier than the robbing and therefore probably associated with the building of the super-

Plate 7 Horizontal squared timber (469) slot trench in Phase IIa town wall foundation as first seen in trench II, area D. Note the voids where vertical timbers once stood and the void of the horizontal timber continuing under the baulk. Looking NW. Scale 0.5m

Plate 8 (right) Rubble and voids in the fill of the Phase IIb construction trench for the tower. Area E. Looking W. Scale 1m

Plate 9   Reconstruction model showing the southern part of the Gateway supermarket site as it might have appeared at the beginning of Phase II, from the north. The granary is being demolished to make way for the town wall

structure itself. However, the stratigraphy was not particularly clear and it may be that these deposits were associated with the building of the town wall (Phase IIa) rather than the tower (IIb). These deposits included several small patches of soil with small rubble, a dump containing copper alloy offcuts (**805**), and some small pits or hollows but the main deposits were two mortar surfaces (see 'Mortar' report) and an intervening gravel surface.

It is not known exactly when the stone of the town wall and tower first began to be removed (Phase III) but traces of this process were visible on sites A, C, D, and E. The robber trench (*455, 802, 803, 819*) had been dug down to the top of the foundation levels of the wall and in places the upper part of the foundations had been removed as well. To the SW of the robber trench lay patches of rubble.

On area B, the post-Roman layers and features (Phase C) were distinguished on the basis of the presence of medieval or post-medieval pottery (fig 4). At the SW end of area B the Phase C deposits were 1.5m deep; at the NE end, over the rampart, they were only 0.54m deep. However, the lower layers (*129, 148*) also contained much Roman pottery and it may well be that they were largely Roman but had been disturbed at a later date, although distinctions were not apparent (Phase C(i)). Two pits, a small hole, and a shallow ditch running NNE–SSW cut these layers and were in turn overlaid by 300mm of silty clay loam with rubble.

The first clearly post-Roman features on the site (Phase C(ii)) were a pit and two possible wells (*137; 145*: not fully excavated). The layer of silty clay loam which sealed these features was 1m deep. Cut through the top of this layer were several features, all of which appeared to be recent in date. The topsoil (100) was 350mm deep.

The post-Roman deposition on the other excavated areas (Phase IV) was less substantial at only 500mm deep. On area D a large pit contained a good medieval pottery group and on area A a post-medieval wooden shed was represented but the remaining features did not seem to indicate any particular pattern.

Layers of clay with 5% gravel, *c* 0.7m thick were revealed by the boreholes and contractor's test pits in the middle and the western part of the area being developed. The origin of these deposits is uncertain but they may, in part at least, have derived from the degradation of the ramparts of the town defences and in part from the ?dump used to raise the ground level prior to the construction of the granary building.

Finds: summary table

Table 2 Summary table of all finds excavated at the Gateway Supermarket site

Type of material	No or wt	Print	Fiche	Comments
Samian	16	Full report, p 19		
Roman pot (other)	1299	Full report, p 20		Figs 10, 11
Medieval pot	529	Summary, p 31	M1:C3	Fig 12
Building materials				
Preserved wood	31+		M1:C7	31 samples kept for analysis: see 'Dendrochronology' and 'Radiocarbon dating'
Stone		Summary, p 33	M1:C8	Samples identified
Ceramic tile	2.277kg		M1:C9	
Stone tile	3.586kg		M1:C11	
Mortar			M1:C12	Samples from town wall, granary, floors analysed
Metalwork				
Copper alloy	32	p 33	M1:C13	Fig 13, inc Polden Hill bow brooch
Lead	1	p 33	M1:C14	
Iron	70	Summary, p 33	M1:C14	Fig 13
Coins	32	p 34	M1:D3	Mainly 3rd/4th C; incl likely late 4th C hoard
Iron slag	small quantity			Not studied
Copper alloy working debris	c 0.2kg	p 34	M1:D4	See also 'Copper alloy', 'Charcoal associated with the copper alloy working'
Bone				
Worked bone	4		M1:D5	Incl knife handle
Human bone	Burial + 13 frags	Summary, p 34	M1:D5	
Animal bone	c 5300	Summary, p 34	M1:D6	Only stratified Roman bone (440 frags) detailed
Ecological remains				
Charred plants	1482	Summary, p 35	M1:D11	Incl hemlock, beet,and wheat
Snails	1 sample	Summary, p 35	M1:E1	Aquatic (with 2 exceptions)
Charcoal associated with alloy copper working	29.8g		M1:E2	Oak and alder predominated in sieved sample
Waterlogged plant remains		Summary, p 35	M1:E3	Sample from borehole N
Other finds				
Glass	2	Summary, p 36	M1:E8	Fragments
Shale	1	Summary, p 36	M1:E8	Bracelet

Samian ware
Margaret (Bulmer) Ward

Introductory note

The abbreviations SG, CG and EG are used to denote South Gaulish, Central Gaulish and East Gaulish origin; ind. denotes an indeterminate sherd. For other terminology, see Bulmer 1979.

While the archive includes a complete record of all the Samian ware recovered from these excavations, the numbered catalogue here has been selected according to intrinsic interest or for dating purposes where the samian may be of significance.

Catalogue

Area B

Phase B

One fragment only B (147): a burnt wall sherd of CG form Dr 38, probably Antonine.

Phase C

1 B (108). CG ind (deep dish or bowl). A large piece of the lower wall, presumably of CG origin, and probably *c* AD 170–200. The sherd has broken across a dovetailed rivet hole, which still bears traces of lead.

The remaining three sherds from area B (Phases B and C) were all fragments of Antonine origin from CG, recovered from contexts (116), (127/1), and (147) – the last sherd being very burnt.

Areas C, D, E

Phase I

2 E (808). CG ind. Hadrianic–Antonine. A tiny fragment, presumably of CG origin, representing the only samian ware retrieved from Phase I.

Phase IIa

3 D (472/3). SG Dr 29. Fragment only of the lower wall with a basal wreath of straight godroons. Probably *c* AD 70–85. A slightly burnt sherd.

Two other residual scraps were recovered, from D (426) and D (449), from later-Antonine CG and Flavian-Trajanic SG respectively.

Phase IIb(–IV)

4 E (806), (811). EG Dr 45. Good orange-red ware with a thick slip. Probably from late 2nd-century or early 3rd-century Rheinzabern, but at any rate manufactured in the range *c* AD 170–260. Two fragments in (806) and one tiny chip in (811) came from the same mortarium as four sherds in Phase IV contexts: area E (800) contained one fragment, and E (801) contained three sherds including rim and base, of which the gritted interior was probably worn from use.
5 E (811). EG Dr 31R. Slightly burnt, reddish ware with a rather coarse fabric. Probably also from late 2nd-century or 3rd-century Rheinzabern. The footring was very worn, presumably by use, while the internal base was battered either before or after breakage.

Two other sherds, one of Antonine date from CG and one probably of late 2nd-century or 3rd-century date from EG, were recovered from C (303) and E (805/1) respectively.

Phase III

One battered fragment only was retrieved from E (804), of Antonine CG manufacture.

Phase IV

Apart from the four sherds listed as No 4 above, three other fragments (probably all of later 2nd-century manufacture) were recovered from D (401) (burnt) and D (510/1) (two sherds, one burnt).

Of the total of 22 sherds representing 16 vessels, 12% originated in South Gaul, 69% in Central Gaul and 19% in East Gaul. As one would expect of samian found in such late contexts, the East Gaulish vessels were of late 2nd-century or 3rd-century manufacture probably from Rheinzabern (2) and Trier (1?). Several of the pieces displayed evidence of use, including Nos 1, 5, and probably 4. Five sherds were burnt.

Table 3 Summary of samian forms and fabrics from all contexts

Fabric	29	31 or 31R	31R	36	38	45	Lud Tg	ind.	Total
SG	1							1	2
CG		1	1	1	1		1	6	11
EG			1	1		1			3
Total	1	1	2	2	1	1	1	7	16

Roman pottery
Rowan Ferguson

This report was written shortly after the excavation was complete and has not been updated to take account of the Gas House Lane pottery. Comparisons *are* made, however, in the discussion of the Gas House Lane pottery.

Excavation in area B produced 728 sherds of Roman pottery weighing 13.109kg. Of this collection only 3 sherds (weighing 0.042kg) came from uncontaminated Roman contexts in Phase B. The remaining 725 sherds were from contexts placed in Phase C, a post-Roman phase. It seemed likely however that many of these contexts, which contained principally Roman pottery, were in fact contaminated Roman contexts. The material from these possibly Roman contexts will be discussed separately (as Phase C(i)) from those layers which were indisputably of a later date (Phase C(ii)). The distribution of the pottery was 43% in Phase C(i) and 57% from Phase C(ii).

The range of fabrics present in area B was consistent with other 4th-century material found in Alcester and included Severn Valley wares, local reduced fabrics, Black-Burnished ware and shell-gritted material amongst the coarse wares whilst the fine ware assemblage was dominated by the Oxfordshire products especially the colour-coated fabric. Three fabrics were present in Phase B (Black-Burnished ware, Severn Valley ware, and samian) each represented by a single sherd. In Phase C(i) there were 25 fabrics of which 8 were only represented by one sherd. Figures for Phase C(ii) contexts were broadly similar (23 fabrics, 3 represented by a single sherd). See table 4.

The material from areas A, C, D, and E will be discussed as one group, in line with the stratigraphic discussion and for the same reasons. A total of 571 sherds weighing 8.016kg was found in these four areas. Of the total number of sherds 45.8% was from medieval and post-medieval contexts (Phases III and IV), and the remaining 54.2% was distributed as follows – Phase I: 38 sherds (6.6%); Phase IIa: 72 sherds (12.6%); Phase IIb: 199 sherds (34.8%). Because of the statistical unreliability caused by the size of the sample there will be no detailed discussion of the chronological trends of the pottery from these areas.

There was a total range of 29 fabrics present on areas A, C, D, and E of which 23 were found in Roman contexts and 22 in later ones (see table 5). Of these, 16 fabrics were common to both periods, 7 fabrics were found only in the Roman layers and 6 fabrics were found only in the later groups. Nine fabrics were represented by a single sherd. The most significant fabrics present were, as on area B, the Severn Valley wares, the local reduced fabrics, and Black-Burnished ware. Shell-gritted wares were not so important here. The only fine ware present in any quantity was the Oxfordshire colour-coated ware.

In view of the small size of the collection, the fact that at least half of it was residual in medieval and post-medieval contexts, and the problem that the upper Roman layers from area B were, at best, heavily contaminated with later material, no detailed discussion of pottery supply and use in this part of the town was possible. The problems of interpretation were further exacerbated by the size of the individual groups: on area B, of the Phase C(i) groups only two contained more than 50 sherds and 11 had less than 10 sherds. In Phases I and II on areas A, C, D, and E only one group consisted of more than 50 sherds and 31 groups had less than 10 sherds. As a result, such interpretative comment as follows must necessarily be extremely tentative particularly with reference to areas A, C, D, and E.

Fine wares

As has been mentioned above the fine ware assemblage was dominated by imports from the Oxfordshire kilns of which the colour-coated fabric (F51) was the most significant. In fact, in area B, the Oxfordshire products were present in greater quantities than any other single group of material (Phase C(i): 95 sherds (30.4%); Phase C(ii): 135 sherds (32.6%)). Table 4 shows the relative proportions in which the different fabric groups were present. It can be seen that the Oxfordshire colour-coated fabric alone represented 26.6% (83 sherds) of the total from Phase C(i) contexts and 27.6% (114 sherds) of the total from Phase C(ii) layers.

In areas A, C, D, and E the Oxfordshire colour-coated ware was less significant and represented 16.5% (51 sherds) of the Phase I and II assemblage and 21.8% (57 sherds) of the Phase III and IV assemblage. (There were only 149 sherds of fine wares in all in these areas – Phase I and II: 72 sherds (23.3%); Phase III and IV: 77 sherds (29.3%)).

As well as the colour-coated fabric the Oxfordshire white *mortarium* fabric (M23) was also present. Where the form could be determined it proved to be Young's type M22 (Young 1977), which he dates *c* AD 240–400. There was also one sherd of the Oxfordshire white ware (W22) from a Phase C(i) context on area B and one from a Phase IIb context on areas A, C, D, and E. The Oxfordshire potters' most successful export to area B at this time, after the colour-coated fabric, seemed to have been the white-coated *mortarium* fabric M43. Although large numbers of sherds were not present in this fabric, the minimum number of vessels present in proportion to the number of sherds was unusually high (11 vessels) and the overall representation of the fabric in the assemblage was also unusually high. The vessels were all of Young's type WC7 (see illustrated vessel no 11). The relative importance of the fabric and the number of vessels in such a limited area might suggest that a 'set' of these *mortaria*, either from someone's kitchen or storeroom, or the stock from a shop or market stall were all abandoned at the same time. Quantities from areas A, C, D, and

Table 4   Area B. Number of sherds of each fabric in Phase C contexts

Fabric description	Source	Warwicks Fab No	Phase C(i)		Phase C(ii)	
			NoSh	%	NoSh	%
Colour-coated Ware	Oxfordshire	F51	83	26.6	114	27.6
White *mortarium* fabric	Oxfordshire	M23	2	0.6	4	0.9
White Ware	Oxfordshire	W23	1	0.3	–	–
White-coated *mortarium* fabric	Oxfordshire	M43	9	2.9	17	4.1
Colour-coated Ware	Nene Valley	F52	20	6.4	49	11.8
Grey-coated Ware	Nene Valley	R24	1	0.3	–	–
White *mortarium* fabric	Mancetter-Harts	M22	1	0.3	3	0.7
White-slipped, oxid. flagon fabrics:	?SW England	Q12	1	0.3	–	–
		Q11	–	–	2	1.4
		Q25	–	–	1	0.7
Samian	all sources	S	1	0.3	3	2.1
Amphora fabric	Spain	A21	1	0.3	–	–
Oxidized fabrics:	Severn Valley	021	13	4.1	18	4.3
		023	20	6.4	20	4.8
		024	25	8.0	23	5.5
		027	5	1.6	7	1.7
	?	081	2	0.6	2	1.4
Reduced fabrics:	?local	R01	14	4.4	21	5.1
		R15	1	0.3	7	1.7
		R19	5	1.6	3	0.7
		R21	2	0.6	9	2.1
		R32	16	5.1	7	1.7
		R41	4	1.2	15	3.6
		R42	–	–	1	0.7
Shell-gritted Ware	?Northamptonshire	C11	45	14.4	62	15.0
Black Burnished Ware	Dorset	B11	31	9.9	24	5.8
Malvernian Metamorphic	Malvern	G44	1	0.3	–	–
Coarse buff storage jar fabric	?SE Midlands	G11	8	2.5	1	0.7
			312		413	

E did not reflect the same popularity, however, and only one sherd (0.4%) was found in a post-Roman context.

The only other fine ware present on area B in significant quantities was the Nene Valley colour-coated fabric, F52. The importance of this fabric was a common feature of later 4th-century assemblages in Alcester (Booth pers comm). Most of the forms present, shallow dishes, flanged bowls, beakers (illustrated vessel no 17) and a lid (illustrated vessel no 18) could all be 4th century in date (Howe *et al* 1980). Nene Valley products were not as important on areas A, C, D, and E but this may reflect the small size of the collection from these areas. Two Nene

Valley fabrics were present, the Nene Valley colour-coated ware and the Grey-coated ware. The grey-coated fabric occurred both here and on area B Phase C(i) (1 sherd (0.7%)) but has not been recognized on other sites in Alcester.

Other fine wares which occurred in very small quantities were samian which is discussed in detail in the samian report; a Spanish amphora fabric, A21; an amphora fabric which may have come from the Aegean, A42, white-slipped flagon fabrics of possible south-western origin; and the Mancetter-Hartshill *mortarium* fabric, M22. The last fabric was the only one which was not definitely residual. The three rim forms present, however, probably date to the early

Table 5 Areas A, C, D, and E. Number of sherds in each fabric in Roman and post-Roman contexts

Fabric description	Source	Fab no	Phase I	Phase IIa	Phase IIb	Total Roman	%	Phase III	Phase IV	Total post-Roman	%
Colour coated fabric	Oxfordshire	F51	3	17	31	51	16.5	33	24	57	21.8
White *mortarium* fabric	Oxfordshire	M23	–	1	2	3	1.0	1	2	3	1.1
White Ware	Oxfordshire	W12	–	–	1	1	0.3	–	–	–	–
White-coated *mortarium* fabric	Oxfordshire	M43	–	–	–	–	–	–	1	1	0.4
Colour-coated ware	Nene Valley	F52	–	–	2	2	0.6	1	1	2	0.8
Grey-coated ware	Nene Valley	R24	–	–	–	–	–	1	–	1	0.4
White *mortarium*	Manc.-Harts	M22	–	–	2	2	0.6	–	4	4	1.5
White-slipped, oxid. flagon fabric	?SW England	Q11	–	1	–	1	0.3	–	–	–	–
Samian	all sources	S	1	3	8	12	3.9	1	8	9	3.4
Amphora fabric	?Aegean	A42	–	–	–	–	–	1	–	1	0.4
Oxidized fabrics:	Severn Val.	O21	7	3	8	18	5.4	1	3	4	1.5
		O22	–	–	1	1	0.3	–	–	–	–
		O23	1	13	18	32	10.4	17	24	41	15.6
		O24	10	13	24	47	15.2	22	19	41	15.6
		O26	1	–	–	1	0.3	–	–	–	–
		O27	–	–	–	–	–	4	6	10	3.8
		O32	–	–	1	1	0.3	–	–	–	–
		O41	–	–	–	–	–	1	–	1	0.4
Reduced fabrics:	?Local	R01	–	2	23	25	8.1	2	12	14	5.3
		R15	–	–	–	–	–	3	2	5	1.9
		R21	4	–	2	6	1.8	1	1	2	0.8
		R32	2	5	3	10	3.0	–	2	2	0.8
		R41	–	2	17	19	6.1	8	6	14	5.3
		R42	1	–	–	1	0.3	2	1	3	1.1
		R52	–	2	–	2	0.6	–	–	–	–
Shell-gritted Ware	?Northants	C11	–	4	9	13	4.2	4	8	12	4.6
Black Burnished Ware	Dorset	B11	8	5	45	58	18.8	13	19	32	12.3
Malvernian Metamorphic fabric	Malvern	G44	–	–	2	2	0.6	–	–	–	–
Coarse buff storage jar fabric	?SE Midlands	G11	–	1	–	1	0.3	–	1	1	0.4
Totals						309				262	

3rd century (see vessels no 16 and no 27 which illustrate two of these forms).

Despite containing the same basic elements the fine ware assemblages from the two areas could be seen to be substantially different. The areas A, C, D, and E group contained a couple of minor anomalies when compared with other 4th-century material from the town, such as the low representation of Nene Valley colour-coated ware, but its small size made it difficult to accept that these represented genuine differences. The area B assemblage, however, seemed to lie much further outside the normal pattern for late groups in Alcester with very high representation of Oxfordshire products. The large quantity of Oxfordshire white-coated *mortarium* fabric was particularly unusual and this affected the proportions represented by all the other fabrics.

The anomalous nature of the area B fine ware assemblage was further underlined by the relative proportions of the different coarse wares and the proportions of different vessel types (see below). It will be suggested below that these features may hint

Table 6 Proportions of different fabric groups present at sites in Alcester
(arranged in descending order of group size)

	Tibbet's Close	64 Bleach-field St	6 Birch Abbey	Gateway Area B	Acorn Ho, Evesham St	Gateway Areas ACDE	34 Eve-sham St	Stratford House
Total number of sherds	1299	1158	1057	725	706	571	266	207
Severn Valley (%)	44.4	17.6	78.6	20.7	35.5	34.7	56.8	33.0
Black Burnished (%)	30.2	8.8	4.4	9.9	–	15.8	6.4	7.5
Local Reduced (%)	5.7	25.9	3.0	13.5	57.4	18.4	11.3	33.0
Shell-gritted (%)	0.7	0.0	–	14.7	–	4.4	–	–
Fine Wares (incl.Samian) (%)	13.8	17.6	13.5	43.2	5.8	26.0	22.8	21.0
(Samian) (%)	7.8	8.8	9.7	0.5	3.7	3.7	11.6	5.3
Date of majority of assemblage (century)	3rd–4th	1st–2nd	2nd–4th	4th	1st	3rd–4th	2nd–4th	2nd

at a very late date for the group, possibly after *c* AD 375.

Coarse wares

The proportions of coarse wares in area B were distorted by the extremely high representation of Oxfordshire products. The Oxfordshire colour-coated fabric alone represented a higher proportion of the total number of sherds than any single group of coarse wares (Phase C(i): 83 sherds (26.6%); Phase C(ii): 114 sherds (27.6%)). This meant that the assemblage was not really comparable with others of a similar period in Alcester. The pottery from areas A, C, D, and E was much closer to other 4th-century assemblages from the town and the proportion of the Oxfordshire colour-coated fabric was less significant (Phases I and II: 51 sherds (16.5%); Phases III and IV: 57 sherds (21.8%)). See table 6 for proportions of different fabrics from other sites in Alcester.

The most significant group of coarse wares in both Phase C(i) and Phase C(ii) contexts was the Severn Valley ware group (20.7%). Five different fabrics were distinguished within this group and they occurred in both periods in approximately similar proportions (see table 4). Severn Valley wares were imported to Alcester from the 1st century and they gradually became more significant until the 3rd century when at sites like Tibbet's Close, they represented 44.4% of an assemblage made up of a narrow range of fabrics. They continued to be present in the same proportion into the 4th century. The differences between Gateway supermarket area B and 4th-century deposits at Tibbet's Close could be explained by a late 4th-century date, possibly after AD 375, for the Gateway supermarket area B assemblage. In late 4th-century deposits at 1–5 Bleachfield Street, Severn Valley wares repre-sented 22% of the total (Booth pers comm), a similar proportion to that present at Gateway supermarket area B.

As on area B, the Severn Valley wares were the most significant coarse wares on areas A, C, D, and E (Phases I and II: (32.6%); Phases III and IV: (37.4%)). A range of 6 fabrics was present in Phases I and II and 5 fabrics in the post-Roman phases. The proportions were more similar to those for Tibbet's Close although the small size of the group made any sort of interpretation unreliable.

Next in importance to the Severn Valley wares were the reduced fabrics, which may have been made locally, and the shell-gritted wares, which were probably imported from somewhere to the east of Warwickshire. The proportions of these two fabrics were almost exactly the same, varying by one or two sherds in either phase. Shell-gritted wares were less significant on areas A, C, D, and E and more in line with other 4th-century groups in Alcester (see table 6 and discussion below).

A range of eight different reduced fabrics was present, of which six were common to both periods. On areas A, C, D, and E there were also 8 reduced fabrics and 5 occurred in both Roman and later phases. Representation of these fabrics in Alcester seemed to vary between 5–12% at sites where occupation was largely 4th-century and 30–60% at sites in use in earlier periods (Ferguson 1985). The proportions in the Gateway supermarket area B assemblage were not much outside the range for 4th-century groups. However the proportions on areas A, C, D, and E did not fit into the 4th-century grouping or the earlier one (Phases I and II: 63 sherds 20.3%; Phases III and IV: 42 sherds (16%)). As the assemblage was known from the stratigraphy to be largely 4th century the relatively high percentages of reduced fabrics here may indicate that 5–12% is an underestimate of the proportions to be expected on 4th-century sites.

Shell-gritted ware has not been seen as an important part of 4th-century assemblages in Alcester (eg at Tibbet's Close there was 0.7%, at 1–5 Bleachfield Street, 1.1% (Booth 1986)) although it was always present during the 4th century. Perhaps the relatively high proportions which were present at AL18 area B should be taken as a pointer to the lateness of the assemblage. This will be discussed further below (see 'Discussion of illustrated vessels'). Illustrated vessel no 4 shows a characteristic form found in these fabrics.

Black-Burnished ware was also only present as a small proportion of the total assemblage on area B (Phase C(i): 9.9%; Phase (ii): 5.8%)) and this too seemed to be at odds with the picture of the 4th-century pottery supply to Alcester hitherto established. Figures for Black-Burnished ware from late 3rd- to 4th-century assemblages were considerably higher at both Tibbet's Close (30.2%) and 1–5 Bleachfield Street (35%). Quantities from areas A, C, D, and E lagged behind these two sites (Phases I and II: (18.8%); Phases III and IV: (12.3%)) but were higher than at area B. Once again the reliability of statistics based on the areas A, C, D, and E figures was seen to be questionable. The usual repertoire of forms was present. Two flanged bowls (nos 2 and 14) and a cooking pot (no 8) have been illustrated.

Two other coarse wares which do not fit into the broad categories described above were also found. Of these only one occurred in both Roman and post-Roman contexts in both areas. This was a coarse oxidized fabric, Fabric G11, which was a common component of late 3rd- to 4th-century assemblages in Alcester and throughout Warwickshire. A source in Northamptonshire or Buckinghamshire is likely for this fabric (Booth and Green 1989). Illustrated vessel no 6 shows the form in which this fabric occurred most commonly.

The other coarse ware present was a Malvernian Metamorphic fabric, G44, of which one sherd was found in a Phase C(i) context on area B where it constituted 0.3% of the assemblage and 2 sherds (0.6%) on areas A, C, D, and E in Phases I and II.

As with the fine ware assemblage the coarse wares from areas A, C, D, and E seemed to be broadly within the normal 4th-century Alcester tradition and it was probable that such anomalies as existed could be attributed to the small size of the collection. The area B assemblage was probably genuinely different in significant aspects from other 4th-century sites in the town in that shell-gritted wares were present in higher proportions than elsewhere, quantities of Severn Valley wares and reduced fabrics were relatively low and those of Black-Burnished ware lower still. As suggested above it may be that these features were characteristic of pottery assemblages of the last quarter of the 4th century in Alcester.

Vessel types

A total of 163 vessels (based on the minimum number of vessels) was present on area B. The range of vessel types present and their proportions are shown in table 7. The vessels were present in 22 different fabrics but over half (110 vessels) were concentrated in four fabrics: Oxfordshire colour-coated ware, a shell-gritted fabric, Black-Burnished ware, and the Nene Valley colour-coated fabric. Of these, the Oxfordshire colour-coated fabric was by far the most significant (46 vessels). Despite the small size of the collection a couple of points could be noted, especially by comparison with other excavated sites in Alcester (see table 9 and below).

On areas A, C, D, and E there was a total of 114 vessels (see table 8). The vessels were present in 21 fabrics (as on area B) and over 70% (84 vessels) were concentrated in just three fabrics, the Oxfordshire colour-coated fabric (23%, 26 vessels), Black-Burnished ware (23.4%, 27 vessels), and the Severn Valley wares (25.3%, 31 vessels).

On area B the unusual predominance of bowls over jars in the vessel proportions (bowls: 31.3%; jars: 28.8%) was probably a result of successful marketing of the Oxfordshire products, especially the colour-coated fabric, rather than a particular demand for bowls; the high incidence of *mortaria* (12.3%) was another example of the achievements of the Oxfordshire potters. The relatively large number of *mortaria* in the Oxfordshire white-coated fabric, M43, is discussed above (see 'Fine wares'). Table 9 shows how unusual these figures were: no other excavated site from Alcester showed such a small difference in proportions of jars and bowls (3%), let alone a situation where bowls were more significant. The proportion of *mortaria* was twice that of any other site. Of the bowls, nearly 65% were in the Oxfordshire colour-coated fabric and 90% of the *mortaria* were Oxfordshire products. This dominance of the *mortarium* market by the Oxfordshire potters was not unusual in 4th-century Alcester. Whilst the relative importance of the different vessel types can be explained by the predominance of the Oxfordshire products it does not clarify whether the percentage of *mortaria* could be attributed to the chronology or the function of the site.

The situation on areas A, C, D, and E was much more in line with that on previously excavated sites in Alcester with jars as the most significant vessel type (40 vessels (35.4%)) and bowls next in importance (34 vessels (30%)). *Mortaria* were also quite highly represented compared with other Alcester sites (9 vessels (8%)) although not as highly as on area B. The *mortaria* were more diverse in the areas A, C, D, and E collection and only 60% were Oxfordshire products.

A second trait apparent in the area B assemblage was the absence of tankards and cups and the consequently low overall proportions of drinking vessels as a class (4.4%). This was not echoed at areas A, C, D, and E where the equivalent figure was 10.6%. However the latter figure seemed suspect when studied further as the only type of drinking vessel present on areas A, C, D, and E (as on area B) was the beaker and the high representation of this

Table 7 Area B. Minimum number of vessels in each fabric

Fabric description	Fabric no	Bowls	Jars	Dishes	Mortaria	Beakers	Storage jars	Flagons/ Jugs	Carinated bowls	Lids	Uniden- tified	No vessels	%
Oxfordshire Colour-coated fabric	F51	30	3	5	2	5	–	–	–	–	1	46	28.2
Oxfordshire *mortarium* fabric	M23	–	–	–	5	–	–	–	–	–	–	5	3.0
Oxfordshire White-coated Ware	M43	–	–	–	11	–	–	–	–	–	–	11	6.7
Nene Valley Colour-coated fabric	F52	5	2	7	–	1	–	–	–	–	–	15	9.2
Nene Valley Grey-coated Ware	R24	–	1	–	–	–	•	–	–	–	–	1	0.6
Samian	S	2	–	–	–	–	–	–	–	–	–	2	1.2
Mancetter-Hartshill white ware	M22	–	–	–	2	–	–	–	–	–	–	2	1.2
White-slip flagon fabrics	Q11	–	–	–	–	1	–	–	–	–	–	1	0.6
	Q25	–	1	–	–	–	–	–	–	–	–	1	0.6
Severn Valley	O21	–	1	–	–	–	–	–	–	–	–	1	0.6
	O23	–	1	–	–	–	1	–	–	–	–	2	1.2
	O24	1	1	–	–	–	–	–	–	–	–	2	1.2
	O27	1	1	–	–	–	1	–	–	–	–	3	1.8
?Local reduced fabrics	R01	1	5	–	–	–	–	–	–	–	–	6	3.7
	R15	–	1	1	–	–	–	–	–	–	–	2	1.2
	R19	1	–	–	–	–	–	–	1	–	–	2	1.2
	R32	1	3	1	–	–	–	–	–	1	–	6	3.7
	R41	2	2	–	–	–	–	–	–	–	–	4	2.4
Shell-gritted Ware	C11	1	21	6	–	–	–	–	–	–	–	28	17.1
BB Ware	B11	6	6	9	–	–	–	–	–	–	–	21	12.8
Malvernian Metamorphic fabric	G44	–	1	–	–	–	–	–	–	–	–	1	0.6
Coarse, buff storage jar	G11	–	–	–	–	–	1	–	–	–	–	1	0.6
No vessels		51	47	29	20	7	3	3	1	1	1	163	
Percentage		31.3	28.8	17.8	12.3	4.4	1.8	1.8	0.6	0.6	0.6		

Table 8 Areas A, C, D, and E, minimum number of vessels in each fabric

Fabric description	Fabric no	Jars	Bowls	Dishes	Beakers	Mortaria	Storage jars	Carinated bowls	Uniden-tified	No of Vessels	%
Oxfordshire Colour-coated fabric	F51	–	13	1	9	1	–	–	2	26	23.0
Oxfordshire *mortarium* fabric	M23	–	–	–	–	4	–	–	–	4	3.5
Oxfordshire White-coated Ware	M43	–	–	–	–	1	–	–	–	1	0.9
Nene Valley Colour-coated fabric	F52	–	–	–	1	–	–	–	–	1	0.9
Nene Valley Grey-coated ware	R24	–	1	–	–	–	–	–	–	1	0.9
Samian	S	–	3	1	–	1	–	–	–	5	4.4
Mancetter-Hartshill white ware	M22	–	–	–	–	2	–	–	–	2	1.8
Severn Valley	O21	3	–	–	–	–	–	–	–	3	2.6
	O23	11	1	–	–	–	1	–	1	14	12.4
	O24	5	2	–	1	–	–	1	–	9	7.9
	O26	1	–	–	–	–	–	–	–	1	0.9
	O27	2	–	–	–	–	–	–	–	2	1.8
?Local reduced fabrics	R01	4	–	–	1	–	–	–	–	5	4.4
	R15	1	–	–	–	–	–	–	–	1	0.9
	R21	2	–	–	–	–	–	–	–	2	1.8
	R32	1	–	–	–	–	–	–	–	1	0.9
	R41	2	1	–	–	–	–	–	–	2	2.6
	R42	1	–	–	–	–	–	–	–	1	0.9
Shell-gritted	C11	2	1	1	–	–	–	–	–	4	3.5
BB Ware	B11	5	12	10	–	–	–	–	–	27	23.4
Malvernian Metamorphic	G44	–	1	–	–	–	–	–	–	1	0.9
Total no. vessels		40	35	13	12	9	1	1	3	113	
Percentages		35.0	30.7	11.4	10.5	7.9	0.9	0.9	2.7		

Table 9 **Vessel proportions on excavated sites in Alcester (in percentages)**

	Tibbet's Close	Gateway B	64 Bleach-field St	6 Birch Abbey	Gateway A, C, D, E	34 Evesham Street	Stratford Ho
Total number of vessels	310	163	150	117	113	49	36
Jars	39.0	28.8	33.3	60.6	35.4	40.8	44.4
Storage Jars	–	1.8	9.3	1.7	0.9	–	–
Flagons/Jugs	1.0	1.8	1.3	0.8	–	4.1	–
Dishes	19.0	17.8	16.7	7.7	11.5	8.2	5.6
Bowls	24.8	31.3	4.0	20.5	30.0	30.6	22.2
Carinated bowls	0.6	0.6	1.3	–	0.9	4.1	5.6
Mortaria	2.6	12.3	2.7	1.7	8.0	6.1	2.8
Amphorae	–	–	0.7	–	–	–	2.8
Lids	0.3	0.6	4.7	0.8	–	–	2.8
Strainers	0.3	–	–	–	–	–	–
Miniature vessels	–	–	–	–	1.8	–	–
Unidentified	–	0.6	8.0	2.5	0.9	–	–
Tankards	8.1	–	8.0	1.7	–	2.0	5.6
Beakers	1.9	4.4	0.7	1.7	10.6	2.0	5.6
Cups	2.2	–	9.3	–	–	–	2.8
Total drinking vessels	12.2	4.4	18.0	3.4	10.6	4.0	14.0

type on areas A, C, D, and E seemed to be as a result of low proportions of other vessel types rather than a genuinely high number of beakers. This must again be attributable to the small size of the assemblage from these areas. The complete absence of tankards from area B was unlikely to have been a result of the probable lateness of the group as the Severn Valley ware potters produced this vessel type throughout the 4th century. Nor were there tankards on areas A, C, D, and E, where there was no reason to suppose that the majority of the assemblage was particularly late.

Discussion of illustrated vessels (figs 10, 11)

The figure in parentheses at the end of each entry indicates the context from which the vessel originated.

Area B

Phase C(i) disturbed Roman contexts

312 Roman sherds 81 post-Roman sherds

1 Oxfordshire colour-coated beaker (127/1)
2 Black-Burnished ware bowl (127/1)
3 Nene Valley ware beaker (127/1)
4 Shell-gritted jar (127/1)
5 Severn Valley ware jar (127/1)
6 Large storage jar (Fabric G11) (148/1)
7 Oxfordshire colour-coated flagon (143/1)

8 Black-Burnished ware cooking pot (143/1)
9 Oxfordshire colour-coated bowl (140)
10 Nene Valley Grey ware jar (140)
11 Oxfordshire white-coated *mortarium* (121)
12 Jar (Fabric R32) (131)

Despite the high proportion of medieval and post-medieval material (21%) it seemed likely that these were Roman contexts which had been extensively disturbed in later periods (see 'Summary of the stratigraphy') as the pottery represented a coherent group of 4th-century material and only two of the contexts in this group contained more than 10 sherds of later pottery.

The assemblage from pit 127 seemed to be a typical 4th-century rubbish pit deposit consisting principally of Black-Burnished ware, Oxfordshire and Nene Valley colour-coated wares, with some Severn Valley wares, reduced and shell-gritted fabrics and the coarse buff storage jar fabric, Fabric G11, which was a characteristic component of assemblages of this period in Alcester. Illustrated vessel no 2, a 4th-century Black-Burnished ware bowl with a dropped flange, established the date of the group beyond doubt. Shell-gritted jars, such as no 4 were not common in Alcester before the 4th century. Vessel no 3 was also 4th century in date. It was a Nene Valley beaker which could not be precisely identified as only the long narrow neck was present but it seemed closest to the group which has been described as 'at the end of the beaker-making tradition in the Nene Valley' (Howe *et al* 1980).

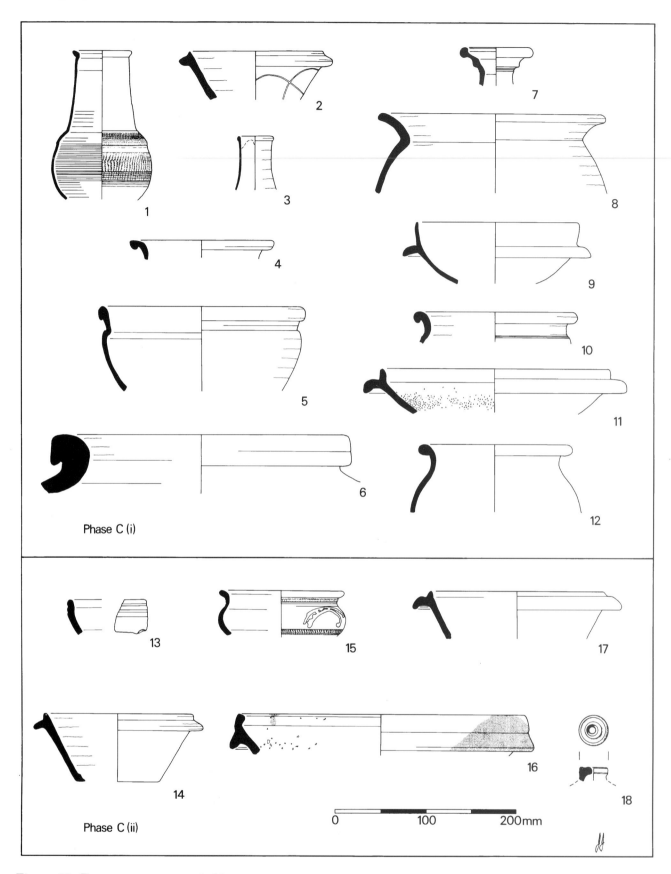

Figure 10 Roman pottery, nos 1–18

Vessels nos 1 and 5 were of types which had slightly wider date ranges: no 1 was an Oxfordshire pentice-moulded beaker, Young's type C23, which he dates *c* AD 270–400 (Young 1977); and no 5 was a Severn Valley ware wide-mouthed jar which would be dated by Webster as late 3rd to 4th century (Webster 1976).

A feature associated with pit 127 was ?ditch 143 which contained a similar assemblage, including the illustrated vessels no 8, a worn 3rd-century Black-Burnished ware cooking pot and no 7, a cup-necked flagon.

The two features discussed above, from which the vessels nos 1–5 and 7–8 came, were both cut through layer 148 which produced a small group of material (10 sherds). Such a small group could not be regarded as significant but vessel no 6, a fragment from a storage jar in a coarse buff fabric, Fabric G11, was felt to be worthy of illustration. This fabric occurred widely in the area in a narrow range of forms of which the vessel type shown was the variant most commonly found in Alcester. For a further discussion of the significance and occurrence of Fabric G11 see Booth and Green 1989. In Alcester the fabric appeared in late 3rd- and 4th-century contexts without known exception.

All the above contexts were sealed by a thick layer which covered most of the trench. This layer was given several context numbers and illustrated vessels nos 9–12 were derived from various of these contexts. Two of these were further examples of Oxfordshire products: no 9 was an extremely worn C51 which Young dates *c* AD 240–400 and no 11 was a white-coated *mortarium* type WC7. Young writes that 'the bulk of the dated examples [of WC7] are 4th century' (Young 1977, 122). This vessel was one example of at least 11 found in Phase C(i). Vessel no 12, also from the same context, was a medium-necked jar in a reduced fabric which could not be traced to a particular source or pinpointed chronologically. The last illustrated example from this phase was no 10, a narrow-mouthed jar in the Nene Valley grey-coated fabric. Very little is known about the occurrence of this fabric in Alcester as it has only been identified at this site, so far, and little further illumination was provided by the only other known finds in the county, three unstratified examples from Tiddington, Warks (Ferguson in Palmer forthcoming, nos 90–92).

The illustrated group from this period, the very small amount of conclusively residual material (which included samian and an amphora fabric: 4 sherds in all), and the worn nature of many sherds which could possibly be 3rd century or earlier (eg vessels nos 8 and 9) suggested that there was very little activity which involved the discarding of pottery prior to *c* AD 300 in this area.

Phase C(ii) Medieval and post-medieval contexts

413 Roman sherds, 629 post-Roman sherds

13 Oxfordshire colour-coated ware dish (104)

14 Black-Burnished ware bowl (108)
15 Oxfordshire colour-coated ware bowl (116)
16 Mancetter-Hartshill *mortarium* (103)
17 Nene Valley colour-coated ware bowl (124)
18 Nene Valley colour-coated ware lid (137/1)

There was no doubt about the post-Roman nature of the contexts in this period and therefore all the illustrated vessels were residual. As with the material from the preceding period the assemblage was consistently 4th century in date although some vessels could be dated late 3rd to 4th century. There was, however, an increase in the occurrence of vessels which were definitely after AD 300 (eg in Phase C(i) only 2 out of 8 Oxfordshire colour-coated ware vessels were in this category but by Phase C(ii) this had become 5 out of 8).

The earliest features in this period were two possible wells and it was from one of these that illustrated vessel no 18, the knob from a Nene Valley colour-coated ware lid, was derived. Although these lids were made from the early 4th century they were concentrated in late 4th-century groups at Great Casterton (Howe *et al* 1980).

These wells were superseded by the principal layer of this phase which was assigned various context numbers and from which vessels nos 14, 15, and 16 were selected for illustration. Vessel no 14 was a 4th-century Nene Valley colour-coated ware flanged bowl and no 15 an Oxfordshire colour-coated ware necked bowl, Young's type C77, which he dates to the late 4th century. The final vessel from this layer was no 16, a Mancetter-Hartshill *mortarium* of late 3rd- to 4th-century date (Hartley pers comm).

The layer mentioned above was cut by several small indeterminate features from two of which came vessel no 14, a 4th-century Black-Burnished ware bowl and no 13, a small Oxfordshire colour-coated dish.

The predominance of pottery which was post-AD 300 and the presence of vessels which might be specifically assigned to late in the 4th century (eg nos 15 and 18) may possibly indicate that in the post-Roman contexts on area B there were the remnants of a very late Roman assemblage.

Areas A, C, D and E

Phases I and II Roman contexts

309 Roman sherds, 5 post-Roman sherds

19 Jar (Fabric R21) (Phase I, D 452/1)
20 Oxfordshire M17 *mortarium* (Phase IIa, D 425/1)
21 Oxfordshire colour-coated wall-sided *mortarium* (Phase IIa, D 619)
22 Nene Valley colour-coated beaker (Phase IIb, C 314)
23 Oxfordshire colour-coated miniature bowl (Phase IIb, E 813/1)

The overall picture of the pottery from Phases I and II supported the 4th-century date suggested by the relationship of the stratigraphy to the

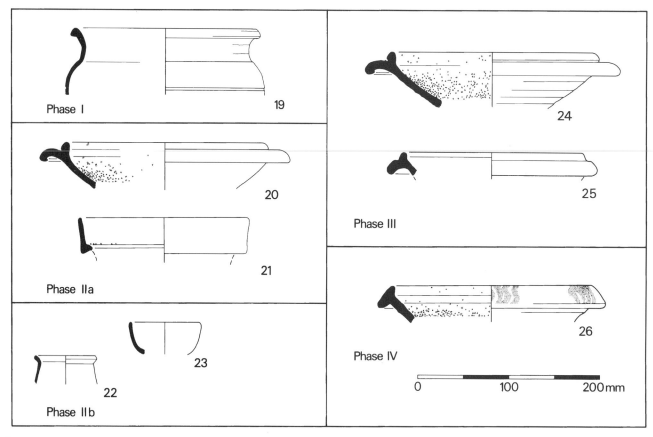

Figure 11   Roman pottery, nos 19–27

Coulters Garage site. Unfortunately the size of the complete assemblage and the individual groups within it was such that the pottery could neither confirm nor disprove the more detailed putative dating put forward. On the whole the sherds from these areas were small and often worn so that vessels which could be illustrated were difficult to select.

Illustrated vessel no 19 was the only example from Phase I. It came from layer 452/1 on area D, an occupation layer possibly associated with the granary and sealed by the rampart for the Phase IIa wall. The vessel was a wide-mouthed jar of a type commonly found in 3rd- and 4th-century deposits in Alcester. It is likely that it was made locally.

The principal activity in Phase IIa was the construction of the town wall and rampart. Vessel no 21 came from the wall construction trench and was an Oxfordshire wall-sided *mortarium*, Young's type C97, which he dates *c* AD 240–400+. He describes the type as 'very common' (Young 1977). This example was very worn and broken into small pieces. The other illustrated vessel from this phase was also an Oxfordshire product, an M17 white ware *mortarium* which Young dates *c* AD 240–300. It was found in one of the rampart layers and must therefore be redeposited.

The remaining illustrated vessels from Roman contexts were from Phase IIb and were in line with the excavator's suggested *tpq* of AD 371 for this phase although the remainder of the assemblage was so fragmentary as to make any definite confirmation impossible. Vessel no 22 from context 314, an indeterminate layer which overlay a Phase I mortar floor, was a Nene Valley beaker of a type very similar to no 3 from area B which probably dates to the late 4th-century (see Howe *et al* 1980, no 57). The other vessel from this phase, no 23, was a small hemispherical cup in the Oxfordshire colour-coated fabric, Young's type C110, about which he says 'the only dating evidence is mid-4th-century but its date range could be longer'. He suggests the range ?AD 300–400+ but with an emphasis on the second half of the period. There was also an intrusive medieval vessel in the metal working hollow (805/1).

The pottery from the Roman contexts in areas A, C, D, and E was not present in sufficient quantities to provide a coherent picture but was consistent with other 4th-century groups from Alcester and contained some residual 2nd- and 3rd-century material as might be expected on a site where much of the pottery was redeposited. It was not possible to provide any detailed dating for the individual phases. However, as suggested above, vessels nos 22 and 23 show there to have been some late 4th-material present on the site although the proportions of different fine and coarse wares present did not indicate any variance from the 4th-century norm.

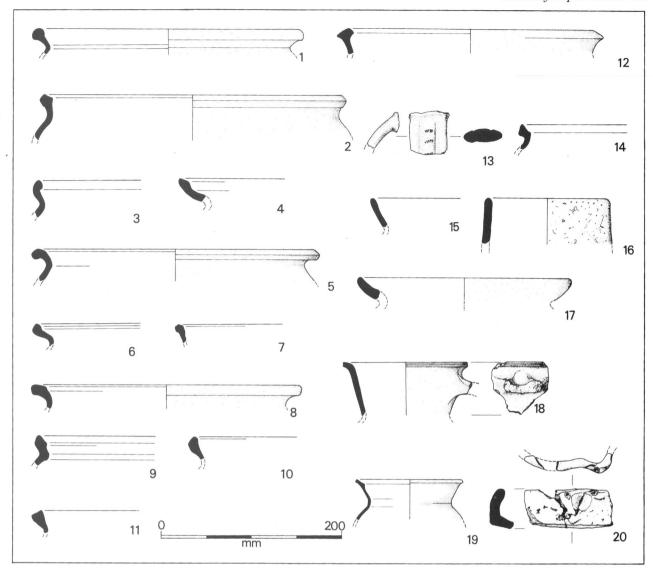

Figure 12 Medieval pottery

Phases III and IV post-Roman contexts

262 Roman sherds, 567 post-Roman sherds

24 Oxfordshire M17 *mortarium* (Phase III, E 804)
25 Nene Valley grey-coated ware bowl (Phase III, C 302)
26 Mancetter-Hartshill hammer-headed *mortarium* (Phase IV, E 800)

As in Phases I and II the assemblage from the post-Roman contexts was made up of the usual components of 4th-century groups in Alcester: Severn Valley wares, Oxfordshire products, local reduced fabrics, Black-Burnished ware, shell-gritted wares, and some residual earlier material such as samian and Malvernian Metamorphic fabrics.

Illustrated vessels nos 24 and 25 show the kind of material found in the destruction rubble of the town wall: a 3rd-century Oxfordshire white ware *mortarium* identical to that found in an earlier context (illustrated vessel no 20) and a Nene Valley grey-coated ware bowl which is dated late 3rd to early 4th century (Howe *et al* 1980, no 21).

Vessel no 26, which came from the topsoil in area E, was a Mancetter-Hartshill hammer-headed *mortarium* for which a later 3rd- to 4th-century date seems most likely (Booth pers comm).

This report was completed in 1989.

Medieval pottery
Stephanie Ratkai

[M1:C3] The medieval pottery report is divided into three sections. A summary is printed below in the text. In microfiche, there is a brief description of the pottery fabrics together with data on their distribution, dating, and frequency, and information on the possible dating of the earliest post-Roman features. The pottery is illustrated in fig 12. In the archive are the detailed fabric descriptions and the basic pottery records.

Summary

There are 529 sherds comprising 81 minimum vessels. The pottery is very fragmentary and there are no

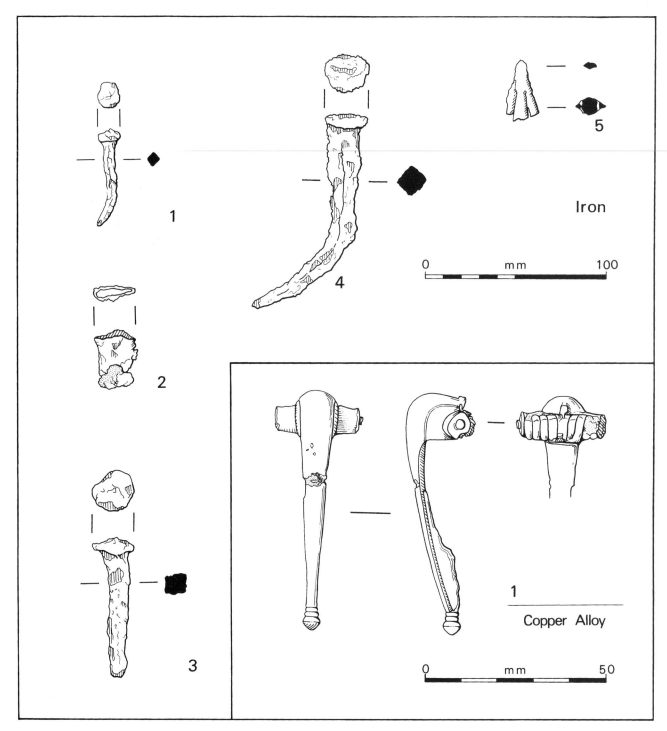

Figure 13 Copper alloy and iron finds

complete vessel profiles. The majority of the pottery is made up of wares produced at a kiln site in School Road, Alcester (Cracknell and Jones 1985) and a significant number of new rim types have been recognized. They may belong to a later phase of production than those recorded by Cracknell and Jones.

The earliest pottery present is probably a few sherds of shell/limestone-tempered ware. These may be ascribed to the 12th century, although the nature of the material and the paucity of the sherds makes it difficult to be certain. Most of the medieval pottery seems to belong to the 13th century or 14th century although three large sherds, which are very hard fired, are probably from the 15th century. These three sherds were not associated with the earliest post-Roman activity on the site.

It seems most likely that the earliest post-Roman activity dates to the 12th century or 13th century.

Illustrated pottery (fig 12)

The number in square brackets after the context number indicates the quantity of rims of the same type found in that context

1 Fabric 1. Everted rim with end thickened internally and externally (B 101, 102, 103[2], 124, 142)
2 Fabric 1. Short, angled everted rim with slight internal bevel (B 102, U/S)
3 Fabric 1. Out-sloping rim, smooth on exterior with pronounced internal roll (D 409 (drawn) and A 4/1; B 102[2], 129[2])
4 Fabric 1. Everted rim with internal thickening (U/S and A 8)
5 Fabric 1. Everted overhung rim (B108)
6 Fabric 1. Everted S-shaped rim with an internal bevel and external thickening (A 8, B 116, 102[2])
7 Fabric 1. Simple everted rim with external thickening and shallow thumbing (B 102)
8 Fabric 1. Thickened, angled rim with slight internal bevel (B 124)
9 Fabric 1. Rim angled out from neck, internal bevel on lower part of rim and an internal ridge at shoulder/neck – ?lidseating (B 103, also A 1 (Fabric 2))
10 Fabric 1. Everted rim with pronounced internal thickening (A 8)
11 Fabric 1. Everted triangular-sectioned rim (A 8)
12 Fabric 1. 'T-shaped' rim (B 103)
13 Fabric 1. Strap handle decorated with two vertical grooves and stabbed decoration along the central section (B 124)
14 Fabric 1. Sharply angled rim, with slightly depressed upper surface and a thickened outer face (B 101)
15 Fabric 1. Simple out-sloping tapered rim (A 1; B 124)
16 Fabric 2. Simple rim with flattened top (B 116; A 1)
17 Fabric 2. Everted rim with internal depression, ?lid-seating (U/S)
18 Fabric 2. Tapered, sharply angled rim from a jug or pitcher with the beginning of a strap handle with a deep central thumb print where handle joins the neck (B 103)
19 Fabric 6. Thin-walled small jug or flask. Internal and external glaze varying in colour from olive green to tan (B 116)
20 Fabric 13. Coarse, handmade shallow vessel with pouring lip and slightly sagging base, perhaps part of a dripping tray (D 418/1)

Building materials

[M1:C8] Sandstone was used for the Phase I building. Jurassic Lower Lias was used in the Phase II town wall foundations and Triassic sandstone was probably used for the superstructure. Oak and alder were used for underpinning the wall and the tower respectively. Ceramic, sandstone, and limestone tiles were also recovered. (Identifications by John Crossling.)

Metalwork

Copper alloy and lead
G Lloyd-Morgan

[M1:C13] There were thirty-two copper alloy objects and fragments and one lead object.

1 An undecorated Polden Hill *fibula* was found with the inhumation on area A. It had slightly crude oval mouldings on either side of the top of the bow, and a neat terminal knob and collar at the foot. The brooch is now a little bent and distorted, and the chord, pin, and part of the catch plate are lost. L 64.6mm (fig 13). (Phase I, A 14/1)

Iron
Quita Mould

Seventy-five iron objects were recovered from the site, occurring in Areas B, C, D, and E. The iron comprised principally of structural fittings, chiefly timber nails (fig 13, 1, 3–4), along with a small quantity of miscellaneous broken fragments (fig 13, 2). The objects found are listed by area and phase in tables 10 and 11 (unstratified objects have been omitted).

Illustrated objects (see fig 13 [M1:C14])

1 Iron nail. Type 1b timber nail with clenched shank of square section and flat head. Complete. Encrusted. Shank L 33/14mm, head L 13mm. (Phase IIb, D 465)
2 Iron sheet, folded. Fragment of folded sheet with minerally preserved organic remains on the exterior, likely to be post-depositional, and small fragments of copper alloy adhering. Also four fragments broken from the above. Incomplete. Encrusted. L 22mm, W 23mm. (Phase IIb, E 805/1)
3 Iron nail. Type 1b timber nail with square-sectioned shank and flat head. Complete. Encrusted. Shank L 66mm, head L 20mm. (Phase IIb, E 811)
4 Iron nail. Large type 1b nail with curved shank of square section and flat head. Complete. Encrusted. Shank L 105mm, head L 21mm. (Phase III, E 804)

Table 10 Stratified iron finds from area B

Object	Phase A	B	C	Total
Arrowhead			1	1
Blade			2	2
Nail			9	9
Nail shank			5	5
Shank, curved			1	1
Sheet			2	2
Strap			1	1
Tine			1	1
Total			22	22

Table 11 Stratified iron finds from areas C, D, and E

Object	Phase I	I/II	IIa	IIb	III	IV	Total
Angle bracket						1	1
Fragment						1	1
Hobnail				1			1
Nail	4	1	4	6	3	10	28
Nailed binding						2	2
Nail shank	3			4	1	5	13
Sheet, folded				1	1		2
Total	7	1	4	12	5	19	48

5 Iron arrowhead. Small barbed arrowhead with lozenge-sectioned head and round-sectioned neck broken before the socket. *London Museum Medieval Catalogue*, type 13 (London Museum 1940, 66 fig 16), comparable with an example dated AD 1241–1263 from Dyserth Castle, Flint (London Museum 1940, fig 17, no 15). Incomplete. L 31mm, max W 17mm, neck diam 9mm. (Phase C, B 101)

Coins
W A Seaby

See [M1:D3] for full details.

Phase	Context	Find No	Identification
I	11	1	270–3
IIa	442	32	270–3
IIa	449	12	later 3rd century
IIa	449	13	later 3rd century
IIb	307	5	260–8
IIb	806	19	259–68
IV	436	9	270–3
–	1290	8	1614–25
U/S	–	23	270–3
U/S	–	24	late 3rd century
U/S	–	29	270–3
U/S	–	30	287–93
U/S	–	31	c 364–75
U/S	–	33	138–161
U/S	–	34	312–337
U/S	–	35	c 360–3
U/S	–	36	c 367–75
U/S	–	37	c 367–75
U/S	–	38	c 380–392
U/S	–	39	380–92
U/S	–	40	1625–c 1648
U/S	–	41	Reckoning counter
U/S	–	42–6	c 368–75
U/S	–	47–9	312–67
U/S	–	50–51	Probably 4th century

Copper alloy working debris
Justine Bayley

[M1:D4] Fragments, including parts of crucibles indicated that copper alloys were being melted on the site.

Bone

Human bone
Ann Stirland

[M1:D5] The skeleton of an adult, age and sex unknown was found on area A (context 14). The ankylosis of the sacro-iliac joint, however, could suggest a male of at least 25 years. A fracture of the right lower arm was caused by a fall or parrying a blow. A further 13 scattered bone fragments were recovered from the rest of the site.

Animal bone
Julie Hamilton

[M1:D6] Only Roman bone (8.3% of identified fragments) is discussed here and in the microfiche. Of the identified fragments, 71 were cattle, 41 sheep/goat (no definite goat), 11 pig, 1 horse, 5 dog, and 1 red deer. In this report the term 'sheep' should be taken to mean sheep or goat although no definite goat was identified. Tables detailing fragment numbers and minimum number of individuals are presented in the microfiche (tables M11, M12). Tables of bone measurements and age data will be kept in the site archive along with all the details of the post-Roman bone (these data are not statistically significant and so not presented here). In common with the format of the rest of the publication, the animal bone is reported in two sections: the bone from area B and that from areas A, C, D, and E.

Area B

Very little bone came from undoubtedly Roman features (table M11). Species present were cattle, sheep, pig, and dog. The number of fragments was really too small to draw any conclusions.

There was a large amount of bone from an extensive layer and other early features which may have been largely Roman. However, since there is no way of distinguishing definitely Roman bone, detailed analysis seems unjustified.

Areas A, C, D, E

Species present were cattle, sheep/goat (no definite goat), pig, horse, dog, and red deer (*Cervus elaphus*) (table M12). Taking meat weight into account, and assuming that these are basically food remains, cattle predominated over sheep, and pig provided a small proportion of meat. Probably red deer was also hunted and eaten.

The majority of the bone was from the fill of the construction trench of the town wall and layers associated with the building of the tower (or possibly the wall). Few fragments were heavily worn. There was evidence of gnawing and butchery. Skeletal part representation was not outstandingly irregular for any species. Low meat value bones were quite common, suggesting butchery waste, probably with some kitchen debris also. There was no evidence of specialized processing of carcasses. Probably advantage was taken of construction work to deposit rubbish of various kinds.

Ecological remains

Charred plant remains
Lisa Moffett

[M1:D11] The Gateway Supermarket site was mainly an investigation of the town defences and it had few contexts with occupation material that might have been expected to produce charred plant remains. However, it was felt to be of value to continue botanical investigations to add to the growing evidence for economic plants in the Roman and medieval town. Most of the samples contained some residual amounts of cereals and weed seeds. One of the most productive samples, a possible Roman occupation deposit, (452/0/1) contained 50 fruit clusters of beet (*Beta vulgaris*) as well as abundant seeds of stinking mayweed (*Anthemis cotula*). Stinking mayweed is now a rare weed of mainly heavy soils. Beet grows wild chiefly in coastal habitats and its presence so far inland is likely to indicate that it was cultivated. The chances of garden vegetable seeds or remains being preserved by charring or waterlogging, and under circumstances where they can be distingushed from their wild relatives, are generally quite rare, and these plants are undoubtedly very much under-represented in the archaeological record. A sample from the Roman context 473/1/1 is peculiar in consisting almost entirely of charred hemlock (*Conium maculatum*) seeds. It is possible that the plant was collected deliberately for medicinal purposes, though hemlock is also a common plant on damp and disturbed ground. Sample 805/1/1 is also Roman, and consists of an almost pure crop of wheat which appears to be a fully threshed and cleaned product ready to be prepared for consumption. It does not resemble in composition the spelt and emmer chaff-dominated

assemblage from Coulters Garage and is probably too late in date to be related to the supposed granary.

Snails
Beverley Meddens

[M1:E1] Samples were examined from near the bottom of the soil profile of borehole AA. Except for two individual terrestrial specimens the assemblage was exclusively aquatic and supports the results of the soil and other analyses showing a river channel with varying flow speeds.

Waterlogged plant remains
James Greig

[M1:E3] The pollen diagram indicates a fairly small amount of woodland, probably mixed with hawthorn (*Crataegus*) and elder (*Sambucus*) scrub (fig 14). Open landscape is represented by grassland plants, and arable land or cereal processing by cereal pollen. This seems to represent the rather open landscape of the Romano-British period, especially in Alcester itself, with less woodland than during the Iron Age.

Soil analysis
Matthew Canti

Four sets of soil samples were taken: a complete borehole core (F), three samples from the Phase A bank (151), three from Phase B material (136) to the SW of the rampart, provisionally thought to derive from it, and three from the Phase I granary construction make-up layer (11). They were analysed in terms of colour, stone content, anthropogenic remains, and

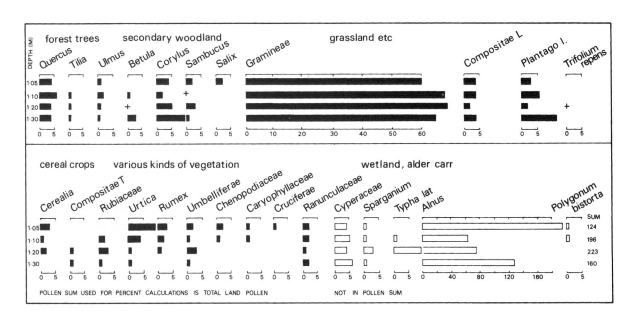

Figure 14 Pollen diagram

particle size to British Standard 1377. Details of the analyses can be found in the site archive and in Canti (1987).

The natural deposits at the bottom of the borehole core appeared to consist of Devensian gravels (1057, 1056) of the first and second river terraces, perhaps deposited by meltwater. They were overlaid by a suite of marsh clays (1050–5) which were very fine at the bottom. This depositional change is best explained by sedimentary factors such as river channel abandonment or barrier accretion. Higher up the deposits were coarser.

The samples from the Phase A bank (151) and the Phase I make-up (11) were distinct from each other and were almost certainly not derived from the marsh clays seen in the borehole core. However they did belong to the same sedimentary regime and could easily have come from other nearby natural deposits.

The analysis showed that the sample of Phase B material (136) was not derived from the surviving bank layer (151), although this does not rule out the possibility of it having been derived from higher rampart deposits which no longer exist. Its particle size analysis was similar to that of the upper (topsoil) layers in the borehole.

Other finds

Glass and shale
Denise Allen

[M1:E8] There were two fragments of glass and part of a shale bracelet.

Radiocarbon dating

[M1:E8] Radiocarbon dates were obtained from four samples of wood piling, two samples from the wall and two samples from the tower foundations. The dates (see table M19) were statistically identical (Ward and Wilson's (1986) T-test):

Wall: HAR-8522 ± HAR-8523: 1715 ± 30 BP (1 sigma: Cal AD 255–380; 2 sigma: Cal AD 230–405)

Tower: HAR-8524 ± HAR-8525: 1695 ± 50 BP (1 sigma: Cal AD 255–410; 2 sigma: Cal AD 230–430).

(Calibrations by Stuiver and Pearson 1986.)

Discussion
Stephen Cracknell

Pre-Roman and early Roman landscape

The River Arrow runs round the east side of the modern town centre but it now seems certain that it once ran round the west side. Indeed, until the flood barriers were built in recent years, the river occasionally broke its banks and flooded the Moorfield area, of which the excavated site forms a part.

Peat and other organic deposits, possibly of several different dates, have now been found over a large area at the south end of Moorfield Road indicating a damp, marshy environment, but no river channel has been identified. (At the other end of Moorfield Rd Mahany found 'an ox-bow lake of the river which had evidently been open in medieval times' in the Rectory Garden (Mahany 1965), but this is some distance away). The contours plotted in fig 3 indicate that the gravel river terrace sloped down to the SW in the supermarket area suggesting that the main channel may be located somewhere to the SW of the Gateway supermarket site and the adjacent Coulters Garage site (site 10 in fig 1). However, it is possible that a channel or channels lay within the area of peat deposit as marked on fig 3, with the peat being laid down only after the flow of water ceased. The soil analysis, the presence of aquatic snails, and the pollen assemblage all confirm that the area was wet at the time when the lowest deposits on top of the river terrace were laid down.

The peat and organic deposits on the Gateway supermarket site were related to those seen by Booth during his investigations of the Coulters Garage site (Booth 1985). Peat was also seen in the excavations at Bulls Head Yard (Phase 1: site 7; Phase 2: site 8), on the Market site (site 9), and in borehole 1 on a site to the west of Moorfield Rd (fig 2, site 14, P Booth pers comm). An attempt has been made to plot the edge of the peaty organic deposits on fig 3.

There are four pieces of dating evidence available for the organic deposits. A deposit at Coulters Garage had a C-14 date of 2410 ± 110 BP (HAR 4905). Secondly, a determination for peat in Bulls Head Yard Phase 1 Hole 7 gave a date of 1760 ± 60 BP (HAR 2257) (1 sigma: Cal AD 215–345; 2 sigma: Cal AD 120–410, Stuiver and Pearson 1986). Thirdly, the town defences were rebuilt in the late 4th century AD extending the circuit to include areas with peaty deposits on the eastern margins of the Moorfield marsh. As there would be little point in enclosing wet land it seems that the marsh must have partly dried out by that time: peat was no longer being deposited. Further east a C-14 date of 2150 ± 50 BP (GU-5137) (1 sigma: Cal BC 355–115; 2 sigma: Cal BC 380–90, Stuiver and Pearson 1986) from twigs on the Gas House Lane site indicates the presence of waterlogged deposits further round the gravel 'island'.

Booth has suggested that in most areas on the Coulters Garage site the accumulation of peat was terminated by the deposition of a layer of clean red clay, derived from Mercian Mudstone outcrops higher up the Arrow valley, a phenomenon first described by Shotton (Booth 1985; Shotton 1978). Nevertheless, in some areas Booth identified a second, later phase of peat deposition. The starting date for the alluviation is given by Shotton as c 660 BC. Clay deposits of various colours have been seen at appropriate levels on the watching briefs in the surrounding area (sites 7–9, 11 on fig 2; details in Warwicks SMR) but it is by no means clear if they were all related. Booth (1985) suggests that as far as the area at the south end of Moorfield Road is concerned the alluviation had substantially finished by the middle of the Roman period. Clean clay deposits were seen at low levels on Gateway supermarket areas D and B and in the boreholes A–L and Z. To the west, these gravelless clay layers were interleaved to some extent with the organic deposits. The clays were various colours (the clay on the Coulters Garage site was normally red). The interleaving of the clay and organic deposits may suggest that the alluviation took place at intervals over a period of time but the evidence of the particle size analysis of the clays in borehole F suggests a more continuous process. Only an extensive sampling programme covering a large part of the marsh is likely to yield a definite answer. There was no evidence from this site about the date and duration of the alluviation but Booth's scheme seems plausible.

Phase A: first town defences

A bank of layers made up from clay and gravel was uncovered at the NE end of area B. This is interpreted as part of the first, earthwork town defences, dating to the 2nd century or later, although it must be admitted that the evidence from this site was insubstantial. The interpretation rests largely on the fact that the bank lay on the supposed course of the defences indicated by other excavations and observations and that it was similar to the remains at Gas House Lane. The ground to the SW of the bank sloped downwards. The front edge of the rampart, as excavated, was a near-vertical face suggesting the presence of a timber revetment. However there were no traces of associated postholes or tie beams.

The Gateway supermarket bank lay on a thick deposit of intermixed clay and gravel, probably 700mm deep at its deepest, which had been laid on the top of the slope of the purer, probably naturally deposited clays discussed in the previous section. Although no dating evidence was recovered it would seem likely that this deposit was laid down in order to level up the sloping ground prior to the construction of the rampart. There was no buried soil horizon under the defences.

There was no certain trace of a ditch outside the rampart. Although the ground did slope down to the SW, as excavation was very limited in this area, it was not clear if the slope was artificial. In any case the slope was not steep, and it cannot have been the edge of the kind of steep-sided ditch that would have been typical at this date. As the SW half of area B was not excavated down to the undisturbed substrata, had the ditch been in that area it would not have been observed. However, this would place the town side of the ditch at more than six metres from the edge of the rampart and this would be an excessively wide berm for a late 2nd-century defensive structure. As mentioned above, some of the earlier deposits at the deepest point of excavation

and in the boreholes AA–DD suggest a damp, perhaps marshy area lay to the SW of the rampart and this factor, combined with a pre-existing slope, may have obviated the need for a formal defensive ditch. On the other hand analysis of the soil deposits suggests that the rampart dump could have been derived from the nearby alluvial clays, dug out of some kind of quarry ditch. It is easier to prove the presence of a ditch than its absence and the evidence from the Gateway supermarket excavations is, in any case equivocal. A similar situation was seen at Gas House Lane: the case against the presence of a formal ditch seems to be growing. There is only one other example of a defended Roman settlement that did not have a ditch and that is Gatcombe (Crickmore 1984, 113) but Gatcombe was certainly not typical of Romano-British small towns and may not have been a town at all.

There were no sherds from the lowest layers of area B on the supermarket site. There were only three sherds from undisturbed Roman contexts dating to the time of the decay of the rampart (an undateable fragment of Severn Valley ware, a fragment of samian dating to AD 140–200, and a small sherd from a 4th-century BB1 bowl with a dropped flange). In so far as it goes, the evidence is compatible with Mahany's suggested date of 2nd century or later for the building of the first defences (Cracknell and Mahany 1994). The most likely date for the building of the defences would seem to be about AD 200 (on the basis of the Gas House Lane site).

Phase I: occupation outside the earthwork defences

There were several structures on areas A, C, D, and E and on the Coulters Garage site which were contemporary with or later than the earthwork defences and earlier than the building of the town wall in the mid-4th century. They were, of course, outside the defended area as then defined, with the earth rampart lying 30m or more away. It was not clear how long the rampart was maintained in good repair and hence it is uncertain to what extent these buildings impinged on any *cordon sanitaire* which would have been kept clear in front of it.

The earliest major structure known from outside the defences was represented in Booth's 1978–9 Coulters Garage excavations (site 10 in figs 1, 2) by a series of posts (Booth 1985). Booth has interpreted this as a possible timber granary with a *terminus post quem* of 'the later 2nd century'. At its nearest point this structure was something like 40m away from the line of the defences, well to the south of the supermarket site trenches.

This building was followed by a stone-walled structure with 1m wide walls (see the reconstruction model in plate 9). Fragments of the stone building were first recorded at the Coulters Garage site and the NE end of the structure was seen on area D.

Booth (1985) thought that the construction of the

stone building was preceded by the dumping of clay to level up the site and that there may have been further dumping while the building was being erected. It seems likely that the extensive Phase I clay dump seen on the supermarket site areas A, D, and E was part of the initial dump. There was no evidence to suggest that the decaying Phase A clay and gravel rampart was used as a quarry for this dump. The layers of gravel seen in the rampart were not represented in the dump and particle size analysis of one of the clay layers in the rampart and one in the dump showed that they were not the same.

The clay dump contained a coin probably dating to the reign of Tetricus I (AD 270–3) which is in accord with the date of around AD 300 proposed for the construction of the stone building. A skeleton was also uncovered within the clay deposit. The finds associated with the burial – a Polden Hill *fibula* and a sherd of BB1 – might together suggest a date of about AD 120–50, although the BB1 could be much later. However, the clay layers above the skeleton were apparently the same as those below it and contained late 3rd-century material. It seems more reasonable to date the burial to late in the 3rd century (and assume that the brooch was an heirloom) than to date it to early in the 2nd century and assume that the skeleton was covered directly by 3rd-century layers without the presence of any intervening soil deposits.

The supermarket excavation revealed the NE end of the Coulters Garage stone building, including a 9.2m length of the end wall on area D and a fragment of the SE wall on area E. The end bay of the building, at 3.1m wide, was similar in size to the other bays to the south-west. Only a very small fragment of the interior of the structure was excavated so the results may not be significant but, as in Booth's excavation, there was no sign of flooring material.

Booth (1985) considered that this building could have been a granary or store building. There was no evidence from the supermarket site either to confirm or to deny this suggestion. The significance of the current excavation lies in what it has to say about the demolition of the structure, rather than about its life. Stratigraphically there was no direct link between the destruction of the granary and the *construction* of the town wall although the destruction of the granary was shown to have been earlier than the *destruction* of the town wall. However, it is inconceivable that a structure as substantial as the granary would have been left standing directly outside the new defences. It is surprising that the granary was not actually included in the new and enlarged defensive circuit. If, as Booth suggests, it was an official building, perhaps a collecting point for the *annona militaris*, it would have been a prime candidate for inclusion within the walls. Its demolition at the time that the wall was built almost certainly shows that it was already obsolete, although it could have been rebuilt on another site.

A few metres to the NW of the granary Booth uncovered a short segment of a wall of similar construction, running at a few degrees from parallel to the long axis of the granary. It was thought possible that this wall represented a second granary. Area A, which was laid out within the supposed area of this building, failed to reveal any trace of it, although this does not rule out the possibility that it existed but terminated further to the SW than expected.

Traces of floors and walls were uncovered in the area to the SE of the end of the granary in the small space not damaged by later structures on area E, and on area C. The first period of occupation was represented by a mortar floor. This had presumably been inside a building although the size of the structure was not determined. Above this floor was a gravelly make-up layer, a possible wall stub (which only just projected into the trench), and rubble probably associated with the destruction of the wall. A third period was represented by a gravel surface. This was overlaid by a mortar floor which had two parallel wall lines associated with it. Both were of post-and-slot construction, though they were rather different in nature. Again the overall dimensions of this structure are not known. The two timber walls appeared to be aligned at right angles to the long axis of the granary. It seems likely that these traces represent a series of outbuildings associated with the construction or use of the granary nearby.

The adjacent trench (T2N) on the Coulters Garage site produced similar remains but it is impossible to be certain exactly how they were related to the remains described above. At Coulters Garage, a clay layer was overlaid by a mortar floor with a rubble make up. The mortar floor was in turn overlaid by dumps of clay and rubble, probably destruction debris (Booth 1985, 80). While not identical, this sequence suggests that the Coulters Garage remains should be equated with the first two periods of occupation on the adjacent parts of areas C and E. However, Booth noted that the features in area 2 were aligned at an odd angle to the granary and that the fragment of stone wall to the NW and the fragments of stone and timber walling to the SE of it were also on this alignment. The alignment is the same as that of the town wall (12° anticlockwise of the granary short axis). It is possible, then, that the structures were connected with the construction of the town wall rather than with the granary, as Booth supposed. Nevertheless, the stone structures at least were too substantial to have been workmen's huts.

There were few finds associated with these buildings but of particular note was a dump of deliberately burned hemlock seeds found in a layer which was sealed by the rampart that backed onto the Phase IIa town wall. Also, seeds of beet were found in an adjacent context. (See 'Charred plant remains'.)

Phase IIa: the town wall

The town wall was probably built shortly after AD 364 (see below). In the SW part of the circuit the defences consisted of a stone wall (robbed out) with a clay and gravel revetment behind it, similar to the remains revealed on the opposite side of the circuit in 1964 (Mahany 1965; 1994). The customary third element of Roman town defences, a ditch, was missing. (Although the Phase I granary was demolished to accommodate the wall, there was no sign of a ditch cutting its 40m length.)

The wall was supported by irregularly spaced timber piles which had been partially rammed into the gravel subsoil at the bottom of a foundation trench. The piles, all made of oak, were pointed but otherwise untrimmed. They had been cut in the late spring or early summer from 36- to 60-year-old trees. The space between them was packed with large angular stones, followed by thinner layers of gravel and then clay. Discontinuous, longitudinal, horizontal, trimmed and squared timber beams were laid on top of the clay and there was at least one cross-beam laid on top of them. The spaces between the beams were packed with stone and lumps of what at the time of excavation was a sandy loam although it may originally have been mortar.

The largest collection of animal bone from the sites was recovered from this trench (Phase IIa) and from layers associated with the building of the tower (Phase IIb) although the overall quantities were small. Domestic, butchery, and kitchen waste were all probably represented.

On the Gateway supermarket site, the foundations would originally have reached up to the contemporary Roman ground level (though subsequent collapse has left the top of the foundations at a rather lower level). It may be that elsewhere on the circuit the timber piling did not project from the base of the trench to such a great extent. The piles supported a network of timber lacing. This feature was not apparent on the NE side of the circuit. However, as the trenches there were dug by machine, the traces of the timber lacing may not have been recognizable.

Although the wall itself did not survive, the timber lacing and the shape of the robber trench demonstrate the width of the wall. The outermost edges of the longitudinal beams were separated by 3.2m and this must have been the minimum width of the wall. The maximum width – 3.5m – is given by the distance between the near-vertical face on the NE side of the robber trench and the edge of a layer of mortar on the opposite side of the trench.

The wall was backed by a clay and gravel revetment bank. There was no surviving stratigraphic relationship between the wall and the bank since the wall had been thoroughly robbed out. The coins from the rampart are not particularly helpful. All three dated to the late 3rd century as compared with a mid-4th century date for the wall. The coins merely provide a *terminus post quem* for the rampart but do not confirm that it and the wall were contemporary. However, there are several reasons for believing that the bank and the wall were built at one time:

1 An earlier defensive rampart existed elsewhere (area B).

2 The surviving part of the revetment bank was made up of soils similar to those which would have been dug out of the top of the foundation trench of the wall. The increased proportion of sandstone fragments in some of the layers could be a product of stone trimming on site during the construction of the wall. The clay layers that would have been dug out of the bottom of the foundation trench were not present in the surviving part of the rampart but as much of the rampart had been eroded this is not surprising.

3 The slope of the layers in the bank indicated that it was piled up against a nearby structure.

While this evidence is not conclusive it seems to show that the revetment bank and wall were indeed contemporary. The evidence from Mahany's site MI is rather more positive (Mahany 1994). The wall construction trench there was more than 5.5m wide, presumably the result of a misjudgement as it was only 3.5m wide in the nearby trench MIII. In consequence earth had to be thrown back into the construction trench behind the wall to fill the gap. The clay-and-gravel rampart was then banked up against the wall, over part of the construction trench. Thus, although the wall was later robbed out, sufficient stratigraphy remained to demonstrate that the rampart was later than the wall construction trench and therefore almost certainly contemporary with the wall itself. Curiously, on Mahany's site MIII there was also a small bank of clay 3m wide by 0.4m high *outside* the wall but this feature was not present on the supermarket site. At Gas House Lane there was no stratigraphic relationship between the construction trench layers and the rampart.

Eventually the tree rings on the timbers removed from the foundation trench may provide an accurate date for the wall (see 'Dendrochronology') but at present the dating relies largely on a single coin. This coin, of Valentinian I and dated to AD 364–7, was found on Booth's Coulters Garage site in a context associated with the robbing of the walls of the Phase I granary, which must have occurred at the beginning of Phase II. The C-14 age determinations from the last twenty rings of the timber piles under the town wall (HAR-8522 + HAR-8523) and those from under the later tower (HAR-8524 + HAR 8525) were not significantly different (Ward and Wilson 1986). The respective mean dates at two standard deviations (95% confidence level) (Cal AD 230–405 and Cal AD 230–430, Stuiver and Pearson 1986) are compatible with a date for the wall in the third quarter of the 4th century, although they do not refine the dating suggested by the coin. The pottery is in general agreement with the other dating evidence, but there was not enough of it in appropriate layers to provide independent confirmation of the proposed *tpq* of AD 364. This date fits in with the intensification of activity noted during the late 4th century at Gas House Lane. The town wall is further discussed in the section on the defences below (p 127).

Phase IIb: external tower or bastion

After a few years, a tower was added to the wall. Like the wall itself, the tower was supported on a bed of piles topped by a lattice of horizontal beams. Dendrochronological analysis of the timbers suggested *tentatively* that the wood was cut down seven years later than the wood used for underpinning the town wall. The C-14 dates for the timbers were statistically identical to those from the wall (see above) as would be expected if there was such a small lapse of time between them. (Combined with the coin evidence from Coulters Garage (discussed in the preceding section) this gives a *tpq* of AD 371.) Alder was used instead of the oak of the main wall. Alder was almost certainly available in quantity in the Alcester area. It was prominent in the pollen records at Coulters Garage during the early Iron Age, although it declined later in the Iron Age along with other recorded tree pollen (Woodwards and Greig 1985). However, it is reasonable to assume that of the trees which remained in the area – presumably at some distance from the town – a good proportion was alder. The use of alder, therefore, seems to represent the sensible exploitation of local natural resources. (Oak may have been more difficult to obtain.)

At ground level, the foundation trench was slightly trapezoidal. None of the superstructure remained but the nature of the foundations gave two clues to its shape. Firstly, the piles covered the whole of the area of the foundation trench. The timber lacing probably covered the same area, presumably indicating that the tower was solid rather than hollow. (At Portchester the timber lacing (such as it was) only ran under the solid part of the walls (Johnson 1983, 196–214).) Secondly, the shape of the robber trench and the position of the demolition rubble suggested that the above-ground structure was a flattened D, semicircular, or perhaps polygonal shape, projecting about 5m from the wall. The shape of the robber trench was too irregular to allow a more precise definition of the shape but it does not appear to have been rectangular. The tower was built at a point 20m from the corner of the wall and about 80m from the likely position of the town gate, at the S end of the modern High Street (Cracknell 1985a).

It is clear that the provision of an external tower here was not a part of the original design of the stone defensive circuit. The structural independence of the wall and tower, the use of alder rather than oak, and the tentative seven year gap between the construction of the wall and the tower all indicate that the tower was an afterthought. The use of alder, a locally available but low-grade wood, suggests that standards had slipped for one reason or another.

Near to the tower was a small hollow which contained relics of copper alloy working, though none of it was *in situ*. Fuel ash slag, dribbles of copper alloys including brass, and sheet metal clippings indicate wrought and cast metal production on a small scale. The charcoal associated with the copper alloy working was predominantly oak and alder. Oak is said to be one of the best woods in terms of its heating value whilst alder is poor (Boulton and Jay 1946, 112). Both these species are known to have existed in the general vicinity of the site (Booth 1985) but more alder than oak was perhaps available locally. This deposit also contained an almost pure crop of threshed and cleaned wheat, presumably by coincidence.

A possible coin hoard was uncovered on the site by a local metal detector enthusiast (after the end of the excavation). Although he did not keep adequate records of the distribution of the coins, it seems likely that they belonged to a hoard deposited in the AD 380s (see 'Coins'). It was placed in the waste ground just inside the defences, in a similar kind of position to the hoard found on the Gas House Lane site.

Much of the pottery from disturbed Roman or post-Roman area B contexts dated to about this time, indicating occupation of the area within the defences right to the end of the Roman period. To the south, in the extra-mural area around Bleachfield Street, occupation also continued in the late 4th century and possibly later. This is in contrast with the Coulters Garage site just outside the defences where late material appears (unsurprisingly) to be virtually absent.

The supermarket site area B pottery assemblage was unusual in terms of the Alcester sites so far excavated in that it contained significantly more Oxfordshire products than normal. However, other 'fine' wares were not over-represented and there is no particular reason to believe that this was a 'table' ware assemblage. The proportion of Oxfordshire products may be partly a reflection of the late date of the group.

Phases III, IV, and C: post-Roman remains

The earliest post-Roman pottery on the site dated to the 12th or 13th century and a limited amount of 13th-century pottery was found in the robber trench of the town wall. The wall must have been demolished in part before that date but it is significant that the robbing was continuing into the 13th century, a time of noticeable activity in medieval Alcester. Indeed most of the post-Roman archaeological remains so far uncovered in the town date to about that time. The pottery waster dumps at School Rd dated to the 12th or 13th century (Cracknell and Jones 1985). A malting kiln or drying oven in Tibbet's Close was probably 13th century (Cracknell 1985a). A stone drying oven and associated features found on the Baromix site in Bleachfield St contained '12th- to 14th-century pottery' (Taylor 1969, 33). A medieval oven was found on Mahany's site C IIIA in association with two almost complete cooking pots dated to the 13th century (Cracknell and Mahany 1994). The medieval pottery at 21 Bleachfield St suggested occupation beginning in the 12th or 13th century (Cracknell 1985a). This is in contrast with the paucity of material dating to earlier years: a 7th-century silver bracelet fragment from Bleachfield St, a few sherds of possibly Saxon pottery from Birch Abbey, Gas House Lane, and Lloyds Bank, and an 11th-century crozier head from the Rectory Gardens.

The archaeological evidence is undoubtedly biased as most of it has come from the periphery of the medieval town but the historical record presents a similar picture, with Alcester beginning to appear more frequently in the historical record from the 13th century onwards. This is probably partly a product of the increase in the use of written records and may not be entirely related to Alcester's increasing significance. Nevertheless, the confirmation of Alcester's status as a free borough in 1251–2 (*VCH*, 9), the formal granting of a market charter *c* 1274 (the market existed as of ancient time), and the grant of an annual fair in 1292 (*VCH*, 13) all speak of a thriving community determined to protect its rights by committing them to paper.

Growth of the town would have led to demand for building stone and may well have resulted in further robbing of the decayed Roman town walls. After the walls had been robbed the trench was quickly backfilled, as the state of preservation of its vertical N side shows. Apart from this there was little archaeological trace of activity in what were already or were soon to become the back yards of the medieval burgage plots. Pits were dug, rubbish was dumped (particularly on area B) and (presumably) gardens were cultivated where once the town wall lay.

Gas House Lane

This report describes the archaeological work which took place at Gas House Lane, Alcester, Warwickshire, from 1988 to 1990 (figs 1, 15; NGR SP0905 5735). At the start of 1988 the site was occupied by small factories, largely constructed around the time of the Second World War. The site was redeveloped for housing in 1990–91.

Work was financed by Tom Pettifer (Contractors) Ltd and Stratford-on-Avon District Council (owners of the site at that time) and by English Heritage. Much of the work was directed by the editor, following a trial season organized by Martin Jones. The finds and site records have been deposited in Warwickshire Museum under the code AL 23.

The objectives of the Gas House Lane dig were defined as:

1 Identification of the nature, density and date of the intramural settlement.
2 Confirmation of the location of the town defences.
3 Recovery of dating evidence for the defences, including timber piles for dendrochronological dating from the second circuit.

Method of investigation

[M1:E9] The archaeological work on the Gas House Lane site was divided into three phases: a trial season in 1988, the main excavations in May–October 1989, and a watching brief the following year.

Five trenches were excavated during the trial season, located in the limited spaces available be-

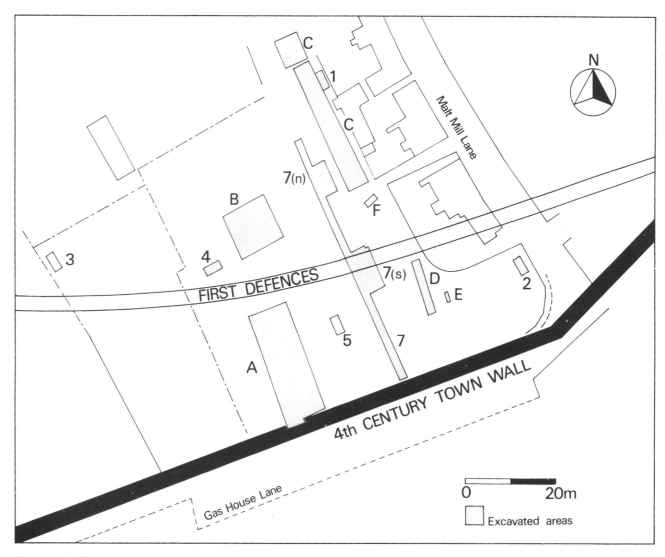

Figure 15 Details of site layout

tween the factories. As a result of this work, areas of archaeological significance were defined on the basis of the state of preservation and uniqueness of the features expected. Preservation was thought to be best in the NW corner of the site (under gardens), in the NE corner of the site (under an access road and raised factory floor), and in the undeveloped areas on the SE edge of the site, near Gas House Lane. The developers were asked to avoid the significant areas or, failing that, to pay for their excavation and publication.

After the development plans had been drawn up five main areas were selected for excavation (trenches A, B, C, 7 south, and 7 north). Trench A was designed to provide a section across the defences. As it turned out, the 4th-century stone wall defences were located in the extreme S of the site and the trench needed to be extended 2.2m to enable their excavation. This trench was excavated largely by machine. Trenches B, C, and 7 north were designed to investigate the intramural settlement. Trenches B, 7 north and the southern part of trench C were successful in this objective, although pressure of time meant that the lowest deposits could not be excavated over the whole area. However, the northern half of trench C (and particularly the detached part of the trench at the NW end) was badly disturbed by post-medieval pits and trenches and no significant Roman remains were recovered. Trench 7 south uncovered the line of the first defensive circuit and provided the most convincing section hitherto brought to light.

Only limited work was undertaken on the three other trenches. Trench D was abandoned after the removal of the topsoil as the deposits were seen to be similar to those in trench A. Trenches E and F were machine-dug trial pits excavated by the developers.

One of the problems in the interpretation of the deposits was the lack of complete buildings available for study, which was a direct result of the excavation strategy, devised in the early stages of developer funding in Warwickshire. At the planning stage, the site was divided into areas of primary, secondary, and lower archaeological importance. Through the planning process, the developers were requested to avoid the areas of primary importance and to contribute to the cost of excavation of any areas deemed to be of secondary importance if the deposits would be destroyed by the development. This *did* ensure that the best deposits survive intact for future archaeologists but it has had the unfortunate consequence that the areas actually excavated were of only moderate quality and their extent was effectively determined by modern development plans. In retrospect a more rewarding strategy would have been the *complete* excavation of any significant ancient structures which would be substantially damaged by the development (as well as avoidance of areas of primary importance).

The main aims of the watching brief were to follow the lines of the two sets of town defences and recover further timber piles if possible. (Further details of the method of investigation are given in microfiche.)

Summary of the stratigraphy

[M1:E12] Throughout the text, features which appear in plans are indicated in **bold**; those which appear in sections are shown in *italic*. Context numbers are only used in the printed section of the report where necessary for the identification of particular features; all contexts are described and listed individually in the microfiche.

The remains on the site have been divided into five main periods:

> Period A: before the construction of the first defences
> Period B: construction of the first defences
> Period C: after the construction of the first defences
> Period D: construction of the 4th-century town wall to *c* AD 410
> Period E: medieval and later

In some parts of the site, at certain times, the intensity of occupation justified the subdivision of these periods into phases (see fig 16). A key to the site plans is shown in fig 17 and a summary of the main structural features appears in fig 18. Phase plans are reproduced as figs 19–26 with sections in figs 27–31.

Period A: before the first defences

There were very few deposits which may have pre-dated the first town defences. The main deposits were in trench B: six linear soilmarks – ploughmarks or lazy beds – some postholes, and an irregular slot appear to date to before the first earthwork defences (fig 19). These features were overlain by what is presumably a plough-disturbed soil (*1138*; fig 28).

At the north end of trench C there was a single pit (2050) containing Iron Age pottery.

In trench 7(s) a layer of clay loam (*7180–81*) on top of the geological layers near to the first defences could itself be natural, or belong to Period A or B (fig 29).

Period B: construction of the first defences

The first defences were sectioned in trench 7(s) (fig 29, plates 10, 11). The rampart was built of layers of clay loam and gravel. It survived as a bank aligned ENE–WSW, 5m wide by 1.35m high. The S side (outside) of the rampart was nearly vertical. This feature has been noted elsewhere on the circuit (at the Gateway supermarket) and has been taken to indicate the presence of a timber revetment although associated postholes or timber lacing have yet to be found. The sharp, vertical nature of the rampart face appears to rule out the possibility of a turf revetment.

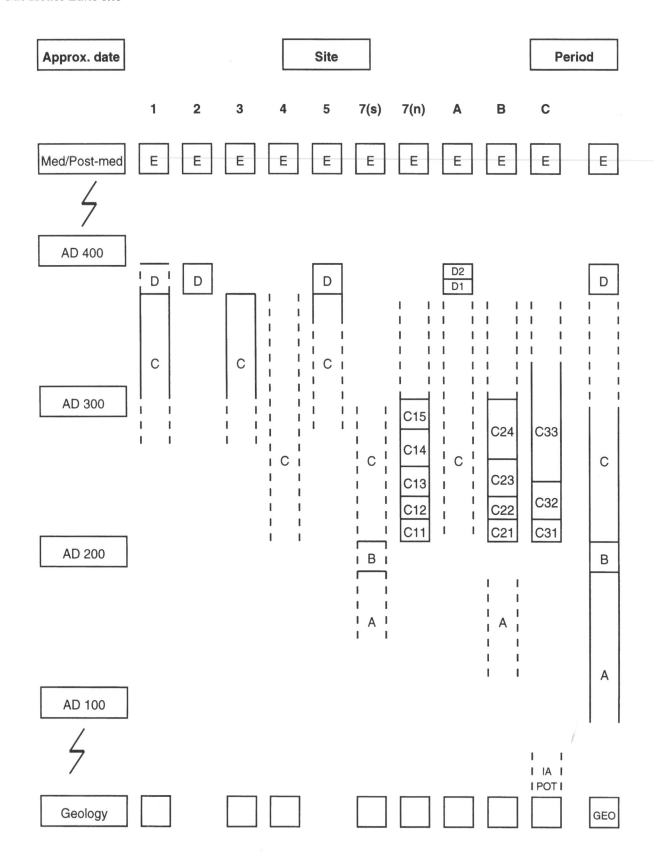

Figure 16 Subdivision of the site into phases with approximate equivalences and dates

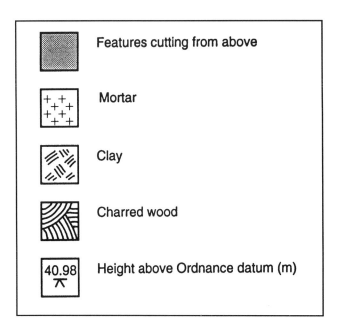

Key:
- Features cutting from above
- Mortar
- Clay
- Charred wood
- 40.98 — Height above Ordnance datum (m)

Figure 17 Key to plans and sections

In front of the rampart was a 1.8m-wide berm before the ground sloped down. The interface between the natural and artificial deposits was not clear and it is uncertain if this slope was the edge of a ditch. (Excavation of trench A revealed a broad zone of marshy deposits which may have obviated the need for a formal ditch.)

Period C: after the construction of the first defences

Deposits dated to after the construction of the first defences were found in all trenches except for trench 2 (which was not fully excavated). Apart from in trench 7(s) this dating is based on the artefacts recovered rather than on any stratigraphic indicators. Most of the deposits date to the 3rd century, with some resurgence of activity from the mid-4th century (see plates 12–14).

The earliest deposit was a series of thick gravelly layers seen in trenches 4, B, 7(n), and the southern part of C. This deposit was up to 330mm thick and had overall dimensions of at least 40m NE–SW by 10m NW–SE (trench 7(n): **7259**; Phase C11; fig 30; trench B: **1059, 1092, 1104**, *1128, 1127*; Phase C21; figs 19, 20, 28; trench C: *2121, 2122*; Phase C31; fig 31). It was probably a make-up layer, partially levelling the area before building commenced in the following phase.

The one other early feature of note was an exceptionally large and possibly isolated posthole (**1132**, Phase C21; fig 19) in the centre of trench B cut through the gravel surface.

Trench 7(n)

In trench 7(n) the extensive gravelly layer (Phase C11) was cut by the stake holes, slot, and postholes

defining building A, which lay mostly beyond the edge of the excavated area (fig 22, Phase C12). In the complex stratigraphy of this area it was difficult to distinguish traces of this structure from those assigned to building B (Phase C13) which followed.

Building B (fig 23, Phase C13) can be regarded as an extension and renovation of building A. The SE corner of the building was demolished and reconstructed on a new alignment, which implies the addition of a second ridge. A combination of cill beams and vertical posts and stakes was again used (with part of one of the cills surviving as a charred timber).

Inside building B was a clay floor which was pockmarked by small holes. The apparent restriction of these features to the area of the building might suggest that they were contemporary with its use. On the other hand, it would be an unusual way to treat the floor of a standing building.

Outside the building were gravel surfaces and occupation deposits. A curious linear band of yellowish brown soil (**7238**) extended parallel to the wall of building B but there was no clear evidence that it was part of the structure.

Building B was demolished, to be replaced by a structure with stone foundations. This structure, building C (fig 24, Phase C14) survived as a two-period wall and various stone features on top of the Phase C13 gravel surface. The NW part of the wall was made of dry stone set directly on the gravel surface. The S part was constructed on a foundation trench which contained six post pads spaced at 0.6m centres. No other walls were found associated with building C but to the S and SW there were mainly soil layers whilst the area to the NE was covered with stone rubble which formed half-recognizable structures. There were further possible traces of building C – stone rubble – in trench C (fig 26, Phase C33). The area which had previously been external now became internal.

Phase C15 saw the demolition of building C and the making of a new structure, evidenced by three postholes (7110–12), a rough line of stones (7161), and an ill-defined slot (7160) (figs 18D, 25). It is by no means certain if this structure was a building or a fence-line; there was no differentiation between the layers on either side of it. The most significant thing about it is the realignment, at 25 degrees clockwise of the previous alignment which had been in use on the site.

The latest surviving Roman feature was a gravel surface covering the eastern two-thirds of the trench.

Trench B

The earliest structure in trench B, building D, was constructed on horizontal timber cill beams, and with wattle and daub, traces of which had survived near the walls (fig 20, phase C22). There was one internal posthole, associated with a partition. The single room that was completely within the trench measured

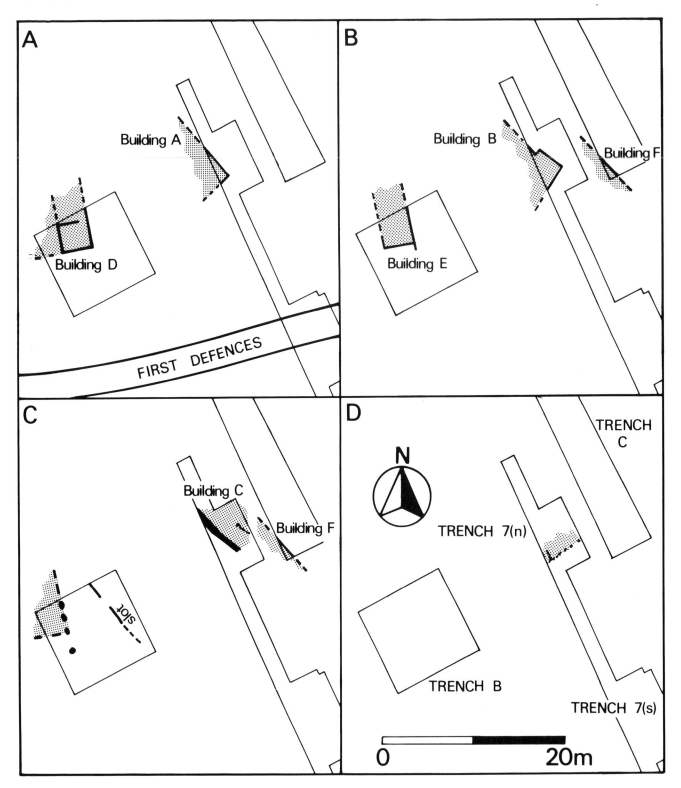

Figure 18   Main structural features on trenches B, C, 7(n), and 7(s). **A: early to mid-3rd century** – *first defences on trench 7(s), Building A (Phase C12), Building D (Phase C22).* **B: mid-3rd century** – *Building B (Phase C13), Building E (Phase C23), and possibly Building F (Phases C32–3).* **C: mid- to late 3rd century** – *Building C (Phase C14), posthole and slot on trench B (Phase C24), and possibly Building F (Phases C32–3).* **D: late 3rd century** – *post settings on trench 7(n) (Phase C15)*

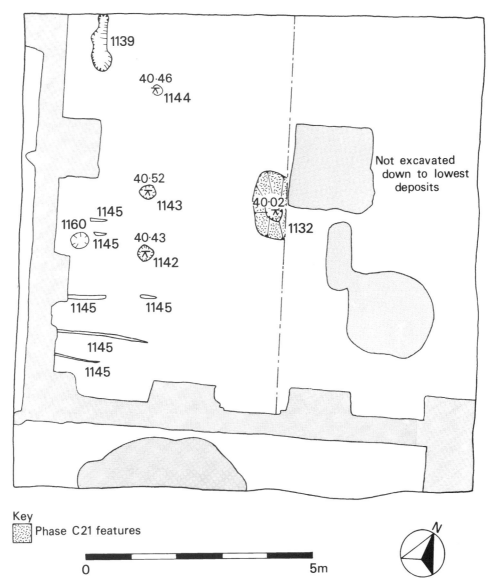

Key
▨ Phase C21 features

0   5m

N

Figure 19   Trench B, early features: Period A and Phase C21

3.6m E–W × 3m N–S; the building certainly extended to the N and may have extended to the W. It was aligned 10 degrees clockwise of the phase A features but this may not be significant. Initially the Phase C21 gravel surface served as a floor but the building was later refloored with silty clay loam which ran over the (presumably demolished) partition.

To the S were two possible stone pads (*1113, 1114*) approximately aligned with the E wall, surrounded by deposits which built up during the occupation of the building.

Building E (Phase C23) was a replacement for building D. Like its predecessor, building E was constructed on cill beams. In contrast, however, there was evidence for postholes, and plaster was used on the walls (fig 21). Again the structure extended beyond the N edge of the trench and may have extended to the W. There was an internal gravel floor. The alignment of a possible beam slot and a posthole suggested that the structure may have extended beyond the apparent SE corner.

The occupation deposits outside the building were cut by several small holes. An irregular line of postholes (**1044, 1061, 1080** etc), perhaps a fence, extended from the SW corner of the building, on the same line as some of the phase A features. There was also a gravel surface in the N corner of the site.

Three large postholes cut the floor of building E marking its demolition (Phase C24). A fourth posthole to the S may have been associated but its spacing was uneven and its fill different. No floor layers contemporary with these postholes had survived the truncation of the site in recent years but it seems most likely that the building lay to the W.

In the E half of the site there was a long narrow slot aligned NW–SE like the structures on sites 7(n) and C, with which it was probably associated.

Building D

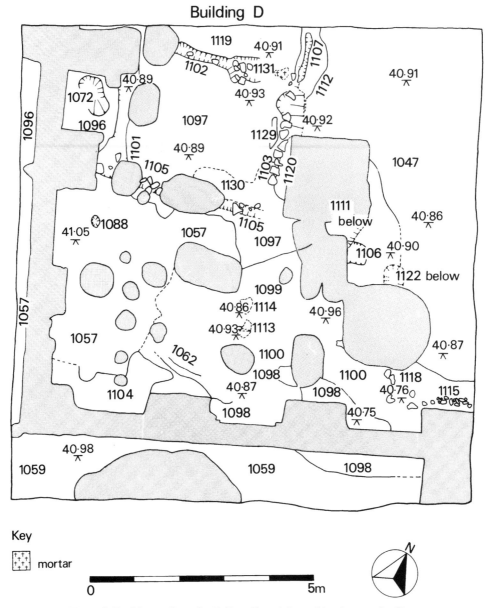

Key

mortar

0   5m

N

Figure 20   Trench B, Phase C22, building D, with earlier layers in S

Trench C

The N end of trench C (both the main trench and the detached section) had been badly damaged after the Roman period and little survived apart from pits. This is in itself significant as few pits were seen elsewhere on the Gas House Lane site. At the southern end of the trench the gravelly layer on top of the natural deposits (Phase C31) was largely overlaid by silty clay loam (Phase C32). The exception was in the SW corner where there was a triangular area of clay with two associated postholes (**2111**, *2138*; figs 26, 31). A possible interpretation of these features is that the clay layer was a floor with the two postholes marking the wall (building F).

In this scheme, the building was later refloored with gravel, probably at the same time as the external area was surfaced (Phase C33). At a later date building F was rebuilt with the replacement of the putative post-built structure with one founded on

a cill beam. No sign of building F was seen in trench C which makes interpretation difficult and conclusions uncertain.

Rubble at the N end of the external gravel surface probably represents further traces of building C (see trench 7(n)).

Elsewhere

The Period C deposits in trench 1 were similar to those at the N end of trench C; the other trenches contained nothing exceptional.

Period D: construction of the 4th-century town wall to AD 410

The only substantial traces of the town's 4th century defences were seen in trench A (Phase D1, plate 15).

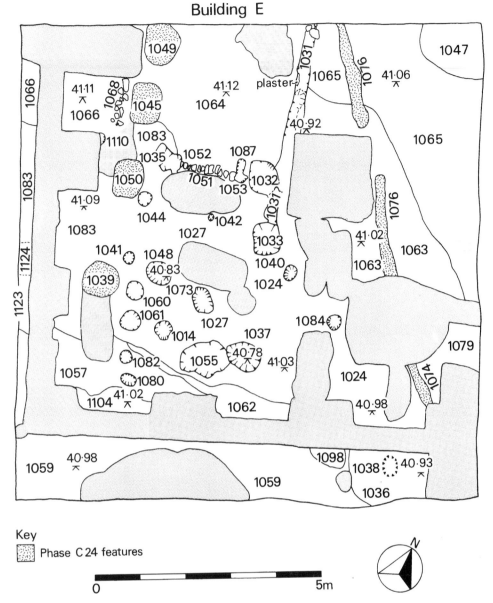

Figure 21   Trench B, Phase C23, building E, with Phase C24 features hatched,
and earlier layers still visible in SW

Parts of the town wall robber and construction trenches were uncovered and waterlogged timber piles removed. Further timber piles were seen during the watching brief. Unfortunately the timbers proved to be too small for dendrochronological analysis. Behind (to the N) of the robber trench was a rampart which survived to a thickness of 0.8m and an overall (eroded) width of 9m. The clay and gravel layers had been dumped over a coffin containing a male inhumation, which had been laid on the contemporary ground surface.

After the construction of the defences, soil accumulated against the back of the rampart, with the area being used for dumping rubbish (Phase D2).

Period D deposits were also identified in trenches 2 and 5. Although these probably date to the period of rubbish dumping they cannot be stratigraphically

related to the defences and so have been ascribed to Period D in general. A related series of layers in trench 2 contained a disturbed coin hoard dating to sometime after AD 388.

Period E: medieval and later

Post-Roman features were present in all trenches, with significant truncation in all areas except trench 3 and trench A. The main post-Roman features were a late medieval stone-lined pit, possibly a tanning pit (plate 16) and a drying kiln (plate 17), both at the N end of trench C. The keyhole-shaped drying kiln was revetted with stone. Possible fragments of a second kiln were seen in trench 2. A sherd of Saxon pottery was found in a post-medieval context in trench 7(s).

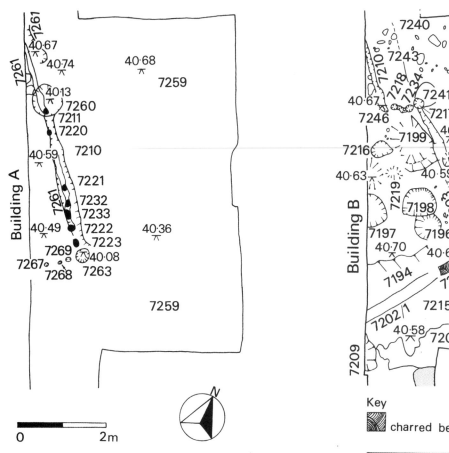

Figure 22   Trench 7(n), Phase C12, building A

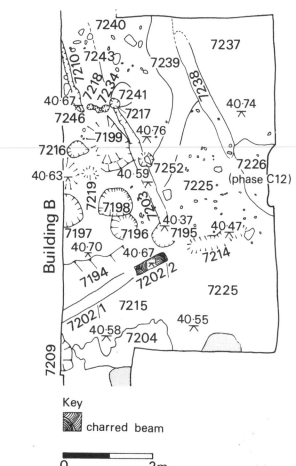

Figure 23   Trench 7(n), Phase C13, building B

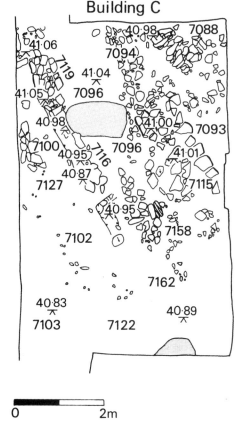

Figure 24   Trench 7(n), Phase C14, building C

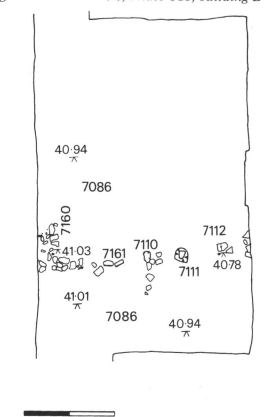

Figure 25   Trench 7(n), Phase C15

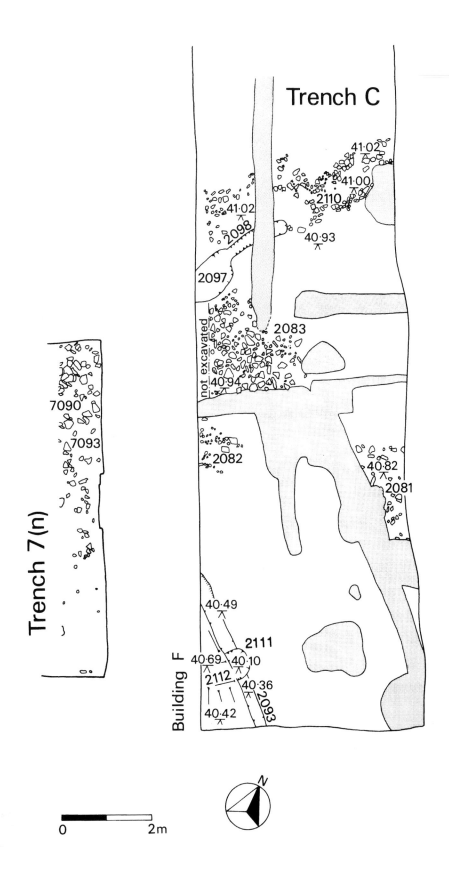

Figure 26 Trench C, south end, showing features of various phases: Phase C32, building F, posthole (2111) and clay floor (2112); Phase C33, building F beam slot (2093); Phase C33, ?more traces of building C, 2081, 2082, 2083, 2097, 2098, 2110, with the E edge of trench 7(n) Phase C14 shown for comparison (see also fig 24)

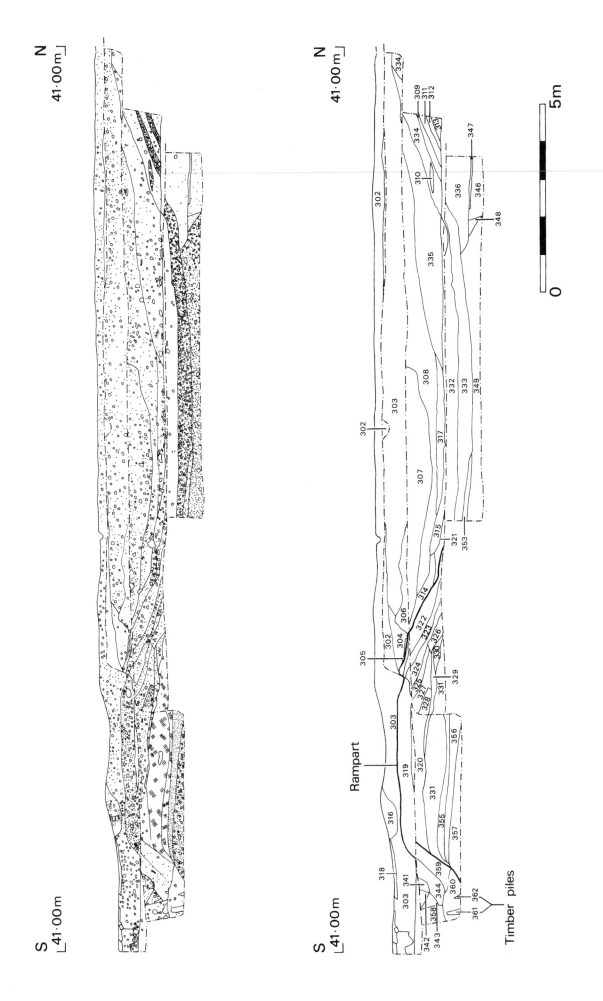

Figure 27 Section showing the SW side of trench A with the 4th century defences at the S end

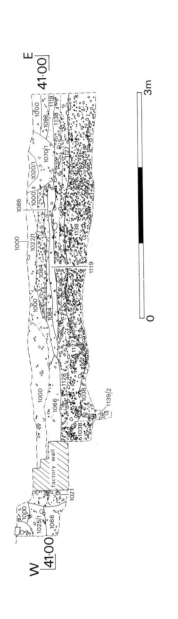

Figure 28 Section showing the western end of the NW side of trench B

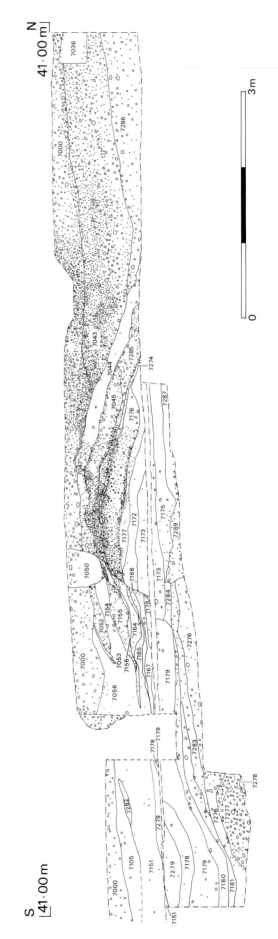

Figure 29 Section showing the SW side of trench 7(s) including the first town defences

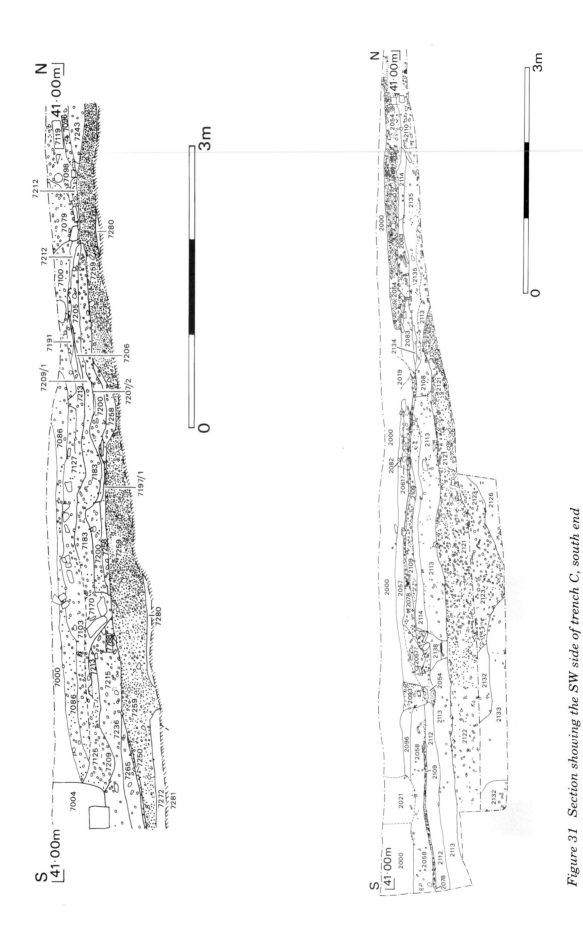

Figure 31 Section showing the SW side of trench C, south end

Plate 10 Trench 7(s), south-west side, Period B, showing the first town defences: with the rampart at top centre and possible ditch deposits in the foreground (see fig 29). Looking W. Horizontal scales 2m; vertical scale 1m

Plate 12 Trench 7(n), Period C. Showing Phase C12 building A slot (7210) and stake holes (see fig 22, and Phase C13 building B (see fig 23). Looking SE. Scales 2m

Plate 11 Trench 7(s), south-west side, Period B, detail of the first town rampart (see fig 29). Looking SW. Scale 2m

Plate 13 (above)   Trench B, Phase C23, building E (see fig 21). (The modern pig burial just to the S of the building had not been excavated at the time of the photograph.) Looking NW. Scales 2m

Plate 14 (left)   Trench C, south end, Phases C32, C33 (see fig 26). Beam slot of building F at lower left; rubble spreads, perhaps associated with building C in centre. Looking NW. Scales 2m

Plate 15 (below)   Trench A, S end, Period D. Showing the 4th-century rampart which backed the town wall. Timber piles associated with the wall were later recovered from the very SW corner of the trench (top left in photo). The dark staining above the tail of the rampart is modern chemical contamination. Looking SW. Horizontal scales 2m; vertical scale 1m

Plate 16 (left)   Trench C, north end, Period E. Late medieval stone-lined pit. Looking S. Horizontal scale 0.5m, vertical scale 1m

Plate 17 (below)   Trench C, north end, Period E. Late medieval drying kiln with partially excavated flue. Looking SW. Scale 0.5m

Finds: summary table

Table 12 Summary table of all finds excavated

Type of material	No or wt	Print	Microfiche	Comments
Roman pot (not samian)	8324	Discussion, p 58	M2:C6	Mostly 3rd/late 4th. Figs 32–39
Samian	799	Summary, p 74	M3:B8	
Post-Roman pot	358	Summary, p 97	M3:C5	One Saxon sherd. Fig 52
Building materials				
Preserved wood	3 samples			From 4th C wall. Undatable by dendrochronology
Stone	12 samples	Summary, p 99	M3:C12	Including ?rosso antico
Ceramic and stone tile	1234	Summary, p 99	M3:C13	Incl *pilae, antefix*, flue tile
Mortar		Summary, p 102	M3:D5	Samples analysed
Burnt daub	84	Summary, p 102	M3:D7	Fig 54
Metalwork				
Copper alloy	81	Summary, p 102	M3:D9	Fig 55
Lead	15	Summary, p 104	M3:E3	
Iron	337 +1050 nails	Summary, p 104	M3:E4	Fig 56
Slag	3070g	p 109	M3:F1	
Coins	26	Summary, p 109	M3:F3	Incl late 4th C hoard
Bone				
Worked bone	17	Summary, p 109	M3:F5	Fig 57
Human bone	Burial + mandible	Summary, p 111	M3:F7	Burial under 4th C rampart
Animal bone	*c* 8300	Summary, p 111	M3:F9	Antler working
Ecological remains				
Charred plants	29 samples	Summary, p 112	M4:A7	Roman asparagus
Preserved pollen	1 sample	Full report, p 112		Pre-Roman
Other finds				
Glass	99	Full report, p 115		Fig 58
Stone objects	71	Full report, p 119		Fig 59

Roman pottery
Jeremy Evans with the samian by Margaret (Bulmer) Ward

Introduction

[M2:C6] The pottery from the Gas House Lane site is of particular interest as it is a reasonably sized collection from a site which saw virtually no occupation before the early 3rd century. As such it provides a useful check on sequences from other sites in the town which saw continuous occupation and, therefore, tend to have had a greater component of archaeologically residual material in 3rd- and 4th-century deposits. The bulk of the material from the site is of early to mid-3rd-century date. There are also useful groups of late 4th-century material from the dumps behind the rampart at the back of the 4th-century stone wall which seem to have a low residual component, and which provide a very useful insight into pottery supply in the town at the close of the 4th century or later. These can be compared with the group from area B of the Gateway supermarket site.

Some 10,400 sherds (148.3kg) of pottery were excavated from the site of which 9,123 sherds (121.2kg) were Roman. The medieval pottery is the subject of a separate report. The Roman pottery has been recorded using the Warwickshire Museum fabric type series and standard recording system. Fabrics have been divided into thirteen major categories which have been further divided by inclusion types and frequency with the aid of a binocular microscope at ×20 magnification. Table M23 (microfiche M2:G13) gives brief fabric descriptions of all fabrics occurring on the site with fuller descriptions of those not previously described. Full descriptions and the fabric type series are held at the Warwickshire Museum where they may be consulted. A concordance of these fabric numbers with the numerical fabric numbering system used in previous publications (eg Ferguson 1985) is also provided so that all reports may be compared (table M23). In several cases a number of fabric descriptions used previously have been combined in the light of further knowledge.

All the material examined has been defined into exact fabric types including the material from post-Roman contexts. Quantification has been performed by sherd counts, weight, minimum number of rims per context, and percentage of rim (RE). Some 15.6% of the Roman pottery (measured by sherd count) occurred in medieval and post-medieval contexts.

The vessel forms from the site are illustrated as a type series within each fabric type (thus fabric B11 will have form types B11.1 to B11.n; figs 40–43). Table M24 (microfiche M3:A11) lists the occurrences of form and fabric by phase for all stratified Roman deposits (forms occurring in the type series but not listed in table M24 come from post-Roman and unstratified deposits). A catalogue citing parallels to the form types is provided in microfiche (Form type series, M2:C10). A summary version of the fabric proportions by phase is given in figs 32–39 for the major fabric types. Table M22 (microfiche M2:E1) gives the detailed figures for all Roman phases containing more than 30 sherds.

Chronology

Iron Age pottery

Seven sherds of Iron Age pottery were found in a pit (2050) at the north end of trench C. The sherds date to the middle to late Iron Age.

Earliest Roman activity

Apart from the Iron Age pottery, there were no sherds from Periods A and B. The earliest Roman structural feature on the site is the construction of the earth rampart (Period B) which would seem likely to have been immediately followed by Phase C11. (See fig 16 for the subdivision of the site into phases with appropriate equivalences and dates). The rampart contained no pottery at all confirming that it represented the primary Roman activity on the site and that little Roman material was spread in the area from which it was excavated. Material in later phases cannot, therefore, be regarded as archaeologically residual from earlier features at Gas House Lane. In Phase C11 a layer of gravel was laid across trench 7(n). This contained 4 sherds including

one BB1 bodysherd with obtuse lattice decoration. In trench B there was also a primary gravel dump in Phase C21 (contexts (1059, 1092, 1104, 1125, 1126, 1127, and 1128)) which contained 36 sherds including one BB1 sherd with obtuse lattice burnished decoration, a 2nd-century Severn Valley ware tankard form (fabric O24, form O24.15), a late 2nd- to 3rd-century Severn Valley ware tankard (fabric O27, form O27.13), and a constricted necked Severn Valley ware jar (fabric O55, form O55.1). The samian from this comprised a single rim fragment, probably Dr 18/31R, of Les Martres (*c* AD 100–140).

The material from Phase C11 (trench 7(n)) is consistent with its being contemporary with that from the gravel dump in Phase C21 (trench B) and it is difficult to escape the conclusion that the site did not commence occupation until BB1 obtuse lattice decoration was prevalent, ie after AD 200 (cf Bidwell 1985, Gillam 1976). This is of note in relation to the site samian collection, some 8.6% of all pottery from the site by sherd numbers, which cannot but have arrived on the site after this date. It cannot be regarded as archaeologically residual on the site. It also cannot easily, for the most part, be regarded as having arrived in building materials brought to the site. This is because of its high overall percentage of the pottery assemblage and the paucity of associated 2nd-century coarsewares, particularly greywares, (for example only 121 of 1086 BB1 lattice decorated sherds are decorated with the acute lattice type). (See 'Samian: a note', p 77 for further discussion of the significance of this point.)

Fig 16 shows the sequence of Period C phases by area of which only C11, C21 and C31 are probably linked by stratigraphy, although C14 and part of C33 may be linked. Given that the site samian list must be reconciled with the coarse pottery, it may be that the date of emergence of obtuse lattice decorated BB1 at 'AD 223–5 at the latest' (Bidwell 1985, 175) ought to be brought down to nearer *c* AD 200 (see below p 70).

Trench B: Period C phases

Phase C21 contains little intrinsically datable material which would help to tie it down more closely within the early 3rd-century date discussed above. (Intrusive post-medieval material is present in context (1132/1)).

Phase C22 contains two sherds of later 2nd- to early 3rd-century Rheinzabern ware amongst the samian, and a BB1 assemblage consistent with an early to mid-3rd-century date. The only *mortarium* represented is a late 2nd-century Mancetter vessel (M22.6). Small quantities of intrusive medieval and post-medieval material are present in contexts (1086) and (1098). This gives a date range of *c* AD 220–230/40.

Phase C23 includes a Young (1977) type M22 *mortarium* (*c* AD 240–400) and Nene Valley bodysherds including some with white painted decora-

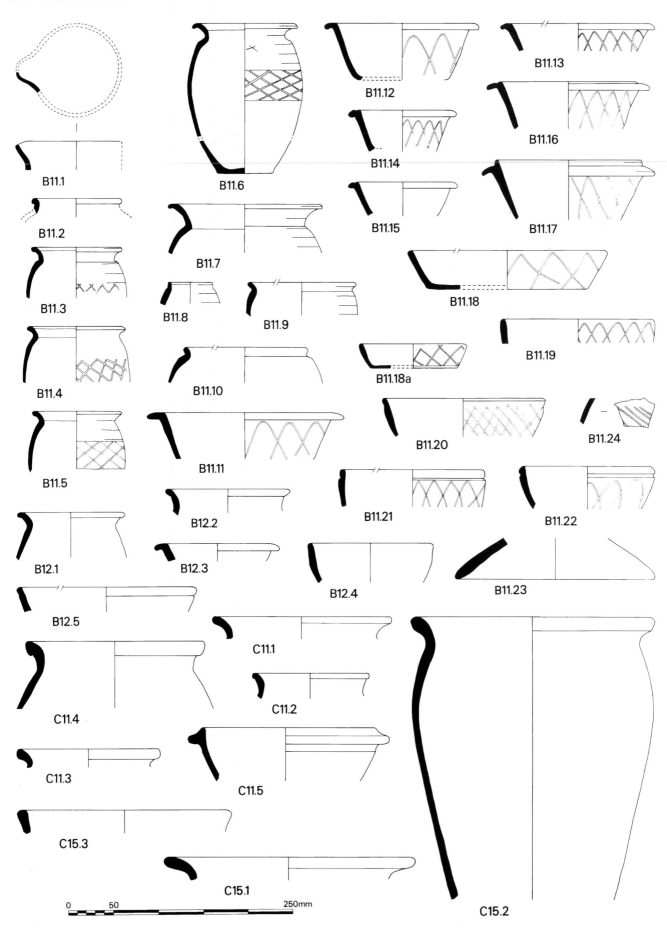

Figure 32   Form type series for fabrics B.11–C.15

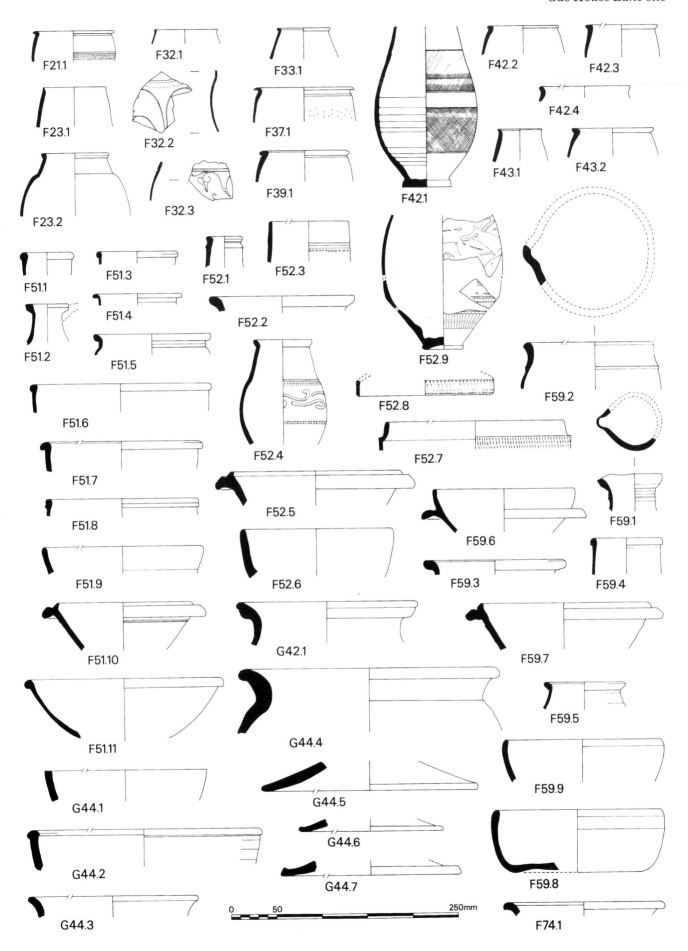

Figure 33 Form type series for fabrics F.21–G.44

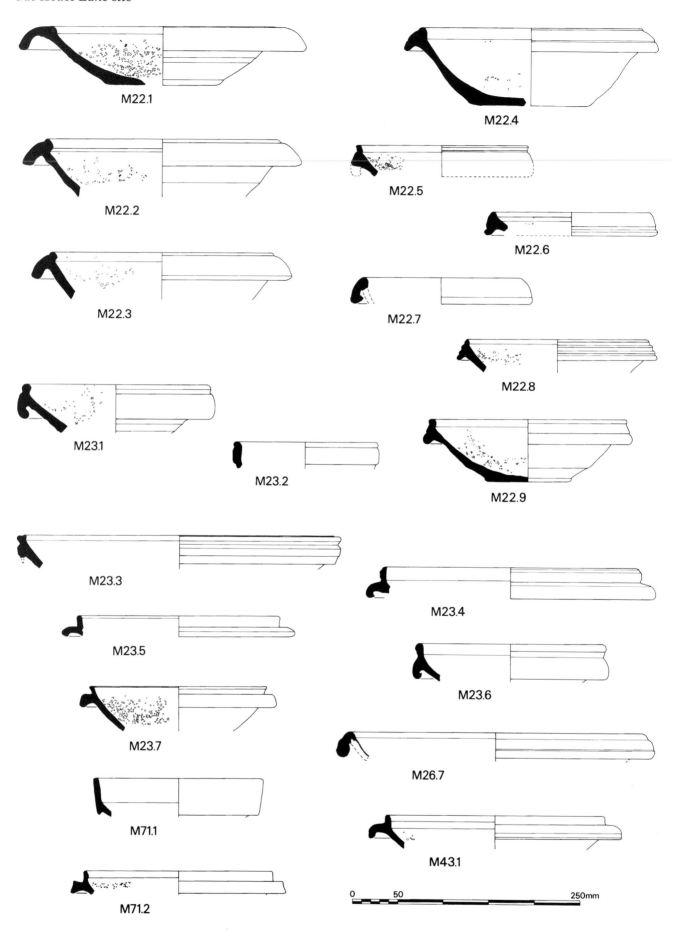

M22.1

M22.4

M22.2

M22.5

M22.3

M22.6

M22.7

M23.1

M22.8

M23.2

M22.9

M23.3

M23.4

M23.5

M23.6

M23.7

M26.7

M71.1

M43.1

M71.2

0   50   250mm

Figure 34   Form type series for fabrics M.22–M.43

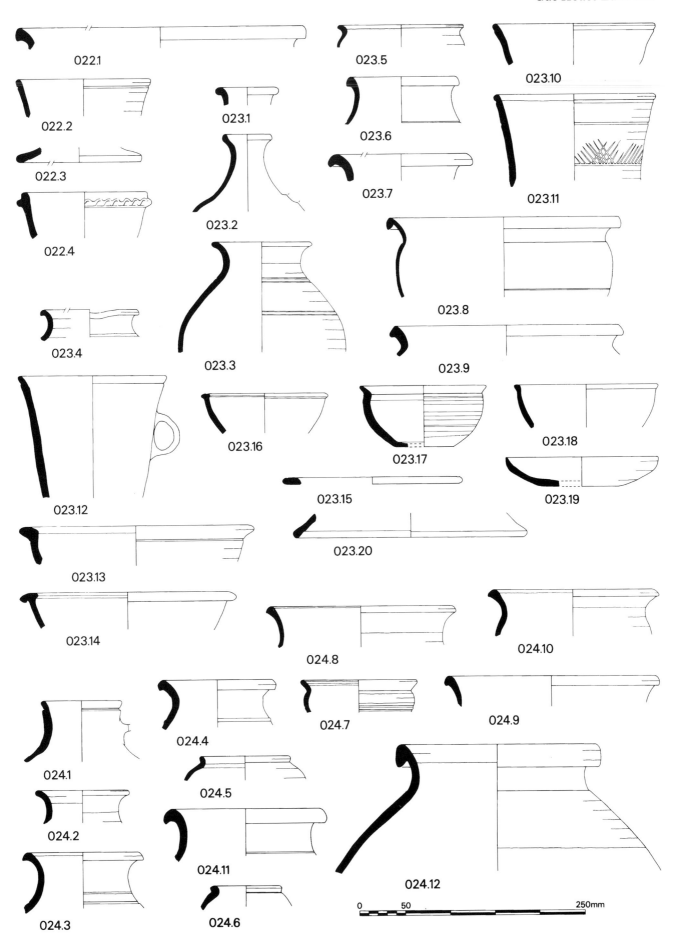

Figure 35 Form type series for fabrics O.22–O.24

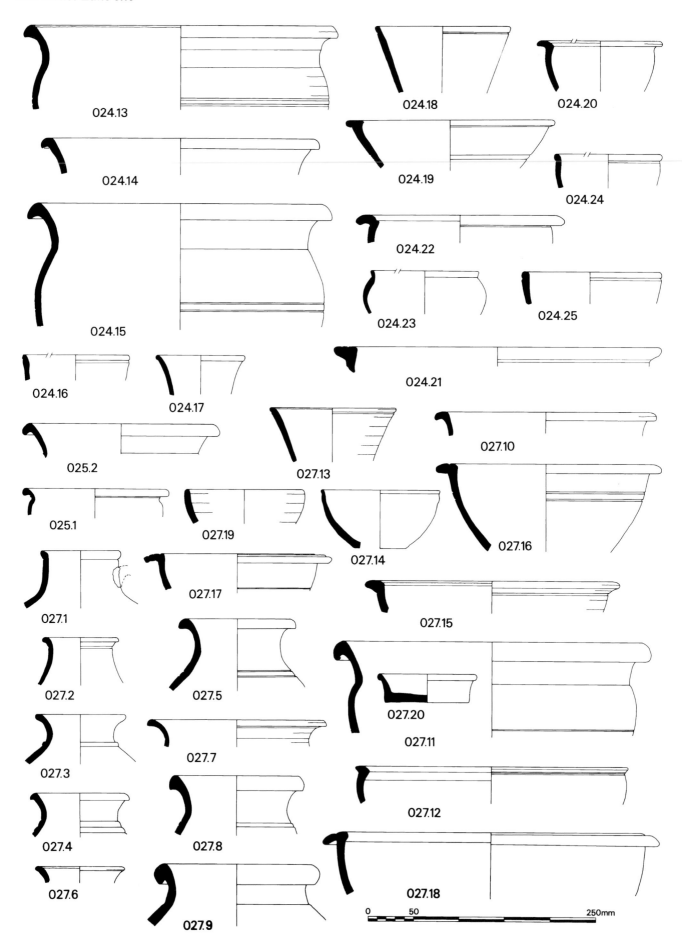

Figure 36 Form type series for fabrics O.24–O.27

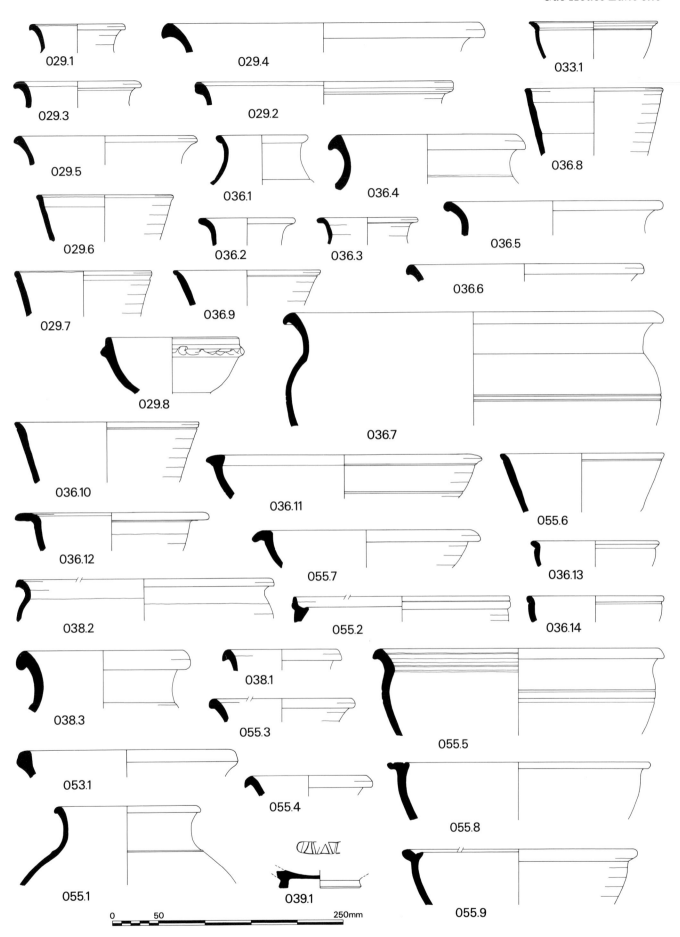

Figure 37   Form type series for fabrics O.29–O.55

65

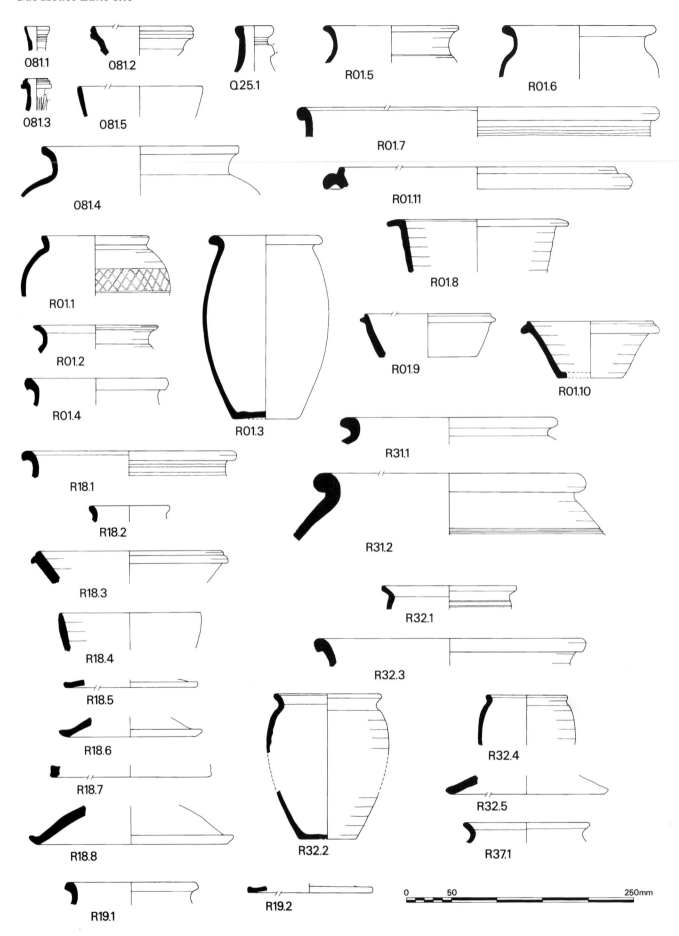

Figure 38 Form type series for fabrics O.81–R.37

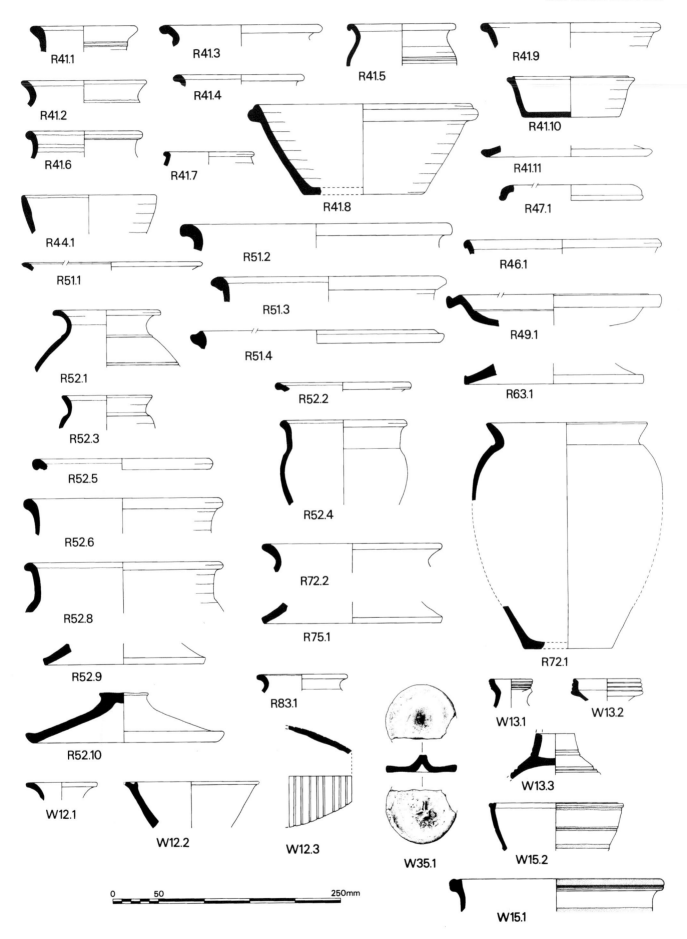

Figure 39 Form type series for fabrics R.41–W.15

tion; but the BB1 assemblage is consistent with an early to mid-3rd-century date. The phase clearly continues after *c* AD 240 and a date range of *c* AD 230/240–250/270 would seem appropriate. Small quantities of intrusive medieval and post-medieval material occur in several contexts (1024, 1035, 1038/1, 1066, and 1083) and this contamination is presumably the source of the intrusive 4th-century shell-tempered ware (C11) from context 1035.

Phase C24 includes amongst a BB1 collection, which is probably largely residual, a later 3rd- to early 4th-century jar rim (B11.7). There is little other intrinsically datable material, but given its succession after C23 a date range of *c* AD 250/70 to *c* 300 might be suggested. Intrusive medieval material occurs in context (1050/3).

Trench C: Period C phases

Phase C31 contains some Hadrianic–Antonine samian ware and a 2nd- to 3rd-century Severn Valley ware flanged bowl (O27.15). However, given its stratigraphic equation with phases C11 and C21 it is, presumably, early 3rd-century.

Phase C32 contains BB1 consistent with an early to mid-3rd-century date, two Mancetter *mortaria* (M22.1 and M22.8) and an Oxford type M11 (*c* AD 180–240). An early to mid-3rd-century date seems appropriate, perhaps *c* AD 220–240/250.

Phase C33 contains a sherd of Oxfordshire red colour-coated ware (F51), some BB1 developed flanged bowls and a number of Oxfordshire *mortaria* including Young types M22 (*c* AD 240–400) and M17 and M21 (both *c* AD 240–300). A date range running from the middle to the end of the 3rd century seems appropriate, perhaps *c* AD 240/250–300. There are intrusive occurrences of 4th-century fabrics C11 and F59 from two contexts (2066/1 and 2059) both of which, along with (2061), include small quantities of intrusive medieval and post-medieval material.

Trench 7(n): Period C phases

Phase C11 contains no rimsherds and is not closely datable beyond the presence of obtuse lattice BB1.

Phase C12 contains a BB1 assemblage of earlier 3rd-century date and an East Gaulish Dr 31R dated *c* AD 170–260. A date range of *c* AD 220–230/40, is likely.

Phase C13 contains an early to mid-3rd-century Nene Valley bag beaker, a Mancetter *mortarium* (M22.5), an Oxfordshire *mortarium* rim (flange missing) which is perhaps of type M22, and a later 3rd-century BB1 jar rim (B11.7). A date range of *c* AD 230/40–250/60 might seem appropriate.

Phase C14 includes an Oxfordshire *mortarium* of Young type M17 (AD 240–300), a BB1 developed flanged bowl of later 3rd- to early 4th-century date, and a Mancetter *mortarium* (M22.3). (There is also a

bodysherd of fabric C11 from context (7113) in trench 7(s) which is not accompanied by other intrusive material and may be the first occurrence of this fabric on the site.) A date range of *c* AD 250/60 to *c* AD 280 might be suggested.

Phase C15 contains BB1 which would appear to be mainly residual earlier 3rd-century material and one each of Young types M18 and M22 Oxfordshire *mortaria* (*c* AD 240–300 and *c* AD 240–400). Given that this phase succeeds Phase C14 but contains no 4th-century material a date range of *c* AD 280–300 might be proposed.

Period C deposits which have not been assigned to individual phases

Apart from the sequences discussed above some comment should be made on those deposits simply phased to Period C. In trench 1 these include contexts (91) and (86/1) containing respectively a later 3rd- to early 4th-century BB1 jar rim and a sherd of South-Western brown slip ware suggesting these features may be of early to mid-4th-century date.

In trench 3 Period C deposits include a small sequence of deposits (contexts 114, 115, 116, 118, 120, 123 and 124: group 0CC) which seem to represent 4th-century activity and include shell-tempered ware (C11), South-Western brown slip ware (F59) and an Oxfordshire red colour-coated *mortarium* (M71). Elsewhere on the site this 4th-century activity seems to have been effectively truncated.

Similarly, in trench 5, Period C deposits include one context (265) which contains South-Western brown slip ware, including a Young type C23 copy, dating to the second half of the 4th century.

In trench C there are two contexts, 2027/1 and 2048/1, containing South-Western brown slip ware and shell-tempered ware (C11), of Period C which probably date to the 4th century.

Period D

In trench 2, the Period D deposit contains a dispersed coin hoard probably deposited *c* AD 390–400 (*see* p 109; Brickstock pers comm). This is associated with a pottery assemblage which has shell-tempered ware (C11) as the principal coarseware. In trench 5, Period D, BB1 is still present in some quantity and it is unlikely to be archaeologically residual given that this area was beyond the earlier defended circuit and contains little earlier activity, whilst shell-tempered ware forms a low proportion of the group, so a date range of *c* AD 370–390 is therefore suggested (the former date derives from the construction date of the stone circuit (*see* Gateway supermarket p 39). The trench A, Phase D2 group tends to be intermediate between these two groups in terms of its composition and might perhaps date *c* AD 380–90.

Period E

The Roman material from Period E deposits is of some interest in its reflection of material truncated by medieval and later activity. Amongst the fine-wares 37% is of Oxford red colour-coated ware (F51), 14.7% is South-Western brown slip ware, and 19.0% is of Nene Valley colour-coated ware (F52). Seventy percent of the finewares from these deposits are, therefore, in fabrics which are very likely to have arrived on the site in the 4th century. The coarse pottery also shows some emphasis on 4th-century material with 2.1% of the 4th-century fabric C11. The proportion of 4th-century material in the coarse-wares is lower because of the notable rise in the proportion of finewares in the late 4th-century deposits (*see* 'Functional analysis'). Overall around 10% of the Roman material from post-Roman deposits might be of later 4th-century date.

Discussion of the major fabric groups

For summary histograms showing the major fabric proportions in each phase see figs 40–43.

Amphorae

There is a comparatively low quantity of *amphorae* from this site, some 0.6% by sherd number and 4.5% by weight, as might be expected given a location distant from the coast and a 3rd- and 4th-century chronological range. The major fabric group is the ubiquitous Baetican Dressel 20, followed by the Gallic Pélichet 47 with a few other fabrics represented by single sherds, including a Baetican Camulodunum 185A and a single sherd of North African *amphora* (Williams pers comm).

Black-Burnished ware

Date of termination of BB1 supply

BB1 is a major component in the Gas House Lane assemblage throughout Period C. However, it seems to be residual in the Period D deposits from trench 2 and Phase D2 deposits from trench A, which appear principally to date to AD 390–400 on the evidence of the dispersed coin hoard from trench 2 (*see* p 109; Brickstock pers comm). These late deposits, which seem to contain fairly little archaeologically residual material, demonstrate that BB1 had ceased to be supplied to Alcester before the end of the Roman Period.

There were none of the latest type of BB1 jars (*see* Catsgore: Leech 1982, fig 109, nos 422–3) with flaring rims, conical bodies, and oblique-line burnished bands on the girth, rather than an obtuse lattice. However, this type of jar has a distribution restricted to the Dorset/north Somerset core area of BB1, where

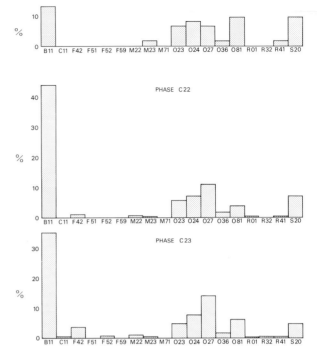

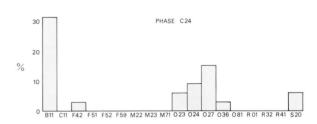

Figure 40 Histogram of major fabric proportions for 3rd-century phases from trench B (by sherd nos)

a number of types are found fairly frequently which rarely, if ever, occur beyond the region. Therefore the absence of this type at Gas House Lane does not necessarily indicate that BB1 had ceased to be supplied to the town.

BB1 clearly ceases to be supplied in northern England after *c* AD 355. It is, however, debatable whether it ceased to be supplied in Wales and the Midlands at this date.

At *Segontium* in North Wales (Webster, P V, 1993) there were large deposits from Phase 10A comprising rubbish dumped in a disused drainage channel, which does not seem to have been archaeologically residual and contained many large fragments, dated after AD 364, including a very substantial proportion of BB1 (*c* 41.8%). On this basis BB1 may still have been in use in the later 4th century in North Wales.

At the 1–5 Bleachfield St Site (AES 76–7) BB1 reached a peak in the assemblage in Period 9 (*c* AD 290–350) at around 35% (Ferguson forthcoming)

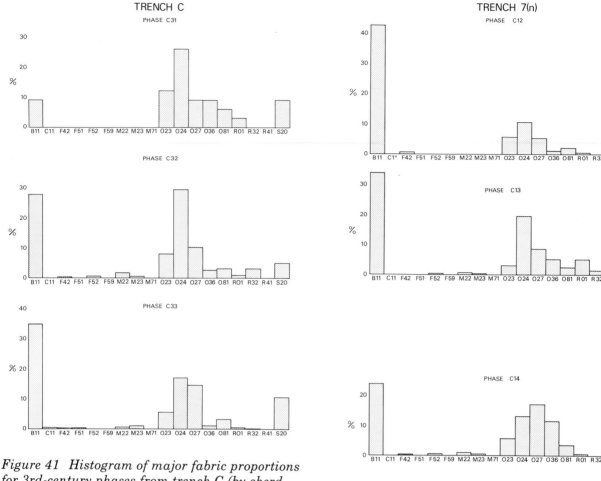

Figure 41 Histogram of major fabric proportions for 3rd-century phases from trench C (by sherd nos)

Figure 42 Histogram of major fabric proportions for 3rd-century phases from trench 7(n) (by sherd nos)

and comprised 30% of the following, Period 10, assemblage (*c* AD 340/50–400+), a considerably higher figure than the 17% maximum it contributed to any period before Period 9. It is far from certain, therefore, that the BB1 from Period 10 was residual. Similarly at the Gateway supermarket site (AL18) areas A, C, D, and E, the pottery from Phase IIb dated to after *c* AD 371 contained 23% of BB1 (n = 199) which may not necessarily have been residual (*see* pp 22). The evidence from Gas House Lane suggests that BB1 was not being supplied at Alcester by *c* AD 390 (trench 2, Period D), however, it may be that BB1 supply in the Midlands and Wales continued after *c* AD 355, perhaps until around AD 385, after which BB1 seems to have receded to supplying its core area in Dorset and north Somerset.

BB1 seems to have suffered from increasing competition from other greywares and Southern Shell-Tempered ware at Cirencester (Keeley 1986, table 27) and even at Dorchester (Andrews forthcoming), where greywares and Devonshire granite-tempered ware appear in the latest 4th-century deposits. Table 13 (after Keeley 1986) shows the decline of BB1 at Cirencester through Periods I to III up to *c* AD 375, although it still comprised about 20% of the group from area DE/DF dated by coinage to *c* AD 375–95.

General trends in the supply of BB1

At the 1–5 Bleachfield St site (AES 76–7; Ferguson forthcoming, fig 42) BB1 supply is shown as low in the 2nd century, rising in the third with the peak coming in the later 3rd or early 4th century. The general trend in BB1 supply at Alcester would seem to become clearer from the Gas House Lane figures. Figs 40–42 show histograms for the three principal areas with 3rd-century sequences at Gas House Lane, trenches B, C, and 7(n). The earliest phases, C21, C31 and C11 respectively, contain 15% of BB1 (fabric B11 and B12) by sherd number when combined (n = 100), a level comparable to the rise at the 1–5 Bleachfield St site at the end of the 2nd century (Period 5, *c* AD 150/70–?240). However the picture from the two sites diverges after this with a marked rise in the early 3rd

TRENCH 5

PHASE   D

TRENCH A

PHASE D2

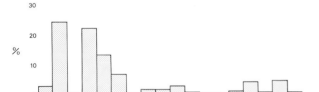

TRENCH 2

PHASE D

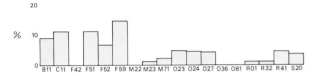

Figure 43 Histogram of major fabric proportions for later 4th-century phases from the site, arranged from earliest to latest (by sherd nos)

century (Phases C22, C32 and C12) at Gas House Lane to between 27% and 43% by sherd number. The figures for the 3rd-century sequence tend to oscillate. The best sequence from trench 7(n), in the sense that it is divided into the greatest number of phases, tends to suggest that there is a dip in supply around the middle of the century, but that this is restored by the end. The other sequences show trends of a slight rise (trench C) and a slight fall (trench B) through the

century which may not be incompatible with the trench 7(n) sequence reflecting the detailed picture.

As noted above ('Introduction') there are few 4th-century deposits before Period D, but there is a small sequence from trench 3 of apparently mid- to late 4th-century date (perhaps *c* AD 340–70; group 0CC) where BB1 comprised 27%. BB1 is still present in some quantity in the Period D deposits from trench 5 (and to a lesser extent in Phase D2 in trench A) where it is unlikely to be archaeologically residual given that this area was beyond the earlier defended circuit and contains little earlier activity. Also the BB1 forms present are consistent with a 4th-century date. The low proportion of Southern shell-tempered ware (C11) and the high proportion of Severn Valley ware fabric O23 in trench 5 both suggest that Period D deposits here precede those in trench 2, which is associated with the coin hoard, and might, perhaps, be dated *c* AD 370–390. It would seem likely that BB1 was current still, although declining, at Alcester in this period.

The 3rd- and 4th-century BB1 figures from Gas House Lane offer a marked contrast to those from the 1–5 Bleachfield St site (AES 76–7), and perhaps a more accurate view of trends in supply, as residual material from earlier periods was clearly a major problem in much of the later sequence from the 1–5 Bleachfield St site.

The general trends of BB1 supply at Alcester as shown at Gas House Lane and from the 2nd-century 1–5 Bleachfield St site (AES 76–7) sequence (Ferguson forthcoming, fig 42) show that BB1 supply is comparatively low in the 2nd century and only rises in the 3rd with the peak coming in the later 3rd or early 4th century. This is similar to the pattern of BB1 supply in northern England where it is really quite a minor component in assemblages in the Pennines and North-East until the 3rd century when it reaches its maximum distribution, after which it retreats from markets in North-East England but becomes even more important in north-western assemblages.

One feature of BB1 supply at Alcester is of interest, that being its comparatively low level. It would seem logical that some of the BB1 supply going to north-western England would have travelled up the Severn to be trans-shipped at Chester. This, however, would not seem to be the case given that Alcester supply

Table 13   Cirencester coarsewares (after Keeley 1986)

Area	CQ			CX/CY			DE/DF
Period	I	II	III	I	II	III	
	%	%	%	%	%	%	
Fabric							
BB1	44	36	25	34	36	26	20
BB1 copy	2	5	10	7	12	8	8
Shell-tempered	0	–	1	0	1	5	20
Greyware	24	23	20	25	20	23	25

Table 14 Frequencies of BB1 forms in period C

Gillam 1976 types	Rim nos	%	% of rim	%
1–4	3	0.9	24	0.9
4–6	3	0.9	38	1.4
5–7	61	17.5	646	23.6
8	67	19.2	730	26.6
9–13	9	2.6	73	2.7
24, 28–29	5	1.5	41	1.5
30,32	1	0.3	12	0.4
34–6, 57	16	4.6	108	3.9
37–41, 54, 56, 58–66	39	11.2	305	11.1
42	2	0.6	13	0.5
43–44	14	4.0	127	4.6
45–49	3	0.9	32	1.2
68–73	8	2.3	34	1.3
74	18	5.1	53	1.9
75	7	2.0	39	1.4
77, 78–81, 83–4	88	25.3	463	16.8
Lids	1	0.3	–	0
	345		2738	

levels are less than those prevailing at Chester (Carrington 1980, mansio well II, 63.5% (excluding samian)) and Old Penrith in Cumbria (Evans 1985, table 7.8, 45%) and it must, indeed, be the case that BB1 was shipped by sea around both Cornwall and Wales (evidence of shipping round Cornwall was given by Holbrook (1989 RB Pot Study Group conference, Southampton) in the differential distribution of BB1 at Exeter and its environs).

Forms

There are few individual BB1 pieces of intrinsic interest (fig 32); one fragment which may be from the lip of a BB1 jug (context (7127), Phase C14, B11.1, cf Wallace and Webster 1989) and a jar bodysherd from context (7215) (B11.24, Phase C12, early 3rd century) which has an oblique-line burnished zone as on the latest 4th-century types. This is securely stratified and Booth (pers comm) points to another from the Tiddington Wellstood collection on an early jar form. There is also a straight-sided lid fragment, B11.23.

The frequencies of occurrence of BB1 forms from the Period C deposits are of some interest given the lack of residual material on the site. The forms present in each individual phase are tabulated in table M24 (microfiche M3:A11). Table 14 gives the occurrence of forms from all Period C deposits by minimum numbers of rims per context and percentage of rim.

It is interesting to note those 2nd-century forms which were still apparently in circulation at the opening of the 3rd century. Gillam (1976) clearly regarded grooved rim dishes (nos 72–4) as continuing until the later 3rd century. However, their frequency at Alcester is very low and it seems doubtful if the general type survived much into the century, excepting type 74. Gillam's (1976) no 73 has very good parallels at Bar Hill (Robertson *et al* 1975, fig 56, nos 14 and 15). The most significant grouping is the flange-rimmed dishes and bowls (Gillam 1976, 34–41 and 53–66) which are clearly still in use in the early to mid-3rd century at Alcester. Given that the grooved-rim flanged bowl (Gillam 1976, nos 43–4) does not appear in the Alcester sequences before Phases C13, C22, and C33, none of which seem to date before the second quarter of the 3rd century, the evidence from Alcester would seem to be consistent with that from *Vindolanda* (Bidwell 1985, 176–8) where the type first appeared in Period 4A/B (mid-3rd century). This suggests that Gillam 1976, type 43 is not at all common before *c* AD 230. This should not be taken to indicate type 42, better represented by Gillam (1970), type 226, with the flange rising above the bead, is 3rd century; its emergence would seem to date to *c* AD 170 (Bell and Evans forthcoming).

To highlight the differences in this group from an Antonine one, table 15 compares the Gas House Lane and Antonine Bar Hill forms on a similar basis, by approximate minimum numbers of rims, using the data provided by Robertson (1975, 162, figs 55–6) for Bar Hill. There is some overlap with the Bar Hill material (only about 40%), the main features being the continued use of handled beakers (Gillam 1976,

Table 15 Bar Hill BB1 forms compared with Gas House Lane Period C

Gillam (1976) types	Bar Hill		Alcester	
	Nos	%	Nos	%
1–3	12	5.6	3	0.9
4–7	87	40.9	64	18.5
17	2	0.9	0	0
19–22	3	1.4	0	0
26	1	0.5	0	0
28–29	4	1.9	5	1.5
34–41, 53–66	80	37.6	55	15.8
35 with grooved rim	1	0.5	0	0
68–70	18	8.5	7	2.0
76 acute lattice	5	2.3	18	5.1*
	n = 213		n = 345 (*total* Period C)	

* intersecting arcs

nos 24–9), flanged rim dishes/bowls, and a few grooved-rim dishes. (Gillam cites a 3rd-century example of a handled beaker in the text although not in the type series (Gillam 1976, 66)). Given the comparatively low overlap between these BB1 assemblages it may be that the best approach to refining the relative chronology of large groups with plenty of BB1 lies in examining the ratios of proportions of the types rather than their presence and absence (cf Millett 1983).

The dishes from Alcester are mainly straight-sided with intersecting-arc decoration; there are also some with intersecting-arc decoration and a slightly grooved rim (cf Gillam 1976, nos 74 and 76 for wall form). There are a very few examples of straight-sided dishes with acute-lattice decoration (8 out of 87) and proportionately more (4 out of 24) of the slightly grooved rim type.

Table 16 shows the functional breakdown of BB1 types from the Gas House Lane site. It is interesting in that it shares the characteristic of a number of sites in the North-West and Wales of having a higher proportion of dishes and bowls combined than of jars (Evans 1985; Evans forthcoming). It seems probable that this reflects a saturated assemblage in terms of BB1, unlike those from north-eastern England where the jar form was predominant, probably because of its premium value as a cooking vessel.

Shell-tempered wares

Two shell-tempered fabrics are represented at Gas House Lane, C11 and C15. The inclusions in both are very similar and the latter is distinguished from the former by its being handmade (this distinction has not been made in previous reports in the Alcester series using the Warwickshire Museum fabric type series). C15 occurs sporadically in 3rd- and early

4th-century contexts. Its first appearances are in Phases C13 and C22, perhaps a little before the mid-3rd century. The only form represented from 3rd-century Period C deposits is a simple handmade rimmed dish (C15.3, fig 32) from context (2061) (Phase C33), if this is not an intrusive piece of wheelmade C11. C15 is principally represented by the almost complete everted-rimmed storage jar, C15.2, from context (79) (Period D), which was probably a setting for it. It probably originates to the east in the Northamptonshire area. C11, the wheelmade Southern Shell-Tempered ware almost certainly originates at Harrold, Bedfordshire (Swan 1984, fiche 1.208; Sanders 1973; Brown and Alexander 1982) and first appears on the site in Phase C14.

In Period D in trenches A and 2, c AD 390–400, fabric C11 is the principal coarseware and it is probably, apart from some of the sandy greywares, one of the few coarseware fabrics represented which is not residual. It must have provided the bulk of the cooking vessels at the very end of the Roman period (these being its almost exclusive form) and it is of considerable interest that these should have travelled to Alcester from Bedfordshire. As will be discussed further below (p 96) it is remarkable that at the end of the Roman period, pottery sources for Alcester do not retreat to more local suppliers, but rather local suppliers seem to die out, and most of the surviving industries are the major regional industries of the 4th century.

Table 16 Functional analysis of BB1 forms from stratified Roman deposits at Gas House Lane

Jars	Bowls	Dishes	Beakers	Jugs	Lids
41.3%	20.1%	36.4%	1.4%	0.5%	0.3%

n = 368 rims

73

**Table 17 Functional analysis of
vessels in fabric C.11**

Jars	Bowls	Dishes
83%	14%	3%?

n = 35

Table 17 shows the functional composition of vessels in C11 from the site, the presence of bowls amongst the collection is not unusual for sites with reasonable quantities of the fabric (cf Cirencester, Keeley 1986 and Barnsley Park, Webster 1982, fig 55, no 145).

Samian ware
Margaret (Bulmer) Ward

Introduction

[M3:B8] While the archive includes a complete record of all the samian ware recovered from these excavations, the catalogue (in microfiche) has been selected according to intrinsic interest or because the sherd may be significant stratigraphically or relevant to the subject of survival (fig 44).

Vessels are listed in order of phase, context, form, and fabric. The abbreviations SG, CG, and EG are used to denote South Gaulish, Central Gaulish, and East Gaulish origin; ind. denotes a sherd of indeterminate form. The following abbreviations have been employed: Oswald, for Oswald 1936; Rogers, for Rogers 1974; S&S for Stanfield and Simpson 1958. For other terminology, see Bulmer 1979.

All stamps with decipherable letters have been listed; all those on plain vessels are basal. I should like to thank Miss B M Dickinson, who kindly gave details of these stamps in her report, which is incorporated in the microfiche. These are recorded here in this order, following the form: the reading of the stamp, any published reference, the potter (i, ii, etc where homonyms are involved), die number, pottery of origin, and date. Ligatured letters are underlined. (a), (b) and (c) indicate:

(a) Stamp attested at the pottery in question.
(b) Potter, but not the particular stamp, attested at the pottery in question.
(c) Assigned to the pottery on the evidence of fabric, distribution and/or form.

Plainware stamps have not been drawn as illustrations will appear in Dickinson and Hartley's definitive catalogue of stamps (forthcoming). For the sake of consistency, numbers following the potters' names here are those employed in that catalogue. Where helpful, these are followed by the style number given in Stanfield and Simpson 1958, thus: Paternus v (II), Do(v)eccus i (I), etc.

For each phase, a quantified summary is provided in the form of tables recording forms and fabrics. Maximum numbers of vessels have been used, since experience has shown that estimation of minimum numbers of vessels based on large quantities of small fragments is little more than a guess.

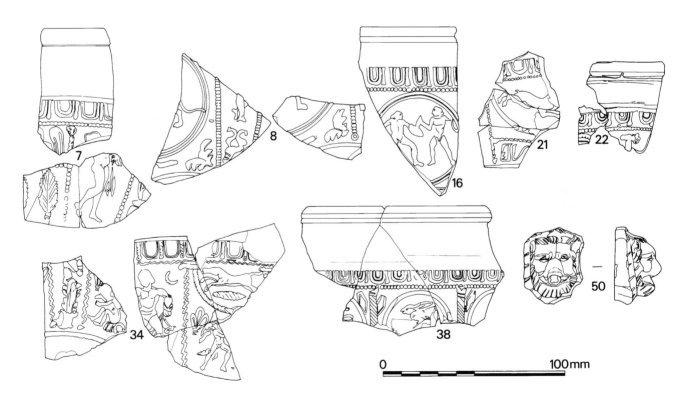

Figure 44 Samian

Table 18 Summary of samian forms and fabrics from all contexts (maximum numbers)

Fab	18/R	18R	18 or 18/31	18R or 18/31R	18/31	18/31 or 31	18/31R	18/31R or 31R	31	31/R	31R	C15	C23	27	33	35
SG	3	1	1	2										1	1	
CG				1	4	10	6	42	61	10	39	2	1	4	101	1
EG									1	1	2					
Total	3	1	1	3	4	10	6	42	62	11	41	2	1	5	102	1

Fab	36	38	43	45	46	72	79etc	80	cup	encl.	bowl	ind.	30	30 or 37	37	Tot
SG										1		15	1			26
CG	7	28		7	1	5	19	5	3	2	5	223	13	1	50	651
EG			1				1					7			1	14
Tot	7	28	1	7	1	5	20	5	3	3	5	245	14	1	51	691

Discussion

The maximum of 691 vessels was composed of 799 sherds. A fairly low proportion of the total was burnt – 9%, ranging from 1% of Phase C32 material to 15% in Phase C14. The preponderance of Central Gaulish samian was overwhelming. Only 4% of the vessels originated in South Gaul, 94% in Central Gaul, and only 2% in East Gaul. This contrasts with, for instance, the Gateway supermarket site (AL18), where the proportions were 12%, 69%, and 19%. Even more marked was the contrast with the earlier material from the 1969 excavations on an extramural site Baromix, Bleachfield St, for which the figures were 57%, 41%, and 2%. Closer were the proportions from Taylor's 1972 excavations at Birch Abbey: 15%, 83%, and 2% (Ward forthcoming (b), Taylor 1972, samian report in site archives). The collection is summarized in table 18 and fig 45. To produce the histogram, illustrating the maximum numbers of vessels according to their date of manufacture, all the samian from the site has been used, despite the drawbacks of including such imprecisely dated material. The stamped or decorated vessels alone were too few to be meaningful statistically, but some form of graphical representation according to date was thought to be desirable.

As one might expect of a late collection, the SG sherds in all phases on the site consisted of tiny pieces. One fragment from Period C was possibly of pre-Flavian or early Flavian origin. None of the others was in any way remarkable. None of the fragments was sufficiently large for evidence of use to be detected.

As noted in the phase summaries, a small number of fragments originated at Les Martres-de-Veyre in the early 2nd century, forming around 2% of the total. One was stamped (no 47); none was decorated. A few pieces, including no 39, were dated to the Hadrianic–early Antonine Period. The shortage of samian ware in the early 2nd century has now been noted at many sites occupied at that time, but here it is perhaps more pronounced. In this collection, much of the material was not closely datable within the Hadri-anic–Antonine and Antonine periods, owing to its fragmentary condition. On fig 45, this tends to exaggerate the quantity of samian appearing under the Hadrianic–early Antonine Period and in the last decade of the 2nd century. The peak in the material around AD 160 seems real enough. A similar, pronounced peak has been recorded at other sites under occupation at this time (see Marsh 1981, fig 11.8, etc).

The quantity of East Gaulish samian was very small: 14 vessels composed of 20 sherds. Their proportion of the total was certainly low even among material admittedly excavated from an inland site outside the military North (*see* Dickinson and Hartley 1971, 130 referring to stamped vessels). In the predominantly late collection at Piercebridge, Co Durham (fort and *vicus*), the overall proportion of EG wares recorded by the present writer was *c* 17% of the total of 5543 vessels (Ward 1993, 16). To judge from the present collection, one might think that samian from East Gaul, particularly decorated ware, was not readily available to the people of Alcester. However, EG products have certainly been recognized at several excavations in the extra-mural area (see above, and Dickinson 1985 *passim*). On the Birch Abbey site, it was noted that the relatively small quantity of CG samian compared with the EG ware

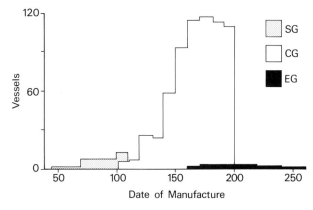

Figure 45 Histogram showing distribution of samian per decade, from all phases; maximum 691 vessels against date of manufacture

75

was indeed unusual for Britain *except* in the 3rd century when Lezoux ceased exporting (Dickinson 1985, 33). One might well have expected more EG samian if the large collection from Gas House Lane was in fact representative of a 3rd-century assemblage. It is, of course, conceivable that the sample is not representative, and that late EG products continued in use through the 3rd century before deposition elsewhere (see below). The difficulty of dating EG samian is notorious, and it was not possible to differentiate here between the products of East Gaul in the later 2nd century and those of the 3rd century. At any rate, all must certainly have been manufactured before *c* AD 260, this being the preferred date for the termination of samian imports into Britain from Rheinzabern and Trier (Ward 1993, 19).

For the rather limited range of forms on this site, see table 18. More than a third of the collection was of unidentifiable form, owing to its fragmentary nature. Among the largest class, that of the dishes, it was not considered wise to prejudice the figures by distinguishing between many instances of, for example, form 18/31R and 31R, where no diagnostic feature survived. On the other hand, it would be very surprising if the majority was not of the latter type. More readily identifiable were the four cups of form 27, produced until *c* AD 160, and those of form 33, made throughout the samian period. Of the latter, the maximum number represented was 102; the minimum was certainly not ascertainable. Among the predominantly late forms the absence of, for instance, Dr 32 and 40 may be explained by the fact that these were more commonly produced by the potters of East Gaul who are under represented. There were five beakers of form Déch 72, one with cut-glass decoration (probably after *c* AD 160) and 25 examples of the Walters 79 group (again after *c* AD 160). There were perhaps eight *mortaria* (manufactured after *c* AD 170), forming a surprisingly low percentage in a late collection (1%). In the predominantly late material at Piercebridge where EG products were much more frequent, the proportion was 8% (Ward forthcoming (a)). It may be relevant to compare the figures of contemporary *mortaria* in non-samian fabrics (cf Ward and Carrington 1981, 31). Note may also be made of the relatively low proportion (10%) of the collection consisting of moulded bowls of forms 30 and 37. This proportion would have been higher had there been more SG ware. Nevertheless, one may speculate that the people of Alcester were more able to afford the presumably cheaper plain wares.

There was a total of nineteen stamps with letters surviving; all are listed in the catalogue. Eleven were attributable to specific potters. The only vessel which was probably not produced at Lezoux was no 47; its maker, Regullus, worked at both Les Martres and Lezoux. Two stamps (11%) were dated to the early or mid-Antonine era (nos 25 and 18). Seven (forming 37% of the stamps) post-dated AD 160. Of these late potters, stamps of five featured in the late group from New Fresh Wharf (Bird 1986, 141, fig 80); stamps of

six occurred in the Piercebridge collection referred to above, four of them from the same dies as at Gas House Lane.

A similar picture is formed by the nineteen moulded bowls with attributable decoration. All the decorated bowls were from Lezoux, with the exception of no 20 which was of uncertain origin in East Gaul (5%). One sherd was probably from a bowl of Hadrianic–early Antonine manufacture, probably by the Pugnus group (no 39). Four vessels (21%) were produced in the early to mid-Antonine era, two by the Pugnus-Secundus group and two by the firm of Cinnamus. The proportion by the latter (11%) is low (see Marsh 1981, 210), but the sample of attributable bowls is small and the majority of the moulded bowls here is late. At least twelve (63%) were in the style of potters working after AD 160, namely Iustus, Advocisus, Banuus, Mercator iv (II), Iullinus – one vessel each; Paternus v (II) and Casurius – two each; Do(v)eccus i (I) – three vessels. The proportion of these late potters among the large collection of CG moulded ware at Piercebridge was 57%, compared with 67% here. There is no need to give further consideration here to recent and continuing speculation that later CG vessels were 3rd-century products (King 1981, 66, etc; for a rejoinder, see Bird 1986, 146, and Ward 1993, 17). In this collection the predominance of these later Antonine vessels and the scarcity of EG ware could be seen as further evidence in the opposite direction.

At least 11% of the samian showed some sign of wear, repair, or reuse. This figure is close to that of around 10.5% recorded by the author at the extramural site at Castle St, Chester (Bulmer 1980, 89) but lower than the 17% recorded at Piercebridge. The percentage in the Alcester collection may be lower because of the condition of the material; this renders difficult recognition of worn, as opposed to battered or abraded, fragments of footrings. Apart from six examples of worn *mortaria*, five vessels had heavily worn interiors; all were bowls or deep dishes, which may have been used as mixing bowls (a feature also noted of 30 vessels at Piercebridge). There seems no need to suggest here the extraction of samian dust (see Marsh 1981, 229). The worn patch on no 15 could represent erasion of a graffito, although there was no evidence on any of the extant portions. There were, however, two graffiti, both apparently numerical and both incised on the bottom of the footrings (nos 3, 36).

There were nine vessels which had apparently been repaired, although it is not possible to say how successful the repair was (see nos 2, 5, 13, 30, 41, 48, 53, 54, 60). All had dovetailed rivet holes, at which most of the pieces had broken. In one case a lead rivet had survived, broken, and there were traces of lead in five other instances. It is likely that such repairs were done by a local handyman. At Prestatyn repair work may have been carried out by metalworkers known to have been active on the site (Ward 1989, 154). All the Gas House Lane vessels were of 2nd-century manufacture and at least five dated after *c* AD 150. From the Baromix 1969 excavations came a further six repaired vessels, of 1st- and 2nd-century manufacture. It has been suggested that a decline in mass-production of samian ware may have resulted in preservation of old stock (see for instance Bulmer 1980, 89); this begs the question of whether the industry declined over a period or suddenly collapsed. Marsh (1981, 227) has noted that the percentage of riveted vessels indeed remains fairly constant whatever the availability of new samian.

There were also several instances of samian which had been reused in a secondary function after breakage. There were no samian spindle-whorls, but there were possibly seven counters, all from the later phases, ranging in date of manufacture from the Trajanic-Hadrianic era (one) to the later 2nd century (at least three). They varied in size between 10 and 15mm (three), 20 and 30mm (three), and 40 and 43mm (one). It should be noted of this last example (no 35, of Trajanic-Hadrianic manufacture) that it is doubtful whether such large discs could be used as gaming counters (Marsh 1981, 229), but this presupposes that all Romano-British games are known to us. As in the Piercebridge collection, there was one lionheaded *appliqué* which appeared to have been sawn off from its *mortarium* (no 50). One base with a footring may have been used after breakage, whether as a lid or inverted as a palette; at Piercebridge there were 50 such reused footrings. Of this last site, it was suggested by the author that handymen working in the *vicus* could have been repairing and reworking the samian, perhaps connected with the metalworking activity known in the *vicus* (Ward 1993, 20). Such pieces could have had a very long life indeed in their secondary function. Samian ware is thought to have survived in use through the 3rd century and beyond (see for instance Hartley and Dickinson 1985, 82 on Saxon West Stow).

The question of residuality and survival in use is clearly a difficult one. Preservation of antique 'heirlooms' may be suggested in late contexts such as the fill of the Castle St wells in Chester (Bulmer 1980, 55–8), the Brougham cemetery (Dickinson, forthcoming), and at Portchester Castle (Morris 1975, 277f). In all these collections the samian ware included 1st- and early 2nd-century fragments as well as late 2nd- to 3rd-century vessels. At Gas House Lane, the presence of repaired and reused pieces originally manufactured in the later Antonine period could indicate their continued use well into the 3rd century. On the other hand, it should be emphasised that the repaired vessels were each represented by a single, small sherd; their successful repair and extended life in use cannot be proved. One might surely have expected less fragmentation and better condition if the samian had indeed represented survival in use until the time of deposition. A large portion of a stamped cup (no 44 from Phase C33) was a rare exception. At least 33% of the collection consisted of indeterminate sherds, even in the earliest contexts.

The large quantity of later Antonine CG ware and the low proportion of EG vessels could suggest two contrasting possibilities. Firstly, that this material was deposited before the 3rd century; as was noted in passing in the Tibbet's Close, Alcester report (Dickinson 1985, 17), the predominance of CG samian is normal for British sites with little or no 3rd-century occupation. Secondly, it is conceivable that any late EG vessels were preserved in use through the 3rd century and discarded elsewhere in Alcester. At 6 Birch Abbey, a large part of a Rheinzabern bowl of late 2nd- or 3rd-century manufacture survived until perhaps the 4th century, as it was found in the latest Roman gravel surface (Dickinson 1985, 36 fig 24). It is more likely that the samian recovered on the Gas House Lane site was already rubbish in the early 3rd century. There were at most three EG vessels of which the fragments showed any sign of wear from use. Of these, two were pieces of footrings of indeterminate form, origin, and date. The other was a *mortarium* Dr 43 of late 2nd- to early 3rd-century manufacture, of which two sherds were recovered from Phases C22 and C23. Arguably, this form could have accumulated signs of heavy use in a relatively short time. It is unfortunate that, owing to the problem of dating plain fragments in particular, none of these sherds can be ascribed firmly to the 3rd century any more than to the later 2nd century. If the samian collection was studied in isolation, the scarcity of EG ware and the relatively small number of any *mortaria* (produced exclusively after c AD 170) might suggest assemblage no later than the end of the 2nd century. From that time, EG imports were left, rather inadequately, in monopoly of the market.

Samian: a note by Jeremy Evans

The origin of the samian ware has been discussed above and it seems difficult to regard its presence on the site as a result of archaeological residuality rather than material currently in use when the site was occupied c AD 200.

Table 19 lists the average sherd weight by phase of the Central Gaulish samian from the site. This shows that average sherd weights for this material in Period C fall after Phases C12, C32, and C21 and this does not correlate with the average sherd weights of the remainder of the Roman material, which tends to suggest that Central Gaulish material became archaeologically residual after sometime in the second quarter of the 3rd century.

Other finewares
Jeremy Evans

The other finewares provide an interesting range of material, particularly for the first half of the 3rd century. Two vessels in the mica dusted ware F23, (F23.1 and F23.2, fig 33) tend to suggest that this was current in the second half of the 2nd century and still available at the end of the century as does the

Table 19 Average sherd weight of Central Gaulish samian by phase

	Trench B			Trench C			Trench 7(n)	
Phase	CGS mean wt (g)	All Roman pot mean wt (g)	Phase	CGS mean wt (g)	All Roman pot mean wt (g)	Phase	CGS mean wt (g)	All Roman pot mean wt (g)
C21	6.8	7.1	C31	(7.0)	8.6	C12	10.5	13.3
C22	4.6	10.7	C32	11.7	21.1	C13	9.0	14.9
C23	4.6	9.0	C33	6.6	11.7	C14	5.2	11.5
C24	(4.5)	16.1				C15	5.0	9.4
E	9.0	11.5	E	7.8	13.3	E	(4.5)	10.1

Figures in parentheses are from unreliably low sample sizes.

occurrence in this fabric of a Dr 38 copy from the 1–5 Bleachfield St Site (Ferguson, forthcoming, no 573). This type is not found amongst the earlier 2nd-century mica-dusted types published from London (Marsh 1978) and it must be suggested that the industry producing F23 was an unusually late survivor of the earlier 2nd-century mica-dusted ware industries. The forms represented also rather suggest this with F23.1 apparently being the rim of a 'Rhenish' type beaker, whilst the shouldered beaker, F23.2, is similar to Howe *et al* (1980) types 40–1, later 2nd to early 3rd century, but without the indentations. Continental imports are not strongly represented with Central Gaulish (?) 'Rhenish' type ware (F32) representing only 3.8% of all finewares from Period C and Trier (?) 'Rhenish' type ware, (F33) representing 11.3%. The greater emphasis on East Gaulish material no doubt reflects its later date range.

There are a number of minor colour-coated wares present, most of them probably from western Britain, of which the most important is F42, 39.4% of all Period C finewares (excluding samian). There is a complete profile of a finely rouletted beaker in this fabric, copying a Central Gaulish or Trier form, F42.1 (fig 33), (cf Greene 1978, fig 2.3, no 4; Gillam 1970, types 47 and 48, *c* AD 200–50). There are also a number of sub-cornice rimmed beakers in this fabric and a necked beaker, F42.4 (Howe *et al* 1980, types 40–1), all suggesting a later 2nd- to early 3rd-century date range. Booth (pers comm) suggests that this fabric is quite common at Chesterton and *Tripontium* and may originate to the east of Alcester. Most of the other minor colour-coated ware fabrics are also likely to be of later 2nd- to early 3rd-century date. It could be suggested that these industries benefited from the decline of samian ware but, as most if not all of their products were beakers, they might be better seen as fulfilling the same demand as Nene Valley ware beakers in south-eastern and northern Britain. Cologne products (F37) are also represented by a single cornice rimmed beaker (F37.1), with clay pellet roughcast decoration with a dark brown colour coat, from Phase C32.

Two minor finewares, F46, represented by the base of an indented beaker, and F57 seem more related to the South-Western brown slip ware, F59, discussed further below.

The Nene Valley wares (F52) from the site form quite an interesting collection. The fabric is rare in the 3rd-century deposits (21.7% of the finewares excluding samian), but its proportion increases in the later 4th century; table 20 shows its occurrence by phase. (In table 20 and similar tables which follow data from Phase C11 has been omitted as there were very few sherds and the figures would be meaningless). It makes its first appearance on the site in phases C13, C23, and C32, perhaps around the middle of the 3rd century, much later than its occurrence in northern England, and at a much lower level, despite the greater distance to the latter region. It seems clear from the rising proportion of F52 through the Period D deposits (trench 5, Period D, trench A, Phase D2 and trench 2, Period D) that the fabric was increasingly important from *c* AD 370 until the end of the Roman period. The phenomenon of an increasing supply of Nene Valley ware in the last quarter of the 4th century is one also seen in northern England (Evans 1985).

The date distribution of the forms represented also reflects the trends shown in table 20. There are two of later 2nd- to mid 3rd-century date (a hunt cup, F52.9, and a barbotine-decorated bag beaker, F52.3), one 3rd century (Howe *et al* (1980) types 49–50, F52.4), and twelve 4th century (one rim as Howe *et al* (1980) type 66, F52.1, three type 79, F52.5, seven type 87, F52.6, and one type 75–7, F52.2).

The functional analysis of F52 (table 21) reflects the fact that most of it comes from late 4th-century contexts with beakers being a very minor component in the assemblage, unlike in 3rd-century contexts where they are predominant.

The first occurrence of Oxfordshire colour-coated ware (F51) is in context (2096), Phase C33, dated towards the end of the 3rd century, and this is probably not intrusive as there is no other material suggesting this from the context. The general lack of Oxfordshire fineware from Period C deposits is of note and contrasts with its appearance in Period 6 at the 1–5 Bleachfield St Site (*c* AD 240–250/60). It is clear from the late 4th-century deposits that the proportion of F51 was rising throughout the last quarter of the 4th century and it seems likely that it was a minor component in the assemblage, before this, in the early to mid-4th century. The Oxfordshire colour-coated ware types which can be identified from the site do not include any exclusively early

Table 20 Proportions of Oxfordshire, Nene Valley, and South-Western Brown Slipped wares by phase

Trench	Phase	% sherd nos				% weight				% by percentage of rim			
		F51	F52	F59	*n*	F51	F52	F59	*n*	F51	F52	F59	*n*
7(n)	C12	0	0	0	467	0	0	0	6234	0	0	0	712
7(n)	C13	0	0.1	0	1010	0	0.1	0	15081	0	0	0	1338
7(n)	C14	0	0.4	0	924	0	1.6	0	10601	0.6	0	0	882
7(n)	C15	0	0.8	0	242	0	0.2	0	2267	0	0	0	256
B	C21	0	0	0	61	0	0	0	470	0	0	0	62
B	C22	0	0	0	815	0	0	0	8708	0	0	0	974
B	C23	0	0.7	0	556	0	0.4	0	4965	0	0	0	553
B	C24	0	0	0	34	0	0	0	533	0	0	0	87
C	C31	0	0	0	34	0	0	0	292	0	0	0	16
C	C32	0	0.5	0	747	0	0.7	0	15783	0	0	0	1737
C	C33	0.1	0.6	0.5*	1449	0	0.5	0.1*	16875	0	0.4	0	1724
	0CC	0	2	4	95	0	0	2	874	0	0	14	79
5	D *c* AD 370–90	8.3	2.8	4.6	108	4.3	0.5	6.5	2372	8.1	0	4.2	261
A	D2 *c* AD 380–90	11	7	15	89	9	8	12	1218	4	42	33	144
2	D *c* AD 390–400	23.9	12.4	6.5	322	13.1	9.5	6.8	2964	18	14.1	10	411

* intrusive

ones and there is a clear emphasis on the 4th century in the material. The types represented are C1–10, C14.1, C20–39, C44, C45, C51, C55, C75, C81–6, and C93 amongst 32 rimsherds. Functional analysis (table 22) of this material shows that it was predominantly composed of tableware bowls with minor proportions of flagons and beakers.

The other major component of the fineware assemblage at Gas House Lane in the 4th century is South-Western brown slip ware (F59, Cirencester fabric 105). This makes its first appearance in the small sequence of 4th-century deposits in trench C assigned to Period C which have been treated here as a separate sub-group 0CC. There are a few pieces in earlier phases, all of which are intrusive (table 20). The fabric seems to be first produced around the middle of the 4th century (Young 1980; Keeley 1986; Evans forthcoming) and to originate in Gloucestershire perhaps near to Wycomb (Young 1980). The functional analysis of the Gas House Lane material in table 23 is basically similar to that from the

1964–66 Birch Abbey site, although there is a greater emphasis at Gas House Lane on dishes and jars. Interestingly there is one flanged bowl which probably belongs with the Wycomb examples in this fabric, a form also reported at Cirencester (Keeley 1986, fig 106, no 75). (This example, F59.7, could possibly be in a Nene Valley oxidized fabric, but it is more likely that it is South-Western brown slip ware, especially as flanged bowls in the Nene Valley oxidized fabric are very rare in northern England and Nene Valley material is even rarer at Alcester.)

The Alcester figures for F59, 16.5% of finewares from Period D, are comparable to the figures from Bath (Green and Young 1985, fig 82) both sites being a similar distance from the putative Gloucestershire kiln site (Evans 1994).

Alcester provides a convenient point at which to examine the relationships between the South-Western brown slip, Nene Valley, and Oxfordshire industries.

Table 21 Functional analysis of Nene Valley ware (F52) from Gas House Lane

Jars	Bowls	Dishes	Beakers	Flagons
7%	27%	47%	13%	7%

n = 15 rims

Table 22 Functional analysis of Oxfordshire colour-coated ware F51 (excluding *mortaria* M71)

Flagons		Beakers		Bowls	
MNR	% rim	MNR	% rim	MNR	% rim
3%	15%	13%	23%	84%	62%

n = 32 rims, 162%

Table 23 Functional analysis of Nene Valley wares (F52) and South-Western Brown Slipped ware (F59) from selected 4th-century groups

	Jars (%)	Bowls (%)	Dishes (%)	Beakers (%)	Flagons (%)	Lids (%)	
F52							
Binchester (Phase 9)	0	27	18	27	5	23	*n* = 22 rims
Beadlam (late 4th century)	0	41	14	36	5	5	*n* = 22 rims
Gas House Lane	7	27	47	13	7	0	*n* = 15 rims
F59							
Gas House Lane	7	13	13	47	20	0	*n* = 15 rims
Wycomb	0	45	0		56	0	*n* = 114 rims
1964–66 Birch Abbey	0	12	0	76	12	0	*n* = 17 rims

Note: the 56% at Wycomb includes both flagons and beakers

Table 24 Relative proportions of finewares from various later 4th-century groups in the south-west

	Oxford (%)	South-Western brown slip (%)	Nene Valley (%)	New Forest (%)
Wycomb	50	44	6	0
Bath 5C	67	24	0	9
Bath 5D	70	16	5	9
Cirencester	81	11	8	0
Alcester	52	17	26	0
Shakenoak	89	>1	10	0

Compared with many sites in the South-West, Nene Valley material is well represented in the late 4th-century finewares and is the second most important fabric, at 26%, compared with 52% Oxfordshire red ware and 17% South-Western brown slip ware amongst the finewares from Period D deposits.

Nene Valley products actually appear to be in direct competition with the Oxfordshire material in the late 4th century at Alcester, 74% being dishes and bowls compared with 84% of bowls amongst the Oxfordshire ware, although the Oxfordshire products are more clearly tablewares whilst the Nene Valley products are in a range which has been described as 'colour-coated coarsewares' (ie predominantly flanged bowls and simple rimmed dishes).

It was observed above that Nene Valley assemblages of late 4th-century date in the North include relatively few beakers compared with earlier groups. However, as table 23 shows, the proportion of beakers in the Alcester groups is less than half that of two typical northern assemblages of the period. This may well be the result of competition from the South-Western brown slip ware industry which was producing a very similar range of products and specializing in beakers.

It is curious that the proportion of beakers in Oxfordshire red colour-coated ware at Alcester (13% by minimum number of rims and 23% by percentage of rim) is greater than that at Cirencester (7.6% by percentage of rim) (Keeley 1986, 189) despite the potentially greater competition from South-Western brown slip ware at Alcester in this range of forms. However demand for drinking vessels at Alcester may have been quite high comparatively, as previously Severn Valley ware tankards had fulfilled this function as well as beakers, but these were now no longer supplied (*see* 'Functional analysis' below).

Gritted wares

The principal wares in this category are the pink grogged ware, G11 (Booth and Green 1989), and Malvernian Metamorphic-tempered ware, G44, both present in very low proportions. The former occurs sporadically at a level of less than 1% in Period C whilst the latter occurs generally at a level of around 1% in Period C; it was probably residual in Period D. It is interesting that one sherd of wheelmade Malvernian material (G46) occurs for the first time at Alcester (Hereford and Worcester fabric 19). The forms represented are principally storage jars and lids, rather than the 2nd-century tubby cooking pots. The proportion of lids in this fabric is truly remarkable (table 25) and it would appear that lids were sold by themselves to serve with vessels in other fabrics. This is perhaps not so surprising given that lids were so rarely produced by other industries supplying the town.

Table 25 Vessels represented in Malvernian ware, fabric G44

Jars		Storage jars		Lids	
Min no of rims	% of rim	Min no of rims	% of rim	Min no of rims	% of rim
27%	9%	14%	20%	59%	71%

n = 22 rims and 131%

Mortaria

The *mortaria* from Gas House Lane represent almost exclusively Mancetter-Hartshill and Oxfordshire products (fig 34). In the early 3rd century, Mancetter products were clearly pre-eminent, as might be expected given the respective distances of 47km and 70km from the kiln sites at Mancetter and Oxfordshire to Alcester. It is notable that Oxfordshire *mortaria* were actually present in Phase C21 in the early 3rd century, in contrast to the evidence from the 1–5 Bleachfield St site (Ferguson forthcoming) where the fabric does not appear before the mid-3rd century. Also in contrast to the 1–5 Bleachfield St Site there are examples of Young types M11, M14, and M16 (dated *c* AD 180–240). By the later 3rd century (for example Phase C33) the proportion of Mancetter-Hartshill material had been overtaken by that of Oxfordshire, and when the site sequence offers further information, in the later 4th century (Phases D and D2), Oxfordshire *mortaria* clearly had a monopoly of supply, after the demise of the Mancetter industry. Oxfordshire white-slip *mortaria* (M43) first appear in the sequence in Phase C23, but do not become fairly common until Period D. Red-slip *mortaria*, Young type M71, do not appear on the site until Period D, when they are the principal *mortarium* type, and the previously common M22s are sufficiently scarce for it to be doubtful if they were still in production. Green and Young (1985, 145) note a similar phenomenon in the 4th-century deposits at Bath: 'within the Oxfordshire products, there is some indication that the two colour-coated fabrics became more common and the white-ware fabric less so as the 4th century progressed'.

Given the road transport distances it would appear that Oxfordshire products were competitively priced or had some other advantage which increased as the industry expanded in the later 3rd century. It is of note that, despite the expanded proportion of Nene Valley colour coated ware from the site in the late 4th century, no Nene Valley *mortaria* were present on the site.

Oxidized wares

The vast bulk of the oxidized wares at Gas House Lane are Severn Valley wares (figs 35–8). The only other oxidized ware to bé reasonably represented is fabric O81. This principally produced a range of 3rd-century flagons and seems to have been current throughout Period C, although it would seem to be entirely residual by the late 4th century.

The main Severn Valley ware fabrics are O23, O24, O27, and O36 (the last group resulting from the division of the former fabric group O21 into the early, heavily organically tempered material (O21) and the later, more lightly organically tempered fabric with limestone inclusions (O36)). Fabrics O25, O27, and O33 are now regarded as probably being points along a continuum and the perception of divisions between them varies slightly from that of previous work (cf Ferguson forthcoming). The latter group of fabrics would seem to be visually indistinguishable from kiln material from Newlands and Great Buckmans Farm, Malvern Link, (Waters 1976) and to match the description of Malvernian Severn Valley ware given by Peacock (1967). Fabric O36 would also seem to be very similar to some of the sherds from the Newlands kiln. Analytical work to test the relationships of these fabrics to the Malvern Link kilns is in progress. Fabric O24 has some visual similarities with the Perry Barr kiln material (Hughes 1961) which may well have continued in production rather longer than the report suggests.

The trends in the Severn Valley ware fabrics are quite interesting. In all the sequences, fabric O24 is the predominant fabric at the beginning of the 3rd century, but in all areas, except trench C, it has been overtaken by the amount of O27 by the end of the century, and in trench C the trend is running in the same direction. Generally O27 seems to be becoming the major Severn Valley ware in the sequences around the middle of the century.

Fabric O36 does not show such clear trends. The evidence from trench 7(n) suggests that its proportion increases after the mid-3rd century (Phase C14) but then declines again later in the century (Phase C15). The sequence from trench B shows no convincing trends and the same is true for trench C when allowance is made for the low numbers and consequent instability of the figures from Phase C31. If O36 is indeed associated with O27, as tentatively suggested above, then its reflection of O27's rise in trench 7(n) may be a real trend but it would not seem to go on to be a major fabric in the 4th century.

Fabric O23 seems to fluctuate in its proportions rather but to remain a fairly constant contributor to the Severn Valley ware assemblage throughout the 3rd century. There are some suggestions that it may have become a more important fabric in the 4th century, or at least that it may have remained in use longer than the other Severn Valley wares. It forms the majority of the Severn Valley ware in Period D in trench 5, where it may not have been residual, it is also important in the Severn Valley wares in

Table 26 Functional analysis of Severn Valley wares from Gas House Lane

Class Fabric	Flagons (%)	Constricted necked jars (%)	Jars (%)	Wide jars (%)	Carinated bowls (%)	Tankards (%)	Bowls (%)	Dishes (%)	Lids (%)	*n* (rims)
O23	3.6	10.7	19.6	14.3	3.6	25.0	21.4	0	1.8	56
O24	5.2	10.4	14.8	27.0	1.7	27.8	12.2	0.9	0	115
O27	4.1	15.5	18.6	19.6	1.0	29.9	9.3	2.1	0	97
O36	3.0	10.0	23.0	26.0	3.0	26.0	10.0	0	0	31
O55	0	22.0	9.0	13.0	0	17.0	39.0	0	0	23

trench A, Phase D2, and in the limited, and probably residual, Severn Valley ware component in trench 2, Period D. Similarly in Period E material there is some tendency for fabric O23 to be strongly represented in areas which show a greater proportion of 4th-century fabrics.

The Severn Valley wares from Gas House Lane appear to show a considerable contrast with those from the 1–5 Bleachfield St site (Ferguson forthcoming) where fabric O21 was recorded as being the dominant fabric until the end of the 3rd century (Period 8). However, it is clear from the high proportion of reduced wares (Ferguson forthcoming, fig 42), much of which is represented by rustic ware jars (dated by Booth (pers comm) as Flavian to mid-2nd century), that there is a very high proportion of residual material in that sequence up to this point.

Table 26 shows the functional analysis of Severn Valley wares from Gas House Lane. There are marked variations in some classes depending upon fabric type. O23 tends to produce more bowls than most, as does O55. O24 has a high proportion wide-mouthed jars, as does O36, whilst O55 has a higher proportion of constricted-necked jars and fewer jars than the other fabrics. These variations do not particularly seem to correlate with the date ranges of the fabrics (O23 has a later emphasis, O24 an early one, and O27 a middle one) but rather reflect some specialization at the kiln sites producing them. (The emphases of O36 and O55 are not clear although both seem to be minor 3rd-century fabrics).

The occurrences of form types by phase and fabric are listed in table M24 (microfiche M3:A11). Unfortunately there seems to be little discernible typological change in the material throughout the 3rd-century Period C sequence.

The principal other oxidized fabric, O81, perhaps from Whitehall Farm, Wiltshire (Cirencester fabric 96/98), would seem to be a consistent component of 3rd-century Period C deposits, but to be residual thereafter. A functional analysis of vessels in the

fabric from Gas House Lane (table 27) shows that the largest classes of vessels are flagons and jars.

Handmade wares

The only material in this fabric group (P) is seven sherds from a pit (2050) which probably dates to the mid–late Iron Age.

White-slipped flagon fabrics

Only 38 sherds in all from this fabric group (Q) are represented, reflecting the decline in this type of flagon after the end of the 2nd century. The most frequently represented fabric is Q13, followed by Q14, Q21, Q22, Q25 and Q12 and Q15. Only one rimsherd in fabric Q25 is represented (Q25.1, fig 38), a ring-necked flagon.

Reduced fabrics

No real trends can be discerned in the reduced ware fabric figures in Period C, which is no real surprise as they represent a very low proportion of the assemblage and it is likely that much of the material is residual after the early 3rd century. In trench C the proportion of reduced wares (fabric R) falls from around 9% in the (rather unreliable) Phase C31 to 6.5% in C32 and 1.6% in C33. In trench 7(n) the figures are 3.7% in C12, 3.5% in C13, 2.6% in C14, and 3.6% in C15 (perhaps suggesting more residual material in Phase C15). These figures offer a marked contrast to those from the 1–5 Bleachfield St site (Ferguson forthcoming) emphasising the marked residual component in the 3rd-century sequence from that site.

In Period D the picture changes at Gas House Lane. In trench 5 reduced wares comprise 22% of the group and are clearly representing contemporary material as forms such as flanged bowls occur. Similarly in trench A, Phase D2, reduced wares are at 14.5% and in trench 2, Period D, they are 13.2%. As the trench 5, Period D group would seem to be of a slightly earlier date than the other two, there may be some suggestion that the importance of these fabrics was declining in the last decade of the 4th century. However, they clearly represented an important part of the fabric supply in the period *c* AD 370–90. The

Table 27 Functional analysis of vessels in oxidized fabric O81

Flagons	Jars	Tankards	Dishes
40%	40%	10?%	10%

n = 10 rims

82

importance of greyware in the latter half of the 4th century is also shown in the figures from the 1–5 Bleachfield St site (Ferguson forthcoming) where the proportion of reduced wares rises in Period 10 and includes contemporary forms such as flanged bowls (Ferguson forthcoming, nos 780–1, 897–8). The source of at least some of this material may be to the south as reduced wares are common in the later 4th century at Stretton-on-Fosse (Booth pers comm, contra Gardner *et al* 1980). They also seem to be increasing in importance in the late 4th century at Barnsley Park, Gloucester (Webster 1982) and are of some importance at Cirencester (Keeley 1986; *see* table 13 above).

The definitions of some of the greyware fabrics are not very precise, but the forms occurring in them do show which have early and late emphases (figs 38–9). Fabric R01 appears both in everted rim jars and BB-derived jar forms in Phase C13, but there are also examples of flanged bowls in a visually indistinguishable fabric from Period E and unstratified contexts. Fabric R18 seems to have a late emphasis, the first rimsherd occurring in Phase C15, and forms including a flanged bowl (R18.3), a straight-walled dish (R18.4), and several lids. Fabric R31 is a well-defined early storage jar fabric, probably residual from shortly after the occupation of the site. Fabric R32, a finer, organically tempered fabric is also early, copying BB1 jars and beakers and occurring most frequently in Phase C13; it is probably residual after the mid-3rd-century. Fabric R41 would seem to be principally late, with all rimsherds occurring in 4th-century or later contexts and including flanged bowls in its repertoire (R41.8).

Fabrics R51 and R52 both appear to be 3rd century, but in contrast to R32 the forms are mainly medium-mouthed everted rimmed jars and lids. Similarly R72 is a 3rd-century fabric mainly of everted rimmed medium-mouthed jars (R72.2).

Whitewares

Whitewares (fabric W) are principally represented by Mancetter and Oxfordshire products (fig 38). Throughout Period C Mancetter products are present at a level of around 1% whilst probable Oxfordshire material appears in Phases C14, C23, and C33 but is never so common as the Mancetter material. It seems probable that Mancetter whiteware (W12) went out of production sometime in the 3rd century although the figures for Period C do not offer any indication of when this might be. It is of note that there are several sherds in fabric W23 which would seem to be the brown-slip Mancetter whiteware. Surprisingly, Oxfordshire parchment ware (W15) is not found in the Period D deposits perhaps suggesting that the type was not reaching Alcester by the end of the 4th century. Most of the parchment ware comes from Period E deposits, which presumably represent truncation of early to mid-4th-century activity on the site. A number of parchment ware (Young 1977) type P24s appear in

Phase C33 and they are accompanied by two examples of whiteware (W13) type W15s (*c* AD 240–300).

Functional analysis

Table 28 shows the functional analysis of the major sequences: from trenches B, C, and 7(n) for the 3rd century; 4th-century figures from group 0CC and trench 5 Period D; and trench 2 Period D, which date from the mid- to late 4th century.

In trenches B and 7(n) there appear to be few chronological developments in Period C, although the proportion of beakers and tankards does seem to rise in trench 7(n) in the later 3rd century and there seems to be a general rise in the proportion of lids through the Period. In trench C the proportions of jars, beakers, and tankards appear to fall in the late 3rd century and those of dishes, bowls, and *mortaria* seem to rise.

There is, however, a marked variation between the functional pattern in trenches 7(n) and B, with trench C starting with a pattern similar to trench B in Phase C32 and developing one more like trench 7(n) in Phase C33. In terms of the higher proportion of dishes and bowls, and later, drinking vessels, from trench 7(n), this would appear to be a higher status assemblage, whilst that from trench B, with a higher proportion of jars would seem to be a more functional, workaday group. Jugs and flagons also seem to be rather commoner in trench 7(n). Turning to table 29, this phenomenon is reflected in the later phases in trench 7(n) (Phases C14–C15), but not in Phases C12–C13.

In contrast to the 3rd-century sequence, the 4th-century one shows marked chronological changes. Constricted-necked jars have disappeared, wide-mouthed jars are much scarcer, whilst tankards, which were a major component of the assemblage, have disappeared entirely. The level of jars (Warwickshire Museum classes 21–36) is similar to that from Period C in trench B and greater than that from trench 7(n), although the overall proportion, if constricted-necked jars and wide-mouthed jar/bowls are included, is lower. The proportion of beakers rises slightly, but this does not compensate for the absence of tankards, thus failing to maintain the proportion of drinking vessels. The proportion of *mortaria* also seems to be higher in the later 4th-century sequence whilst dishes and bowls have now increased to over 50% of the assemblage, a considerable increase even on the trench 7(n) figures in the 3rd century.

In comparison with table 28, table 29 shows the Alcester function figures calculated by percentage of rim (RE). The trends remain fairly consistent but there are some minor variations owing to discrepancies between the methods, as a similar exercise at Catterick also revealed (Bell and Evans forthcoming). Generally open vessels of greater diameter, ie dishes and bowls, receive a lower representation and closed forms, jugs, jars, and constricted-necked jars a greater one.

83

Table 28 Functional analysis of Gas House Lane pottery by minimum number of rims per context

Phase	Jugs (%)	Constricted necked jars (%)	Wide mouthed jars/bowls (%)	Other jars (%)	Beakers (%)	Tankards (%)	Carinated Bowls (%)	Bowls (%)	Dishes (%)	Mortaria (%)	Lids (%)	Other bowls/ jars (%)	Amphorae (%)	n
Trench B														
C22	2	5	5	31	4	14	1	19	16	1	3	0	0	106
C23	0	5	5	32	2	14	2	20	12	5	6	0	0	66
Trench C														
C32	3	3	10	35	2	15	1	22	7	3	0	1	0	118
C33	3	6	6	22	2	9	2	22	20	4	3	2	0	181
Trench 7(n)														
C12	1	2	7	26	1	17	0	22	22	0	1	0	0	85
C13	2	4	7	24	1	12	1	31	14	2	2	0	0	140
C14	2	2	6	25	1	20	1	25	13	2	4	0	0	110
C15	0	5	0	21	5	16	3	16	26	5	3	0	0	38
Trench C														
0CC	0	0	0	33	8	33	17	0	0	0	0	0	0	12
Trench 5														
D	0	0	4	19	4	0	11	33	15	11	7	0	0	27
Trench 2														
D	6	0	0	35	0	0	16	18	20	4	0	0	0	49

Table 29 Functional analysis of Gas House Lane pottery by percentage of rim (RE)

Phase (%)	Jugs (%)	Constricted necked jars (%)	Wide mouthed jars/bowls (%)	Other jars (%)	Beakers (%)	Tankards (%)	Carinated (%)	Bowls (%)	Dishes (%)	Mortaria (%)	Lids (%)	Other bowls/ jars (%)	Amphorae (%)	n
Trench B														
C22	2	17	3	31	5	18	1	16	7	0	1	0	0	958
C23	0	6	2	38	6	13	2	19	5	4	6	0	0	525
Trench C														
C32	4	5	12	41	1	12	0	16	3	4	0	1	0	1724
C33	11	10	3	28	2	7	3	15	12	5	5	1	0	1706
Trench 7(n)														
C12	11	4	6	34	2	10	0	22	12	0	1	0	0	699
C13	3	8	9	36	0	14	1	18	9	1	2	0	0	1286
C14	12	2	7	25	1	24	0	15	9	2	3	0	0	816
C15	0	4	0	27	10	9	2	12	17	14	5	0	0	256
Trench 5														
D	0	0	17	21	4	0	0	30	20	7	0	0	0	270
Trench 2														
D	18	0	0	35	0	0	7	17	18	4	0	0	0	396

Table 30 Comparative functional analysis from Silchester, Ilchester, and Cirencester

	Flagons and constricted necked jars (%)	Beakers (%)	Mortaria (%)	Jars (%)	Bowls (%)	Dishes (%)	Bowls (%)	Lids (%)	Amphorae (%)	Other dishes (%)	n
Silchester											
Group 2.9	17	0	0	54	6	1	17	1	0	0	0
Flavian											
Group 2.5	0	17	0	39	11	24	0	3	0	0	3.95 eve
Hadrianic-Antonine											
Group 4.1, late 3rd	13	15	0	39	13	16	0	3	0	0	4.32 eve
Group 5.4, late 4th century	3	6	7	30	30	21	0	1	0	0	5.85 eve
Ilchester											
Per I – 1st century	18	12	0	38	25	7	0	1	0	0	103
Per II – 1st–2nd century	5	11	2	38	22	15	0	4	0	0	144
Per III – 2nd–3rd century	10	10	1	42	15	20	0	1	1	0	163
Per IV – 3rd–4th century	6	11	1	43	19	18	0	1	2	0	431
Per V – 5th–7th century	4	13	5	34	31	11	0	1	1	0	180
Cirencester											
Area CQ											
Per I	7	4	4	61	12	9	0	2	0	1	13.73 eve
Per II	9	3	11	46	24	4	0	4	0	0	25.06 eve
Per III	10	5	11	40	20	10	0	3	1	1	45.99 eve
Area CX/CY											
Per I	14	14	4	42	8	16	0	0	1	0	22.63 eve
Per II	7	7	5	54	20	15	0	0	0	1	24.63 eve
Per III	6	3	10	43	23	12	0	1	1	1	105.82 eve

To view the Alcester function figures against their background it is worth comparing them with other sites. Millett (1979, fig 13), published sequences from Neatham, Chichester, and *Verulamium* (although excluding samian ware which will have skewed the 1st- and 2nd-century figures (Millett and Graham 1986, 91)) suggesting a general pattern of a high proportion of jars and a low proportion of tablewares in the early Roman period gradually developing to the reverse of this in the 4th century. However, whilst this picture might be valid for south-eastern towns it is clearly false for the North where, in 3rd- and 4th-century assemblages, both urban and military, the proportion of jars rises markedly in the later 4th century (Evans 1985).

Table 30 shows comparative figures from the Silchester defences (Fulford 1983), Ilchester (Leach 1982), and Cirencester (Keeley 1986, 189). Figure 46 shows Chichester, *Verulamium* (after Millett 1979, fig 13) and Neatham (Millett and Graham 1986; excluding the well deposits which often have a very different functional composition to other parts of the site assemblage (cf Rudston, Rigby 1980; Evans 1985)).

The Alcester figures generally conform to Millett's pattern of a declining proportion of jars, and are comparable with the figures from Neatham and Silchester. There are, however, curious differences when set against the Cirencester figures (from the Beeches) and Ilchester. The pattern and levels at Silchester and Alcester are similar to those at *Verulamium* and Chichester (fig 46; Millett 1979) whilst the general level of jars at Neatham is rather higher and nearer to the high levels from Ilchester and Cirencester. Neither Ilchester or Cirencester show any clear trends. Given that a high proportion of jars is generally a more rural picture, it is of interest that this group (Ilchester, Neatham and Cirencester) is of two small towns, one almost without stone buildings, and an 'urban' site of a villa-like building from which the coin list 'would have to be equated with substantial West Country villas, farms, and small settlements' (Reece 1986, 103) and which the excavator suggested 'represent a group of farms with their smithies' (McWhirr 1986, 78).

Turning to direct evidence for the use of vessels on the site, the incidence of sooting and white internal limescale(?) deposits has been recorded. Its incidence by fabric type is shown on table 31.

The incidence of sooting is very much as might be expected, comprising principally cooking ware fabrics, BB1 (B11) and BB1? (B12), shell-tempered ware (C11 and C15), Malvernian ware (G44), and coarsely sand-tempered greyware (R01). This is very much the same as with northern assemblages (Evans 1985) and once more points to the usefulness of coarsely sand-tempered wares as cooking pots despite the reservations of Rye (1976). Woods has confirmed this point in practical experiments (1983).

The incidence of internal white deposits, assumed to be limescale, is a little different. Most of the

Table 31 Incidence of sooting and limescale (?) by fabric

Fabric	% sooted	% limescale(?)	n
B11	14.6	6.8	2861
B12	8.9	–	78
C11	15.4	3.1	130
C15	9.4	–	53
G44	14.4	0.9	111
O23	0.4	2.4	548
O24	0.09	4.7	1162
O27	0.3	3.4	1018
O29	–	4.3	115
O36	–	1.2	428
O38	–	5.5	36
R01	29.8	24.6	114
R18	4.5	–	22
R19	11.0	–	9
R31	–	4.2	24
R32	–	0.5	193
R41	6.0	–	50
R51	11.0	–	9
R52	1.0	1.0	102
R63	100.0	–	1
R72	5.7	–	35

cooking ware fabrics are reasonably represented, the low figure for Malvernian ware (G44) probably reflecting the large number of lids in this fabric (*see* p 95). The principal Severn Valley ware fabrics and the organically tempered reduced storage jar fabric (R31) are also reasonably represented. The forms (where determinable) amongst the Severn Valley wares appear to be jars and tankards. Ratkai (pers comm) points out that similar deposits are found on medieval vessels without evidence of sooting, and that they are quite common on vessel forms such as jugs. It is quite possible that some of the deposits, rather than being limescale, are the result of the storage of urine, or some other liquid or even possibly from a bain-marie type heating process (Ratkai pers comm).

Finewares

Table 32 shows the proportion of finewares in the three main trenches for Period C and for Period D by sherd count and weight, and the percentage of glassware by sherd count (as if this were to be calculated as part of the pottery assemblage). There do not seem to be any clear chronological trends in the data in Period C and neither are there any very

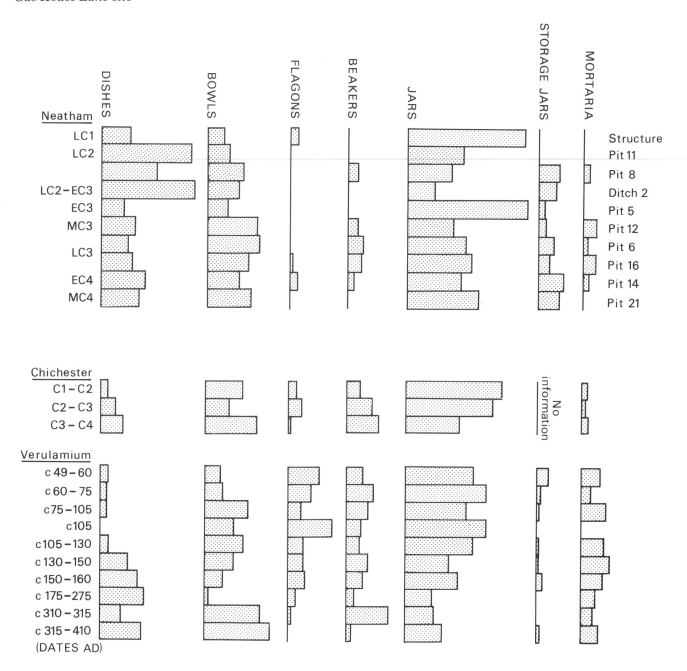

Figure 46 Function figures for Neatham, Chichester, and Verulamium, after Millett (1979) and Millett and Graham (1986)

clear spatial differences between trenches. The glass-ware offers a similar picture except that in trench C Phase C33 and in trench 7 Phase C13 there is a rather stronger representation, possibly suggesting higher status activity.

There is, however, a very consistent trend in the data running from Period C, group 0CC (a small early to mid-4th-century group), through trench 5, Period D (perhaps *c* AD 370–90) to trench 2, Period D (*c* AD 390–400) of a consistent rise in the proportion of finewares to a peak at the very end of the 4th century. This is not necessarily to suggest an increase in the status of the assemblage, but needs to be compared with data from other sites (table 33). Table 33 shows the proportion of finewares from

various other mainly urban sites in the south-east and south-west. It can readily be seen that the trends in the Alcester data find a strong reflection at Cirencester (Keeley 1986), Silchester (Fulford 1984), Great Dunmow (Going and Ford 1988), Chelmsford (Going 1987), London (Orton 1977), and Portchester (Fulford 1975b), although not in the figures from Neatham (Millett and Graham 1986) and Barnsley Park (Webster 1982) whilst the Towcester, Catsgore, and Bath figures may show the effect slightly. It is not simply an urban/rural division as the 55.3% by minimum vessels, 27.8% by weight from the minor rural site at Bishopstone, Sussex shows (Green 1977). Neither can it be seen as simply due to the proximity or otherwise of fineware production cen-

Table 32 Gas House Lane: proportions of pottery finewares and glass compared with the total quantity of pottery and glass combined

Phase (%)	Sherd nos (%)	Wt	Glass (%)
Trench B			
C21	19.0	11.0	–
C22	9.2	5.0	0.4
C23	11.4	5.8	0.6
Trench C			
C32	6.0	3.7	0.4
C33	13.3	6.8	1.1
Trench 7			
C12	12.0	8.7	0.2
C13	8.5	4.9	0.8
C14	13.3	6.4	0.5
C15	12.0	7.1	0.4
Trench C			
OCC	21.0	19.0	–
Trench 5			
D	25.8	19.5	0.2
Trench 2			
D	46.8	32.0	0.2

tres (although this would seem to be the case in large part for Bishopstone itself), for at Alcester all the suppliers in the latest phase were in production in the mid-4th century and most were in production in the late 3rd century. It may be, quixotically, that the phenomenon is rather determined by the available supply of local coarsewares or its absence, as Fulford (1975a, 134) has suggested. Neatham was immediately adjacent to the Alice Holt industry, which was in production until the very end of the 4th century. At Barnsley Park, Bath, and Bradley Hill, greywares were still readily available and at Catsgore, in the core area of BB1 production, that industry was still in production and supplying most of the needs. At Alcester, certainly, one of the remarkable features of the pottery at the end of the 4th century is the complete absence of any potentially local material. The Severn Valley ware industries have come to an end and supplies come from Bedfordshire (*c* 90km), Oxfordshire (*c* 70km), the Nene Valley (*c* 110km), northern Gloucestershire (*c* 35km), and within the Gloucestershire area or perhaps the East Midlands (Trent Valley?) for the greywares (*c* 50/90km). There is no source of supply within 30km of the site, in which circumstance finewares may well have been relatively cheap ceramics, if not the cheapest, because they were at least a little less bulky and were organized for long-distance trade (probably through *negotiatores*).

Repairs to vessels

Seventeen sherds show evidence of repairs to vessels in the form of rivet holes, six of these in oxidized wares and the remainder amongst the samian ware. The samian rivets were all of the X cut-slot type. All those on coarseware were circular drilled holes into which a lead cylinder would have slotted, to be soldered onto a lead strip on each face. The more delicate style of rivet reserved for the samian ware was presumably too weak for functioning coarseware vessels. The lack of examples of riveting in reduced wares no doubt reflects their infrequency in the coarseware assemblage and the fact that BB1 jars, as cooking vessels, could hardly have been so repaired. The disproportionate riveting of samian ware is usual (cf Bell and Evans forthcoming) and emphasises samian's perceived value. There is no evidence that later samian was riveted any more than early material (Marsh 1981) and this is confirmed here with a riveting rate of 1.4%, identical to that from Bainesse Farm, Catterick (Bell and Evans forthcoming) and similar to the 1% from London (Marsh 1981). There is one rivet from Phase C13, one from C22, two each from Phases C32 and C33 and C, one from the 0CC group, two from Period D, and six from medieval and later contexts.

Taphonomy

An attempt has been made to complete cross-joins between vessels within each trench but no such general attempt has been made between the different areas, except for the samian ware. In practice this task may have been fairly successful for the rarely occurring fabrics, but much less so in the commonly occurring ones where matches are almost entirely restricted to rimsherds: very few joins were successfully identified amongst the hand-made fabrics such as BB1. The results are, therefore, very partial, and if they were used to 'correct' the fabric figures they would almost certainly introduce more distortion than they 'corrected'.

Table M20 (microfiche M2:C6) tabulates the cross-joins between contexts in trenches B, C, and 7. The proportion of conjoining sherds and sherds from the same vessel varies between trenches from 1.9% in trench 2 (number of conjoining vessels as a proportion of the total minimum number of rims per context in each trench), 4.5% in trench C, 6.3% in trench 7, and 10.7% in trench B.

The low proportion in trench 2 reflects the lack of a long stratigraphic sequence here and the little post-Roman disturbance. In trench C, 7 of the 19 cross-joins show post-Roman disturbance and two disturbance of C32 deposits from C33; the remaining 10 merely reflect internal disturbance or the spread of debris mainly in Phases C33 and Period C.

In trench B, 11 of the 27 cross joins show post-Roman disturbance and 12 disturbance of Roman deposits within the Roman period, mainly of Phase C22

Table 33 Proportion of finewares from various Roman sites in southern England

i) Neatham finewares (wt) (Millett 1986)

Feature	Ditch 2	Pit 17	Oven 1	Pit 5	Well 3	Well 2	Pit 12
Date	LC2/EC3	EC3	MC3	EC3	MC3	LC3	MC3
Fineware (%) by wt	3.0	1.6	0.2	4.1	2.4	6.7	9.3
Feature	Pit 6	Pit 16	Well 1	Well 6	Pit 14	Pit 21	Well 5
Date	M-LC3	LC3	MC4	MC4	EC4	MC4	LC4/EC5
Fineware	9.4%	3.6%	3.8%	5.3%	5.1%	4.4%	4.7%

(%) by wt

ii) London Riverside wall period 3 (Millett 1980)

Finewares: 20.2% by sherd count

iii) London, Angel Court (Orton 1977) ER1582 AD 370

Finewares: 22% by sherd count; 38% eve

London, Angel Court ER1581 c AD 370/410 or Saxon

Finewares: 27% by sherd count; 35% eve

iv) Barnsley Park (Webster 1982)

Period	PS6	PS7	PS8	PS9	PS10
Date	c AD 360–75	c AD 375–85	c AD 380–400	c AD 400+	C5th
Fineware	5.4	0	4.5	1.1	7.0

(%) by sherd count

v) Great Dunmow post AD 350 shrine late group (Going and Ford 1988)

Finewares: 26.2% by weight, 48.8% rim equivalent (RE)

vi) Towcester Grammar School (Brown and Alexander 1982)

Phase and date	Phase 4D	E–MC4	Phase 5	Occupation M–LC4	PS5 Collapse	LC4–C5
Sherd nos	Min vessels	Sherd nos	Min vessels	Sherd nos	Min vessels	
Finewares (%)	11.1	4.5	20.3	31.6	17.0	18.9

vii) Towcester, Alchester Road (Woodfield 1983)

Phase	Phase 3	Phase 4A	Phase 4B	Phase 4B*
Date	c 270–330	c 330–355	c 355–70	c 370+
Fineware (%) by sherd no	17.5	24.35	17.5	20

viii) Chelmsford mansio etc (Going 1987)

Phase	Phase 6	Phase 7	Phase 8
Date	260/75–300/10	300/10–360/70	360/70–400+
Fineware (%) (RE)	2.99	4.38	17.43

Table 33 Proportion of finewares from various Roman sites in southern England

ix) Portchester (Fulford 1975b)

Date	c AD 300–325		c AD 325–345		c AD 345–400	
	Nos	**Min vessels**	**Nos**	**Min vessels**	**Nos**	**Min vessels**
Fineware (%)	21	40	35	41	53	46

x) Bath (Green and Young 1985)

Period	**Period 3**	**5A**	**5B**	**5C**	**5D**	**5E**
Date	**EC4**	*c* **AD 350**	*c* **AD 390**			*c* **AD 400+**
Fineware (%)	10	19	25	28	25	20

xi) Bishopstone, Sussex (Green 1977)

Date: 4th century, mainly later

Finewares: 55.3% by min vessels; 27.8% by weight

xii) Cirencester (Keeley 1986)

Area	**CQ**			**CX/CY**			**DE/DF**
Period	**I**	**II**	**III**	**I**	**II**	**III**	
Fineware (%) (RE)	8.0%	18.3%	31.2%	17.9%	19.8%	31.7%	24.5%

xiii) Silchester defences (Fulford 1984)

Period and date	**G2.8 Flavian**	**G2.7 Flavian-Hadrianic**	**G5.4 later 4th century**
Fineware (%) (RE)	11.2%	24.3%	19.1%

xiv) Bradley Hill, Somerset, 4th century (Leech 1981)

Finewares: 10.8% by sherd nos

deposits by C23 (8 examples). In trench 7 in contrast, only 3 of the 26 cross joins show post-Roman disturbance; 12 show Roman disturbance mainly of Phase C13 by C14, although also of C12 by C13. Although much of the material in phase C15 and C24 appears to be residual the cross-joins do not seem to be of much use in highlighting this at first. If allowance is made for the quantity of material in the different phases, however, then in trench B, 1.9% of cross joins between phases link with C22, 13.6% with C23, 28.6% with C24, and 17.9% with E which probably gives a more reasonable reflection of the trends in residuality in the sequence. In trench C there are no cross joins from C32 and only 1.1% from C33 with a rise, but only to 8.3%, in Period E. In trench 7 there are 2.7% cross-joins in Phase C13, 10.0% in C14, and 7.9% in C15, with a rise to 37.5% in Period E. Obviously all the material in Period E is derived from Roman deposits, but much of it is clearly from the truncation of the 4th-century stratigraphy and thus the variations in the proportions of cross-joins would not relate to this. The variations ought to reflect the level of disturbance of the remaining Period C stratigraphy, or perhaps, indirectly, the level of redeposited 3rd-century material in 4th-century deposits in turn truncated by Period E activity. Certainly the variations in the level of cross-joins in Period E deposits do not seem to reflect the recorded levels of modern disturbance. Trench 7, with apparently the least disturbed stratigraphy, has the most cross-joins with Period E. Trench B, with some disturbance, has a good few cross-joins, whilst trench C, with apparently, much disturbance, has least.

This said, the sequences within Period C do seem to conform more to expectations, with in all cases a rise in the number of cross-joins as the sequences progress. In trench B there is quite a marked rise in Phase C23 and a further doubling in Phase C24 where, as observed above, (p 68) much of the pottery seems to be residual. In trench 7 the rise is much more gradual and the rise in C15 is not marked although much of this material too seems to be residual. This would suggest that this material is

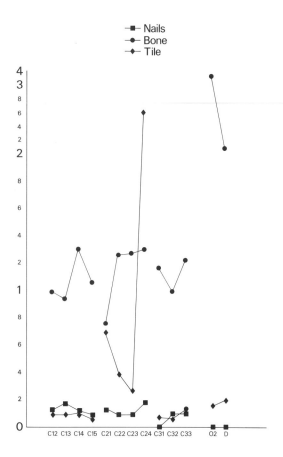

Figure 47 Common finds by phase from Gas House Lane (numbers of bones are derived from site lists and are counted on a different basis to the numbers given in the bone report). The vertical logarithmic scale indicates the number of examples of a particular material divided by the number of pottery sherds from the same phase

introduced as a result of the dumping of earlier material from elsewhere rather than from the disturbance of earlier deposits.

In trench C there is a very low level of cross-joins within Period C with only 1.1% in Phase C33. This seems to match the internal evidence of the pottery where much less of the material from phase C33 would seem to be residual than in the other late 3rd-century groups.

One point of note is the nature of the deposits from which the vast majority of Period C cross-joins occur. Almost without exception they are from layers of stratigraphy, not from pit fills cutting earlier deposits as might be expected (the main exception being slot 1076 in Phase C24), suggesting that much of the material is derived from the recycling of earlier deposits as levelling materials in later phases.

Turning to other methods of analysis, figure 47 shows the ratios of numbers of tile fragments, nails, and animal bone fragments relative to the amount of

pottery from the three Period C sequences and from the Period D deposits. The nail and tile figures are generally rather stable with the exception of Phase C24 when there is relatively a large amount of tile. It would seem to be no coincidence that this is the only Roman phase yielding *pilae* and would seem to offer evidence of the demolition or refurbishment of a hypocausted building somewhere in the vicinity.

In all three Period C sequences the animal bone/pottery ratio is fairly stable fluctuating around 1:1. A marked change takes place in Period D with a doubling of the ratio. This tends to suggest either a decline in the absolute quantity of pottery, or a breakdown in previous waste disposal practices with more waste being left on the site. The latter explanation is favoured as this pattern is not unique to the Gas House Lane site, which merely provides a weaker echo of the sequence from the fort of *Segontium*, fig 48. There it is very difficult, given the quantity of ceramics from its late phases, to suggest an absolute decline in the amount of pottery in use, but the dumping of refuse in a virtually disused quarter of the fort would seem probable. Although ratio plots are not available, a similar pattern of the breakdown of previous discard and waste disposal patterns seems to be suggested by the deposit on the berm outside the town wall at Lincoln (Darling 1977) and by the large dump of pottery and animal bone including several pole-axed cattle skulls behind the back of the 'Commandants House' at the Roman fort at Binchester, County Durham.

Ceramic small finds

This catalogue includes some samian items which are also recorded in the samian report.

Spindle whorls

1 About 50% of a pierced ceramic disc made from a chamfered dish base sherd in BB1 (fabric B11), probably a spindle whorl. The edges are filed smooth. Diameter of central hole 8mm, diameter of whorl 38mm. Wt 6.5g. (Phase C33, C 2062, SF 232). Fig 49

Counters

2 About 30% of a ceramic disc probably made from a BB1 jar base (fabric B11). Diameter probably originally *c* 65mm. (Phase C22, B 1096)

3 A roughly shaped ceramic disc made from a Central Gaulish (S20) samian sherd, Dr 37 (*c* AD 150–200) *c* 22 × 25mm. Samian catalogue no 31. (Phase C22, B 1099)

4 A roughly shaped ceramic disc made from the upper wall of a Severn Valley ware jar (fabric O27). Diameter 42mm. (Phase C23, B 1063)

5 A small ceramic disc made from a Central Gaulish (S20) samian wall-sherd, form indeterminable (*c* AD 150–200) roughly chipped to shape, probably a gaming counter. Diameter 15mm. Samian catalogue no 49. (Period E, B 1000)

6 A roughly shaped ceramic disc made from a Central Gaulish

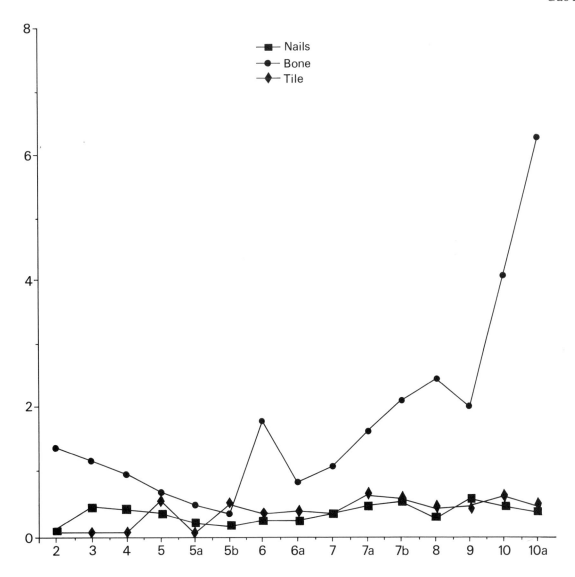

Figure 48   Common finds ratios by period from Segontium, North Wales

(S20) samian wall sherd from a Dr 31R. Dimensions *c* 25 × 30mm. Samian catalogue no 51. (Period E, B 1021/1)

7 A roughly shaped ceramic disc made from a Les Martres (S21) samian wall sherd, Dr 18R or 18/31R, (*c* AD 100–30). Dimensions: *c* 40 × 45mm. Samian catalogue no 35. (Period C32, C 2113)

8 A neatly cut small ceramic disc, probably a gaming counter cut from a vessel in fabric O81. Diameter 12mm. (Period C33, C 2058, SF 384)

9 Slightly more than half of a small ceramic disc made from a Central Gaulish (S20) wall sherd (*c* AD 120–200), form indeterminable, probably a gaming counter. Diameter: *c* 15mm. Samian catalogue no 42. (Period C33, C 2058)

10 A small ceramic disc made from a decorated Central Gaulish (S20) samian Dr 30 wall sherd (*c* AD 140–200), probably a gaming counter. Diameter: *c* 10mm. Samian catalogue no 43. (Phase C33, C 2059)

11 A small ceramic disc cut from the wall of a Severn Valley ware vessel (fabric O27). Diameter 27mm. (Phase C33, C 2062)

12 A roughly shaped ceramic disc made from the wall of a large greyware jar (fabric R01), decorated with three parallel burnished lines. Diameter 68mm. (Period E, C 2018/1)

13 A roughly shaped ovoid ceramic disc made from a Central Gaulish (S20) samian Dr 37 lower wall sherd (*c* AD 140–200). Dimensions: 30 × 35mm. Samian catalogue no 56. (Period E, C 2038/1)

14 Fragment of a base(?) sherd in greyware (R42) consisting of part of a ceramic disc with ground edge; probably a gaming counter. Diameter: *c* 5mm. (Phase C13. 7(n) 7125)

15 A neatly cut small ceramic disc, probably a gaming counter cut from a vessel in BB1 (fabric B11). Diameter 13mm. (Phase C15, 7(n) 7086, SF 199)

Other

16 A Central Gaulish Dr 18/31 or 31 base (*c* AD 120–180) with a hole drilled through the centre of the base. Samian catalogue no 47. (Period E, 3 113/1)

17 A lionheaded spout from a Central Gaulish Dr 45 (*c* AD 170–200) which has been deliberately cut out from the vessel. Samian catalogue no 50. (Period E, B 1020/1, SF 126)

18 Base sherd of a large jar in Severn Valley ware (fabric O24) into the wall of which a circular hole has been drilled which penetrates the vessel at the level of the bottom of the interior. Diameter of hole 6mm. The hole is rather large and a little distant from the break for it clearly to have been a rivet hole, and it is possible it was inserted in order to drain the contents of the vessel. (Phase C32, C 2113)

19 Two joining sherds from the shoulder of a Severn Valley ware

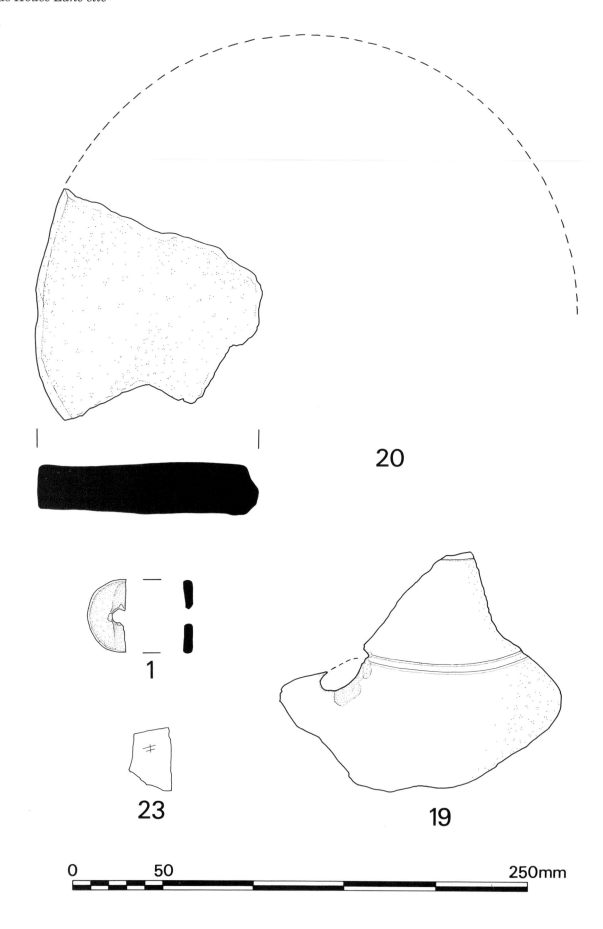

20

1

23

19

Figure 49 Ceramic small finds and graffiti

(O24) constricted-necked jar. After firing, an oval hole *c* 30 × 10mm has been chipped through the shoulder, possibly for secondary use as a money box. (Phase C24, B 1076/1). Fig 49.

20 Fragment of the circumference of a baked clay disc. Thickness *c* 24mm, diameter *c* 270mm. The fabric is coarsely sand tempered with a red-brown core and brown upper surface and side, but with a blackened base. Perhaps used as a griddle for products such as chappatis. There are other examples from Birch Abbey (Ferguson, 1994) and this type of disc is also found in Oxfordshire (Sanders 1979). (Phase C13, 7(n) 7216/1). Fig 49.

Discussion

The fourteen counters comprised four in reduced fabrics, three in oxidized fabrics and seven in samian ware. The last, therefore, had clearly been preferentially selected for such treatment. It seems probable that reduced fabrics had also been preferentially selected as they are not this frequent in the pottery assemblage: perhaps they were selected to offer contrasting-coloured counters to the samian ware. Spatially the counters are not randomly distributed, but confined to trenches 7(n), B, and C. They are not found beyond the earth defences, as they are not in Period D, suggesting that all originate from Period C deposits within the earth defences. The size ranges of the counters shows a similar distribution to those from Birch Abbey (Ferguson 1994) and similarly there is a slight tendency for samian counters to be smaller than the average.

Graffiti

21 BB1 dish or bowl base with a cross 'X' scratched on the underside of the base. A numeral 10, an illiterate mark of ownership, or an apotrophaic symbol. (Period C, 3 124)

22 BB1 jar with obtuse lattice decoration of early 3rd-century form with a cross 'X' inscribed on the burnished shoulder after firing. Presumably an illiterate mark of ownership. Form B11.6. (Period C, C 2040/1). Fig 32

23 This base sherd is an Oxfordshire red colour-coated ware, probably from a beaker. (Probably a later 3rd to 4th century). On the underside is a finely scratched double cross made after firing. Either an illiterate ownership mark or perhaps, given its location on the vessel, an apotrophaic symbol. (Period E, C 2003/1). Fig 49.

24 A Central Gaulish (S20) footring from a DR 18/31R or 31R with a straight cut graffito 'XI' or 'IX' on the base of the footring. Presumably the number 9 or 11 or a mark of ownership. Samian catalogue no 36. (Phase C32, C 2113)

25 A Central Gaulish (S20) bowl footring (*c* AD 140–200) with a graffito 'X' on the base of the footring. A numeral 10, an illiterate mark of ownership, or an apotrophaic symbol. Samian catalogue no 3. (Period C, C 2040/1 joining Period E, C 2038/1)

Discussion

As usual a disproportionate number of the graffiti are on plain samian ware. The incidence of graffiti, one in 1,825 sherds, may be compared with around one in 1,400–1,500 from a 1st to later 3rd-century group from Catterick (CEU site 46, a roadside settlement) and one in 1,676 from a later 2nd- to 4th-century group

from Catterick (CEU site 240, part of the extra-mural area of the town). In comparison the more rural Catterick CEU site 273 just outside the town had a ratio of one in 5,028 sherds and the village site at Catsgore, Somerset (Leech 1982) produced a ratio of one in 12,500 suggesting, as might be expected, greater urban literacy (Evans 1987).

Discussion of the Gas House Lane pottery assemblage

The Gas House Lane pottery sequence provides a very good guide to the material in use in the town in the 3rd century and again at the end of the 4th century. The sequence starts with BB1 obtuse lattice decoration being predominant and a late 2nd-century Central Gaulish samian list. It tends to suggest that obtuse lattice decoration on BB1 had become predominant *c* AD 210 or even *c* AD 200, rather than 'AD 223–5 at the latest' (Bidwell 1985, 175). The sequence also tends to suggest, like the *Vindolanda* one, that the grooved-rimmed flanged bowls did not generally emerge until some time into the 3rd century (although Swan (pers comm) points to earlier examples from Carpow) and that the flange-rimmed dishes and bowls had a rather longer lifespan than Gillam (1976) suggested.

The sequence provides useful evidence for the seriation of Severn Valley ware fabrics in the town, with the suggestion that the O25, O27, and O33 group, perhaps from the Malvern Link kiln complex, had become the major supplier by the later 3rd century; analytical work may shed further light on this. Unfortunately there seems to be little evidence of any useful chronological indicators within the Severn Valley ware form repertoire in the 3rd century at the site.

The *amphorae* collection from the site is small and mainly dominated by Dressel 20s with some Pélichet 47s. A single sherd of north African *amphora* represents the oil trade in the 4th century. The *mortaria* supply to the site is almost completely limited to Mancetter-Hartshill and Oxfordshire products, perhaps surprisingly, there being no Nene Valley products, even in the late 4th century when Nene Valley colour-coated wares formed a substantial part of fineware supply to the site. In the early 3rd century Mancetter products are predominant, although Oxfordshire examples seem to have been supplied from the beginning of the century. By the later 3rd century Oxfordshire products seem to have been predominant, suggesting major problems for the Mancetter industry, given its much closer location to Alcester and that the inception of the Crambeck industry in East Yorkshire at the time must have added to the Mancetter industry's problems in its main northern markets. The small Malvernian assemblage from the site is mainly represented by jars and lids, the latter being so frequent that it is difficult to escape the suggestion that they were being sold separately for use with

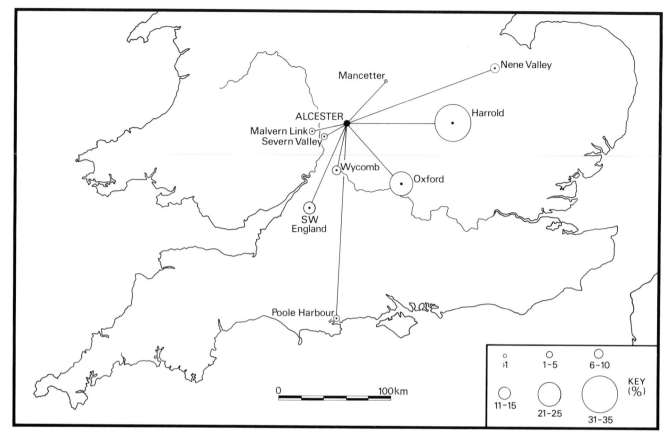

Figure 50 Map showing principal sources of fabrics at Alcester in the late 4th century by fabric weight (trench 5, Period D). Greywares are attributed to south-west England and South-Western Brown Slipped Ware to the vicinity of Wycomb.

other fabric types. Given the predominance of jar forms apart from the lids, and the location of Droitwich (*Salinae*) roughly between the kiln site and Alcester it might be that some of these vessels acted as containers for salt, although they seem to be good cooking pots and there is little about the distribution of the ware to support this (Peacock 1967, fig 2).

Finewares at the site in the 3rd century were principally supplied by Central Gaulish samian potters in the first half, but the other major component in the period came from an apparently fairly local fineware fabric (F42) of unknown source but possibly to the east of Alcester. This provided no substitute for samian, the form repertoire being exclusively limited to beakers, but rather must have been in competition with Nene Valley and imported beaker fabrics. No replacement for fineware bowls appears on the site until the late 3rd century when Oxfordshire red-slipped ware first appears, but in very low quantities.

Reduced wares form a very low proportion of the 3rd-century assemblage from the site, demonstrating the residual nature of much of the material in phases of this period at the 1–5 Bleachfield St Site (Ferguson forthcoming).

When the site sequence resumes in the later 4th century the picture of supply has changed markedly (fig 50) in comparison with the 3rd century (fig 51).

Severn Valley wares have ceased to be supplied and greywares make a much increased contribution, although one that declines towards the end of the century. Harrold shell-tempered wares (C11) increase in importance, being the principal source of cooking wares by the end of the century whilst most of the rest of the assemblage is made up of finewares from Oxford, the Nene Valley, and north Gloucestershire(?). The rise in the proportion of finewares in the assemblages is remarkable, especially given that for the most part it is not caused by new suppliers appearing nearer to the site; rather, the industries which seem to have been more locally situated have ceased production. The Malvernian Severn Valley ware industry, and all the others, seem to have collapsed and it is quite likely that the greyware component in the assemblage is not local either. In many ways the high proportion of finewares may well reflect this. The transport of coarsewares over long distances, when on average they tend to be more bulky, should make finewares relatively cheaper, and thus more common except for functions they could not serve, ie as cooking vessels.

The late 4th-century fineware pattern at Alcester is neither unique nor universal, but it *is* reflected on many sites in southern England (table 33). There is very little fineware at Neatham (Millett 1986) and no late 4th-century rise. It is, of course, adjacent to the Alice Holt coarseware kiln complex which was active

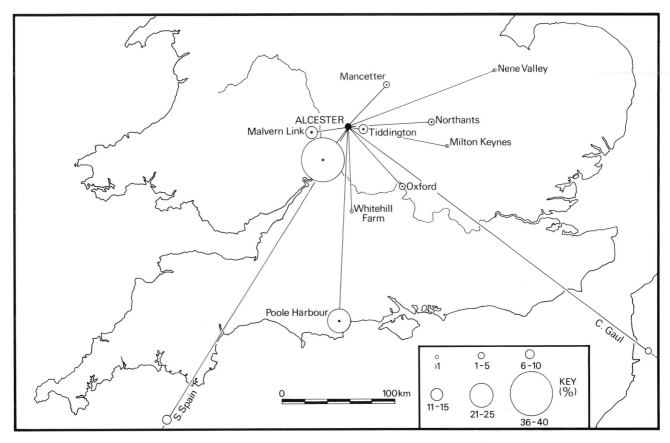

Figure 51 Map showing principal sources of fabrics at Alcester in the early 3rd century (figures taken from Phase C13 by fabric weight). Severn Valley wares are attributed to lower Severn Valley and greywares to Tiddington area arbitrarily.

until the end of the 4th century. The Towcester Grammar School (Brown and Alexander 1982) and Alchester Road (Woodfield 1983) figures are also not so high: here the Harrold kiln site is comparatively nearby and the pink-grogged ware industry (Booth and Green 1989) seems still to have been active in the late 4th century. The sites at Bradley Hill, Somerset (Leech 1981) and Barnsley Park, Gloucestershire (Webster 1982) both have low figures: both are rural (and thus perhaps further removed from an urban-based distribution network for finewares) and appear to be served by local greyware industries until the end of the 4th century.

The phenomenon of collapsing local industries seen at Alcester was suggested at Towcester by Woodfield (1983, 79):

the impression given here, and in a deposit in the 370s from the villa currently under excavation at Piddington is that of the death of the local pottery industries, the material from Piddington comprising mainly of shelly wares, Oxford and Nene Valley colour-coats in more or less equal quantities, Much Hadham products and burnished grey wares, possibly of Trent Valley origin, in less quantity . . . At Towcester the equivalent levels produce approximately one-third soft pink grogged, one-quarter shelly wares and about one-sixth greywares . . . plus a little material from Alice Holt and Much

Hadham. All this looks more like the survival of large production centres outside modern Northants serving an area which had lost its local industries.

Alcester's Roman pottery needs to be seen in a regional context but there is not space here.

This report was finished in 1991.

Post-Roman pottery
Stephanie Ratkai

[M3:C5] The Gas House Lane excavation produced 358 medieval sherds and 794 post-medieval sherds. The range of medieval fabrics found was similar to that recovered from previous Alcester excavations at the 1–5 Bleachfield St site (Ratkai forthcoming (b)) and the Gateway supermarket site but there were also ten new fabrics. Additionally a layer in trench 7(s) (7080), which was stratigraphically above the 2nd-century rampart, produced one large (33g) sherd of early to mid-Saxon pottery. Unfortunately the context also contained a clay-pipe stem. The sherd has a fine sandy matrix with sparse golden mica, angular quartzitic rock fragments (up to 1mm), and rounded soft brownish inclusions (possibly clay pellets or ferruginous). It is thick walled, approximately 10mm thick, and reduced throughout. The external and internal surfaces show signs of burnishing.

Similar types of pottery have been found elsewhere in Warwickshire, eg Wasperton and Burton Dassett (P Booth pers comm) and recent re-examination of the pottery from the Lloyds Bank 1975 excavations has identified Saxon sherds (J Evans pers comm). However, there have been but few Saxon finds from the town or its environs apart from an ivory tau cross crozier head (British Museum 1907, 158–9), an unstratified 7th-century silver bracelet fragment from Bleachfield Street (Wilson 1963), and a small enamelled and inlaid early to mid-Saxon sword mount, found near the Roman cemetery by metal detectors in 1990 (Wise, pers comm).

The dominant fabrics were locally produced Alcester fabrics (fabric 1, 32%, fabric 2, 6%) and fabric 31 (19%), a sandy fabric with some calcareous inclusions, of unknown source. It is possible that this fabric was produced fairly locally since there are limestone outcrops to the south of Alcester. Fabric 38, a late medieval/post-medieval transitional Malvernian fabric was also well represented (14%). It often occurs with Cistercian ware, fabric 50 (10%). This is the first time that any quantity of late medieval pottery has been found in Alcester. The remaining fabric which was reasonably well represented was a sandy grey ware, fabric 26A (4%). This grey ware is commonly found in Warwickshire in 13th- and (?)early 14th-century contexts. It occurs at Bridge End, Warwick, (fabric 122, Ratkai 1987), the Bard's Walk, Stratford (fabric 19, Ratkai forthcoming (a)) and Burton Dassett (fabric 58, Ratkai forthcoming (a)). This grey sandy ware is typified by an angular everted rim, with a slightly concave upper surface, which springs from the neck. As with other Alcester sites, non-local pottery came from Brill (fabric 104), Chilvers Coton (fabrics 14 and 14A) and the Malverns (fabric 23/37), and possibly North Oxfordshire (Banbury-Brackley type ware, fabric 25/30). There were also a few sherds of White Slip Decorated ware (fabric 109). However, each of these non-local fabrics only forms between 1 and 2% of the assemblage.

Ten new fabrics were recovered from this excavation. These were: fabric 41 a sandy buff ware; fabric 42, a sandy buff ware with grey pellets (possibly a variant of Alcester fabric 2); fabric 43, a rough laminated buff ware with elongated voids; fabric 44, a slightly sandy orange ware; fabric 45, a greyish brown sandy calcareous ware; fabric 46, a fine very sandy grey-brown or orange ware; fabric 47, a brown or grey fabric with a fine sandy matrix with sparse large rounded quartz grains visible to the naked eye; fabric 48, a slightly sandy late medieval/post-medieval transitional type ware; fabric 51, a coarse reduced sandy cooking pot ware with sparse calcareous inclusions; and fabric 52, a smooth oxidized sandy ware with clay pellets and organic inclusions.

There were some possible variants of existing fabrics which have been given a letter code to the existing number code. As nearly all the pottery recovered from Alcester has been very fragmentary, with very few complete vessel profiles it is difficult to be certain of what is a distinct fabric group and what constitutes mere variants of existing fabrics.

The most significant finds were from trench C; discussion of the remainder of the sherds will be found in microfiche.

Trench C (number of sherds: post-medieval 175, medieval 132)

The two main features in this area were a stone-lined pit (2001) and a drying oven (2007). The pit group was dominated by late medieval/post-medieval transitional fabrics. There were nineteen Cistercian ware sherds representing a maximum of seven cups. Two of the cups were three handled. One was decorated with applied white clay circular pellets, the other with a simple foliate design (fig 52, no 5). The late Malvernian ware, fabric 38, was also present in quantity (fifteen sherds). Most of these sherds had a tan glaze, where the glaze was present, although a bowl (no 6) had an internal olive glaze. The dominant rim form was the infolded rim. One vessel (no 7) may have been part of a double-handled tripod pipkin (a small unglazed foot was also found in the stone-lined pit). There were two other vessels in this fabric with an internal glaze on the base, presumably from bowls. The pit also contained two 'Tudor Green' cup sherds (fabric 49) and another fine red ware sherd (fabric 39A). There were three residual earlier medieval sherds in fabrics 1, 28, and 32. The presence of Cistercian wares suggests a date in the late 15th century or early 16th century for when the pit went out of use. It is unlikely that the vessels found in the pit were in any way connected with its use. However the group does point to the clearing out of reasonably high quality domestic debris which may suggest a comparatively well off household living in one of the nearby houses on Malt Mill Lane.

The drying oven contained only eleven sherds. These were made up of fabric 1 (six sherds), fabric 31 (one sherd) and fabric 47 (one sherd). These sherds are all most likely to be 12th or 13th century. The oven also contained a sherd of fabric 38, and an overfired/burnt glazed sherd which it was not possible to type. However, there was an intrusive 19th/20th century English stoneware sherd in the kiln which makes it difficult to say whether the overfired sherd and the fabric 38 sherd were intrusive also. The date of the use of the kiln is therefore in doubt. Evidence from elsewhere in Alcester suggests that malting kilns were most common in the 13th and 14th centuries but this may merely result from a lack of excavation in appropriate areas of the town.

Pits (2017), (2022), and (2066) all contained sherds of fabric 38. Pit (2022) also contained a Black ware sherd. This may indicate that fabric 38 continued in use until the 17th century. The other two pits may be contemporary with, or connected with, the use and abandonment of the stone-lined pit (2001). A layer (2020) contained a similar group to that from the stone-lined pit (2001): fabric 38, (six sherds) together

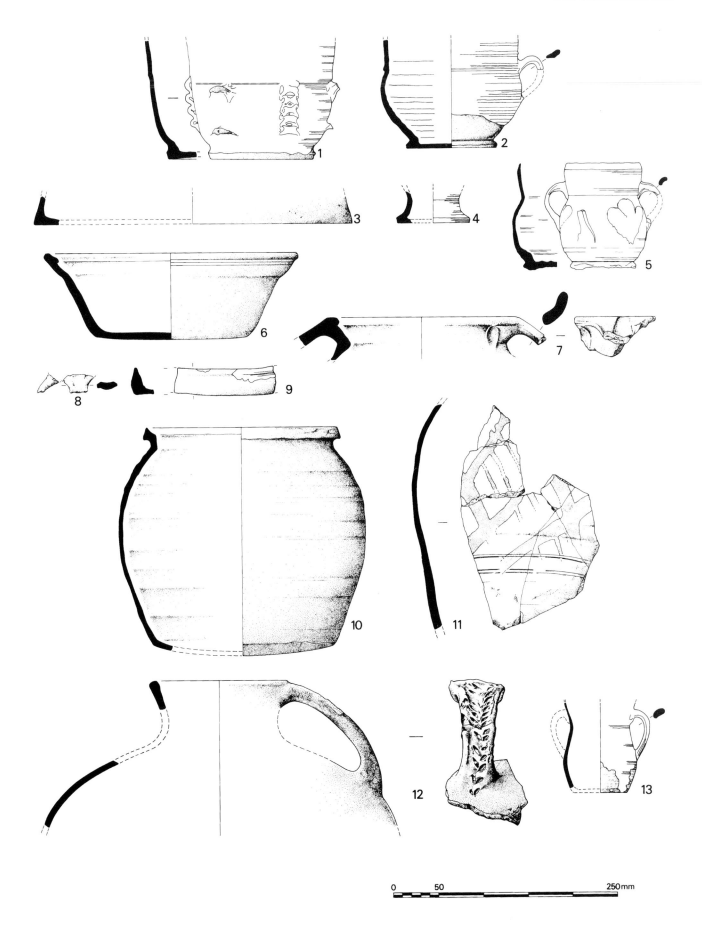

Figure 52   Medieval pottery

with six 'Tudor Green' (fabric 49) sherds. The remaining three sherds were earlier residual material. In layer (2020) there was part of a shallow dripping tray (fabric 38) with a good quality internal tan glaze speckled with dark green. This vessel had a thick external soot deposit.

Earlier medieval features appear to have been two pits (2002 and 2074). The well (2018) contained 51 medieval sherds dating to no later than the 14th century. The majority of the sherds were local fabrics 1 and 2 and possible local fabric 31. There were twelve Warwickshire grey ware sherds (fabric 26A) and one white slip decorated ware sherd (fabric 109) (see above). The well produced the greatest quantity of fabric 2 sherds from anywhere on the site. This is interesting in view of the fact that the majority of pitchers are made in this fabric (Cracknell and Jones 1985). There were at least five jugs/pitchers represented in the group. The pottery suggests that the well may have been in use during the 12th or 13th century but had fallen out of use by the mid-14th century at the latest.

The post-medieval pottery from the trench spanned the 17th- to 20th-century range and most of the features could not be dated accurately but a stone structure (2008) contained Yellow ware, Black ware, coarse wares (including a pie crust edged dish with internal brown glaze), and slip ware. This suggests that this feature belongs to the early 18th century.

The Gas House Lane excavations have furnished some new information on the late medieval and early post-medieval pottery. However, they have been disappointing in terms of establishing the date and nature of the earliest post-Roman occupation or activity in the area. Medieval activity in this area does not appear to have been great, even allowing for post-medieval and modern levelling etc in the area as few medieval sherds occur, even residually. Trenches A and C produced the greatest amount of medieval pottery. A general date of 12th to 13th century can be given for the earliest substantial post-Roman activity (although the Saxon sherd from trench 7(s) (7080) may indicate some limited earlier use of the area) which concurs with the information from the Gateway supermarket site.

Illustrated vessels (fig 52)

1 Blackware posset pot, three-handled, int and ext black glaze over (?)int and ext slip. (113/1)

2 Blackware ?posset pot, int and ext black glaze over int and ext slip. (113/1)

3 Fabric 1. ?West Country base. (306)

4 Fabric 50, Cistercian Ware pedestal base, int and ext mid-brown glaze. (2000)

5 Fabric 50, Cistercian Ware cup, three handles interspersed with applied trefoil decoration in white clay. One of the motifs is poorly applied and has become smudged with red clay. (2001/1)

6 Fabric 38, wide-mouthed bowl, patchy int olive glaze. Wheelthrown but with separately applied base. (2001/1)

7 Fabric 38, tripod pipkin, int tan glaze, knife trimmed at junction of handle and rim. (2001/1)

8 Fabric 38 foot from tripod pipkin possibly from illustrated vessel 7 (2001/1)

9 Fabric 38, dripping tray, int mottled tan glaze, thick band of ext soot. (2010)

10 Fabric 26A, cooking pot/jar, unsooted. (2018/1)

11 Fabric 2, wall sherd from large pitcher, patchy ext olive glaze red slip (?)lattice decoration. (2018/1)

12 Fabric 2, large pitcher, badly decayed ext glaze, ext abrasion with patches of a limey deposit (?mortar) int and ext. (2018/1)

13 Two-handled Cistercian ware cup, internal and external brown glaze. (2020)

Building materials

Stone buildings materials
Lorraine Webb

[M3:C12] The stone building materials comprise twelve items and included three pieces of tufa (presumably from a hypocaust), four limestone *tesserae* (see microfiche), and a fragment of marble. This was a small broken fragment of dull red to purple fine-grained marble, 70mm by 50mm, 9mm in thickness, with ?saw marks along one edge. Possibly *rosso antico* from Cape Taenarum at the tip of southern Greece. *Rosso antico* seems to have been little distributed outside of Italy (Dodge 1988), although in Britain fragments have been found in Colchester (Crummy 1984). The Alcester piece may have been used either as part of a wall veneer or as *opus sectile* but was probably a palette. (Phase C15, trench 7(n), (7086).) (Identification by D F Williams.)

Ceramic and stone tile
Lorraine Webb

[M3:C13] There are 1234 pieces of tile from the site with a cumulative weight of 75.316kg. Most of the tile was placed into fabric groups but little could be defined as a specific tile type because the fragments were small. The stone roof tiles were virtually all made of limestone. Amongst the ceramic tiles which could be identified there were 234 *tegulae*, 87 floor tiles, 10 *imbrices*, 7 *pilae*, 1 antefix, and 1 flue tile.

The *pilae* appear in phase C24 and are possibly from the phase C23 building E (from a part beyond the edge of the site) or some contemporary structure. The single flue tile was found in a phase D2 context in trench A; its origin is unknown.

The largest quantity of identified ceramic tile in a single phase was the 140 *tegulae* fragments found in trench B in phase C22, mostly from an occupation deposit (1100, 1108) outside building D. It is possible that these tiles came from the demolition of building D although these layers were thought to be contemporary with the use of the building rather than with its demolition. On the other hand they may have come from another structure altogether. Elsewhere the quantities of tile were small: sufficient to indicate roofs covered with ceramic tile in the vicinity but not sufficient to identify their location.

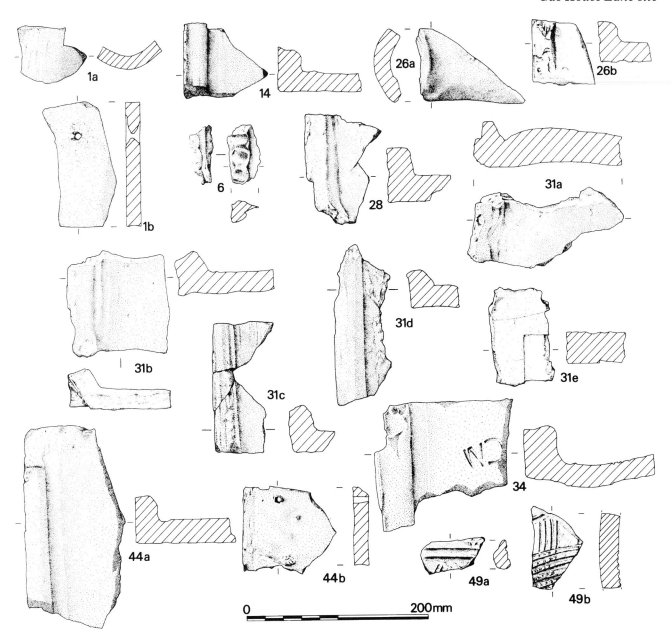

Figure 53   Ceramic and stone tile

Of the stone roof tiles 24 came from phase D (largely trenches 2 and 5) and 20 from trench B, phase C21. No buildings are known from the vicinity.

Catalogue of illustrated items (fig 53)

Period C

1 One *imbrex* (fig 53, 1a), (118/1) and one limestone roof tile (124) (fig 53, 1b) were found in trench 3 where there were possible signs of building activity.

Phase C13

6 One *antefix* (fig 53, 6) was found inside building B. (7(n) 7169/1)

Phase C14

14 Two *tegulae* fragments were found, one of which is drawn (fig 53, 14). (7(n) 7127).

Phase C23

26 One *imbrex* (fig 53, 26a) (B 1024), 2 *tegulae* (one of which is drawn, fig 53, 26b) (B 1037) were found outside building E.
28 Two *tegulae* (one of which is shown in fig 53, 28) were found in the earliest phase C23 layer to the east of building E. (B 1063).

Phase C24

31 There were three large postholes which cut through the phase C23 floor layers. They contain 23 *tegulae*, 4 of which are drawn (fig 53, 31a (B 1048/1), 31b, 31c, 31d (B 1050/1)) and one drawn decorated fragment (fig 53 31e) (B 1050/1).

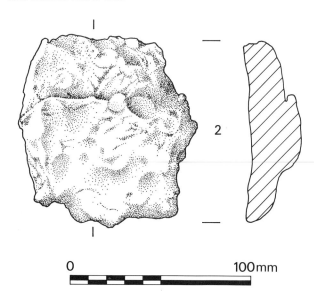

0   100mm

Figure 54 Burnt daub

Phase C32

34 Four *tegulae*, one of which is drawn (fig 53, 34), were found in the lowest deposit ascribed to this period. They are possibly associated with building F (C 2113). The illustrated example was stamped]CM , probably TCM originally. The 28mm-high letters are sharply cut suggesting a metal die. It is not clear if they were cut individually or all at once. McWhirr and Viner (1978) report 20 TCM tiles from the region with examples from Baginton (1), Kenilworth (3), Ebrington (6), Hucclecote (8), and Cirencester (2). They suggest that the tiles were the product of itinerant tile makers or possibly come from some Gloucestershire tilery.

Two other tile stamps are known from Alcester. TCD stamps are relatively common with at least three examples in Warwickshire Museum (Booth 1980, 5). The lettering on these stamps is, however, quite distinct from the]CM lettering, being only 10mm high and imposed all at once, with the rectangular outline of the die clearly visible.

The other stamp reads]ER [and was found on Taylor's 1973 Flood Barrier excavations (Taylor 1973). To the right of the surviving lettering is a vertical stroke, part of a further damaged character. This is the last character, as slight traces of the rectangular die show.

Phase C33

44 Five *tegulae*, 2 of which are drawn (fig 53, 44a and 44b) were found in a spread of rubble which is possibly associated with building F or may form part of building C (C 2110). One of the illustrated examples, 44b, has a peg hole, an unusual feature in *tegulae*.

Phase D2

49 Thirteen fragments, 2 of which are decorated (fig 53, 49a and 49b) were found in layers containing limestone chips – possibly from a wall (A 308, 335).

Mortar and plaster
Graham Morgan

[M3:D5] All the mortar and plaster from the site was studied, by chemical analysis, particle size distribution analysis, and microscopic examination. In gen-

eral the samples were comparable with other samples from Alcester. One piece (from phase C23 (1031/2)) was found *in situ* at the base of the timber-framed wall of building E. See microfiche for details.

Burnt daub
Lorraine Webb

[M3:D7] There are a total of 84 pieces of daub from the site with a cumulative weight of 962g. There were no pieces of daub which definitely came from a specific building. One piece of intrinsic interest was no 2.

2 Curved piece of daub which is probably from the rounded corner of a wall. It is made from two overlapping, roughly rectangular clay plates which form part of a series of plates covering the wall. The formation of the plates is shown by the finger prints on their backs: they seem to have been moulded in one hand, the other pulling the clay onto the palm. There is a clearly visible ridge where the two plates have been joined together (Period C, trench 1, (95/1)). Fig 54.

Metalwork

Copper alloy
Glenys Lloyd-Morgan

Illustrated objects (fig 55)

For full catalogue see [M3:D9].

1 Lower part of a *fibula* consisting of a 'fan-shaped' or trapezoidal section with a small protruding circular foot and a deep, undecorated, catch plate. The lower part of the bow appears to have been filled with ?solder, presumably for the attachment of a sheet metal plaque with repoussé decoration. The height and solidity of the fragment suggests that the original brooch was a substantial piece – and from the depth of the catch plate it would appear to have been used for a heavy cloak or similar garment. Present length 46.0mm, max width 22.4mm. (Phase C13, 7(n) 7091, SF345).

2 Langton Down derivative, with a panel of simple, laterally incised decoration on the upper section of the bow and a small series of transverse hatchings towards the foot. The head and part of the catch-plate are chipped and damaged and the hinged pin is now lost, though most of the iron swivel is still present. Length 51.7mm. (Phase C13, 7(n) 7096, SF355).

Compare the example from Shakenoak, Oxon where the type is dated by Mackreth 'from the Conquest to *c* AD 75' (Brodribb *et al* 1973, 108, 115–6, fig 53, no 178); another by Maryport, Cumbria was dated by Webster to the 1st century AD (1986, 49, 51, fig 1, no 1), and a third, much closer parallel from Wroxeter came from pit 58 dated to between the late 1st and early 2nd century (Bushe-Fox 1916, 23, pl XV, no 4).

6 Trumpet brooch, Collingwood Type R(iii), rather corroded but with remains of lightly moulded patterning on the upper section of the bow. The integrally cast head loop is broken and the tip of the pin is now lost but the brooch is otherwise intact with the spring. Length 55.4mm. (Phase C14, 7(n) 7093, SF257).

Compare the example from Wroxeter, said to have come from a deposit dated *c* AD 110–30 (Bushe-Fox 1913, 26, fig 9, no 7). A fragment from the mid-section of the bow of a near identical

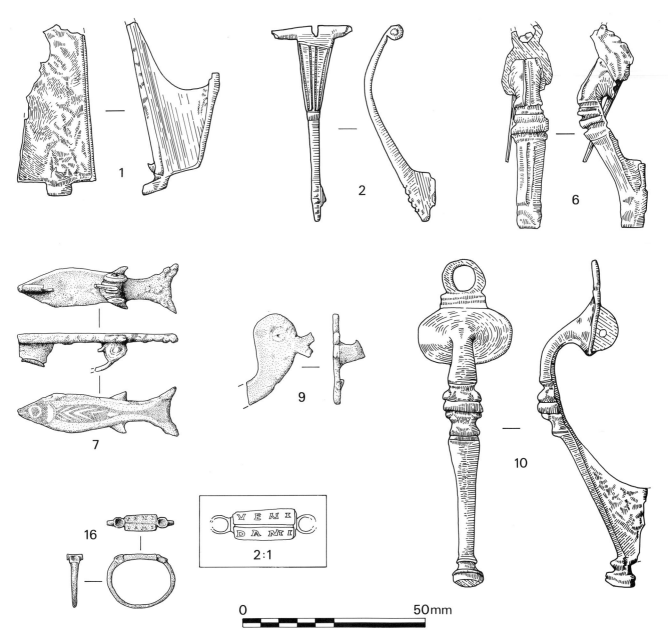

Figure 55 Copper alloy objects

unpublished fibula was found at Bear Field, Cowbridge, Glams, SF no 67/1334 188.

7 Plate brooch in the form of a fish with details picked out in enamel, now green and orange. Part of the pin is now lost. The spring is still in *situ*. Length 44.1mm. Phase C32, C 2113, SF356).

A fish brooch with white and green enamel but otherwise identical is noted from London (Wheeler 1930, 98, fig 29, no 40 inv no A19537, illustrated upside down); a further example has a 2nd-century date suggested by Hattatt (1987, 244, 247, fig 77, no 1198).

9 Part of a plate brooch in the form of a fish, consisting of the head section with fleshy dolphin-like lips, rounded head, engraved dot-and-circle for the eye, and stylised scales. Only part of the snake-like body has survived. The catch plate on the reverse of the head is intact. Present size 20mm × 23mm. (Phase C33, C 2057/1, SF383).

Potter notes the find of the tail and end section of a fish brooch of this type from Ravenglass, with a date from mid-1st to the second half of the 2nd century (1979, 67, fig 26, no 3). Hattatt illustrates another fragment from Augst (1987, 154–6, fig 51g).

However a 1st-century date is given to the two fragments (?of the same brooch) from Rottweil (Planck 1975, vol 1, 180 for discussion and dating; vol II, Taf 71, no 5 tail section, no 6 head only).

10 Trumpet brooch, Collingwood Type R (iv), in two pieces but complete apart from the loss of the pin and spring and some slight damage to the catch-plate. The upper section below the integral loop is decorated with two lines of rocked engraving, and a single line has been incised as a border round the edge of the head. There is a slight moulding on the bow on either side of the acanthus petalling in the central area of the bow. Length 87.7mm. (Phase C33, C 2110, SF322).

16 Finger ring, virtually complete with narrow hoop, and elaborate bezel consisting of a rectangular panel divided horizontally by an engraved line, and inscribed VENI / DAMI To either side of the panel is a circular setting for enamel. One of the settings still contains remains of the enamel now a pale green colour; the other setting is a little damaged. External diam of ring 18.7mm × 15.8mm, internal diam of ring 15.8mm × 13.5mm, height of hoop *c* 1.3mm, bezel 8.7mm × 4.7mm. (Period E, B unstratified, SF135).

103

The style of the ring suggests that it may belong to Henig's group VIIIa rings 'with pronounced shoulders' (1974, vol 1, 50), and is related to the ring from the Legionary Baths at Caerleon from a deposit dated AD 160–230 (Zienkiewicz 1986, 144, fig 47, no 13).

The inscription, which may be translated as 'Come, give (yourself) to me', represents an interesting example of a lover's message given as a gift to a sweetheart or wife. It can be contrasted with the dedicatory inscriptions on rings given to the Gods. These include 'DEO SUCELO' – 'To the God Sucelus' on a silver ring from St Maurice Road, York, found in 1875 (RCHM 1962, 133a, sect 140, pl 65), or 'DEO MARTI' – 'To the God Mars' on a more recent find from Piercebridge 1987 (Hassall and Tomlin 1989, 337), or a more secular good wish 'ITERE/FELIX' – '(Have a) good/lucky journey' on a 2nd-century gold ring now in the collection of the Victoria and Albert Museum (Bury 1984, 19, no 19B acc no 502–1871). Amongst the lover's messages on a small sample of rings from Roman Britain published recently, are two with 'AVE/AMA' which has been read as 'Hail, beloved' and 'Greetings Love'. Both are on copper alloy rings, one from St Oswald's Priory, Gloucester 1975–6 (Heighway and Parker 1982, 58, fig 11, no 4), the other from Piercebridge 1988 (Hassall and Tomlin 1989, 337). A gold ring from *Vindolanda* is inscribed to 'AN/IM/A/ME/A' – 'My life' or 'Darling' (Wright and Hassall 1971, 301); a silver ring from the fort at Castell Collen recalls an 'AMOR/DULCIS' – 'Sweet Love' (Boon 1973, 18, no 3, pl 1, no 3, fig 1); whilst only one ring from Brandon, Suffolk, comes out with a direct proposal of marriage – in Greek – 'CYN/H H' – 'Marry me' (Hassall and Tomlin 1978, 481, pl 32A).

Discussion

Much of the material from this site can be paralleled amongst the finds from other parts of Roman Alcester, and other sites within the region. There are, however, a few exotic items such as the two fish-shaped plate brooches, of which no 7 has several parallels and variant types recorded from elsewhere in Britain. The damaged no 9 is more unusual with almost comparable examples coming from the German *limes* and the settled frontier areas of the north-western provinces rather than Britain. There is also the large, damaged, lower portion of an elaborate *fibula*, no 1. All the brooches can be dated to the 1st to 2nd centuries AD. Another 1st-century item is the damaged spoon no 71, a type which is well known in Alcester as on many other Romano-British sites.

Although three or four of the rings were probably used as crude links for harnesses or other outdoor activity, there are also two finger-rings. The inscribed no 16 with its coaxing message for the beloved fits in well with other British finds.

Apart from the other few items of modest jewellery and fragments of domestic utensils, and fittings, the largest category of material consists of wire, sheeting, offcuts, and general waste. This waste, including the casting fragment no 45 and later slag, 46, suggests that some industrial activity was going on at the site, or in its immediate vicinity. This may account for the presence of early material (originally intended for recycling?) in an area of generally later occupation and use. There is also the possibility that dumping of material from clearance elsewhere in Alcester could account for the conflicting dating

evidence suggested by these finds in comparison with other classes of material. There is the usual modest selection of medieval and later items.

Lead objects
Glenys Lloyd-Morgan

[M3:E3] Most of the lead from the site can be classed as waste either from the manufacture of lead or lead alloy objects, or produced during the finishing stages, as for example offcuts which were lost before recycling. The only item of major interest is the fragment of medieval lead window came, which is of no relevance to the Roman occupation. The full catalogue of lead objects can be found in microfiche.

Iron objects
Quita Mould

Introduction

[M3:E4] This report comprises a discussion of the Roman ironwork accompanied by a catalogue of the illustrated material and a separate catalogue in microfiche of all the material found during the excavations. The catalogues are arranged by function in phase order. Individual objects mentioned in the text are followed by their catalogue number in square brackets [ ]; those objects with published illustrations are preceded by an asterisk *.

A total of 335 iron objects were examined, see table 34. In addition 1050 timber nails were found, details of which are summarized in the full catalogue. Forty-one percent of the iron objects came from post-Roman contexts and whilst residual Roman objects are discussed, the remainder receive little further comment here.

Nature of the assemblage

The range of iron finds was limited to a small number of craft and agricultural tools, writing equipment, domestic utensils, and structural fittings, see table 34. No items of weaponry were found from the excavations. There appears to be little to distinguish this iron assemblage, coming from within the town defences, from that from Birch Abbey (Cracknell and Mahany 1994) situated outside the defences. The functional categories of ironwork found on each site are similar, differing only in the more restricted range of artefact types recovered from Gas House Lane. However, this may simply be a reflection of the size of area excavated on each site.

General distribution

Very little ironwork was recovered from trenches 1, 2, 3, 5, and A. The largest group of objects (38.5%)

came from trench C; a further 21% occurred in both trench B and 7(n). The nails showed a similar distribution, although occurring in different proportions; 35% coming from trench 7 (60% of these from 7(n)), 34% from trench C, and 20.5% from trench B. There would seem from the distribution of the ironwork to have been little activity in trench A between the first defences and the 4th-century town wall.

Material found within each period

No ironwork was recovered from contexts belonging to Periods A or B. The majority, some 53% of the iron objects found, derived from Period C contexts dated late 2nd century to *c* AD 370, with a further 5% coming from Period D contexts dated *c* AD 370 – *c* 410. The relative quantities of the ironwork suggest that there was little activity in the area prior to the beginning of the 3rd century with the *floruit* of the occupation occurring in that century and ending with it.

Period C (*c* AD 200–370)

Tools A square file [*29] came from a gravel layer (1095) outside building D: its closely set teeth suggest it to be a metalworking file. A possible chisel or knife blank [*30] was found in an occupation deposit associated with building D (1096). In addition a small iron filing or shaving [38] was found inside the building. Although slight, the iron finds may suggest some small-scale metalworking in the vicinity, possibly a smithy producing and repairing tools and cart fittings (a linchpin was also found in building D, see below 'Transport').

The nail puller [*28], found in a gravel surface (trench B (1128)), is comparable with other short claw nail pullers from Pompei (Gaitzsch 1980 vol ii, fig 30, 148–58 and fig 31, 151). There was also a fragment with a gently U-shaped profile [40], possibly a gouge blade fragment.

Two broken, round-sectioned stems from needles or pins [18,48] were also found in Period C contexts, indicating domestic textile working.

Agricultural implements Oxgoads were relatively well represented in the assemblage, the three recovered all coming from trench 7(n) in Period C contexts. Oxgoads are usually regarded as indicative of traction ploughing, although they would also be used to drive stock to market. Two [*25, *19] have triple spiral ferrules of Rees type I (1979, 75–9), the other [*3] has a narrow collar ferrule of Rees type II (1979, 75–9). All are fine examples, one [*19] having a particularly long point. One oxgoad was found outside building A [*3] and another outside building C [*19] which suggests that the area was used for agricultural purposes during this phase.

An unusual implement [*49] found in a layer associated with building F (2058) appears to be another type of goad. The object comprises a tang and point separated by a small, central, flanged socket. The socket contained a small amount of minerally preserved wood indicating it was originally hafted. Presumably the tang projecting from the socket was tied to the handle with twine to further secure the implement. The long point ends in a blunt tip suggesting the implement to be a goad or prod rather than a hole boring tool.

A possible broken rake tooth or hoe tine was found in an occupation layer (trench B (1115)).

Transport A small spatulate-headed linchpin [*33] of Manning's type 2b (1985, 74 and fig 20) was found in an occupation deposit in building D (1097) and a broken two-link snaffle bit [*11] was found in a layer outside building B (7091).

Writing equipment Three styli were found, all of Manning's type 4 (1985, 85) decorated with transverse mouldings and bands of inlaid non-ferrous metal. All were from Period C contexts.

Dress fittings Hobnails from nailed footwear occurred in several contexts.

Domestic utensils Knives were poorly represented, with only fragments being recovered [43, 44, 52]. Two three-toothed, L-shaped lift-keys [*53, *54] were found in trench C. The terminal of a bucket handle mount [*13] and a possible handle were found in trench 7(n).

Structural ironwork A small range of structural fittings were represented including the terminal of a loop hinge strap [23], wallhooks [6, 55], split spiked-loops [14, 55], joiner's dogs [45, 26], and timber nails. Nearly three-quarters (73.5%) of all the nails and nail fragments found during the excavations occurred in Period C. Of the classifiable nails recovered from the phase, 98.5% were of type 1b (Manning 1985, 134–7).

Period D (*c* AD 370 – *c* 410)

Less than 5% of the iron objects found during the excavations came from Period D contexts, see table 34. A pin/needle stem fragment [65] was found in a layer of probable dumping after the building of the 4th-century town wall (trench 2 (13/3)). No other tools or domestic items were recovered, but a small number (9) of hobnails were found. A single joiner's dog [67] was found in the lowest layer excavated in trench 2 (23). Very little metalwork was recovered from trench 1; however, a nailed binding terminal [70] occurred along with an almost complete shelly ware pot in the fill of a hole (trench 1 (79/1)) belonging to Period D. Period D contexts contained less than

3% of the nails and nail fragments recovered from the site.

Coffin nails Four small type 1b nails and a further four broken shanks were recovered associated with a human skeleton (Period D, trench A, (337)) on the ground surface below the earth rampart. All the nail shanks were broken, the longest surviving to a length of 58mm; those with heads had a head length of 16mm. Three nails only were recorded during excavation, all aligned longitudinally. The distance of 2.05m recorded from the nail at the head to the two at the feet may represent the original length of the coffin. The other nails recovered came from the west of the burial, those from the east side are thought to have been lost during machining. No minerally preserved organic deposits remained.

Period E (post-Roman)

Residual Roman finds The most interesting item of domestic equipment [*81] occurred residually in a post-medieval or modern soil layer (trench 7(s), (7028)). It comprises numerous small fragments from a shallow flat-bottomed vessel together with a fragment of a flanged socket and is tentatively identified as a frying pan. Frying pans with folding handles, made in both copper alloy and iron, are occasionally found in Britain in civilian contexts, chiefly occurring as part of late Roman metalwork hoards (cf Manning 1985, 104, P32, P33 and pl 50 for discussion and comparanda). The main feature of trench 7(s) where the vessel fragments were recovered was the earth bank and ditch of the first town defences and it is likely that the fragments derive from these deposits originally.

A small quantity (6) of hobnails also occurred residually in Period E.

Post-Roman material

The fill of a stone-lined pit (2001/1) in trench C contained an oxshoe [76], a bone handled knife [78], a wooden knife handle with copper alloy fittings [79], a broken rake tine [75], a loop hinge strap terminal [82], a nailed binding fragment [88], a copper alloy nailed iron plate [*93], and a nailed sheet fragment [90]. Diagnostic iron finds from the pit are of post-Roman date; the bone scale tang knife handle with geometrically incised decoration can date no earlier than the mid-14th century, whilst the wooden handle with copper alloy fittings appears to be post-medieval. The rectangular plate [*93] with two groups of three copper alloy nails/studs and a central one between is reminiscent of a piece cut from *lorica segmentata*. However, this interpretation has to be dismissed for a number of reasons. The strip has no discernible longitudinal curvature and is too narrow, the cuirass pieces from the Corbridge Hoard (Allason-Jones and Bishop 1988)

being almost double the width. In addition, the configuration of copper alloy studs is not consistent with the known arrangement of fittings and strap attachments present on *lorica segmentata* pieces.

A small quantity of fine iron filings or shavings [101, 102] were retrieved from soil sampled from the fill of the medieval drying kiln (2007/1/3). Two similar filing/shavings occurred in Period C contexts. The filings indicate metalworking, but occurred in too small a quantity to be of significance.

Catalogue of illustrated objects (fig 56)

This catalogue is arranged in phase order. Object types represented are: craft tools (28–30), agricultural tools (3, 19, 25, 49), transport (11, 33), writing equipment (4, 20, 51), keys (53, 54), domestic equipment (13, 81), miscellaneous (93) (fig 56).

Phase C12

3 Oxgoad with narrow collar ferrule of rectangular section, and pointed tine. Length 30mm, tine length 20mm, diam 18mm. (Phase C12, 7(n) 7236)
4 Stylus. Round-sectioned stem thickening to a shoulder before the pointed tip. Decorative mouldings with bands of non-ferrous metal inlay present at the shoulder. Length 70mm, max diam 5mm. (Phase C12, 7(n) 7236)

Phase C13

11 Snaffle bit: two articulating links of rectangular section with looped terminals, other ends broken. Fractured. Link length *c* 65mm, loop diam 20mm. (Phase C13, 7(n) 7091)
13 Bucket handle mount: nailed strap fragment with centrally-pierced, rounded terminal. Length 40mm, width 28mm. (Phase C13, 7(s) 7125, SF337).

Phase C14

19 Oxgoad: fine example with triple spirally coiled ferrule and very long pointed tine. Length 45mm, tine length 35mm, diam 12mm. (Phase C14, 7(n) 7103, SF269).
20 Stylus with simple wedge-sectioned eraser, round-sectioned stem with a distinct shoulder and a point. A series of transverse mouldings is present above the shoulder. Length 103mm, eraser width 8mm, diam 6mm. (Phase C14, 7(n) 7094)

Phase C15

25 Oxgoad with triple spirally coiled ferrule and short, rectangular-sectioned tine. Length 42mm, tine length 20mm, diam 18mm. (Phase C15, 7(n) 7086, SF222)

Phase C21

28 Nail puller with flat, round, possibly burred head, straight neck of similar thickness bifurcated into two tines with broken tips. Length 90mm, head diam 28mm. (Phase C21, B 1128)

Phase C22

29 Square file with short, pointed tang expanding to a distinct shoulder before tapering to a long, blunt point. In radiograph one face can be seen to be covered by a series of fine, closely spaced horizontal teeth. Length 111mm, max width *c* 12mm. (Phase C22, B 1095, SF142)

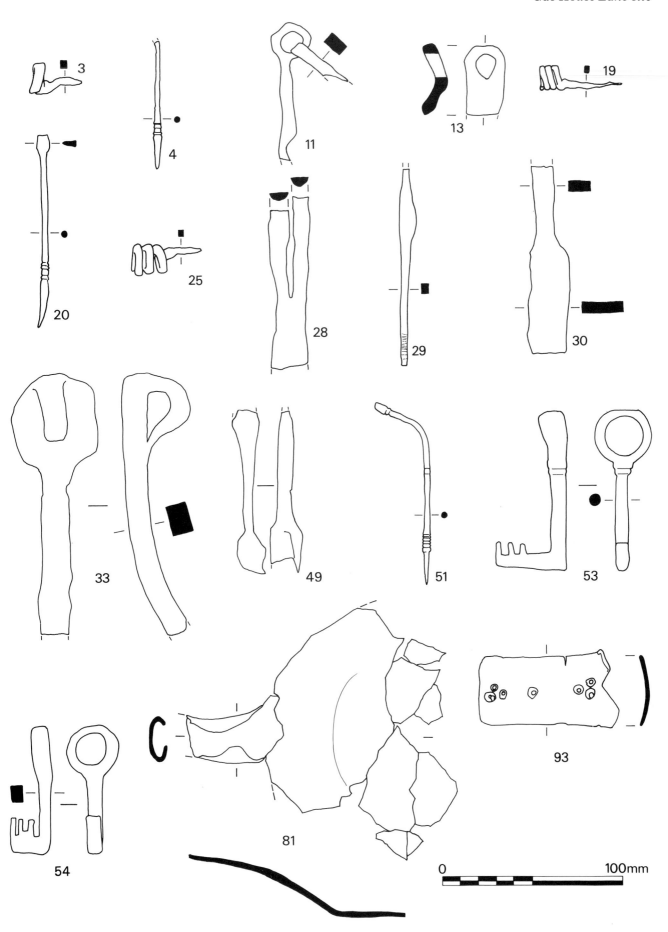

Figure 56 Iron objects

Table 34   Iron objects

Object type	Period C	D	E	U/S	Object type	Period C	D	E	U/S
Tools, craft					*Domestic equipment*				
File, square	1	–	–	–	Bucket handle mount	1	–	–	–
Nail puller	1	–	–	–	Frying pan	–	–	1	–
?Chisel/blade	1	–	–	–	Handle	1	–	–	–
?Gouge fragment	1	–	–	–	*Structural fittings*				
Pin/needle stem	2	1	2	–	Hinge, loop	1	–	1	–
Tools, agricultural					Wallhook	2	–	1	–
?Rake tooth/hoe tine	1	–	1	–	Split spiked-loop	2	–	–	–
Oxgoad	3	–	–	–	Joiner's dog	2	1	1	–
Tools, miscellaneous					Cramp	–	–	1	–
?Implement, goad	1	–	–	–	Nail	765	27	235	14
Socket/ferrule	1	–	–	–	Nail, coffin	–	8	–	–
Ferrule, collar	1	–	–	–	*Miscellaneous*				
Transport					Ring	2	–	–	–
Linchpin	1	–	–	–	Link	–	–	1	–
Snaffle bit	1	–	–	–	Nailed binding fragment	4	1	2	–
Oxshoe	–	–	1	–	Strap fragment	4	–	3	–
Writing equipment					Strip fragment	5	–	–	–
Stylus	3	–	–	–	Sheet, nailed fragment	–	–	1	–
Dress fittings					Sheet fragment	3	1	3	–
Hobnail	212	9	6	1	Plate, copper alloy nailed	–	–	1	–
Locking mechanisms					Stem fragment	1	–	2	–
Key	2	–	–	–	Wire fragment	–	–	2	–
Blades					Pierced shank	–	–	–	1
Knife	1	–	–	–	Filing/shaving	2	–	6	–
Knife handle	–	–	2	–	Fragment, unidentifiable	4	1	10	–
?Blade fragment	2	–	2	–					

30 ?Blade or chisel blank. Rectangular section with straight sides and end constricting at one end into a wide rectangular tang with a bevelled edge, possibly the result of flaking. No edge is present. Length 104mm, width 22mm. (Phase C22, B 1096, SF148)

33 Linchpin with small spatulate head with turned over loop and rectangular-sectioned stem, slightly curved. Length *c* 140mm, head width *c* 50mm. (Phase C22, B 1097, SF159)

Phase C33

49 Double tined implement with small, central, flanged socket containing a small amount of minerally preserved wood. One tine, possibly the tang, has a square section; the other, possibly the point, is rectangular. Fractured. Length 145mm, point width 10mm, socket diam 18mm. (Phase C33, C 2059, SF275)

51 Stylus with simple semi-circular eraser, round-sectioned stem with decorative transverse moulding at the neck, and expanded shoulder and point. Length 102mm, eraser width *c* 8mm, max diam 4mm. (Phase C33, C 2061)

53 L-shaped **lift-key** with round bow and round-sectioned stem with three decorative transverse mouldings below the bow and a

long rectangular bit with three small teeth at right angles to the stem. Length 87mm, bow diam 32mm, bit length 30mm. (Phase C33, C 2058, SF274).

54 L-shaped **lift-key** with large round bow, rectangular-sectioned stem, and large bit with three long teeth at right angle to the stem. Length 68mm, bow diam *c* 25mm, bit length 15mm. (Phase C33, C 2067/1, SF243).

Period E

81 Frying pan, fragments of flat bottomed shallow vessel and fragment of flanged socket of U-shaped section. Remaining length *c* 115mm, width 118mm, height *c* 10mm, socket width *c* 30mm. (Period E, trench 7(s), (7028)).

93 Riveted plate: rectangular plate with gently curved profile. One end is straight, the other has a large V-shaped nick cut from it. In radiograph two groups of three non-ferrous metal rivets/studs with a central one between are visible. Shadow around the stems indicate that the studs had round heads. Flaking. Length 77mm, width 36mm. (Period E, trench C, (2001/1), SF173).

Coins from the Gas House Lane site

Phase	Trench	Context	SF No	Date
C12	7	7224	377	98–117. Very worn.
C15	C	7086	194	Possibly later 3rd or 4th century
C33	C	2059	226	c 347–8
D	1	73/1	9	c 367–75
D	2	13	63	Probably not Roman.
D	2	13/3	8	c 388–92
D	2	13/4	30	c 364–7
D	2	13/4	31	probably c 364–78
D	2	20	18	Probably c 364–78
D	2	20	32	c 367–75
D	2	20	34	c 367–75
D	2	20	40	c 350–65
D	2	20	43	c 367–75
D	2	20	44	later 4th century
D	2	20	48	c 364–75
D	2	20	52	c 364–78
E	B	1022/1	102	c 337–40
E	C	2002/1	168	c 146–175
E	7	7000		Possibly later 3rd or 4th century
E	7	7000	192	Possibly 355–365
U/S	A	380		Possibly 355–65
U/S	A	380		Just possibly 287–96
U/S	B	2000	188	later 3rd century
U/S	U/S	U/S	163	c 367–75
U/S	3	U/S	67	17th-century
U/S	3	U/S	76	late 3rd or 4th century

Iron Slag
Gerry McDonnell

[M3:F1] The only diagnostic slag recovered was a very small quantity of smithing slag lumps (1.8kg). One fragment of hearth lining and less than 0.5kg of cinder was also identified. The material classed as 'other' mainly comprised un-diagnostic iron objects. This quantity of slag is considered to be a background level of slag, ie fragments of slag that were accidentally included in other domestic rubbish. A full listing by context is given in table M45 in microfiche.

Coins: summary list
W A Seaby

[M3:F3] The coins found are tabulated above. In trench 2, the Period D deposit contains a dispersed coin hoard probably deposited c AD 390–400 (Brickstock pers comm). A hoard in a similar position and also dating to late in the 4th century was found on the Gateway site (see p 34).

Bone

Worked bone
Glenys Lloyd-Morgan

[M3:F5] The worked bone from the site comprised eleven pins, two shafts of pins or needles, two needles or bodkins, a fragment probably from a tabular, and a bracelet handlegrip. Nine of the pins and shafts were found in Phase C33 contexts in trench C, with a further four objects from other Period C contexts.

Although the number of worked bone items of Roman date is too small for any meaningful statisti-

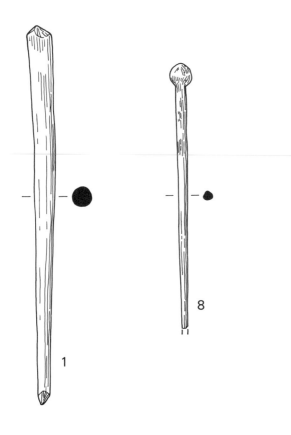

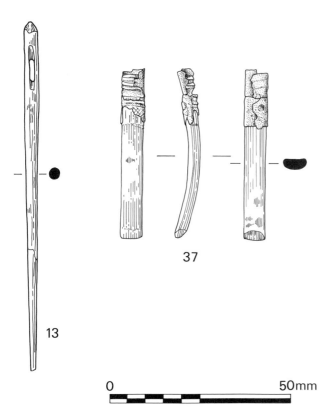

Figure 57 Worked bone objects

cal survey to be made, it is interesting to note that the items which are represented are nicely paralleled by finds on other Alcester sites. This is especially true of the pins where Crummy Types 1 and 3, which are the only ones represented on this site, are also the two types most commonly found on other local excavations. The Type 1 pin has been dated to *c* 70–200/250, and although some pieces may be in part residual, it seems likely that the majority may be contemporary with the Type 3 pins whose time span runs from AD 200 through until the formal end of the Roman occupation. The generally late date for the use of the site is suggested by the find of an undecorated 4th-century bracelet fragment no 17, which has a parallel (SF168) from the 1–5 Bleachfield St site which also yielded two more elaborate examples (Booth, Chadderton, and Evans, forthcoming). The finds of the ubiquitous needles might have been expected, though the lack of any gaming counters may be a little surprising. In total, the small sample is not unexpected for the site.

There were no items made of antler despite the presence of discarded antlers in Period D contexts.

Illustrated items (fig 57)

1 Pin with low conical head, the tip may have been repointed in antiquity. Length 100.2mm, max diam shaft 6.7mm. (Phase C33, trench C, (2058), SF236).

Crummy Type 1 pin with suggested date range *c* AD 70–200/250 (1979, 159–60, fig 1 no 1). One example from *Vindolanda* came from a demolition layer *c* AD 223–5 (Bidwell 1985, 128, fig 45 no 7); another from Neatham, Hampshire was found in a mid-3rd century context (Millett and Graham 1986, 124, fig 86 no 409). Compare also the earlier finds from Alcester including ALC 64–66 BO8B; 65; ALC 72 SF45; and Bleachfield Street AES 76–7 SF132 and SF46.

8 Pin with subspherical head, the tip and part of the lower shaft now lost. Length 70mm, diam head *c* 6.5mm. (Period D, trench 5, (261) SF68).

Crummy Type 3 pin with a suggested date range of *c* AD 200–late 4th/early 5th century (1979, 161, fig 1 nos 3, 4). One example from Wadham House, Dorchester, Dorset came from an early 4th century context (Draper and Chaplin 1982, 24, fig 12 no 5); with further pieces from Neatham, Hampshire (Millett and Graham 1986, 217, fig 86 no 416, dated mid- to late 3rd century; no 417, 418 dated mid- 3rd century; 128, fig 88 no 448 dated late 3rd century; no 450 early to mid 4th century; 130, fig 89 no 473 dated early 3rd to 4th century; no 473 dated 3rd century). The type is well represented in Alcester with over three dozen examples, and some nine pieces from Tiddington, Warwicks.

13 Needle or bodkin, in two pieces but virtually complete, as above. Length 92.4mm. (Phase C13, trench 7(n), (7225), SF397).

17 Bracelet consisting of two fragments of the terminals with oval cross-section, and with the remains of transverse notches on the outer face. The copper alloy binding which held the ends together survives in part, along with one of the rivets still *in situ* on the reverse side. The binding has been pressed into the transverse ribbing of the bracelet hoop underneath, and at one end there is also some decorative light cross-hatching still visible. Overall length *c* 47mm, cross-section 3mm × 6.5mm, length of copper alloy binding 15mm. (Period D, trench 2, (20), SF37).

Compare the other examples of bone bracelets with ribbed sleeves or binding from the Lankhills cemetery, Winchester (Clarke 1979, p 313–4 Type A: no 49 fig 70 Grave 63 dated

AD 370–380; no 138 fig 76 Grave 137 AD 330–70; no 160 fig 77 Grave 143 AD 350–370; no 286 fig 82 Grave 265 AD 390–395; no 348, 349 Grave 336 AD 350–370; no 457, 458 fig 86 Grave 327 AD 350–70; no 503 fig 96 Grave 396 AD 370–90). A closely related but more complete undecorated bone bracelet was found during excavations at Bleachfield Street, Alcester 1976–7 AES 76–7 SF168 (Booth, Chadderton and Evans, forthcoming).

Human bone
Christine Osborne

[M3: F7] The skeleton buried in a coffin beneath the 4th-century town defences (Phase D1, trench A, (337)) is that of an adult male, probably in his late 20s–30s and with a stature of 1.75m ± 39mm. A separate adult mandible was found in an unstratified context.

Animal bone
Julie Hamilton

[M3:F9] Only bone from the Roman period is discussed here. This is divided into Period C (apparently domestic buildings within the defended area (c 7,000 bone fragments)) and Period D (rubbish deposits associated with the second, stone, defences (c 1,300 fragments)). These are probably at least partly contemporary, but the deposits are distinct and are generally analysed separately. Age and measurement data, where there were no discernible differences, are combined. Subdivisions by area or phase within Period C proved not to be useful. Bone recovered from sieved samples (Period C) gave interesting information, particularly on fish remains.

The major species present were cattle (45% of identified fragments, NIF; 24% of minimum number of individuals, MNI), sheep (44% NIF, 62% MNI), and pig (10% NIF, 14% MNI; for all Period C contexts together). The disparity between NIF and MNI proportions reflects the relatively better preservation of cattle. A crude calculation of meat weights (based on MNI, and taking no account of turnover or age or sex proportions: cf Grant 1991, 451) suggests that cattle provided at least 70% of the meat eaten, sheep 20%, and pig up to 10%. There was relatively more cattle and pig, and less sheep, in the Period D deposits (chi-square, P<0.05). Minor species (horse, dog, cat, red deer, roe deer (Period C only) and hare) made up more of the Period D material (C, 1.3%; D, 18%, or 10% omitting red deer antler). The difference is related to the different nature of deposition, also reflected in rates of butchery (commoner in Period C), burning (rare throughout, possibly commoner in Period C), gnawing (mainly by dogs, commoner in Period D), and overall preservation (better in Period C, in spite of greater fragmentation of meat-bearing limb bones of cattle). I interpret the phase C deposits as a mixture of domestic refuse and the waste from primary butchery (on the basis of skeletal element proportions; cf Maltby forthcoming). The Period D deposits include much more non-domestic refuse and

higher proportions of animals that were not eaten, and are mainly from dumping in the area behind the stone wall. The Period C deposits included many cattle horncores (but scattered over several contexts) which were discarded after horn removal, and in Period D there was a deposit of waste from antler working, probably comb-making.

The cattle were mainly short-horned (Armitage and Clutton-Brock 1976) and had a mean withers height of 1.16m (range 1.09–1.23m, plus one animal 1.30–1.35m; metapodial lengths multiplied by factors from von den Driesch and Boessneck 1974). This is similar to contemporary Cotswold/Thames Valley sites (eg Kingscote, Frocester, Barton Court Farm, Farmoor, Ashville: Luff 1982; Noddle 1984) but larger than at Exeter (Maltby 1979). The various methods of age estimation give a somewhat confused picture for the younger age groups, but agree in indicating that a majority of cattle died as adults. There is no evidence for specialised dairy/veal production. The age profile represents a compromise between the uses of cattle for traction, dairying, breeding, and meat supply to the town; cattle by-products include manure (while living) and horns and hides (when dead). There is evidence for both of the latter from butchery data. The evidence for sex structure was equivocal. Males, females and castrates were all present, but the ratios are uncertain. Some mandible and joint pathology was seen, but not at a high rate.

The sheep (there was no definite evidence of goat) included a high proportion of hornless ('polled') animals (6/11 skulls, and there may have been preservation bias against hornless skulls). Mean withers height was around 600 mm (range 510–700 mm: radius, tibia, metapodial lengths multiplied by factors from von den Driesch and Boessneck 1974). Like cattle, they seem larger than those from Exeter, and probably similar in size to Cotswold/Thames Valley sheep, though sample variation complicates comparison. Unlike cattle, sheep tended to be killed young, in their second or third year, suggesting that meat production was their major function, though no doubt secondary products (milk, wool) and by-products (manure, horns, skins) were also important. Again, sex data are inadequate. Rates of pathology were low.

The pigs were clearly reared primarily for meat, and the great majority slaughtered at 1–1.5 years, with a few kept as breeding stock. A high proportion of pig remains may be associated with high status at some Roman period sites (Grant 1989), but the proportion here is well within the normal range (King 1978).

Horse and dog appear regularly but in low proportion: cat was also present. These were clearly not kept for food, but had other functions (eg transport, hunting, and pest control). The low proportions found reflect lower population turnover, but also differences in disposal. The predominant bird was the domestic fowl, raised for meat and eggs, though it is hard to assess its relative importance. Like pigs, fowl may be kept as backyard recyclers of waste. Goose and duck bones were found, in small numbers, and not certainly domestic.

Wild animals (including birds) are found in very low proportions. They include the occasional bone of hare and red and roe deer, and a few wildfowl and other birds, such as woodcock, which may have been eaten. The status of corvids, particularly the raven, is uncertain (see Parker 1988). The use of red deer antler as a raw material leads to occasional accumulations, such as the comb-making waste deposit from Gas House Lane Period D. The house mouse (a human commensal, and pest) was present. A few bones of mice, voles and small mustelid(s) were found in the sieved samples. The importance of fish cannot be estimated, because rather little sieving has been done to recover fish remains, and it is difficult to integrate the results with the rest of the faunal data. Freshwater species that were probably caught locally were present (eel, roach). Perhaps more interesting is the presence of herring and ray, definitely marine and transported quite a distance to this inland site. They could have been preserved by drying, smoking, pickling or salting.

Conclusions

The animal remains from Alcester fit into the pattern of evidence from other urban sites (King 1978; Maltby 1979; 1984; Grant 1989). Cattle were the major suppliers of meat, followed by sheep and pig. Domestic fowl were present. Wild animals were very rare. Both freshwater and marine fish, and oysters, were eaten. Of particular interest is the emerging evidence for differences among Alcester sites related to carcass processing and distribution, as well as site use. The faunal evidence has great potential value in analysis of economic/social relationships within the town and between the town and the hinterland, and this should be borne in mind when planning future excavations in the area.

Ecological remains

Charred plant remains
Lisa Moffett

[M4:A7] Samples for charred plant remains were taken on a judgement basis by the excavator in consultation with the author. Contexts chosen for sampling usually were those which had other occupation material or where there was visible charred material. A list of all the species found is given in table 35. Detailed data from each sample, excluding those with no remains, is given in microfiche and in microfiche table M49.

Roman

All but one of the Roman samples came from Period C. The single exception was a sample from trench A (317/0/1) which was from Period D. This sample did not appear to be significantly different from the Period C samples. None of the samples represented material charred *in situ*.

The crop plants found were emmer (*Triticum dicoccum*), spelt (*Triticum spelta*), a free-threshing wheat (*Triticum* sp. free threshing), hulled barley (*Hordeum vulgare*), bean (*Vicia faba*) and asparagus (*Asparagus officinalis*). Spelt, emmer, and hulled barley are all typical Roman crops. There was one rye grain (*Secale cereale*) which could have been either a crop or a weed. A few oat grains (*Avena* sp.) were also found. It is not possible to distinguish wild from cultivated oats on the basis of the grains alone, but since oats from Roman period sites, when identified, are usually wild, it is assumed here that these were wild oats. Beans are less commonly found than cereals, probably because they are less likely to be exposed to fire and are therefore under-represented (Dennell 1976). They can be cultivated either as a field or as a garden crop. Asparagus has previously been found in Roman Alcester (Moffett 1988) but as of this writing has not yet been reported from elsewhere in Britain.

Other plants found included a fragment of *Prunus* sp. (which could have been sloe, bullace, damson, or cherry) and a fragment of hazel (*Corylus avellana*), both of which could have been collected for food. Most of the other plants were weeds which could have grown in cornfields, gardens, or other disturbed ground.

Many of the samples also had fragments of dicotyledonous taproots. The identification of archaeological parenchymatous tissue including root and tuber fragments is still in its infancy although the pioneering work of Hather (1991) has shown that progress can be made in this area. A time-consuming project of this nature, however, could not be included within the framework of this excavation report and the identification of these fragments must await future work.

The type of material in the samples for the most part did not seem to vary significantly. Only one sample stood out as significantly different from the others. One of the layers from trench C (2121/0/1) produced a relatively large amount of glume wheat chaff, most of it too poorly preserved to be identifiable to species, though what was identifiable was primarily spelt. This material closely resembles the fine sieve by-product of spelt processing (step 12 in Hillman 1981, fig 5) which consists of small dense chaff fragments such as glume bases and rachises, small dense weed seeds and some undersized cereal grains (tail grains). This fine sieve by-product might simply have been burned as waste or used as tinder or fuel.

Post-Roman

The two main post-Roman features sampled were a drying kiln and a possible tanning pit, both medieval. Another post-Roman feature contained residual

Table 35 **Total list of plants represented by charred and ?chemically preserved remains**

Species	Roman	Post-Roman	Common name
Cultivated plants			
Triticum dicoccum Schübl. spikelet forks/glume bases	+	–	emmer
Triticum dicoccum / spelta spikelet forks/glume bases	+	–	emmer/spelt
Triticum spelta L. rachises/spikelet forks	+	–	spelt
Triticum spelta L. glume bases	+	+	
Triticum spelta / aestivum grains	+	–	spelt/bread wheat
Triticum sp. grains/free-threshing grains	+	+	wheat
Triticum / Secale grains	+	+	wheat/rye
Secale cereale L. grains	+	+	rye
Hordeum vulgare grains/hulled grains	+	+	barley
Avena sp. grains	+	+	oat
Avena / large Gramineae grains	+	–	oat/large grass
Cereal indeterminate grains	+	+	
Cereal/large Gramineae culm nodes	+	–	
Vicia faba L.	+	+	bean
Vicia / Pisum / Lathyrus	+	–	bean/pea/vetchling
Ficus carica L.	–	+	fig
Asparagus officinalis L.	+	+	asparagus
Wild plants			
Brassica oleracea / Sinapis alba	+	–	wild cabbage/white mustard
Raphanus raphanistrum L.	+	–	wild radish
Polygala sp.	+	–	milkwort
Agrostemma githago L.	+	–	corncockle
Stellaria media type	–	+	chickweed
Caryophyllaceae indet.	–	+	
Chenopodium hybridum L.	+	–	maple-leaved goosefoot
Chenopodium sp.	+	+	fat hen
Chenopodiaceae indet.	+	–	
Ulex sp. leaves (uncharred)	–	+	gorse
cf. *Lathyrus aphaca*	+	–	yellow vetchling
Vicia / Lathyrus	+	+	vetch/vetchling
Medicago / Melilotus / Trifolium	+	–	medick/melilot/clover
Leguminosae indet.	+	–	
Rubus fruticosus (uncharred)	–	+	bramble
Prunus sp.	+	–	sloe/bullace/damson/cherry
Conium maculatum L.	+	–	hemlock
Umbelliferae	–	+	
Polygonum aviculare agg.	+	–	knotgrass
Polygonum persicaria / lapathifolium	+	–	persicaria/pale persicaria
Rumex acetosella agg.	–	+	sheep's sorrel
Rumex sp.	+	+	dock
Corylus avellana L. fragments	+	+	hazel

Table 35 Total list of plants represented by charred and ?chemically preserved remains (*continued*)

Species	Roman	Post-Roman	Common name
Quercus sp. buds (uncharred)	−	+	oak
Salix sp. buds (uncharred)	−	+	willow
Solanum nigrum L.	−	+	black nightshade
Rhinanthus sp.	+	−	yellow rattle
Lamium sp. (mineralized)	−	+	deadnettle
Galeopsis tetrahit agg./*speciosa* (uncharred)	−	+	hempnettle
Plantago lanceolata type	+	−	ribwort plantain type
Galium mollugo/*verum*	−	+	hedge bedstraw/lady's bedstraw
Galium aparine L.	+	−	cleavers
Galium sp.	−	+	cleavers/bedstraw
Sambucus nigra (uncharred)	−	+	elder
Carex sp.	+	+	sedge
Carex sp. (uncharred)	−	+	
Lolium perenne L.	+	−	rye-grass
Bromus hordeaceus / *secalinus*	+	−	lop-grass/rye-brome
cf. *Danthonia decumbens*	+	−	heath grass
Gramineae indet.	+	+	grasses
Dicotyledonous taproot fragments	+	+	
Root/rhizome fragments	+	+	
Unidentified tree buds	+	+	
Moss fragments	−	+	
Unidentified	+	−	
Unidentified (mineralized)	−	+	

Roman artefacts. It had little in the way of plant remains but it did produce two asparagus seeds. The plant remains from the kiln yielded no evidence of malting.

The majority of the botanical remains in the tanning pit were not charred. Most of the material consisted of elder seeds (*Sambucus nigra*), gorse leaves (*Ulex* sp.), and tree buds, including willow (*Salix* sp.) and oak (*Quercus* sp.). A few fig seeds (*Ficus carica*) and possibly bramble seeds (*Rubus fruticosus* agg.) suggest the presence of human faecal material. There were also many fragments of stem and leaf which could not be further identified. It seems highly probable that this represents the residues of material used in the tanning process. Elder berries, oak and willow are all high in tannins, and the possible faecal material could derive from liquid latrine waste which may also have been used in the tanning process. The reason for the presence of gorse is not known.

The preservation of the botanical remains is somewhat unusual in that most of it has not been preserved by the usual processes of charring, waterlogging, or mineralization. Possibly the chemical conditions in the tanning pit have helped to preserve it.

Plant remains from trench A
James Greig

Introduction

The sample consisted of organic material from a ditch or river channel (Period A). The various samples apparently represent the same basic deposit: the material was organic and woody, with shells. Some material from contexts (336) and (346) was examined (on a presence and absence basis to save time) (for location see fig 27). Some identifications were left at a fairly low taxonomic level. A small pollen count was made on one sample from (346). Plant names follow Clapham *et al* (1987). Wood fragments for the radiocarbon dating were sorted from 1 litre of the sample from (336) and dated by the Scottish Universities Research and Reactor Centre.

Results

The macrofossil floras and pollen spectrum show various kinds of vegetation. Several fully aquatic plants were found such as *Ranunculus* subg. *Batra-*

chium (water crowfoot), *Ceratophyllum* sp. (hornwort), *Lemna* sp. (duckweed), and *Zannichellia* sp. (horned pondweed). The water snails also indicated wet conditions although they were not identified to species. The ditch was therefore water filled.

There were also plants of damp streamsides and marshes, such as *Filipendula* ulmaria (meadowsweet), *Apium nodiflorum* (fool's watercress), *Hydrocotyle vulgaris* (pennywort), *Berula erecta* (water parsnip), *Alisma* sp.(water plantain), and *Carex* sp. (sedge). *Montia fontana* grows on damp stony ground, as is found at the sides of streams. This shows that the ditch carried vegetation along its banks. Such an aquatic and bankside flora is fairly commonly found since it grows in places where plant remains may be easily preserved in wet sediments.

A rather different aspect of the flora was the presence of many seeds of woody plants together with twigs and buds (some of which may be identifiable) and thorns from hawthorn or sloe. Seeds of *Crataegus* sp. (hawthorn), *Prunus spinosa* (sloe), *Acer campestre* (field maple), *Alnus glutinosa* (alder), and *Rhamnus catharticus* (purging buckthorn) were present (the last two somewhat unusually). The pollen record shows abundant *Alnus*, *Rhamnus*, traces of *Prunus* and *Crataegus* (which are poorly represented) and adds *Ulmus* (elm), *Hedera* (ivy), and *Euonymus* (spindle). This pollen probably represents the vegetation of the immediate surroundings because there are corresponding macrofossil records in so many cases. Macrofossils from other woodland and hedgerow plants include *Moehringia trinervia* (three-nerved sandwort), with *Rubus fruticosus* (bramble), *Urtica* species (nettles), the *Carduus*, *Cirsium*, and *Sonchus* thistles, and *Sambucus nigra* (elder).

The main vegetation represented seems to be something like hedgerow or scrub. The number of species is great which might be a sign that it was then a long-established hedge. *Acer* is not uncommon in Midland hedgerows now, but rarely found subfossil (Solihull moat, Greig unpublished). *Rhamnus* and *Euonymus* are not uncommon today, and grow mainly in the south of the country on the calcareous soils but are recorded from Alcester (Cadbury *et al* 1971). They are infrequently encountered as subfossils or pollen, though.

Some weeds are present, showing signs of more open, cultivated land, such as *Stellaria media* (chickweed) and *Atriplex* (orache), and especially *Valerianella* (lamb's lettuce) and *Raphanus raphanistrum* (runch), which are mainly cornfield weeds. There are just traces of crop plants in the form of some wheat chaff remains: a charred *Triticum* sp. spikelet fork and a piece of glume. Other direct signs of human activity include black soot particles in the pollen preparation showing that there were fires nearby.

There are also records from a few plants of managed grassland such as *Rhinanthus* sp. (yellow rattle) seeds and some *Plantago lanceolata* (ribwort plantain) pollen. This could either represent local vegetation or deposited material such as dung.

The radiocarbon date was done on good material,

twigs. The determination (GU-5137) gave a radiocarbon age of 2150 ± 50 BP so that the 1 sigma range lies between 354 and 116 Cal BC.

Discussion

These samples can be compared with other material from Alcester. The sample from the Coulters Garage site (various authors, in Booth 1985) consisted of waterlogged material dated a little older (2410 ± 110 bp, HAR 4905). This had a fairly similar flora of aquatic, wetland, and grassland plants and weeds. The woodland and hedgerow plants from Coulters Garage are very different, however, consisting of the selection normally found, with none of the interesting hedgerow species which make the Gas House Lane site so special. This suggests that 'hedge' plants were not part of the general vegetation.

The suite of hedgerow plants found in this material suggests that the ditch was bordered by a hedge, quite possibly managed for keeping domestic livestock in or out. The signs of chaff and soot suggest that there was settlement close by.

Other finds

Roman glass
Denise Allen

Roman glass vessel fragments total 99, of which the great majority (68 fragments) are natural blue-green in colour. A further seventeen fragments are yellow-green, eight are colourless, five are pale green, and there is one chip of amber glass. In addition, there are eight fragments of window glass and three beads. Two of the latter are very small, plain and annular, but one is much larger and extremely fine, and probably acted as a spacer separating several strands of a necklace.

In common with the overwhelming majority of glass assemblages in Britain and elsewhere, most of the blue-green fragments are from bottles, which would have been brought to the site for their contents. There are 36 fragments in all (nos 12–15 and following list). These vessels were significant in terms of dating. The longest-lived, and therefore the commonest, was the square bottle, in production from before the middle of the 1st century AD to at least the end of the 2nd century and possibly beyond. Nine fragments here can be certainly identified as coming from such vessels, and most of the further 21 fragments recognizable only as coming from prismatic (as opposed to cylindrical) bottles are also likely to belong to this category. The apparent absence of cylindrical bottles, which went out of use early in the 2nd century, must have some significance in the overall dating of the assemblage.

Only one fragment can be identified as representing a bottle type other than a square, and this is no 15, from a small, thin-walled hexagonal bottle.

Gas House Lane site

Very much larger bottles of this shape occur from the late 1st century to the second quarter of the 2nd, but there does seem to have been a smaller, thinner-walled variety which was later in date. One example 111mm high came from a late 3rd/early 4th century inhumation burial at York (RCHM 1962, 137, no H.34C, fig 88), and there are two more from Tongres in Belgium, one undated (Vanderhoeven 1962, 40, no 72), the other from a grave of the second half of the 3rd century (information from W Vanvinkenroye).

Basal trade-marks on bottles occur in great variety, and the geometric patterns surviving on nos 12–14 here are typical.

A container of a different type is represented by no 10, a small looped handle of blue-green glass. This is most likely to be from a globular-bodied bath-flask, which would have held perfumed oil, and been carried to the bath-house suspended from the wrist. The general form was long-lived (Isings 1957, 78–81, form 61), spanning the second half of the 1st to the 3rd century, and there was much variety within the type. However, there is some evidence to suggest that a small, thin-walled version, to which this fragment bears most resemblance, was introduced during the 2nd century. Many examples, with handles virtually identical to no 10, came from a drain deposit dated *c* AD 160–230 at the fortress baths at Caerleon (Allen 1986, 104–7, nos 32–42, fig 41). Parallels of 2nd-century date are discussed with reference to these.

The remaining catalogued vessel fragments come into the category of tableware, brought to the site as items to be used, rather than for their contents.

The one bowl rim (no 2) is of blue-green glass, and is insufficiently diagnostic to allow close identification or dating.

There are five rims of drinking vessels. No 1 represents the commonest cup form of the later 2nd and earlier 3rd centuries. This is a colourless, cylindrical vessel, usually with two concentric base-rings (Isings 1957, 102–3, form 85b). These often occur in quite large numbers on British sites: more than 60 have now come from *Verulamium* (eg Wheeler 1936, 186, fig 29:24), and about 40 from Caerleon (eg Allen 1986, 111–13, nos 68–9, fig 43).

Rim fragments 4–6 are from equally popular drinking vessels, but are typical of the 4th century. The yellow-green colour, cracked-off rims, and faint wheel-incised lines are all characteristic of a variety of bowl and beaker or cup forms at this late date. Probably the commonest, and that most likely to be represented here, is a tall truncated-conical beaker (eg Harden 1979, 212–4, class IIA, fig 27, from Lankhills Cemetery, Winchester).

Jugs or flasks are represented by two handle fragments (nos 8–9), neither of which can be closely identified or dated, and two colourless rim fragments (nos 7 and 11). Both are of a type commonly used for a variety of jug, flask, and bottle forms during the 3rd and 4th centuries (eg Isings 1957, forms 102, 120, 122, 126, 127).

Two of the three beads (nos 21 and 23) are common

Roman types which cannot be closely dated. The third (no 22) is the most unusual and interesting individual item in the assemblage. From what remains, it appears to have been a long, flat, oval piece, with two or probably more horizontal perforations. The most likely explanation for these is that it was used as a spacer between several strands of a necklace. It has been carefully bevelled so that one face is larger than the other, and the larger face has been cased with a layer of what was probably opaque white glass, with marvered streaks of opaque yellow, pale green, and pale blue. Whether this would have been the front or the back it is now impossible to say. No parallel is known to me at present.

The eight fragments of window glass are all of the cast, matt-glossy variety, in use to about AD 300 (Boon 1966). Four are blue-green, and four are colourless.

In summary, the assemblage ranges in date from the 2nd century (and probably the later rather than earlier part) to the 4th century. Containers and tableware of types in common usage are represented, but no vessels of exceptional quality. The finest piece is the polychrome spacer bead.

Catalogue (fig 58)

Bowls, cups, and beakers

1 Rim fragment of a cup of colourless glass. Rim fire-rounded and thickened and turned slightly inward, diam *c* 90mm. (Period C, trench C, (2040/1)).
2 Rim fragment of a bowl of pale blue-green glass. Rim folded outward and downward twice, then turned inward, diam *c* 150mm. (Phase C33, trench C, (2079), SF313).
3 Rim fragment similar to nos 4–6 below, but thinner-walled; surface iridescent. Diam indeterminable. (Phase D2, trench A, (317/0/1)).
4 Rim fragment very similar to no 6 below, but outflared lip a little more pronounced, and wheel-incised lines slightly lower down side. Diam of rim *c* 100mm. (Phase D2, trench A, (335)).
5 Rim fragment similar to nos 4–5 above; surfaces dulled and streaky, rim itself chipped. Diam of rim *c* 110mm. (Period E, trench 2, C5).
6 Rim fragment of a beaker or cup of yellow-green glass; some flaking whitish iridescence on outer surface. Rim outflared, broken off flat and roughly wheel-polished; faint horizontal wheel-incised lines further down side. Diam of rim *c* 110mm. (Period E, trench A, (303), SF139).

Jugs/flasks

7 Two joining rim fragments of a flask or jug of colourless glass; surfaces dulled. Rim outflared and folded outward, upward and inward, diam *c* 40mm. (Period C, trench 3, (135), SF90).
8 Fragment of a handle of blue-green glass; part of one outer rib extant. (Phase C32, trench C, (2113)).
9 Lower handle fragment of pale green glass; flaking patches of iridescent weathering. Part of one outer rib extant, extended into a claw to grip vessel body; small fragment of vessel wall still adheres, its angle suggesting a conical body shape. (Phase C33, trench C, (2058/0/1), SF385).

Bottle fragments not numbered in the catalogue

Trench	Context	Small find no	Description	Phase
7	7245		1 body frag, prismatic bottle	C12
7	7096	359	1 rim frag	C13
7	7097	302	1 body frag, square bottle	C13
7	7125		1 body frag, prismatic bottle	C13
7	7125	369	1 body frag, prismatic bottle	C13
7	7126		1 body frag, prismatic bottle	C13
7	7170		1 body frag, square bottle	C13
7(n)	7199/1		1 body frag, prismatic bottle	C13
7	7225	367	1 body frag, prismatic bottle	C13
7	7116/1		1 body frag, prismatic bottle	C14
7	7122		2 body frags, prismatic bottle	C14
B	1047		1 body frag, prismatic bottle	C22
B	1100		1 body frag, prismatic bottle	C22
B	1119	158	1 body frag, prismatic bottle	C22
B	1024		1 body frag, prismatic bottle	C23
B	1063	129	1 body frag, prismatic bottle	C23
B	1065	119	1 base frag, prismatic bottle	C23
C	2113		1 body frag, prismatic bottle	C32
C	2113	352	1 body frag, square bottle	C32
C	2059		1 neck frag	C33
C	2065		1 body frag, prismatic bottle	C33
C	2065	235	1 body frag, square bottle	C33
C	2080		2 body frags, prismatic bottle	C33
C	2093	291	1 rim and handle frag	C33
C	2093/2		1 handle frag	C33
C	2101	304	1 body frag, square bottle	C33
C	2000		1 handle frag	E
C	2020/1		1 body frag, square bottle	E
7	7005/1		1 body frag, square bottle	E
7	7254		1 body frag, prismatic bottle	E

10 Upper loop of a handle of blue-green glass. Small part of rim and neck still adhering. Max width of handle *c* 7mm. (Period E, trench C, (2000), SF204).

11 Rim fragment of a flask or jug of greenish-colourless glass; flaking iridescent surfaces. Rim outflared, fire-rounded, and thickened, diam *c* 30mm. (Period E, trench 7, (7000), SF284).

Bottles

12 Side and base fragment of a square bottle of blue-green glass; whitish-iridescent surfaces. Surviving side slightly distorted inward; moulded basal mark with part of one circle extant. Width of sides 79mm. (Phase C14, trench 7, (7090), SF247).

13 Base fragment of prismatic bottle of blue-green glass. Surviving part of moulded basal marking shows the centre as a cross, with a short section of another, apparently curved, line. (Phase C15, trench 7(n), (7086)).

14 One base and three body fragments of a square bottle of blue-green glass; flaking whitish iridescence. Surviving part of moulded basal mark shows a raised dot in two of the corners. Width of sides 54mm. (Phase C33, trench C, (2057)).

15 Two joining body fragments of a small hexagonal bottle; thin-walled, with many bubbles and impurities within the metal. Width of side *c* 17mm. (Phase C33, trench C, (2058), SF241).

Gas House Lane site

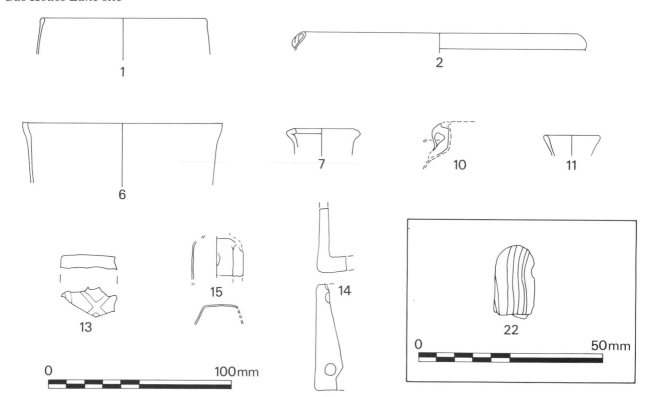

Figure 58 Roman glass

Miscellaneous fragments, vessel forms uncertain

16 Two joining base fragments of colourless glass. Pushed-in solid base-ring, with central pontil mark on underside. Diam of base-ring *c* 40mm. (Phase C33, trench C, (2058), SF238).

17 Base fragment of blue-green glass: pushed-in tubular base-ring, diam *c* 50mm. (Period D, trench 2, (13/4), SF35).

18 Small, thin-walled body fragment of yellow-green glass; flaking iridescent surfaces. Part of a fine, applied self-coloured trail extant. (Phase D2, trench A, (308), SF141).

19 One fragment, pale green, burnt and distorted; possibly Roman. (Phase C33, trench C, (2059)).

20 One fragment, blue/green, indeterminate, Roman. (Phase C33, trench C, (2059)).

Beads

21 Tiny annular bead of colourless glass. Diam 2mm; depth 2mm. (Phase C22, trench B, (1086/0/1), SF279).

22 Fragment of a ?spacer bead of green glass. The surviving piece is parallel-sided, with a rounded end, the edges being evenly bevelled so that one face is smaller than the other. The larger face has been cased with another layer of glass, so badly weathered that its colours are difficult to determine. The background may be opaque white, with marvered longitudinal streaks of (from l to r) ?opaque yellow, pale green, ?pale blue, and opaque yellow. There are two surviving horizontal holes, pierced from side to side, the lower being where the piece has broken. Width 11mm; surviving length 19mm; total thickness of opaque white layer *c* 1.5mm. (Period D, trench 2, (20), SF23).

23 Small cylindrical bead of opaque green glass; perforation slightly off-centre. Diam 7mm; depth 4mm. (Period E, trench C, (2005/0/1), SF178).

Window glass

Window glass was all of the cast, matt-glossy variety (see table).

Window glass

Trench	Context	Small find no	Description	Phase
3	118/1		1 frag, greenish-colourless	C
7	7245		1 frag, blue-green	C12
7	7258		1 frag, blue-green	C12
B	1086		1 frag, blue-green	C22
B	1066		1 frag, greenish-colourless	C23
C	2113	354	1 frag, blue-green	C32
C	2058	266	1 frag, colourless	C33
C	2059		1 frag, colourless	C33

118

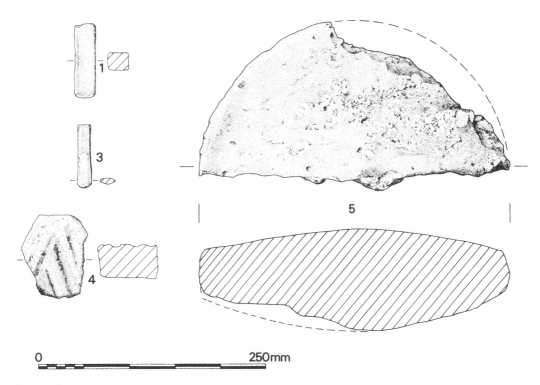

Figure 59   Stone objects

Stone objects
Lorraine Webb with contributions by John Crossling

Including the building materials listed separately, there were 71 stone objects and fragments.

Catalogue of identifiable objects (fig 59)

Whetstones

1 Rectangular-sectioned rod-like whetstone, worn smooth on all sides. Length: 77mm, width: 20mm, thickness: 19mm. (Phase C22, trench B, (1047), SF number 117). *Geology*: 'Calcareous sandstone with an abundant fauna comprising bivalves, echinoderms, ostracodes and foraminifera' (Dr Paul Smith, Lapworth Museum) which are minute marine animals. It comes from the Hythe Beds in Kent and was a 'rock used extensively by the Romans as a building stone in London' (Wells and Kirkaldy, 1966, p 382).
2 Bar-shaped whetstone, worn smooth at the edges, with rough surfaces (not illustrated). Length: 90mm, width: 39mm, thickness: 9mm. (Phase C21, trench B, (1127), SF number 164). *Geology*: Micaceous siltstone with a lot of parallel scratches – this may have been worked but it is alternatively possibly a natural stone. It is uncertain where the stone came from – Wales is the most likely source; it is not from Warwickshire. It is possibly from coal measures.
3 Rod-like whetstone, worn smooth. Length: 65mm, width: 14mm, thickness: 5mm. (Period E, trench C, (2018/2), SF number 186). *Geology*: This is a very fine grained stone with mica inclusions. It is possibly a very low grade metamorphic rock – metamorphous mud/siltstone – or phylite, although there appear to be no records, in reports, of any other phylites appearing in Alcester. It is not local, but is possibly from the Lake District or Scotland.

Quernstones

4 Mauve/grey-coloured quernstone or millstone fragment. Only part of the face of the grinding surface survives. This is cut in

harps. Length: 86mm, width: 67mm, thickness: 46mm. (Period D, trench 1, (13/2)). *Geology*: This is a coarse grained sandstone or fine grained gritstone. It is predominantly composed of roughly rounded grains of milky coloured quartz and a lesser amount of pink feldspar grains. It is probably a millstone grit, with possible locations of Derbyshire or Staffordshire as the nearest sources. It is a little pinker than usual and is carboniferous.
5 Half of the lower stone of a rotary quernstone with pecked vertical side and irregular base. The grinding surface is quite well worn with no evidence of surface treatment. Diameter: 344mm, width of fragment: 163mm, thickness: 168mm. (Phase C22, trench B, (1113/1), SF number 149). *Geology*: This is a Forest of Dean conglomerate, which is a very coarse stone, and is slightly pink in colour. The pebbles are quartz with a spot of sandstone and a vein of quartzite. It is possibly carboniferous.

Missing items

6 One quern. (Period D, trench 2, (21), SF number 39).

Stone tiles

These are detailed in the section on tiles.

Discussion

One whetstone was in an occupation deposit to the east of building D and one quernstone to the south of the building.

One whetstone was found in a post-Roman pit or service trench and another in a gravel surface; neither apparently came from a building. One quernstone and 25 small worked fragments were found in the area used for dumping after the construction of the town wall.

There were a further 28 small worked fragments of stone, 18 of which came from Period E; 6 were found in and near buildings.

Radiocarbon dating

Wood fragments for radiocarbon dating were sorted from 1 litre of a sample (from 336) examined by James Greig (see 'Plant remains from trench A'). This sample lay at a stratigraphically low level in trench A. The result (GU-5137) was a date of 2150 ± 50 BP (1 sigma: 354 and 116 Cal BC, 2 sigma: 380–90 Cal BC, Stuiver and Pearson 1986).

Discussion

Period A: before the construction of the first defences

As the first town defences were only visible in trench 7(s) there are few deposits which can be said to predate them with any certainty (for trench locations see fig 15). A couple of the lowest (sterile) layers on trench 7(s) might predate the defences or be part of them, and a pit containing Iron Age pottery on trench C must predate them.

On trench A, an age determination of twigs from waterlogged soils by radiocarbon produced a calibrated date range at two standard deviations (95% confidence level) of 390–90 Cal BC (GU-5137). This ties in with observations of peaty waterlogged deposits on the south side of Gas House Lane (site 13 on fig 1), at Royal Oak passage (site 12 on fig 1), and at the Gateway supermarket (AL 18) (see pp 7, 10). It seems very likely that the river originally flowed down the west side of the modern town centre, probably on a line just to the east of Moorfield Road, before turning east to run in the area between Gas House Lane and Stratford Road. An archaeological evaluation in 1991 at 52 Stratford Road (on the north side of Stratford Road, to the south-east of site 13) failed to locate any traces of the marshy deposits. By the start of the Roman era, the Gas House Lane site would have been divided into two parts with the area of trench A being low-lying and prone to flooding whilst to the north there was a rise onto the gravel terrace and Mercian Mudstone.

In this dryer area, on trench B, there were linear soilmarks – perhaps ploughmarks or lazy beds – and a 300mm-thick soil layer which can be interpreted as plough-disturbed and may indeed be a ploughsoil (fig 19). Nearby there were a few possible postholes. These features and the soil were overlain by an extensive gravel dump which is taken to mark the start of the intensive occupation of the site (Period C) and which can be dated to about AD 200 but there was no dating evidence for the features themselves. Nevertheless, the lack of activity which can be dated

to the first half of the Roman era accords well with the situation at Tibbet's Close (Cracknell 1985a, 12–24), suggesting that the north-east part of the Roman town was not extensively developed before that date (see discussion of the defended area for further details). The presence of charred remains of garden crops on several sites including Gas House Lane may indicate one use of the area.

Period B: construction of the first defences

The Gas House Lane site provides the clearest evidence so far for the structure of the first town defences (fig 29, plates 10 and 11). They were made of layers of clay loam and gravel, surviving 1.35m high by 5m wide. The front edge seemed to have been revetted although the exact nature of this revetment has yet to be elucidated. No timber lacing was visible. There was a 1.8m-wide berm, in front of which the ground sloped away into what was presumably still a marshy area. There was no formal ditch.

There was no direct dating evidence for the defences on this site. The proposed dating – about AD 200 – relies on an assessment of the main occupation of the site, which it is assumed began shortly after the defences were created. (There was no stratigraphic link between the defences on trench 7(s) and the buildings on trench 7(n) although the trench between them was excavated in the hope of establishing such a connection.) The earthwork defences are discussed further below in the general discussion, taking into account evidence from all the Alcester sites (see pp 127–30).

The lack of finds in the defensive bank is an important piece of negative evidence as it confirms that there was no significant occupation of the site before the defences were built.

Period C: after the construction of the first defences – mainly 3rd century

Note: Period C has been subdivided into phases, with a separate series for each trench – see fig 16 for equivalences and dates.

The first activity was the deposition of a gravel make-up layer, seen on trenches 4, B, 7(n), and on the southern part of C. The ready availability of gravel has made gravel layers a common feature in Alcester and it was used extensively for both make-up and flooring.

A series of buildings was constructed on top of this gravel although none was completely excavated. The different alignments of the buildings on trench B from those on trenches 7(n) and C suggests that two building plots were represented (figs 18, 19–26, plates 12–14). The boundary between them would initially have been somewhere between trench B and trench 7(n) although by the mid- to late 3rd century it appears that the north-east plot was encroaching

Table 36 Stray finds of building materials perhaps indicating well-appointed buildings nearby

Material	Possible source	Context	Trench	Phase	Phase date
tufa	hypocaust	2113	C	C32	220–240/50
tessera	floor	2079	C	C33	240/50–300
tufa	hypocaust	7090	7(n)	C14	250/60–280
tessera	floor	7103	7(n)	C14	250/60–280
tessera	floor	7093	7(n)	C14	250/60–280
pilae (7)	hypocaust	large postholes	B	C24	250/70–300
??marble veneer	wall	7086	7(n)	C15	280–300
tessera	floor	20	2	D	370–390

on the south-west one, with the slot shown in fig 18(C) marking the boundary line. Before the end of the 3rd century the situation seems to have changed again with a row of post settings (fig 18(D)) on a completely new alignment.

South-western building plot

There were two, perhaps three successive structures on this site. Building D was constructed on timber cill beams and had wattle and daub walls and an internal partition. At some stage the partition was demolished and a clay floor inserted. Building E, its replacement, used a combination of cill beams and vertical posts. It was plastered and had a gravel floor.

As a result of truncation in recent years, there were few deposits dating to later than building E, but a line of large postholes (fig 18(C)) probably indicated a further building in a new position to the west of its predecessors.

North-eastern building plot

The structures in this area were more difficult to interpret than those to the south-east. In particular, building F, in the south-west corner of trench C survived as no more than a triangular fragment of clay floor bordered by two postholes (phase C32), which were replaced by a gravel surface and beam slot (phase C33). None of the structures on trench 7(n) appeared to be related although they were less than 5m away. The area between the two trenches was so heavily disturbed by modern foundations that further investigation would have been pointless.

The buildings on trench 7(n) were more complete. Building A, which was built on stakeholes, a slot, and postholes, was extended by the addition of a wing (building B). This wing was on a slightly different alignment and its construction implies a second ridge. When it was demolished it was replaced by a stone structure – the dwarf wall of a building which was largely constructed of timber (building C). Very little of the internal detail survived but the building may have run into trench C. The last phase on trench 7(n) was represented by a line of post settings on a new alignment. As with sites B and C, the 4th-century layers were missing presumably as a result of the modern truncation as well as a possible diminution of activity. This truncation is also reflected in the low quantities of early 4th century pottery recovered from the site. In one trench (no 3), however, there were mid-4th century deposits. This was well to the north-west of the main sites and had not been built upon in recent years.

Although evidence is slight, the later buildings seem to be better appointed than the earlier ones – with the use of plaster in building E and stone in building C. However, stray finds which probably derive from nearby buildings suggest that this may not have been a general pattern, with examples from well-appointed buildings from all but the earliest phases (see table 36).

Tiles were found in several phases but never in sufficient quantity to substantiate their use on any particular building. Apart from the structures and the external gravel surfaces (mainly on trench B) the other feature of Period C was the concentration of pits at the north end of trench C.

Economy

There was little in the nature of the Roman structures or finds to suggest a specific economic function or functions for the site and indeed the economic activities may have changed as the 3rd century progressed. There was, however, evidence for copper alloy working in the shape of offcuts, casting fragments, and slag. This activity seems to have been located on the north-east building plot; the wide spread of dates and locations may indicate casual activity or the occasional visits of an itinerant worker. It is likely that both building plots, like the town as a whole, had connections with agriculture and perhaps horticulture.

In more general terms, pottery is a useful economic indicator. *Mortaria* were supplied almost exclusively from Mancetter/Hartshill and Oxfordshire with the latter coming to dominate by the end of the 3rd century. The finewares largely comprised Central

Gaulish samian with little East Gaulish ware, a peculiarity which is discussed further below. The pottery assemblage also demonstrates trading connections predominantly with the Severn Valley basin, rather than with areas to the east at this time although in the late 4th century pottery from the Nene Valley plays an increasingly important part.

The iron finds represent the usual range of agricultural and domestic equipment, writing implements and structural fittings which are found throughout the town. Most examples came from trenches C and 7(n), in common with other material types.

Most of the animal bone was associated with the Period C deposits. The major species present were cattle, sheep, and pig (70:20:10 – cattle:sheep:pig), with cattle overwhelmingly dominant in terms of meat weight. The Period C deposits were a mixture of domestic refuse and waste from primary butchery whilst the Period D deposits included more non-domestic refuse and a higher proportion of animals which were not eaten. Oysters and freshwater and saltwater fish were also present. The most significant feature of the Roman charred plant remains was the presence of asparagus, a garden crop which has been detected previously in Alcester, but not so far elsewhere.

Period D: construction of the 4th-century town wall to the end of Roman occupation

There were four noteworthy discoveries dating to the very end of the Roman era: the foundations of the town wall, a human burial, fragments of sawn antlers, and a coin hoard.

The rampart and town wall foundations were seen at the south end of trench A and during the watching brief adjacent to the development boundary (fig 27, plate 15). The wall line was recognized by the presence of the typical vertical timber piles. Unfortunately dendrochronological analysis proved fruitless, and no other dating evidence was recovered from the wall and rampart construction deposits, although medieval sherds were found in the robber trench. Only a small length of the wall trench was investigated: it appeared to be similar to the better-preserved deposits at the Gateway supermarket site (see above). One detail which the Gas House Lane work has filled in is the overall width of the rampart – 9m – although it is not clear what proportion of this was *in situ*. It has been noted above that there was no dating evidence from the foundation trench or rampart and the dating of this structure relies on the Gateway supermarket site. A limited number of layers on trench A were stratigraphically above the rampart and have been assigned to Phase D2; the layers and other features on trenches 1, 2, and 5 which are attributed to Period D have been identified on the basis of the artefacts recovered.

The burial – the skeleton of a male in his late 20s or 30s – had been laid in a coffin on the Roman ground surface. It was directly covered by the rampart which backed the wall, a convenient way of disposing of a body without the labour of digging a grave. The antler bones were sawn and trimmed, clearly industrial waste, with at least two pieces trimmed to form the side plates of composite combs. The coin hoard was found in trench 2 directly behind the 4th-century defences. There were twelve late 4th-century coins within a small area – a dispersed hoard – with a deposition date in the AD 390s. This is reminiscent of the hoard found behind the defences on the Gateway supermarket site (p 34).

Period E: medieval and later

Evidence for the immediately post-Roman period is restricted to a single large early to mid-Saxon pottery sherd, from a layer stratigraphically above the first rampart. The sherd was not *in situ* as it was found with a clay pipe stem. The modern truncation of some parts of the site may well have destroyed post-Roman remains. No traces of Saxon activity were recovered from the hand-dug trial trenches, which suggests that any losses from the machining of the site are likely to have been minor.

It was somewhat later before more pottery was deposited on the site – in common with several other Alcester sites renewed activity can be dated to the 12th or 13th century. At about this time a drying kiln was built (plate 17). This structure was situated at the N end of trench C, well behind the modern and medieval street frontages. This 'backyard' location is typical of the drying kilns found in Alcester. Given the presence of a malthouse at the top of the nearby Malt Mill Lane as well as the 16th-century reference to a house with a malt mill, the primary use of the kiln was almost certainly for drying malt – even though the structure was some centuries earlier than the historical and architectural evidence for malting. Samples taken for charred plant remains proved inconclusive.

A full-scale reconstruction of the drying kiln at the Alcester Street Market in 1990 showed that the addition of only a few stones to the surviving remains would make a functional structure. With the flue roofed at a height of 0.6m and the drying floor set at 0.8m, a 40mm layer of green malt was drying well after 8 hours, when the whole structure burnt down. The malt was supported on wooden laths covered by sacks filled with about 60mm of straw. Temperatures high enough for malting (60–90°C) could easily be achieved. It may be that the original structure had safety features which have not survived.

A second stone-lined feature at the N end of trench C represents a later phase in the history of the site. This was a bath-shaped clay-lined structure, designed to hold liquids, and backfilled about AD 1500 (plate 16). The plant remains recovered from it have some bearing on its interpretation. Two samples were taken, one from the lowest few centimetres of fill (2001/2/1) and one from higher up (2001/1/1) but as they contain virtually all the same species they can be treated as a single sample. Most of the

Table 37 Proportions of South, Central, and East Gaulish samian and total numbers of sherds from various Alcester sites with over 50 samian sherds

Site	Gas House Lane AL23	Baromix ALC69	Flood barrier ALC73	Flood barrier ALC70
Total samian	691	756	170	50
% SG of samian	4	57	15	30
% CG of samian	94	41	83	64
% EG of samian	2	2	2	6

Site	Baromix (2) ALC72/2	Tibbet's Close AL12	6 Birch Abbey AL10	1964–6 site A
Total samian	249	92	67	360
% SG of samian	25	4	15	14
% CG of samian	66	56	25	81
% EG of samian	9	40	60	5

Site	1964–6 site C	1964–6 site D	1964–6 sites B + H	1964–6 sites E,F,J,P
Total samian	341	517	287	192
% SG of samian	39	26	33	26
% CG of samian	57	70	61	64
% EG of samian	4	4	6	10

Site	1964–6 site G	1964–6 site M		
Total samian	561	74		
% SG of samian	33	1		
% CG of samian	58	91		
% EG of samian	9	8		

Note: the percentages sometimes refer to numbers of sherds and sometimes to vessels. Not all sherds from the 1964–6 excavations were identified: the statistics from these sites are based on about 80% of the retained sherds.

remains were uncharred and there was no evidence for waterlogging or mineralization. The species represented included elder, oak, and willow which are all high in tannins, and fig and bramble seeds which could have been introduced with human faeces. It is suggested that this was a tanning pit and that the unusually good preservation was due to the chemical conditions. The animal bone assemblage is not easily interpreted as most of the material came from the backfilling and not from the primary use of the feature. The collection contained fourteen very young piglets and fish bones including a very large cod.

Dating

Intensive occupation of the site began around AD 200, on the basis of the inclusion of obtuse-latticed BB1 in the lowest Period C layers. The dating of the start of the occupation of the site relies heavily on the assessment of the coarse pottery (see pp 59, 68). However, there are two problems with this dating which, whilst not invalidating the scheme, suggest a note of caution. Neither the samian nor the copper alloy brooch assemblages are quite what might be

expected on a site which was first used intensively at the start of the 3rd century.

The samian comprised 4% South Gaulish ware (with a date range of AD 45–110), 94% Central Gaulish ware (AD 100–200), and 2% East Gaulish ware (AD 160–260). The South Gaulish ware was in tiny pieces and there is no problem in regarding this as residual. Comparison with other sites shows that those in the NE part of the town – Gas House Lane, Tibbet's Close, and 1964–6 (Mahany) site M – all have very low proportions of South Gaulish ware (table 37).

The East Gaulish picture, however, is less clear. Most sites over the whole area of the town have between 4 and 10% of East Gaulish ware. Gas House Lane, Baromix (ALC 69), and the Flood Barrier site (ALC 73) have significantly less (all 2%), whilst at Tibbet's Close and 6 Birch Abbey East Gaulish ware is well represented. These variations do not seem to reflect the differing intensities of occupation in the period AD 160–260+ when East Gaulish ware should have been in circulation and making its way into the ground. Certainly, the 2% figure for East Gaulish ware at Gas House Lane is remarkably small for a site which appears to have been occupied in the 3rd century.

The dominance of the Central Gaulish ware at Gas

House Lane cannot easily be explained as residuality-in-the-ground and Jeremy Evans suggests on the basis of a study of sherd size that it was still in use until sometime between AD 225 and AD 250 although Margaret Ward does not agree. It is beyond the scope of this report to analyse survival-in-use and residuality-in-the-ground in any detail but it is clear that virgin sites occupied part way through the pottery production period can provide significant data. In the case of Gas House Lane, survival in use of both Central and East Gaulish wares could account for the presence of the former and the paucity of the latter.

The copper alloy brooches, it should also be noted, are dated or find parallels in the 1st or 2nd centuries.

This is perhaps less surprising as examples of late brooch types are rare in Alcester anyway and the brooches could be regarded as heirlooms or metal-working scrap.

The other finds are rarely datable with any precision but it is notable that cylindrical glass bottles, which went out of use early in the 2nd century, were completely absent. The glass in general dates 'from the 2nd century (and probably the later rather than the earlier part) to the 4th century'.

It is also worth mentioning in passing that there was only one stratified coin dating to before the late 3rd century, and that a very worn Trajanic example (SF 377) so that, in so far as it goes, the coin evidence supports the dating derived from other sources.

Defences and defended area

Introduction

This section brings together the Gateway supermarket and Gas House Lane sites with other sites on the defences and within the defended area and attempts to provide an overview of this part of the town and to highlight those points which are significant for Romano-British studies in general. It begins with the presentation of some small unpublished pottery groups and short sections specifically treating the pottery and animal bones and is followed by a more general discussion.

Davis Collection and other unpublished pottery from the defended area of the town
Jeremy Evans

There is pottery from three identifiable finds spots within the walled area from the Davis Collection made in the late 1920s (see fig 1 for location).

1 A bodysherd from a BB1 (fabric B11) dish or bowl with mortar adhering, from Meeting Lane (probably no 1 (19 on fig 1)) described as 'on a concrete floor 4 foot (1.2m) deep'.

2 Two joining large bodysherds from a Severn Valley ware wheelmade storage jar in fabric O36 from 'between Malt Mill Lane and Gas House Lane behind the High Street' ie in the vicinity of the Gas House Lane site. The vessel was probably complete on recovery.

3 A collection of material from 'Alcester Builder's Yard, north side, High Street' at a depth of about 6 feet (exact location unknown). This consists of rimsherds and bodysherds and,

Table 38 Alcester High Street Builder's Yard fabric proportions

Fabric	Measured by	
	Sherd no (%)	Wt (%)
BB1		
B11	37	22
Severn Valley Ware		
O23	10	6
O24	13	18
O27	7	22
O36	22	22
O55	3	3
Reduced Wares		
R01	3	2
R18	5	6

although lacking samian and small bodysherds appears to be a reasonably complete collection of restricted date range, dating from the early 3rd century. This contains 60 sherds and has been quantified for comparison with material of a similar date from the Gas House Lane site.

Table 38 shows the fabric proportions for the Builders Yard group. Severn Valley Wares comprise the largest proportion of the group, between 55% and 71%, followed by BB1 with between 22% and 37% and a very minor component of greyware, around 8%. The BB1 forms are all consistent with an early 3rd-century date, whilst the lack of greywares, which are generally frequent at Alcester in the 2nd century (cf Lee and Pickin 1994; Ferguson forthcoming), suggests that the group does not begin before the end of the 2nd century. The forms present, classified according to the Gas House Lane type series, are given in table 39.

Table 40 shows the function figures for the group, although given the possibility of some material, especially samian, being lost from the assemblage, the results are not very reliable. There seems to be a higher proportion of jars in the groups and a lower one of dishes and bowls than amongst those from Gas House Lane, although this may, at least in part, be a consequence of the absence of the samian ware. Lids also seem to be rather strongly represented. However, it should be noted that the numbers are too small to be really meaningful.

Apart from the above there is a very small group of material from a watching brief undertaken by Paul Booth in Malt Mill Lane in 1982 (site 14 on fig 1). The unstratified material includes Oxfordshire rimsherds of types C51 (AD 240–400) and C100 with a rouletted rim (AD 300–400) suggesting occupation in the area continued into the 4th century. The very small stratified group from the 'bottom layer' contains a Severn Valley ware tankard with grooved rim (fabric O23?) with the typical splaying profile of

Table 39 Occurrence of forms in the High Street Builder's Yard group

Fabric	Forms
B11	B11.3, B11.5(x5), B11.6, B11.11, B11.12, B11.20
O23	O23.2
O24	O24.2
O27	O27.8
O36	O36.7; a reeded-rimmed flanged dish
R01	Lid, form as R18.6
R18	R18.6(x2)

Table 40 Function figures for Alcester High Street Builder's Yard

Jars	Wide mouth jars	Bowls	Dishes	Flagons	Constricted-necked jars	Lids
41%	6%	12%	12%	6%	6%	18%

n = 17

examples from the later 2nd century onwards, a Mancetter whiteware bodysherd, a BB1 bodysherd with obtuse lattice decoration, a BB1 flange rim bowl with intersecting arc decoration, a rather hooked BB1 jar, and a cavetto-rimmed BB1 jar. The material tends to suggest a date in the first half of the 3rd century for this initial occupation.

Ceramic evidence for the occupation of the defended area
Jeremy Evans

The Gas House Lane (AL23) site has produced by far the largest pottery assemblage from the defended area; there are, however, small collections from 27 High Street (Cracknell 1985b; 16 on fig 1), Tibbet's Close (AL12; Ferguson 1985; 15 on fig 1), the Gateway supermarket site (AL18; see above, pp 19–31), Mahany's site M (Cracknell and Mahany 1994; site 1 on fig 1), the Davis collection material from the Builder's Yard to the north of the High Street (p 125), and material from a watching brief in Malt Mill Lane (site 14 on fig 1; p 2).

The combined evidence from these sites would seem to suggest that little if any activity took place within the area before the early 3rd century. The sequence from Tibbet's Close (AL12) seems to be particularly revealing, with a little Iron Age activity, a ploughsoil (Phase II) assigned to the 2nd to 3rd century, followed by a series of phases of 3rd century activity including cill beam buildings, succeeded by a stone structure in the 4th century.

There is no direct dating evidence for the first defences at Gas House Lane and significantly no Roman pottery was found within them, suggesting very little activity in the area prior to their construction. The situation was different on the northern side of the town, where Mahany's site M produced some evidence of Roman occupation prior to the rampart construction (and another Iron Age pit; Cracknell and Mahany 1994). Several features from this pre-rampart sequence produced mid- to late Antonine Central Gaulish samian, including a Dr31 stamped by Tempera giving a late 2nd-century *terminus post quem* for the construction of the defences. Sites producing the earliest groups, Tibbet's Close, Davis' Builders Yard collection, Malt Mill Lane, and Gas House Lane, all produce apparently contemporary material, characterized by a good supply of BB1 and Severn Valley wares, with very little greyware and a reasonable proportion of samian ware, mainly Central Gaulish. Elsewhere in Alcester greywares form a major component of 2nd-century assemblages and the low quantities of them

from all the defended area groups must be of chronological significance. Similarly the Severn Valley wares from the defended area are generally consistent with a 3rd-century or later date and specifically early types are generally lacking. The BB1 assemblages are very consistent, and in all the early groups they start with early 3rd-century jar types with obtuse lattice decoration. It is difficult to see how these could be dated to before *c* AD 200 and they are now generally dated to AD 220 or later (Bidwell 1985).

The evidence from Gas House Lane suggests that activity within the defended area was at its most intense in the first half of the 3rd century and this seems to be replicated at Tibbet's Close. The 4th-century sequence is badly truncated at Gas House Lane, but Tibbet's Close and the Gateway Supermarket both suggest a reasonable level of activity in the early- to mid-4th century.

Material consistent with occupation within the defended area in the late 4th century seems much scarcer. There are the small dumps from behind the town wall at Gas House Lane, but there is very little from Tibbet's Close and a small quantity from the defended area at the Gateway supermarket site (area B).

At present, therefore, occupation of the defended area would appear to commence about the beginning of the 3rd century and to be most intense in that century, especially in its first half. Occupation, perhaps at a less intense level, would seem to have continued until the mid-4th century, after which there seems to have been more scattered activity in the last quarter of the century or just beyond.

Animal bone
Julie Hamilton

The Gas House Lane animal bone is the largest assemblage so far uncovered from within the defended area. Several other sites of early and later Roman date, within and without the defended area, have comparable faunal data. The collection from 1–5 Bleachfield Street (Maltby forthcoming), outside the defences, is large enough for some detailed comparisons. Other sites within the defences (Tibbet's Close (15 on fig 1; Cracknell 1985a), Gateway Supermarket (AL18 on fig 1)) and outside (6 Birch Abbey, 34 Evesham Street; both Cracknell 1985a) yielded much smaller faunal samples, but were analysed by compatible methods (Hamilton 1985 and above), and also provide useful comparisons on a cruder scale.

Species composition

The deposits at all sites seem to include both domestic waste and the waste from primary butchery. At all sites and periods, domestic animals account for over 95% of identified fragments, and the range of species is similar (with fewer species at sites with low fragment numbers). Variations in proportions of fragments of major species were not clearly related to period. Sites with the highest cattle percentages (Birch Abbey, Evesham Street) also had high proportions of butchered cattle scapulae. They were outside the defences and probably not domestic in character (Cracknell 1985a). They may represent areas of intensive processing (secondary butchery) and distribution of beef. Excluding these, there seems to be a tendency to a higher proportion of sheep fragments at intramural sites. This may reflect a difference in diet, but could also be because sheep were processed and distributed in a less specialised way than cattle. They would certainly be easier to handle in a domestic setting, being smaller. Within-site differences in species composition (eg Periods C and D at Gas House Lane) can also be related to the differential disposal of food remains and other types of rubbish. Though there are usable data from half a dozen sites, this is still not enough to generalize about differences due to situation (intra/extramural) or period (pre-/post-defence construction).

Gas House Lane (Period C) and 1–5 Bleachfield Street (late Roman)

The large and well-analysed collection from the extramural site at 1–5 Bleachfield Street (Maltby forthcoming) allows direct comparisons with Gas House Lane.

The types of cattle and sheep present are identical, judging by direct comparison of metrical and horn core data. There is a higher proportion of cattle fragments at Bleachfield Street, probably because relatively more cattle were slaughtered/butchered/disposed of – but not necessarily eaten – at the extramural site. Skeletal element distributions are similar. Possibly the cattle at Gas House Lane show a slightly earlier peak of slaughter and a higher proportion of juvenile/immature animals; and, even more tentatively, a higher proportion of males. Such differences must reflect selective marketing, and it is interesting that two sites so close to each other show this differentiation. Sheep age profiles are similar at the two sites, but there seem to be slightly more very young and very old animals at Bleachfield Street. This could, again, reflect selective marketing, and gives a slightly more 'rural' flavour with more 'production' than 'consumption' at Bleachfield St. Though fish remains from Bleachfield Street were scant, due to lack of sieving, many oyster shells were found, demonstrating the use of marine resources here as at Gas House Lane.

Discussion
Stephen Cracknell

Alcester is the only Romano-British town where there have been more excavations outside the walled area than inside it. Other volumes in the Alcester series (Mahany 1994, Cracknell and Mahany 1994, Booth, Chadderton, and Evans forthcoming) and occasional papers (Booth 1985, Cracknell 1985a) have reported work on the extramural area and it was the purpose of the present volume to complete the picture with a study of the defences and defended area, emphasising the differences between areas inside and outside of the walls so that, by analogy, the structure of unexplored suburban areas in other small towns could be better understood. In fact the main thing to emerge from the study of Alcester is the similarity of function and status of the buildings inside and outside the walls.

At this point a note of caution should be inserted. It is becoming increasingly apparent that the term 'small town' is an archaeological construction encompassing a wide variety of settlements. The better the towns are known, the more varied they appear to be and several details of Alcester's history point to its particular uniqueness. In this respect the most important factors to highlight now for discussion below are, firstly, that the overall size of the town (at up to 35ha) was at the top end of the range for 'small towns'; secondly, that the NE part of the town was under-developed before the defences were built around AD 200; and thirdly, that the stone wall was one of the last to be built in Roman Britain, dating as it does to the third quarter of the 4th century.

Alcester was near the edge of 'fully Romanized' Britain (see Jones and Mattingly 1990, map 5:9) and also not far from the 'highland' zone of Wales. There are few villas in the vicinity. Towns in this kind of situation must have provided more of a contrast to the surrounding countryside and villages than those in the south-east would have done and comparisons between towns in these two different situations should be made with caution.

Defences

There have been thirteen archaeological investigations of the town defences since they were first identified in the mid-1960s, see table 41. It is now clear that there were two defensive circuits, firstly an earthen bank, followed some considerable time later by a stone wall.

First defences

Structure

The earthen bank has been positively identified at Mahany's site M (site 1 in fig 1), at Gas House Lane (AL23), and at the Gateway supermarket site (AL18).

Table 41 Excavations on the defences

Site	Location on fig 1	References
Mahany's site M	(1)	(Mahany 1994; Cracknell and Mahany 1994)
Mahany's site K	(6)	(Mahany 1994; Cracknell and Mahany 1994)
Tomlinson's Tibbet's Close site	(2)	(unpublished; no extant records)
9 Meeting Lane (AL 14)	(3)	(Cracknell 1985a)
11 Meeting Lane (AL 24)	(3)	(Warwicks SMR WA5835)
Taylor's Malt Mill Lane site	(4)	(unpublished; no extant records)
The Bear Inn	(5)	(unpublished; no extant records)
Bulls Head Yard Phase 1	(7)	(Warwicks SMR WA506)
Bulls Head Yard Phase 2	(8)	(Warwicks SMR WA 506)
The Market site	(9)	(Warwicks SMR WA 3792)
Gateway supermarket (AL 18)	(AL 18)	(this volume)
Gas House Lane (AL 23)	(AL 23)	(this volume)
Rectory Garden 1991	(17)	(Warwicks SMR WA 5837)

Less certain identifications have been made at nos 9 and 11 Meeting Lane (3), in the Rectory Garden (17), and at Bull's Head Yard (8). Tomlinson's Tibbet's Close site was adjacent to Mahany's site M and is said to have identified similar remains but no records survive. Taylor saw some kind of defences at Malt Mill Lane but little is known (P Booth pers comm). The excavators at the Bear Inn car park (5) and at Mahany's site K (6) failed to identify any remains although the records of the latter site can be reinterpreted as including a bank.

The structure of the first defences was clearest at the Gas House Lane site, period B, the only place where an uninterrupted section has been excavated under controlled conditions. The rampart survived to a height of 1.35m and measured 5m from front to back. It was constructed of layers of clay loam and gravel, with marked banding delineating the tip lines (fig 29, plates 10, 11). The outer edge of the rampart was, in places, near-vertical suggesting that it had been revetted though no traces of this revetment were found despite hand excavation of a 5.6m length. In front of the bank was a 1.8m-wide berm before the land began to slope away. However, the slope was gradual and it was certainly not a formal defensive ditch.

All these characteristics were also present at the Gateway supermarket site (figs 4, 5, plates 1, 2), although the full width of the rampart was not uncovered and it only survived to a height of 0.65m. The area in front of the rampart was cleared for a distance of over 6m and no trace of a significant ditch was found. The bank was also identified at Mahany's site M but at that point it was cut away by the later trench for the stone wall.

As noted above, the front edge of the rampart at Gas House Lane and the Gateway supermarket sites was a near-vertical face suggesting the presence of a timber revetment. However, so far no traces of associated postholes or tie beams have been identified. Most civilian Roman defensive banks in Britain have survived as simple mounds of earth, perhaps revetted by turf. Presumably the remains of any palisades which might have surmounted the banks would have long since disappeared. However, in several cases timber revetment of one kind or another has left traces. At Ilchester, the first clay rampart may have been given a timber frame and a palisaded front (Leach 1982, 9). At Leintwardine, which may have been a fort or a defended civil settlement, the clay rampart was supported on a log corduroy and had timber lacing (Crickmore 1984, 120). At the *vicus* of Melandra Castle the evidence for the first defences was in the form of a ditch with a berm of 3–5ft (0.9–1.5m) wide separating it from a near-vertical step in the subsoil. This step, which was 3–18in (0.07–0.45m) high, was taken to indicate the front of the rampart (Webster, P V 1969, 75). No explanation of this vertical step was offered in the report but in later phases the rampart was partly timber revetted (the wood itself had survived) and it seems probable that timber was involved at the earlier stage as well. At Silchester, the front of the bank near to the SE gate was revetted by a wattle fence (Fulford 1983, 86). At Lincoln, the legionary defences, which were reused for the *colonia*, were supported by timber (Jones 1983, 48–9). These examples represent a variety of approaches to retaining the bank in place. Whilst the Alcester defences were clearly less sophisticated than those at Lincoln – there was trace of neither a log corduroy nor a trench for the front revetment – they appear to have been supported by something more substantial than a rough wattle fence. The cross-sectional area of the surviving rampart is approximately 4sq m, giving a total volume of earth of 4,400cu m for the whole circuit of 1.1km.

An unusual feature of the Alcester defences is the

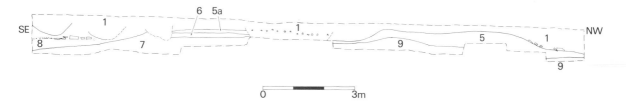

Figure 60 Section showing the SW side of Mahany's site K XIV

apparent lack of any formal ditch and it appears that the natural defences provided by the river and marshes were considered sufficient. Nevertheless, it may be that the shallow slope in front of the rampart at the Gateway supermarket site and at Gas House Lane was an informal ditch created when the area was used as a quarry source for the bank. There is only one other example of a defended Roman settlement which did not have a ditch: Gatcombe (Crickmore 1984, 13).

Circuit

Apart from the Gateway supermarket site and Gas House Lane there have been several other sightings of the defences (table 41). At Christine Mahany's site M the first defences were partly obscured by the traces of the later wall (site 1 in fig 1). The 0.75m-high loam bank (M III 19) was cut by the robber trench of the town wall and, as it was also sealed under the rampart which backed the wall, it seems likely that this loam bank was the bank of the first defences. A layer of clay (M III 32) lying below the loam and a couple of small pits or postholes (M III 18/25 and M III 27/28) might also be associated with the bank.

A few metres to the SE (site 2), R A Tomlinson directed the excavation of another trench across the wall. He is said to have confirmed Mahany's impressions but none of his work has been published. Further round the circuit, excavations of small trial pits at 9 Meeting Lane (3) identified a widespread layer of clay with sandstone which might represent rampart material belonging to either the early or late defences, though other explanations are possible (Cracknell 1985a, 49–50). An evaluation at 11 Meeting Lane (also 3 on fig 1) revealed a similar clay layer but so little of it was excavated that it is impossible to provide a convincing interpretation.

At the SE end of Malt Mill Lane (4), S J Taylor apparently saw traces of both a clay bank and the wall robber trench during building works (P Booth pers comm). Ullin Place excavated a long, narrow trench by machine stretching north from Gas House Lane in 1967 (5). He failed to identify the town defences but other excavators who visited the site thought there were some traces of them (Mahany pers comm).

To the west of the modern town centre, excavations at site K (Rectory Gardens; 6 in fig 1) directed by Christine Mahany 'failed to find any trace of the western defences, or of Roman occupation at all. A

section was cut across what was thought to be an ox bow lake of the river which had evidently been open in medieval times' (Mahany 1965, 3). However, the site records identify a bank (K XIV 5): 'a thick layer of apparently redeposited red clay' (fig 60). It overlies a layer (K XIV 9) of 'dirty, apparently disturbed gravel below clay and above undisturbed natural at N end of section. Similar in nature to, and may well be same as, 7'. The red clay bank was over 6m wide by 0.5m high. It is not clear if any or all of the gravel layer below (K XIV 9) was part of the bank. There were no finds. The position of the bank and the use of red clay and possibly gravel are very reminiscent of the defences on the Gateway supermarket site and it is possible that this bank is in fact part of the first defensive circuit. Further work in the Rectory Gardens in 1991, an evaluation directed by the author, uncovered a 15m-wide bank of clay with some gravelly layers. It may be that this was a remnant of the first defences though other explanations are possible (full report in Warwicks SMR WA 5837).

To the south of the Rectory Gardens, Paul Booth observed both Phases 1 and 2 of the construction of the Bulls Head Yard car park in 1976–8 (7, 8 in fig 1) and the Market site car park (9) in 1982 (Warwicks SMR WA 506, WA 3792). A machine-cut trial trench was also excavated during Bulls Head Yard Phase 2 (see fig 2 for a detailed location plan of this area). Gravel and clay layers similar to those seen at the NE end of the supermarket site area B were recognized in Bulls Head Yard Phase 2, holes 7 & 8 and in the trial trench. It seems possible that the layers represent material piled up as part of the defensive rampart. Peat deposits were noted in holes 2, 3, and 4 on the west part of the site but were not visible in the east showing that the bank was near to the edge of the ancient Moorfield marsh but not actually on it. Part of the marsh area was still damp when the circuit was built as a C-14 date of 1760 ± 60BP (HAR 2257) from the peat in hole 7 of the Bulls Head Yard car park Phase I shows.

Alcester's first defences only protected about 8ha, one-quarter of the total area of the town – perhaps 35ha at that time – and measured about 1.1km in circumference. As Esmonde-Cleary points out, although at *civitas* capitals the majority of the town might be enclosed by a defensive structure, in small towns much, often most of the town was normally unprotected (Esmonde-Cleary 1985, 75). The defences appear to have been positioned to take advantage of the protection provided by three natural features: the River Alne to the north and east, the marsh to the west, and the low-lying and perhaps marshy area to the south. To have enclosed the whole of the town would have required a circuit of about 3km. Clearly this was considered impracticable.

The town gates, both at this time and when the circuit was renewed in the 4th century, would have been at the southern end of the modern High Street, itself probably overlying a Roman road. As yet, there is no evidence for a second set of gates on the opposite side of the circuit.

Dating

There is very little direct dating evidence for the first defences.

The main evidence derives from Mahany's site M where there were deposits associated with the first bank, although it must be remembered that this identification is itself tentative (*see* Mahany 1994, fig 106).

The defences (M III 19) were ascribed to phase I which was terminated by the deposition of an extensive black loam (M III 6B/14). Mid- to late Antonine samian was found in phase I contexts M III 15, 17, and 23, a posthole, a pit, and a beamslot respectively. The coarseware was rather more varied. The small pits (M III 27/28), which from their position could be associated with the defences, contained mid-Iron Age sherds. There was a small reduced rimsherd, possibly a 1st-century carinated beaker, from M I 22. The remaining coarse pottery from the phase is rather later with contexts M III 19, 20, and 24 all containing obtuse-lattice decorated BB1 jar bodysherds (3rd–4th century) and M III 20 having a 3rd-century jar rim fragment. In effect the rampart (M III 19) is dated by the obtuse-lattice decorated BB1 which Jeremy Evans suggests (above p 59) may have been reaching the town from AD 200 onwards.

At the Gateway supermarket site there were no datable finds from the lowest layers on the site and only three sherds from undisturbed Roman contexts dating to the time of the initial decay of the rampart: an undateable fragment of Severn Valley ware, a fragment of samian dating to AD 140–200, and a small sherd from a 4th-century BB1 bowl with a dropped flange.

None of the bank layers on the other sites, including Gas House Lane, contained any dating evidence although I am convinced that it is possible to infer the date of the defences from the date at which this part of the town began to be intensively occupied (see below).

Fourth-century town wall

Structure

Nowhere has the wall itself survived; the structure of the foundations is best known at the Gateway supermarket site where a 17m length was exposed (figs 7, 8, plates 4–7, 9). There, the defences consisted of a stone wall (robbed out) with a clay and gravel revetment behind it. There was no ditch but an external tower was added, probably seven years after the wall was constructed. The wall itself was built on a 4.1m wide (max) foundation trench and was supported on oak piles which had been partly rammed into the subsoil. The space between the piles was packed with large angular stones, followed by thinner layers of gravel and then clay. At the Gateway site (and possibly elsewhere though not recognized) the clay supported discontinuous, longitudinal, horizontal, squared timber beams. Three longitudinal and also one lateral beam survived. The spaces between the beams were packed with stone and lumps of what may once have been mortar.

There are a number of parallels for this method of construction in the Roman world. Gloucester's 1.8m-wide west wall was supported on pitched lias which was packed between timber piles (Hurst 1972, 36), a system identical to that used for the lowest part of Alcester's foundations. The Gloucester wall is not accurately dated. The Roman riverside wall at Baynard's Castle in London was set on a foundation of neat rows of squared oak piles (Hill *et al* 1980). They were capped by a thick chalk raft. Where the gravels gave way to clay subsoil timber piling was no longer utilized. The wall has now been dated by dendrochronology to *c* AD 255–70 (Miller *et al* 1986, 84).

On the Continent, at Xanten, Germany, the foundations of the eastern wall and the 'Mole' tower were set on untrimmed oak piles where they approached an ancient tributary of the Rhine (Precht 1983, 34–5). The timber was dated to AD 105. At Tongres, Belgium at least part of the first wall circuit was supported on regular rows of squared timbers each nearly 5m long (Mertens 1983, 44–5). The piles were closely packed with only a couple of centimetres between them. On top of the piles was a solid layer of mortar on which the wall was built.

Piling is also known to have been used in military contexts such as the Saxon Shore fort at Pevensey (Johnson 1979, 57) and elsewhere. At Pevensey the piles seem to have projected 0.6m from the bottom of the trench. They were packed with flint and chalk and then covered with another layer of flint and chalk on top of which a framework of timber lacing was set.

The purpose of the piling in all these cases was to stabilize the ground. Vitruvius advised that walls on marshy ground should be supported on charred piles of willow, olive or oak, driven in as closely together as possible (Hartshorne 1845, 7). The water should be pumped out, the soil excavated and the space filled with charcoal. While it is likely that the engineers responsible for the construction of the Alcester wall were trying to follow principles similar to those mentioned by Vitruvius, they seem to have failed to understand what they were doing and in consequence their efforts can have done nothing to stabilize the wall. Where there is no alternative, close-packed timber piles are a good way of supporting a wall but here the timbers were packed with large stone rubble which would have been impossible to consolidate properly: settlement over the years would allow gaps to open up. In any case the gravel subsoil into which the timbers were driven would have been a perfectly good base on which to build the wall. The ground on the north-west side of the circuit was undoubtedly marshy and there the timber piles (which have been seen in watching briefs) would have performed a useful function. At the Gateway supermarket, Gas House Lane, and Mahany's site M the logical method of construction would have been either to set the wall directly on the subsoil or to fill the foundation trench with a more readily compactible material without using the piles.

On both the Gateway supermarket site and at Gas House Lane, the foundations would originally have reached up to the contemporary ground level (though subsequent collapse has left the top of the foundations at the Gateway site at a rather lower level). It may be that elsewhere on the circuit the timber piling did not project from the base of the trench to such a great extent. These two sites lie at the low points on the wall circuit and in order to keep the footings at roughly the same level the Roman engineers may have decided to increase the depth of fill in this area beyond the normal level. At Dukes Place, London, the base of the wall was similarly elevated, even to the extent of having the footings above ground level, apparently in order to maintain the plinth at a pre-determined level (Maloney 1983, 100). On the other hand, elsewhere in London the Riverside Wall foundation trench was filled to contemporary ground level (Hill *et al* 1980) and it may be that this is what the Alcester engineers were aiming at.

The only other evidence for how far the piles projected from the base of the foundation trench comes from Mahany's site M (site 1 on fig 1). At that point the wall was at its highest level and at the edge of a steep slope down to the river which would have made it potentially unstable. In a section across the wall the postholes are shown projecting a mere 400mm above the base of the trench (Mahany forthcoming) but, as their tops were apparently cut and possibly damaged by a trench which robbed the wall, the piles may originally have been longer.

At Alcester oak was used for the timber piling under the wall (although alder was used under the later tower). Elsewhere, oak seems to have been the most commonly used wood, in accord with Vitruvius' recommendation. It seems likely that the whole stone wall was supported on timber piles as they have now been identified in four different parts of the circuit.

The piles supported a network of timber lacing. This feature was only apparent on the south-western side of the circuit. However as the trenches elsewhere were dug by machine or only clipped the circuit, the traces of the timber lacing may not have been recognizable.

Timber lacing is well known from other Roman contexts. On the Continent, according to Butler (1983, 126), the clearest instances are on military sites and timber lacing has, as far as I am aware, only been reported in military contexts in Britain (except for in London where the lacing was in the wall itself rather than in the foundation trench).

The wall of the Saxon Shore fort of Pevensey was supported on piles and, just below the level of the plinth, on a lattice of horizontal beams (Bushe-Fox 1932, 60–2). The lattice consisted of two continuous, longitudinal beams, one just inside the outer face and the other just inside the inner face of the wall. These were supported on a repeating pattern of transverse beams and crossing diagonal beams, a system which extended under the contemporary external towers. Timber lacing was also noted at Portchester, Richborough, and Burgh Castle.

There were three significant differences between the Pevensey and the Alcester lacing. The transverse beam at Alcester – only one was found in the relatively short length of trench which was intact at the appropriate level – was set on top of the horizontal longitudinal beams. Secondly, at Alcester, there were no diagonal beams to increase the strength of the lattice. Thirdly, there was clear evidence at Alcester that one of the beams was discontinuous, with a gap of 600mm between the end of one beam slot and the start of its continuation. The last two factors must have reduced the effectiveness of the timber lacing, although the presence of a third, axial beam under the Alcester wall may have gone some way to rectifying these deficiencies. Cunliffe (1975, 15) suggests that the purpose of the lacing used in the Saxon Shore forts was to impart an element of lateral strengthening to the walls. So far only one lateral beam has been discovered under the wall at Alcester though beams were seen running in both directions under the later tower. As there would be little point in providing extra longitudinal support for the wall, it may be that there were normally more lateral beams elsewhere on the circuit.

Although none of the superstructure survived, the position of the timber lacing and the shape of the robber trench can be used to indicate the width of the wall. At Pevensey the longitudinal beams both lay under the wall but were quite near to its edges. At the Gateway supermarket site, the equivalent beams were 3.2m apart (external dimension) and this can be taken as an absolute minimum width for the wall. The robber trench was defined on its NE side by a near-vertical face where the bank had been exposed during the robbing of the wall, probably by pulling the facing stones out after the wall core had been removed. As there was very little bank material in the robber trench, this face must have survived almost intact. The position of the opposite face of the wall was not as well defined because the edge of the robber trench at that side was not clear. However, a layer of mortar which overlapped the edge of the foundation trench was discovered. A similar layer was found on the external side of the wall at Dukes Place, London (Maloney 1983, 100 and fig 95) and mortar layers have also been seen in or under revetment banks associated with Roman walls (eg at Dukes Place and Baynard's Castle in London (Maloney 1983, 100 & fig 95 and 111); and at *Verulamium* (Frere 1983, 50). It seems likely that the mortar layer in Alcester was a working surface associated with the construction of the later external tower nearby, although it could have been associated with the construction of the wall itself. Its edge could then indicate the outer face of the wall. This would give the wall a maximum possible width of 3.5m and it is likely that this was indeed its actual width. This measurement is well within the range of widths of contemporary defensive walls, if slightly above average for civilian sites.

On the opposite side of the defensive circuit in Mahany's trench M III (site 1 on fig 1) the wall construction trench was also 3.5m wide and this can be taken to indicate the width of the wall at that point. (The figure of 2.7m given in the interim report (Mahany 1965, 2) is an error.) The lack of *in situ* stonework in the wall trench is not an unknown phenomenon and there is no reason to believe that the defences were unfinished.

The relationship between the wall and the revetment which backed it has been investigated at the Gateway supermarket site and on Mahany's site M. At Gas House Lane the robber trench of the wall had destroyed any possible stratigraphic relationship. The contemporaneity of bank and wall was best demonstrated at site M where the bank ran over the construction trench of the wall, which had been dug too wide at that point. At the Gateway supermarket site the evidence is more circumstantial but in agreement: the presence of an earlier bank elsewhere all but rules out the possibility that this revetment could be part of an earlier circuit.

The lack of a ditch at this date has also been demonstrated conclusively. There was no ditch on site M, where Mahany excavated a trench for a distance of over 10m in front of the wall. And on the Gateway supermarket and the adjacent Coulters Garage sites the well-defined foundations of a large stone building which predated the wall stretched undisturbed for a distance of over 40m in front of the circuit (Booth 1985).

The construction of the wall was a substantial undertaking as the following statistics show. There were about 32 piles per metre length of wall, each *c* 2m long by *c* 180mm diameter. Including the lacing, the design required about 67.5m of timber for each metre length of wall, ie a total length of 80km of timber. The trees used were 36- to 60-years-old and might have provided 8m of timber each, so the defences required about 10,000 trees. This must have depleted local resources (cf Hanson 1978, 297 for forts). The timbers are unlikely to have been seasoned. Both the horizontal lacing and the vertical piles would have been subject to wet conditions and seasoning would not have been necessary (Hanson 1978).

Taking the width of the wall to be 3.5m and its height to be 7m to the top of the crenellations, say 5m

to the wall walk – based on the size of the Canterbury wall (Tatton-Brown 1978, 81) – gives a volume of 25,000 cubic metres of stone – allowing for the foundations.

It is also possible to make an estimate of the original size of the rampart. At both Gas House Lane and Mahany's site M the full cross-section of the rampart was exposed. Although it is difficult to determine the area with accuracy it appears to measure about 8sq m. (At site M there was some clay *in front* of the wall as well but this may belong to the earlier circuit.) This figure presents something of a problem as the foundation trenches at both site M and the Gateway supermarket site were only about 4sq m in section and it is quite clear at both sites that there was no formal ditch. On the basis of the 8sq m cross section, construction of the rampart would have involved the digging of 9,600cu m of earth.

Circuit

Traces of the 4th-century town wall were first recognized by Christine Mahany on site M (1 on fig 1) and have since been noted by Tomlinson at Tibbet's Close (2 on fig 1), by Taylor at Malt Mill Lane (4 on fig 1), at Gas House Lane (AL23), at the Gateway supermarket (AL18), and at Bull's Head Yard, phase I (7 on fig 1). The possible ramparts at 9 and 11 Meeting Lane (3 on fig 1) could belong to either of the defensive circuits.

The 4th-century wall probably followed the same line around the eastern part of the circuit as the earlier bank (sites 1, 2, and 4). However, on the S and SW side of the town the wall was on a different line to the earlier defences, increasing the enclosed area of *c* 8ha by about 15%. Timber piles were seen during Phase I of the construction of the Bulls Head Yard Car Park (site 7; figs 1, 2). Paul Booth observed the earthmoving which consisted of topsoil stripping and the excavation of nine drainage holes notionally 2m square by 2m deep. In hole 4 the timber piles 'varied in length, some being as much as 1.5m long, and the average diameter was 0.15–0.20m. They had pointed ends to facilitate driving into the ground. The tops of these piles occurred at 1.4m below the surface but they appeared later than the peat deposit, if not subsequent layers' (Warwicks SMR WA 506). In hole 8 their tops were 'only 0.8–0.9m below the level of the made-up surface and (they) were surrounded by grey sandy clay'.

This evidence, along with the results of the excavation and watching brief at the supermarket site and at Gas House Lane allows the plotting of the wall for the S and the SW corner of the circuit. As the wall was straight in the excavated sections it has been plotted as straight lines rather than curves on figures 1 and 2 although the evidence is at present insufficient to completely justify this assessment.

The course of the wall around the NW part of the circuit is rather more problematic. In 1965, Mahany excavated a series of trenches stretching SE from

Moorfield Road into the old Rectory Garden (site 6) but failed to identify any traces of the defences. Instead she uncovered an ox-bow lake which had been open in medieval times (Mahany forthcoming). It now seems highly likely that the town wall did run through this area. Presumably all trace of it had been removed by erosion before the ox-bow lake was cut off from the river, although this remains to be proved.

The circuit took in an extra 1.3ha, bringing the enclosed area up to 9.3ha, with a circuit measuring 1.2km. This size is at the top end of the range for Romano-British small towns and such an increase in size must be almost unique for a small town.

Dating

The wall is thought to date to the third quarter of the 4th century. However, this is not beyond question. The main evidence is a coin found in the destruction rubble of the Coulters Garage store building and dated to AD 364–7 (Booth 1985, 84). The building was demolished to make way for the wall. The problem is that there may have been more than one period of demolition and the coin may have been introduced after most of the building had been levelled and after the town wall was built. However, there are several other indicators which show that this date cannot be far out. The construction of the store building is dated to about AD 300. If it had an official function and if it was still in use at the time of the construction of the wall it would surely have been included in the defended area. Since it was not included it follows that it must have gone out of use. It is unlikely that this would occur within 50 years of its construction so this provides a second *tpq* for the town wall of about AD 350.

At the Gateway supermarket site, the general character of the pottery confirms the 4th-century date for the store building and the defences. More specifically two coins were found in the rampart which backed the wall. The coins, both Antoniniani (from 449: see fig 7) provide a *tpq* of AD 273.

At Gas House Lane there was no direct evidence for the date of the defences but there were significant quantities of late 4th-century pottery and coins from nearby areas.

The pottery from Mahany's site M does not add to the above dating evidence with most vessels dateable to the 2nd century and none certainly 4th century. The date of AD 330–70 given in interim reports (Mahany 1965) was based on the presence of a black-burnished ware dish (Cracknell and Mahany 1994, type CB.23, illustration B.67), which was erroneously dated by parallels with Crambeck products. In fact this pottery type is not closely dateable although it mostly belongs to the 2nd century.

If the late dating is finally confirmed, Alcester will be seen as one of the few towns which remained without a stone wall until so late in the 4th century. Other examples are Bitterne (AD 364 on) and Mild-enhall (AD 360 on) (see Crickmore 1984, 182–205 and Millett 1990, table 6.4).

External tower or bastion

An external tower was discovered on the Gateway supermarket site. Despite the late date of the wall, three factors make it clear that the tower was added to a pre-existing structure (*contra* Burnham and Wacher 1990, 95). Firstly there was a small wedge of possibly natural clay separating the SW edge of the construction trench of the wall from the NE edge of the construction trench of the tower. If the two structures had been contemporaneous the wedge of clay would have been removed. Secondly, whilst the piles under the wall were all oak, those under the tower were alder. And thirdly, dendrochronological analysis tentatively suggests that the alder was cut down seven years later than the oak. The foundation trench for the tower was slightly trapezoidal with the side against the wall measuring 6.2m and the opposite, parallel side measuring 5.4m. The trench projected 5.4m from the wall. Like the wall it was supported on a lattice of timber but none of the superstructure survived. Nevertheless the nature of the foundations suggested a flattened D, a semi-circular or perhaps a polygonal shape with a solid base.

Late Roman towers have been uncovered at a score of towns in recent years to add to those still visible on the Saxon Shore forts. Examples of rectangular or subrectangular foundation trenches associated with D-shaped or polygonal superstructures are fairly common. At Cirencester, Bastions 1 and 2 had square bases, but obtuse-angled facing stones suggested that the superstructure was polygonal. Bastion 3 also had a square base but the evidence for the supposed polygonal superstructure is less convincing. Bastion 4 was polygonal but did not have a square base (Cullen 1970). At London, Bastion 4A had a rectangular foundation with rounded corners but a D-shaped superstructure was implied by the impressions of large blocks of stone in the top of the foundation (Maloney 1983, 105 and 108). At the Saxon Shore fort of Portchester the hollow U-shaped towers were built on timber beams set at right angles to each other running under the arms of the 'U'. Bastion 2 was tied in with the wall. At Alcester the post-Roman robbing of the stonework had removed the traces of the timber beams at the appropriate point but, as the tower was an addition to the original wall, the timber lacing in the two structures could not have been tied together.

The Alcester tower was built at a point 20m from the corner of the wall and about 80m from the likely position of the town gate, at the S end of the modern High Street (Cracknell 1985a). It is possible that towers were only present on the southern part of the walled circuit where the natural defences of the river and marsh were missing (cf the London wall (Maloney 1983, 105 and fig 100)). The position of the tower near to but not on the corner of the wall seems to suggest that its primary purpose was to provide for forward rather than flanking fire. Graham Webster (1983, 119–20) has indeed suggested that this was the main purpose of towers although there is some uncertainty as to what kind of weapons might have been installed on them (Jones and Bond 1987, 85).

Towers are an important facet of late Roman defensive architecture in Britain. They first appear prominently on Saxon Shore forts built in the late 3rd century. Some of the forts were initially constructed without external towers (eg Burgh Castle) whilst at others the towers were an integral part of the structure (eg Portchester) (Johnson 1983, 196–214). *Civilian* sites, with the possible exceptions of Canterbury, St Albans (Frere 1984, 63) and Gloucester (Hurst 1986, 121) seem to be later. At Mildenhall and Caistor-on-the-Wolds the towers and the walls were contemporary. Unfortunately only Mildenhall is well dated, by a coin of AD 360 found under the wall (Crickmore 1984, 127). Elsewhere, towers seem to have been added to pre-existing walls, with *termini post quem* in the middle of the 4th century, eg Great Casterton *tpq* AD 337, Caerwent *tpq* AD 348, London Bastion no 6 *tpq* 341.

It has been argued that the provision of towers for *towns* was the result of a central policy decision (see for example Frere 1977, 248) but there are several problems with this. If towers were an innovation in *military* architecture in the late 3rd century it might be expected that they would be added to towns from the same date, or at least integrated when new walls were built. Hurst has used this proposition in the dating of the Gloucester *colonia's* second and third walls. The second wall was built without towers and the third wall with them (Hurst 1986). This, he argues, shows that the interval between the two works spanned the period when towers were first introduced, which he takes to be the late 3rd century (relying on parallels with the Saxon Shore forts). However, if a similar thesis is used for the Alcester wall and tower we would have towers being introduced to small towns in the 3rd quarter of the 4th century, considerably later. There remains an unbridgeable gap between the dating of towers on forts and those on several towns. This is a good illustration of the dangers of trying to marry historical and archaeological data. If the supposition of central control is removed, the archaeological data is consistent and suggests the gradual adoption of a military innovation over a long period.

Significance of Alcester's defences

There has been much discussion of both the date and significance of the defences which were first erected around many British towns in the second half of the 2nd century (eg Frere 1965, Jarrett 1965, Wacher 1962, Frere 1987, 239–44). Some aspects of Alcester's defences are unique to the town and may have no wider import but there are several factors of note.

Towards the end of the 2nd century the main built up area of the town covered something like 27ha, probably centred around the E–W thoroughfare Street A (fig 1). To the NE was a less well developed, virtually uninhabited, area which was partly cut off from the rest of the town by marshes and uninhabitable ground. However, the NE area was blessed with natural defences in the form of the marshes and the river and it was this area which was chosen for defending. The initial earthwork circuit, which was without a formal ditch, enclosed an area of 8ha. This area was then rapidly developed, though not to the detriment of the rest of the town.

About AD 300 a large store building was erected outside the defences (at Coulters Garage, 10 on fig 1; Booth 1985) and an official function might be postulated for this structure and its timber predecessor. By this time the earthwork circuit had fallen into neglect. By the third quarter of the 4th century the marsh to the west of the town had receded so that when a new defensive circuit was constructed it could enclose a further 1.3ha in a circuit which measured 1.2km. Once again there was no formal ditch. The store building was demolished to make space for the wall. After (probably) seven years, at least one external tower was added to the circuit.

There are several points in this potted history. The first is that if Alcester's defended area is compared with other towns it falls into the top of the range for small towns, yet the majority of the town lay outside. If the extramural area is brought into account Alcester can readily be compared with medium-sized *civitas* capitals so its selection for defending needs to be seen in this context.

Secondly, the enclosure of an underdeveloped area shows that the defences were not undertaken simply as a matter of civic pride, one of the motivations suggested for undertaking defensive works. Equally, the choice of the most easily defended area, rather than the most populous, suggests that a threat was anticipated.

Thirdly, the walls did not enclose a pre-existing market area, thus expediting the collection of taxes on goods, another suggested (presumably secondary) function of defences. In fact the postulated market area at the north end of Birch Abbey, outside the defences, continued in use.

Fourthly, the 4th-century stone wall was not built to defend the one postulated official function of the town – grain collection and storage – as the store building was knocked down to accommodate the defences.

It is not known why the town wall was on a different line to the earlier defences, though the retreat of the marsh must have been a factor. Although an extra *c* 1.3ha was included within the new defences the area could not have been particularly good building land. On the west side of the circuit a C-14 date of 1760 ± 60 BP (HAR 2257) from peat in hole 7 on Bulls Head Yard Phase 1 (Warwicks

Table 42 Excavations within the defended area

Site	Location on fig 1	References
Coin hoard, Butter St, 1638	(exact location unknown)	(Booth 1980, 2; Booth, Seaby, and Palmer forthcoming)
Baptist Chapel	(18)	(Cracknell 1985a, 23)
No1 Meeting Lane/38 Henley St	(19)	(Cracknell 1985a, 23)
Old Police Station, Henley St	(20)	(Cracknell 1985a, 23)
Davis' Builder's Yard site, High St	(exact location unknown)	(pottery only: in Warwicks Museum)
Mahany's site M	(1)	(Mahany 1994)
The Bear Inn	(5)	(unpublished)
Booth's Malt Mill Lane site	(14)	(Warwicks SMR WA 465)
Tibbet's Close	(15)	(Cracknell 1985a, 12–25)
27 High St	(16)	(Cracknell 1985b)
Gateway supermarket	(AL 18)	(this volume)
Gas House Lane	(AL 23)	(this volume)

SMR WA 506) indicates that the area was still decidedly marshy in the middle of the Roman era. (The presence of a medieval ox-bow lake in the Rectory Garden (site K; 6 on fig 1) shows how slow the marsh was to drain.) Roman organic deposits are also known from the Coulters Garage site. On the south side of the circuit peaty deposits are also known from Royal Oak Passage (12 on fig 1, P Booth, pers comm), from the area to the south of Gas House Lane (13 on fig 1; observed by the author in 1991) and on the Gas House Lane site itself, where they were dated at 2150 ± 50 BP (see 'Radiocarbon dating'). None of these deposits necessarily continued to exist into the Roman period although the areas would certainly have been liable to flooding.

There are a number of examples of towns which have two or more defensive circuits, with the second and subsequent circuits on a different alignment to the first, ranging from the *coloniae* downwards. At Colchester the defensive lines may have moved to take account of the changing shape of the town until they became fossilized by the building of the *colonia* wall early in the 2nd century (Crickmore 1984, 57–8). At *Verulamium* the unfinished Fosse earthwork enclosed a very much larger area than the original defences and it projected further to the SW. Yet when the walled circuit was finally built the area in the SW was excluded although additional space was enclosed in the south (Crickmore 1984, 58–9). It is not clear if *Verulamium* was continuously defended or how much of the SW area enclosed by the Fosse earthworks was developed. At Silchester, the street grid was laid out over the first earthwork and the new defences may only have been erected later (Crickmore 1984, 60). Examples of small towns with defensive circuits on new alignments are Mildenhall (Crickmore 1984, 127) and Thorpe-by-Newark (Crickmore 1984, 131). Changes in alignment may reflect an actual change in the size of the town, as at Colchester, or an anticipated change, as at Sil-

chester. Alternatively, the circuit may be smaller than it would otherwise have been because of the need to build the defences quickly or cheaply, or for topographic reasons.

At Alcester, very little excavation has taken place in the area between the two defensive circuits, but the preliminary indications are that the area was never extensively developed.

Defended area

The excavations and other observations which have taken place in the NE part of the town, which was defended about AD 200, are listed in table 42.

Before the defences

Three sites have produced significant information about the NE part of the town before the first defences were built: Tibbet's Close (Cracknell 1985a, 12–24), Gas House Lane (this volume), and Christine Mahany's site M (Mahany 1994). All three produced limited quantities of Iron Age pottery but none dating to immediately before the Roman occupation.

At Tibbet's Close the lowest layers on the site (phases I–V) contained few finds or features but did contain the charred remains of asparagus, aquilegia, and peas, with aquilegia and more asparagus found in phase VI. Asparagus seeds are not edible and the presence of charred seeds here indicates production nearby. At Gas House Lane, in trench B, the lowest soilmarks could well be ploughmarks or lazy beds and the layer above a plough soil, although the evidence would admit of other interpretations. Once again the early layers were virtually sterile. None of the early soils were sampled for charred plant remains as there were no signs of burning or of charcoal concentrations. In retrospect this was a mistake: the later layers included asparagus (which might be taken as evidence of horticultural activity) and beans.

On Christine Mahany's site M there was evidence of structures and more in the way of finds. However, the overall impression is that, until the defences were erected, parts – probably large parts – of the area were not built up and might have been used for horticulture. This conjecture might be supported by the discovery of beet and hemlock – the latter perhaps a medicinal plant or garden weed – on the periphery of the defended area at the Gateway supermarket site (this volume). Of the eight Iron Age coins found in the town none is known to have been found in the NE part of the town. So there appears to be no continuity between the scattered traces of mid-Iron Age occupation and the intensive Roman occupation which seems to have begun early in the 3rd century.

Dating the occupation of the north-eastern part of the town

The defended area has not been investigated as much as the southern suburbs and consequently the pattern of development is less well known. The excavations at Gas House Lane (AL23 on fig 1), Tibbet's Close (15), and Mahany's site M (1) again provide the bulk of the data. In addition, from time to time, chance finds have been reported to the Warwickshire Museum. (For details of the pottery evidence, see 'Davis collection and other unpublished pottery from the defended area of the town' above.)

Pottery

At Gas House Lane the earliest finds were sherds of mid-Iron Age pottery found in a pit on trench C. The first clear signs of occupation on the site were the construction of an earth rampart and the dumping of considerable quantities of gravel make-up. Unfortunately, there was no stratigraphic relationship between the earth rampart and the gravel make-up but it seems most likely that the rampart was the first feature on the site as it contained almost no finds (and none which were dateable); if occupation had already been well established surely more would have been found during the excavation of the 5.6m length of the circuit. (The foundation trench of the 4th-century wall, for example, was much more productive.) It may be that the rampart and the gravel make-up were contemporary; even if they were not it seems unlikely that they could have been greatly separated in time.

The date of the defences might therefore be determined by reference to the date of the gravel make-up. Again, there were relatively few sherds from these layers but, significantly, two sherds of BB1 with obtuse lattice decoration were recovered, leading to the conclusion that the gravel was depos-

ited after about AD 200. Finds from subsequent phases show that there was intensive occupation through the 3rd century. There was relatively little surviving early 4th-century occupation – probably largely as a result of the truncation of the deposits – but there was a resurgence of activity in the second half of the century (leaving its traces in different areas), during which time the stone town wall was built.

At Tibbet's Close (Cracknell 1985a, 12–25) there were also some Iron Age sherds and limited traces of occupation but it was not until the early 3rd century, during Phase VI, that substantial buildings began to be built. Over 95% of the sherds found were manufactured in the 3rd and 4th centuries, clearly demonstrating the late date of the site.

At Christine Mahany's site M (Mahany 1994), in addition to the defences themselves there were some traces of earlier occupation. In this case several periods of Roman occupation appear to predate the putative first defensive bank. This seems to be one area where there was intensive occupation before the building of the first defences although, given the narrowness of the trenches, it is impossible to put together a useful structural history of the site.

At Malt Mill Lane (14), Paul Booth noted mortar and rubble spreads during the excavation of the foundations for new houses on the street frontage. A small group of pottery was recovered. Fragments from the 'bottom layer' included a Severn Valley ware tankard dating to the later 2nd century onwards and a BB1 sherd with obtuse-lattice decoration, suggesting that occupation began in the first half of the 3rd century.

At 27 High Street the structures were more substantial but less well dated (Cracknell 1985b; 16 on fig 1). The main feature of the site was a 10.7m long by 1.4m wide stone-filled foundation trench. Only a few sherds of pottery were recovered but care was taken to ascertain their context if possible. They were 3rd or 4th century in date. There was no evidence of structures in trench B at the Gateway supermarket site which was outside the first defences but inside the stone wall. Most of the pottery from this trench dated to the 4th century. The Bear Inn trench was pronounced by the excavator as negative: no records survive.

Older observations of the north-eastern part of Roman Alcester are often enigmatic. During the construction of the Baptist Chapel in Meeting Lane a tessellated pavement was found but no dating evidence is recorded (Warwicks SMR 474; 18 on fig 1). At no 1 Meeting Lane and the adjacent 38 Henley Street, Bernard Davis, a local amateur archaeologist in the 1920s, found traces of stone walls, floors of *opus signinum* and stone, painted plaster, and *tesserae* (Davis *Notes*; 19 on fig 1). Only one sherd in Warwickshire Museum's collection can now be identified as probably originating on this site: a bodysherd of a BB1 dish or bowl (dating to after AD 120). There are also references to Roman pottery, a large building, and coins from behind the Old Police

Station in Henley Street (see Cracknell 1985a, 23; 20 on fig 1) but no dating evidence.

A useful group of 60 sherds from 'Alcester Builder's Yard, north side, High Street', also part of the Davis collection, appears to be a reasonably complete collection of restricted date range, dating from the early 3rd century.

Coins

Over 1600 Roman coins have been found in Alcester but relatively few of them are certainly from the north-eastern part of the town. In 1638 a hoard of coins was found in Butter Street, near to the churchyard. There were said to be 'sixteen pieces of gold . . . and about 800 pieces of silver, and yet no two of them alike, and the latest of them above fourteen hundred years old: They contained the whole History of the Roman Empire from Julius Caesar till after Constantine the Great's time; each of the Silver pieces weighed about sevenpence, and each of the Gold, about fifteen or sixteen shillings' (quoted in Booth, Seaby, and Palmer forthcoming). The hoard has since been dispersed and the original description cannot be relied upon, particularly given the internal inconsistency of the latest coin being 'above fourteen hundred years old' in 1638 and yet there being issues 'till after Constantine the Great's time'. A study of Alcester's coinage by Booth, Seaby, and Palmer (Booth, Seaby, and Palmer forthcoming) suggests that the weights indicate that the coins ranged from the 1st century AD to the first half of the 4th century.

Many of the coins found by Davis in the 1920s have made their way into the Warwickshire Museum but only one is known certainly to come from the north-eastern part of the town: a coin which 'may be of the time of Allectus' (AD 293–6) (Davis 1927, 288–9). A better provenanced collection is that owned by John Bunting, all from the north-eastern part of the town. Fourteen of the coins were found behind (to the west of) no 5 High Street. The earliest was a coin of Claudius II Gothicus (AD 268–70). One other coin, of Carausius (AD 287–93), was found at the 'back of Church St property near Malt House', which would put it very close to the northern end of the Gas House Lane excavations. A further two coins were found by E W Jepchott, near the High Street. One was of Hadrian, the other of Antoninus Pius (Booth, Seaby, and Palmer forthcoming).

At Gas House Lane, 25 Roman coins were recovered including twelve in a hoard dating to the AD 390s. The other thirteen comprised one coin of Trajan (AD 98–117), one of Faustina II (*c* AD 146–75; unstratified), four possibly or certainly later 3rd century, and seven mid-4th century coins. The predominance of mid-4th century coins when the hoard is excluded results from many being recovered from unstratified or post-Roman contexts; their presence probably reflects the truncation of early to mid-4th-century deposits.

Three coins were recovered from Tibbet's Close (Cracknell 1985a, 12–25), dating from the reigns of Septimus Severus (AD 200–201), Gallienus (AD 257), and Valentinian I (AD 364–7).

A rather larger collection of coins was found on the Gateway supermarket site although, as this borders on the defended area, it may not be as relevant as those collections from within the area proper. There were 29 Roman coins of which 17 were probably part of a hoard deposited in the AD 380s. Of the remaining twelve only one, a *Sestertius* of Antoninus (AD 138–61) dated to before the middle of the 3rd century.

In summary, excluding the hoards, a total of 46 coins from the north-eastern part of the town have been identified. Of these only five date to before AD 200. Given that chance finds are likely to be later rather than earlier in date as these coins will be nearer to the surface, and given the predominance of late coinage in Roman assemblages, these figures are not exceptionally helpful. Whilst the coin evidence is consistent with initial occupation of the north-eastern area halfway through the Roman era, it is not sufficient to confirm the proposition conclusively. Nevertheless, taking all the evidence together, a strong case can be made for the occupation of this part of the town beginning around AD 200.

Layout

No Roman roads have been excavated within the defended area but one of the roads known from the extra-mural area appears to be heading towards it (fig 1). If continued, its SSW–NNE alignment would run approximately under the modern High Street and Butter Street. It seems likely that these modern streets do lie over a Roman predecessor although, as at Winchester, it may be that the implied position of the gate near one end of the High Street was more influential on the modern layout than were the Roman roads. Limited excavations on the N side of the River Arrow near Gunning's Bridge (for location see Cracknell 1985a, no 67 on fig 4) failed to reveal any continuation of this road to the NE and no Roman road is known on this side of the town.

Some of the building alignments within the defended area appear to reflect the SSW–NNE alignment of what must have been the main thoroughfare. At Tibbet's Close (Cracknell 1985a, 12–24) the 3rd-century stone and timber building is on a slightly different alignment to its insubstantial predecessors, but all the structures approximate to the SSW–NNE alignment. At 27 High Street (Cracknell 1985b) the stone building is a few degrees out of line.

At Gas House Lane, however, the picture is more varied (fig 18). Buildings A, B, C, and F on the NE building plot, dating to the early to mid-3rd century (phases C12, C13, C14, and C32–3) were aligned approximately SE–NW. There was also a late gully (1074, 1076) in trench B on the same line. On the other hand, the early to mid-3rd century buildings D and E on the SW plot on trench B (phases C22 and

C23) were aligned SSE–NNW. The late 3rd-century building or fence line on trench 7(n) (phase C15, fig 25) was on a different alignment again. On present evidence then, it appears that the defended area, like the extra-mural area, was not laid out on any grid pattern. Although the excavations at Tibbet's Close (Cracknell 1985a, 12–25) and at Gas House Lane have demonstrated occupation of the sites in the 3rd and 4th centuries and other finds suggest a substantially built-up defended area by the middle of the 4th century, the picture is still somewhat ill-defined (for example Place's trial trench at the Bear Inn (5 on fig 1) failed to locate any remains).

The building of the earthwork defences does not seem to have had a great effect on the intensity of occupation outside the town, with new structures appearing in various parts of the extra-mural area (Mahany 1994) although Booth and Evans have put the case for some diminution of activity in the northern part of the extra-mural area (Booth, Chadderton, and Evans forthcoming). Nevertheless, I believe that the change in the town's morphology is better described as settlement 'growth' rather than as settlement 'shift', indicating a vigorous and assertive community at that time, rather than a 'defensive' one. Burnham and Wacher (1990, 314–15) characterize the 3rd century as a time during which the larger small towns fared well at the expense of the smaller ones and the contrasting fate of Alcester which expanded, and nearby, smaller Tiddington where occupation partly ceased (Palmer 1983, 41) fits well into this pattern.

The area between the two defensive circuits appears never to have been intensively developed. At first sight it seems illogical that an apparently undeveloped area on the margins of the town was enclosed by the town wall whilst much of the built-up area was left undefended. However, it may be that at Alcester the change in the circuit was not related to any changes in the actual or anticipated size of the town. As the Moorfield marsh dried out it may have been expedient to advance the defensive circuit westwards so that it was again bounded by a muddy, impenetrable barrier. Additionally, such a blank area might have been used to provide secure accommodation for mobile field army units or for other purposes (Booth pers comm, and see Frere 1987, 346). On the two main sites, the Gateway supermarket trench B and at Gas House Lane trench A, the deposits appeared to represent rubbish dumping rather than building although a small gravel surface was identified at the Gateway supermarket (context 129). However, the trenches were largely excavated by machine and timber buildings might not have been recognized. Investigation of the area between the defences is now a priority.

Buildings

The variety of Roman buildings excavated within the defences mirrors the variety outside, although rela-tively little is known about them. There were buildings with timber foundations with cill beam construction (at Gas House Lane), with posthole construction (at Gas House Lane and at Tibbet's Close), and with a mixture of methods (at Gas House Lane). Stone foundations were used at Tibbet's Close (in a building which was partly supported on posts), at Gas House Lane, and at 27 High Street. The foundations at the latter site were the most substantial yet found in Alcester, at 1.4m wide, and indicate a stone superstructure.

Floors were made of *opus signinum* (27 High Street), clay, and gravel. Wooden floors have yet to be identified although they certainly must have existed. Painted wall plaster was used both on timber buildings (eg building E at Gas House Lane) and on stone (27 High Street) and finds of daub are commonplace. Davis (*Notes*) writes of stone structures with *opus signinum* floors, *tesserae*, and *pilae* at no 1 Meeting Lane and *tesserae* were also found under the nearby Baptist Chapel, at Gas House Lane, and at 27 High Street. (It should be noted, however, that the evidence of patterned mosaics is perhaps less strong than has been suggested in the literature (eg Booth and Cracknell 1986, 8, fig 5); the sightings, made some time ago, may well refer to plain tessellated pavements.) Another stone building was noted behind the Old Police Station, Henley Street (20 in fig 1). Hypocaust *pilae* and tufa fragments indicate a well-appointed building in the vicinity of the Gas House Lane site. If the marble fragment from this site really is wall covering rather than a palette or reused fragment then the building from which it came must have been remarkably opulent. The quantity of both ceramic and stone tile in general indicates a modicum of tiled buildings although most must have been thatched. The standard of the better class of buildings is similar to those found lining both sides of street A, the main E–W axis through the extra-mural area (Mahany 1994), whilst the other buildings can be compared with those elsewhere outside the walls. As yet there is only limited evidence for a progression from timber buildings to stone and then back to timber – at Gas House Lane – as Booth postulated for the extra-mural area (Mahany 1994).

It is notable that, despite the number of buildings now known from both within and outside the defences, very few strip buildings have been recorded and there is no evidence for land being at a premium with the concomitant packed structures that this might entail.

Economic and social activities and status

Specific activities cannot be assigned to many of the structures or sites within the defences. There is only the hint of antler carving at Gas House Lane and of minor metal working at both Gas House Lane and the Gateway supermarket site, in the latter case probably associated with the building of the tower.

There is no evidence for zoning within the defended area.

In terms of discarded material possessions the defended area seems similar to the extra-mural area, with the usual scatter of exotic items, eg the marble fragment (stone catalogue no 7) and the fish-shaped plate brooches (fig 55, no 9) from Gas House Lane. All three of the coin hoards found in the town come from the defended area (at Butter Street, Gas House Lane, and the Gateway supermarket) – a fourth hoard was found beyond the river to the south of the town – but this only indicated that it was a place of safety rather than a place of wealth. The animal bones from all sites include both domestic waste and refuse from primary butchery (and are discussed in more detail above, pp 126–7). As with other Romano-British sites cattle predominated. It is notable that the assemblage includes both oysters and saltwater fish.

The limited excavation within the defended area has not added greatly to our appreciation of the status and role of the town but has confirmed the growing impression of an unusually large 'small town'. It is clear that from an early stage Alcester was well above a village in size, originating at a route centre with the additional magnet of a fort (presumed to have been in Bleachfield Street (Booth, Chadderton and Evans forthcoming). There is only very limited evidence of immediately pre-Roman activity (mostly centring on artefacts from the southern suburbs), although there is the possibility of an Iron Age hillfort at Oversley Castle a few kilometres to the south.

Alcester falls into the class of larger small towns which had development not only on the street frontages but also well away from the roads. In terms of size and structure it lies well towards the urban end of the urban–agricultural continuum which encompasses nucleated Roman settlement. Yet agriculture must have played a dominant part in the town, with much of the land in the area being worked from the town. There is positive evidence for this in the presence of farming activities at 1–5 Bleachfield Street but perhaps the negative evidence is more important. There is only one possible villa known in the immediate area, in great contrast to the number around the *civitas* capital at Cirencester, and only one possible farmstead is known. (However, little survey has yet been done.)

The town seems to have provided a variety of services without focusing on any one in particular. It is possible to make a case for an official function for the town if the granary found on the Coulters Garage and Gateway supermarket sites (dating to *c* AD 300) is interpreted as a collection point for the *annona militaris*. One problem with this, however, is that the granary was demolished to make way for a clearly official project – the 4th-century town wall – rather than the wall being built to protect it. It has also been argued that a well appointed early building in the extra-mural area could be a *mansio* but the evidence is thin (Booth in Mahany 1994).

With the subdivision of Britain into four provinces in the early 4th century, there was a trend towards devolution. At this stage, and possibly earlier, the town may have become the centre for a northern Dobunnic *pagus* (cf Burnham and Wacher 1990, 39). This status would in some part explain the decision to re-wall the town, though it does not fully explain the late date of the works.

The end of Roman Alcester

It would seem likely that, if Alcester continued as a town into the sub-Roman period, the evidence for it should be found within the defended area but at present the evidence is limited to outside. At the Explosion site (1–5 Bleachfield St) the long sequence of activity might run into the 5th century (Booth, Chadderton, and Evans forthcoming). Further to the south, on Mahany's site F there are three phases of building which belong to after AD 353, and just to the south of street A, on Mahany's site G, phases VI to X date to after AD 337. There are also several 4th-century phases on Mahany's site D (Mahany forthcoming; Cracknell and Mahany forthcoming). The other post-Roman finds are all later in date, with Saxon pottery in a beam slot from Lloyd's Bank (Booth, Chadderton, and Evans forthcoming) being the most positive trace of activity. However, it was not until the 13th century that Alcester again begins to appear in the archaeological and historical record (Saville 1986).

Future work on Roman Alcester

Many of the details of Roman Alcester are now known and at this point I would like to signal four areas worthy of further study, the first three with implications which stretch well beyond the limits of the town itself.

Small towns are increasingly seen as only one element in a landscape which had no sharp divisions between farms, villages, roadside settlements, small towns, and towns. In order to understand this 'small town' better, much more work needs to be done *outside* the town limits.

Secondly, the addition of a newly defended area to the town about AD 200 provides scope for the study of residuality-in-the-ground and residuality-in-use (heirlooms). Although some mention of the opportunities and problems has been made in the Gas House Lane report, particularly with reference to the pottery, this kind of study can only really be pursued in the context of a wider study of the town as a whole and must be left for the future.

Thirdly, another fruitful area could be the study of the economic connections of the town. At various points in the CBA Alcester Series it has been noted that the finds demonstrate trading connections with the Severn Valley: any future synthesis of archaeological work in the town would need to investigate this further.

Fourthly, very little work had been done on the major cemeteries which are known to exist to the west of the town. This is a huge gap in our knowledge. The roads, houses, economy and life styles are broadly known: what is needed now are human beings to populate this ancient townscape.

Bibliography

Allason-Jones, L, and Bishop, M C, 1988 *Excavations at Roman Corbridge: the hoard*

Allen, D A, 1986 The glass vessels in *The legionary fortress baths at Caerleon, Vol II* (J David Zienkiewicz), 98–116

Andrews, A H, and Noddle, B A, 1975 Absence of premolar teeth from ruminant mandibles found at archaeological sites, *J Archaeol Sci*, **2**, 137–44

Andrews, J, forthcoming [The Roman pottery] in [report on excavations at Dorchester, Dorset] (D Batchelor)

Armitage, P, 1982 A system for ageing and sexing the horn cores of cattle from British post-medieval sites, in *Ageing and sexing animal bones from archaeological sites* (eds B Wilson, C Grigson, and S Payne), BAR **109**, 37–54

Armitage, P L, and Clutton-Brock, J, 1976 A system for classification and description of the horn cores of cattle from archaeological sites, *J Archaeol Sci*, **3**, 329–48

Backhouse, J, Turner, D H, and Webster, L, 1984 *The golden age of Anglo-Saxon pot*, British Museum

Baillie, M G L, 1982 *Tree ring dating and archaeology*

Baker, J, and Brothwell, D, 1980 *Animal diseases in archaeology*

Barker, D, 1986 North Staffordshire post-medieval ceramics – a type series. Part two: Blackware, *Staffordshire Archaeol Stud*, Museum Archaeology Society Report New Series, **3**, 58–75

Bell, A, and Evans, J, forthcoming The pottery from the CEU excavations, in *Excavations at Catterick 1956–88* (ed P R Wilson), HBMC Archaeol Rep

Bidwell, P T, 1985 *The Roman fort of Vindolanda at Chesterholm, Northumberland*, HBMC Archaeol Rep, **1**, London

Bird, J, 1986 Samian wares, in Miller *et al* 1986, 139–85

Bishop, M C, and Dore, J N, 1988 *Corbridge. Excavation of the Roman fort and town 1947–80*, HBMC Archaeol Rep, **8**

Boessneck, J, 1969 Osteological differences between sheep and goat, in *Science in Archaeology* (eds D Brothwell and ES Higgs), 331–58

Boon, G C, 1966 Roman window glass from Wales, *J Glass Studies* **8**, 41–5

— 1973 Finds from Castell Collen Roman fort 1911–1913, *Trans Radnorshire Soc*, **43**, 8–22

Booth, P, 1980 *Roman Alcester*, Warwickshire Museum

— 1985 Roman store buildings at Alcester, *Transactions*, **94**, 1985 (1989), 63–106

— 1986 Roman pottery in Warwickshire – production and demand, *J Roman Pottery Stud*, **1**, 22–41

— forthcoming Excavations at 1–5 Bleachfield Street, Alcester (the Explosion site) 1976–77, in *Roman Alcester: northern extramural area* (ed P Booth, J Chadderton, and J Evans), CBA Res Rep

Booth, P, and Cracknell, S, 1986 Alcester, from prehistory to the Norman Conquest, in *Alcester – a history* (ed G E Saville), 5–25

Booth, P, and Green, S, 1989 The nature and distribution of certain pink, grog tempered vessels, *J Roman Pottery Studies*, **2**, Oxford

Booth, P, Chadderton, J, and Evans, J, forthcoming Roman Alcester: northern suburbs, CBA

Booth, P, Seaby, W A, and Palmer, N, forthcoming Iron Age and Roman coins from Alcester, Warwickshire

Boulton, E H B, and Jay B A, 1946 *British timbers*

British Museum, 1907 *Medieval guide*

Brodribb, A C C, Hands, A R, and Walker, D R, 1971 *Excavations at Shakenoak part II: Sites B and H*

— Hands, A R, and Walker, D R, 1973 *Excavations at Shakenoak part IV: Site C*

Brown, A E, and Alexander, J A, 1982 Excavations at Towcester 1954; The Grammar School site, *Northants Archaeol*, **17**, 24–59

Bulmer, M, 1979 An introduction to Roman samian ware, with special reference to collections in Chester and the North-West, *J Chester Archaeol Soc*, **62**, 1979 (1980), 5–72

— 1980 The samian, in Mason, D J P, *Excavations at Chester, 11–15 Castle Street and neighbouring sites 1974–8, a possible Roman posting house (mansio)*, Grosvenor Museum Archaeological and Survey Reports No 2, *passim*

Burnham, B, and Wacher, J, 1990 *The 'small towns' of Roman Britain*

Bury, S, 1984 *An introduction to rings*, Victoria and Albert Museum, London

Bushe-Fox, J P, 1913 *Report on the excavations on the site of the Roman town at Wroxeter, Shropshire 1912*, Rep Res Committee Soc Antiq London, **1**

— 1914 *Second report on the excavations on the site of the Roman town at Wroxeter, Shropshire 1913*, Rep Res Comm Soc Antiq London, **2**

— 1916 *Third report on the excavations on the site of the Roman town at Wroxeter, Shropshire 1914*, Rep Res Committee Soc Antiq London, **4**

Bibliography

— 1932 Some notes on Roman coast defences, *J Roman Stud*, **22**

Butler, R M, 1983 The construction of urban defences, in Maloney and Hobley 1983, 125–9

Cadbury, D A, Hawkes, J G, and Readett, R C, 1971 *A computer-mapped flora; a study of the county of Warwickshire*, Academic press, London

Canti, M G, 1987 Alcester Gateway Store site. Soil report. *Ancient Monuments Lab Reports* 102/87.

Carrington, P, 1980 The pottery, in *Excavations at Chester; 11–15 Castle Street and neighbouring site, 1974–8* (D J P Mason), Grosvenor Museum Excavation and Survey Reports, **2**

Charlesworth, D, 1966 Roman square bottles, *J Glass Stud*, **8**, 26–40

Clapham, A R, Tutin, T G, and Warburg, E F, 1962 *Flora of the British Isles*, 1 ed, Cambridge

— 1987 *Flora of the British Isles*, 3 ed, Cambridge

Clarke, G, 1979 *The Roman cemetery at Lankhills*, Winchester Studies 3: Pre-Roman and Roman Winchester part 2

Clutton-Brock, J, Dennis-Bryan, K, Armitage, P L, and Jewell, P A, 1990 Osteology of the Soay sheep. Bull Brit Mus (Natur Hist) **56** (1), 1–56

Colledge, S, 1985 Charred plant remains, in Booth 1985, 88–91

Columella, *De Re Rustica* vol 3 Forster, E, S, and Heffner, E (eds) 1955, Loeb Classical Library

Conolly, A P, 1971 Plant remains, in The Roman villa at Denton, Lincolnshire, part III (Greenfield), *Lincolnshire History and Archaeology*, I, no 6, 29–57

Cowgill, J, de Neergaard, M, and Griffiths, N, 1987 *Medieval finds from excavations in London. 1: knives and scabbards*

Cracknell, S, 1985a Roman Alcester: recent archaeological excavations, *Trans Birmingham Warwickshire Archaeol Soc*, **94**, 1985 (1989), 1–62

— 1985b 27 High Street, Alcester: a watching brief, *Trans Birmingham Warwickshire Archaeol Soc*, **94**, 1985 (1989), 123–4

— 1987 Bridge End, Warwick: archaeological excavation of a medieval street frontage, *Trans Birmingham Warwickshire Archaeol Soc*, **95**, 1987 (1991), 17–72

Cracknell, S, and Ferguson, R, 1985 The builder's yard site, Bleachfield St, Alcester, 1987: salvage recording, *Trans Birmingham Warwickshire Archaeol Soc*, **94**, 1985 (1989), 126–32

Cracknell, S, and Jones, M, 1985 Medieval kiln debris from School Road, Alcester, *Trans Birmingham Warwickshire Archaeol Soc*, **94**, 1985 (1989), 107–22

Cracknell, S, and Mahany, M, 1994 *Alcester Excavations 1964–66*, Part 2: finds and discussion, CBA Res Rep

Crickmore, J, 1984 *Romano-British urban defences*, BAR Brit Ser, **126**

Crummy, N, 1979 A chronology of Romano-British bone pins, *Britannia*, **10**, 157–63

— 1983 *The Roman small finds from excavations in Colchester 1071–9*, Colchester Archaeol Rep, **2**

— 1984 The stone architectural fragments, in *Excavations at Lion Walk, Balkerne Lane and Middleborough* (P Crummy), Colchester Archaeol Rep, **3**, 29

Cullen, P R, 1970 Cirencester: the restoration of the Roman town wall, 1967–68, *Britannia*, **1**, 227–39

Cunliffe, B W, 1968 *Fifth report on the excavations of the Roman fort at Richborough, Kent*, Rep Res Committee Soc Antiq London, **23**

— 1971 *Excavations at Fishbourne 1961–1969 vol II: the finds*, Rep Res Committee Soc Antiq London, **27**

— 1975 *Excavations at Portchester Castle*, vol 1, Roman, Rep Res Comm Soc Antiq London

Darling, M, 1977 *A group of late Roman pottery from Lincoln*, Lincoln Archaeol Trust Monogr Ser, **16**

Davis, B, 1927 Discoveries at Alcester, *Trans Birmingham Warwickshire Archaeol Soc*, **52**, 1927 (1930), 288–9

— undated *Notes*, unpublished notes on excavations and finds dating to the 1920s–1930s

Dennell, R, 1976 The economic importance of plant resources represented on archaeological sites. *J Archaeol Science*, **3**, 229–47

Dickinson, B, 1985 The samian pottery, in Roman Alcester: recent archaeological excavations (S Cracknell), *Trans Birmingham Warwicks Archaeol Soc*, **94**, 1985 (1989), *passim*

— 1986 Potters' stamps and signatures on samian, in Miller *et al* 1986, 186–98

— forthcoming The Brougham samian ware, in Report on excavations at Brougham fort cemetery (J Andrews and G Green)

Dickinson, B, and Hartley, K F, 1971 The evidence of potters' stamps on samian ware and on mortaria for the trading connections of Roman York, in *Soldier and civilian in Roman Yorkshire* (ed R M Butler), 127–42

Dodge, H, 1988 Decorative stones for architecture in the Roman Empire, *Oxford J Archaeol*, **7**, 65–80

Draper, J, 1985 *Excavations by Mr H P Cooper on the Roman site at Hill Farm, Gestingthorpe, Essex*, E Anglian Archaeol Rep, **25**

Draper, J, and Chaplain, C, 1982 *Dorchester Excavations vol 1*, Dorset Natural Hist Archaeol Soc Monogr Ser, **2**

Driesch, A von den, 1976 *A guide to the measurement of animal bones from archaeological sites*, Peabody Museum Bull, **1**

Driesch, A von den, and Boessneck, J, 1974 Kritische Anmerkungen zur Widerrist-hoehenberechnung aus Laengenmassen vor- und frühgeschichtlicher Tierknochen, *Säugetierkundliche Mitteilungen*, **22**, 325–48

Elling, W, 1966 Untersuchungen über das Jahrringverhalten der Schwarzeerle, *Flora*, **156**, 155–201

Esmonde-Cleary, S, 1985 The quick and the dead: suburbs, cemeteries and the town, in Roman urban topography (ed F Grew and B Hobley), CBA Res Rep, **59**, 74–7

Evans, J, 1985 *Aspects of later Roman pottery assemblages in northern England*, unpublished PhD thesis, University of Bradford

— 1987 Graffiti, the evidence of literacy and pottery use in Roman Britain, *Archaeol J*, **144**, 191–204

— 1994 Discussion of the Birch Abbey Roman pottery in the context of Roman Alcester in *Alcester Excavations 1964–66*, part 2 (ed S Cracknell and C Mahany)

— forthcoming The pottery from Bryn Eryr, in [report on excavations at Bryn Eryr, Gwynedd] (ed D Longley)

— in prep Synthesis of the Roman pottery from Alcester

Evans, J G, 1972 *Land snails in archaeology*

Ferguson, R, 1985 Roman pottery, in Roman Alcester: recent archaeological excavations (S Cracknell), *Trans Birmingham Warwickshire Archaeol Soc*, **94**, 1985 (1989), 1–62

— forthcoming The Roman pottery, in Excavations at 1–5 Bleachfield Street, Alcester (P Booth)

— 1994 Pottery and ceramic small finds, in *Alcester excavations 1964–66*, part 2 (ed S Cracknell and C Mahany)

Frere, S, 1965 Town defences in Roman Britain, *Antiquity*, **39**, 137–9

— 1972 *Verulamium excavations I*, Rep Res Comm Soc Antiq London, **28**

— 1983 *Verulamium excavations II*, Rep Res Comm Soc Antiq London, **41**

— 1984 British urban defences in earthwork, *Britannia*, **15**, 63–74

— 1987 *Britannia* (3rd edition)

Fulford, M, 1975a *New Forest Roman pottery*, BAR, **17**, Oxford

— 1975b The pottery, in *Excavations at Portchester Castle I: Roman.* (ed B W Cunliffe), Soc of Antiq Res Rep, **32**, 270–366

— 1984 *Silchester Defences 1974–80*, Britannia Monogr Ser, **5**, London

— 1983 The defensive sequence at Silchester, in Maloney and Hobley 1983, 85–9

Gaitzsch, W, 1980 *Eiserne römische Werkzeuge. Studien zur römischen Werkzeugkunde in Italien und nordlichen Provinzen des Imperium Romanum. 2 vols*

Gardner, P J, Haldon R, and Malam, J, 1980 Prehistoric, Roman and medieval settlement at Stretton-on-Fosse; excavations and salvage 1971–6, *Trans Birmingham Warwickshire Archaeol Soc*, **90**, 1980 (1982), 1–35

Gillam, J P, 1970 *Types of Roman coarse pottery vessels in Northern Britain*, Newcastle-upon-Tyne

— 1976 Coarse fumed ware in north Britain and beyond, *Glasgow Archaeol J*, **4**, 57–80

Going C, 1987 *The mansio and other sites in the south eastern sector of Caesaromagus: the Roman pottery*, CBA Res Rep, **62**, London

Going, C, and Ford, B, 1988 The Romano-British pottery, in *Excavations at Great Dunmow, Essex* (N P Wickenden), E Anglian Archaeol, **41**, 61–76

Grant, A, 1982 The use of tooth wear as a guide to the age of domestic ungulates, in *Ageing and sexing animal bones from archaeological sites* (eds R Wilson, C Grigsson, and S Payne), 91–108

— 1989 Animals in Roman Britain, in Research on Roman Britain 1960–1989 (ed M Todd),135–46

— 1991 Animal husbandry, in Danebury an Iron age hillfort in Hampshire, Volume 5, (B Cunliffe and C Poole), 447–87

Green, C, 1977 The pottery, in Excavations at Bishopstone, Sussex (M Bell), *Sussex Archaeol Collect*, **115**, 1–291

Green, S, and Young, C, 1985 The Roman pottery, in *The temple of Sulis Minerva at Bath, Vol 1(1) The site* (B Cunliffe and P Davenport), 143–60, OUCA Monogr, **7**, Oxford

Greene, K, 1978 Imported fine wares in Britain to AD 250: a guide to identification, in *Early fine wares in Roman Britain* (ed P Arthur and G Marsh), BAR, **57**, 15–30, Oxford

Grieve, M, 1980 *A modern herbal*

Groves, C, 1987 *Dendrochronological analysis of wood from Alcester* 1985–86, Ancient Monuments Lab Rep Ser, 134/87

Hamilton, J, 1985 The animal bones, in Roman Alcester: recent archaeological excavations (S Cracknell), *Trans Birmingham Warwickshire Archaeol Soc*, **94**, 58

— forthcoming The animal bones, in *Burton Dassett Southend – excavations 1986–1988* (ed N Palmer)

Hanson, W S, 1978 The organization of Roman military timber supply, *Britannia*, **9**, 293–306

Harcourt, R A, 1979 The animal bones, in *Gussage All Saints: an Iron Age settlement in Dorset* (G J Wainwright) Department of the Environment Archaeol Rep, **10**, 150–60

Harden, D B, 1979 Glass vessels, in *Winchester Studies 3 Pre-Roman and Roman Winchester part II: The Roman cemetery at Lankhills* (G Clarke), 209–20

Hartley, B R, 1961 The samian ware, in Excavations at Mumrills 1958–60, *Proc Soc Antiq Scot* (K A Steer), **94**, 100–10

— 1983 The enclosure of Romano-British towns in the second century AD, in *Rome and her northern provinces* (eds B R Hartley and J Wacher), 84–95

Hartley, B, and Dickinson, B, 1985 The samian pottery from Anglo-Saxon contexts, in *West Stow, the Anglo-Saxon village* (S West), E Anglian Archaeol Rep, **24**, 82

Hartley, K F, 1967 *Mortaria* from Mancetter 1964, in Excavations at *Manduessedum*, 1964 (C Mahany), *Trans Birmingham Warwickshire Archaeol Soc*, **84**, 1967–70 (1971), 28–34

Bibliography

Hartshorne, C H, 1845 The history and architecture of Portchester Castle, *Proc Archaeol Inst*,

Hassall, M W C, and Tomlin, R S O, 1978 Roman Britain in 1977 II: Inscriptions, *Britannia*, **9**, 473–85

— 1989 Roman Britain in 1988 II: Inscriptions, *Britannia*, **20**, 327–45

Hather, J, 1991 The identification of charred archaeological remains of vegetative parenchymous tissue, *J Archaeol Sci*, **18**(6), 661–75

Hattatt, R, 1982 *Ancient and Romano-British brooches*

— 1987 *Brooches of antiquity. A third selection of brooches from the author's collection*

— 1989 *Ancient brooches and other artefacts. A fourth selection of brooches together with some other antiquities from the author's collection*

Heighway, C M, and Parker, A J, 1982 The Roman tilery at St Oswald's Priory, Gloucester, *Britannia*, **13**, 25–77

Henig, M, 1974 *A corpus of Roman engraved gemstones from British sites*, BAR, **8**

Hill, C, Millett, M, and Blagg, T, 1980 *The Roman riverside wall and monumental arch in London. Excavations at Baynard's Castle, Upper Thames Street, London 1974–6*, London Middlesex Archaeol Soc Special Pap, **3**

Hillman, G C, 1981 Reconstructing crop processing from charred plant remains, in *Farming practice in British prehistory* (ed R Mercer), 123–62, Edinburgh

— 1982a Crop husbandry at the medieval farmstead, Cefn Graenog, in The excavation of a medieval farmstead at Cefn Graenog Clynnog, Gwynedd (R S Kelly), *Bull Board Celtic Stud*, **4**, 901–6

— 1982b Evidence for malting spelt, in *Excavations at Catsgore 1970–1973, A Romano-British village* (R Leech), Western Archaeol Trust Excavation Monogr, **2**, 137–41

— 1983 Crop processing at 3rd-century Wilderspool, in *Excavations at Wilderspool 1966–1968* (J Hinchcliffe and J H Williams), Cheshire County Council Monogr

Hinton, D, 1973 *Medieval pottery of the Oxford region*, Ashmolean Museum

Hobley, B, 1983 Roman urban defences: a review of research in Britain, in Maloney and Hobley 1983

Howe, M D, Perrin, R, and Mackreth, D, 1980 *Roman pottery from the Nene Valley: a guide*, Peterborough City Museum Occ Pap **2**, Peterborough

Hughes, H V, 1961 A Romano-British kiln site at Perry Barr, Birmingham, *Trans Birmingham Warwickshire Archaeol Soc*, **77**, 33–9

Hurst, H, 1972 Excavations at Gloucester 1968–1971, *Antiq J*, **52**, 24–69

— 1986 *Gloucester, the Roman and later defences*, Gloucester Archaeol Rep, **2**

Isings, C, 1957 *Roman glass dated finds* (Groningen, Djarkarta)

Janus, L, 1965 *The young specialist looks at land and freshwater molluscs*

Jarrett, M G, 1965 Town defences in Roman Britain, *Antiquity*, **39**, 57–9

Jarrett, M G, and Wrathmell, S, 1981 *Whitton. An Iron Age and Roman farmstead in South Glamorgan*, Cardiff

Johnson, S, 1979 *The Roman forts of the Saxon Shore*, Elek, London

— 1983 *Late Roman Fortifications*, Batsford, London

Jones, B and Mattingly, D, 1990 *An atlas of Roman Britain*, Blackwell, Oxford

Jones, M, 1983 *Coloniae* in Maloney and Hobley 1983, 90–5

Jones, M J, and Bond, C J, 1987 Urban defences, in Schofield and Leech 1987

Kaye, N, 1936 *Brewing, a book of reference*

Keeley, J, 1986 The coarse pottery, in McWhirr 1986, 158–89

Kerney, M P, 1976 A list of fresh- and brackish-water mollusca of the British Isles, *Journal of Conchology*, **29**, 26–8

King, A, 1978 A comparative survey of bone assemblages from Roman sites in Britain, *Bull Inst Archaeol Univ London*, **15**, 207–31

— 1981 The decline of samian ware manufacture in the north-west provinces: problems of chronology and interpretation, in *The Roman west in the third century, contributions from archaeology and history* (eds A King and M Henig), BAR Int Ser, **109** (i), 55–78

Knörzer, K H, 1970 Novaesium IV, Römerzeitliche Pflanzenfunde aus Neuss, *Limesforschungen*, **10**

— 1973 Römerzeitliche Pflanzenreste aus einem Brunnen in Butzbach (Hessen), *Saalburg Jahrbuch*, **30**, 71–114

— 1984 Aussagemoglichkeiten von palaeoethnobotanischen Latrinenuntersuchungen, in *Plants and ancient man* (eds W van Ziest and W A Casparie), 331–8

Leach, P, 1982 Roman pottery, in *Ilchester Volume I; Excavations 1974–5* (P Leach)

Leech, R, 1981 The excavation of a Romano-British farmstead and cemetery on Bradley Hill, Somerton, Somerset, *Britannia*, **12**, 177–252

— 1982 *Excavations at Catsgore 1970–73, A Romano-British village*, Western Archaeol Trust Monogr, **2**

Lee, F, and Pickin, G, 1994 Romano-British coarse pottery, in *Excavations at Alcester 1964–6*, part 2 (ed S Cracknell and C Mahany)

Levine, M A, 1982 The use of crown height measurements and eruption-wear sequences to age horse teeth, in *Ageing and sexing animal bones from archaeological sites* (eds B Wilson, C Grigson and S Payne), BAR **109**, 223–50

Levitan, B, 1985 A methodology for recording the pathology and other anomalies of ungulate mandibles from archaeological sites, in *Palaeobiological Investigations*, (eds N R J Fieller, D D Gilbertson and N G A Ralph), BAR Int Series **266**, 41–54

London Museum, 1940 *London Museum Medieval Catalogue*, HMSO

Luff, R-M, 1982 *A zooarchaeological study of the Roman north-western provinces*, BAR Int Ser,**137**

Macan, T T, 1969 *Key to British fresh- and brackish-water gastropods*, Freshwater Biological Association Scientific Publication, **13**, 3 ed

MacGregor, A, 1978 *Roman finds from Skeldergate and Bishophill, The Archaeology of York*, **17** (2) CBA for York Archaeol Trust

— 1985 *Bone, Antler, Ivory, and Horn*

McWhirr, A, 1986 *Cirencester Excavations III, Houses in Roman Cirencester*, Cirencester

McWhirr, A, and Viner, D, 1978 The production and distribution of tiles in Roman Britain with particular reference to the Cirencester region, *Britannia*, **9**, 359–77

Mahany, C, 1965 Alcester excavation committee, *W Midlands Archaeol News* Sheet, **8**, 2–4

— 1987 *Excavations in Alcester, Warwickshire, 1964–66*, draft report in Warks SMR

— 1994 *Roman Alcester, 1964–1966 excavations. Part 1: stratigraphy and structures*, CBA Res Rep **96**

Maloney, J, 1983 Recent work on London's defences, in Maloney and Hobley 1983, 96–117

Maloney, J, and Hobley, B, 1983 *Roman urban defences in the west*, CBA Res Rep, **51**

Maltby, J M, 1979 The animal bones from Exeter 1971–1975, Exeter Archaeol Rep **2**

— 1984 Animal bones and the Romano–British economy, in *Animals and archaeology: 4. Husbandry in Europe* (eds C Grigson and J Clutton-Brock), BAR Int Ser **227**, 125–38

— forthcoming The animal bones, in Excavations at 1–5 Bleachfield Street, Alcester (P Booth), in *Roman Alcester: northern extramural area*, (ed P Booth, J Chadderton, and J Evans), CBA Res Rep

Manning, W H, 1985 *Catalogue of Romano-British iron tools, fittings and weapons in the British Museum*

Marsh, G, 1978 Early second-century fine wares in the London area, *Early fine wares in Roman Britain* (ed P Arthur and G Marsh), BAR **57**, 119–223, Oxford

— 1981 London's samian supply and its relationship to the development of the Gallic samian industry, in *Roman pottery research in Britain and north-west Europe* (ed A C and A S Anderson), BAR Int Ser, **123** (i), 1981, 173–238, Oxford

Mayes, P, and Scott, M, 1984 *Pottery kilns at Chilvers Coton, Nuneaton*, Soc Medieval Archaeol Monogr Ser, **10**

Mellor, J E, and Pearce, T, 1981 *The Austin Friars, Leicester*, CBA Res Rep, **35**

Mertens, J, 1983 Urban wall-circuits in Gallia Belgica in the Roman period, in Maloney and Hobley 1983, 42–57

Miller, L, Schofield, J, and Rhodes, M, 1986 *The Roman quay at St Magnus House, London*, (ed T Dyson), London Middlesex Archaeol Soc Special Pap, **8**

Millett, M, 1979 An approach to the functional interpretation of pottery, in *Pottery and the archaeologist* (ed M Millett), Inst of Archaeol Occ Pub, **4**, 35–49

— 1980 The Roman pottery, in *The Roman Riverside Wall and Monumental Arch in London* (C Hill, M Millett, and T Blagg), *London Middlesex Archaeol Soc Special Pap*, **3**, 95–6

— 1983 *A comparative study of some contemporaneous pottery assemblages from Roman Britain*, unpublished PhD thesis, University of Oxford

— 1990 *The Romanization of Britain*, Cambridge

Millett, M, and Graham, D, 1986 *Excavations on the Romano-British small town at Neatham, Hampshire 1969–79*, Hampshire Field Club Monogr, **3**, 63–94, Gloucester

Moffett, L, 1986 Crops and crop processing in a Romano-British village at Tiddington: the evidence from the charred plant remains, *English Heritage Ancient Monuments Laboratory Report*, 15/86

— 1988 Gardening in Roman Alcester, *Circaea*, **5**, 73–8

— 1985a Charred plant remains, in Cracknell and Jones 1985, microfiche M2:G5–M2:G8

— 1985b Charred plant remains, in Cracknell 1985a, 23

Morris, J, 1975 The samian, in *Excavations at Portchester Castle, vol I, Roman* (B Cunliffe), Rep Res Comm Antiq London, **32**, 276–8

Nash-Williams, V E, 1930 The samian stamps found at Caerwent (*Venta Silurum*), *Bull Board Celtic Stud*, **5**, no 2, 166–85

Neal, D, 1976 Northchurch, Boxmoor, Hemel Hempstead Station: the excavations of three Roman buildings in the Bulbourne Valley, *Hertfordshire Archaeol*, **4**, 1–135

Noddle, B A, 1984 A comparison of the bones of cattle, sheep, and pigs from ten Iron Age and Romano-British sites, in *Animals and archaeology: 4. Husbandry in Europe* (eds C Grigson and J Clutton-Brock), BAR Int Ser, **227**, 105–24

Orton, C, 1977 Roman pottery (excluding samian), in Excavations at Angel Court, Walbrook, 1974 (T R Blurton), *London Middlesex Archaeol Soc*, **28**, 30–55

Oswald, A, 1962 Interim report on the excavations at Weoley Castle 1955–60, *Transactions*, **78**

Oswald, F, 1936 *Index of figure-types on terra sigillata*, Univ Liverpool Annals of Archaeology and Anthropology Supplement 1935–1936.

Bibliography

Palmer, N, 1983 Tiddington Roman settlement: second interim report, *West Midlands Archaeol News Sheet*, **26**, 37–47

— forthcoming *Tiddington Roman settlement*

Parker, A J, 1988 The birds of Roman Britain, *Oxford J Archaeol* vii, 197–226

Partridge, C, 1981 *Skeleton Green: A late Iron Age and Romano-British Site*, Britannia Monogr Ser, **2**

Payne, S, 1973 Kill-off patterns in sheep and goats: the mandibles from Asvan Kale, *Anatolian Stud*, **23**, 281–303

Peacock, D P S, 1967 Romano-British pottery production in the Malvern district of Worcestershire, *Trans Worcestershire Archaeol Soc*, **1**, 15–28

Pearce, J E, Vince, A G, White, R, 1982 A dated type series of London medieval pottery: Mill Green Ware, *Trans London Middlesex Archaeol Soc*, **33**, 266–98

Planck, D, 1975 *Arae Flaviae I. Neue Untersuchungen zur Geschichte der römischen Rottweil*, Forschungen und Berichte zur Vor- und Frühgeschichte in Baden-Württemberg, 6/I+II

Platt, C, and Coleman-Smith, R, 1975 *Excavations in medieval Southampton 1953–1969 vol II: the small finds*

Pliny, *Natural History* vol 4 Bostock, J, and Riley, H T (eds), 1856

Plouviez, J, 1976 The pottery, in The Romano-British site at Icklingham (S E West and J Plouviez), *East Anglian Archaeology*, **3**, 85–102

Potter, T W, 1979 *Romans in north-west England. Excavations at the Roman forts of Ravenglass, Watercrook, and Bowness on Solway*, Cumberland Westmoreland Antiq Archaeol Soc Res Ser, **1**

Potter, T W, and Trow, S W, 1988 *Puckeridge-Braughing, Herts: the Ermine Street excavations 1971–2*, Hertfordshire Archaeol, **10**

Precht, G, 1983 The town walls and defensive system of Xanten – *Colonia Ulpia Traiana*, in Maloney and Hobley 1983

Rahtz, P A, 1969 *Excavations at King John's Hunting Lodge, Writtle, Essex 1955–57*, Soc Medieval Archaeol Monogr Ser, **3**

Ratkai, S, 1985 The medieval and post-medieval pottery from Dudley Castle, *W Midland Pottery Res Grp Newsletter*, **5**

— 1987 The medieval and post-medieval pottery, in Bridge End, Warwick: archaeological excavation of a medieval street frontage (ed S Cracknell), *Trans Birmingham Warwickshire Archaeol Soc*, **95**, 1987 (1991), 33–58

— 1994 Medieval pottery, in 'Bard's Walk', Wood Street, Stratford-on-Avon. Medieval structures excavated in 1989 (ed S Cracknell), *Trans Birmingham Warwickshire Archaeol Soc*, **98**

— forthcoming (a) Medieval pottery, in *Burton Dassett Southend – excavations 1986–1988* (ed N Palmer)

— 1994 Medieval pottery, in Excavations at 25–33 Brook Street, Warwick, 1973 (eds S Cracknell and M W Bishop), *Trans Birmingham Warwickshire Archaeol Soc*, **97**, 1–40

— forthcoming (b) The medieval pottery, in Excavations at 1–5 Bleachfield Street, Alcester (the Explosion Site) (ed P Booth), in Roman Alcester: northern extramural area (eds P Booth, J Chadderton, and J Evans), CBA Res Rep

RCHM, 1962 *An inventory of the historical monuments in the city of York vol I:* Eburacum, Roman York, Royal Commission on Historical Monuments

Reece, R, 1986 The coins, in *Cirencester Excavations III; Houses in Roman Cirencester* (A McWhirr), 100–3, Cirencester

Rees, S E, 1979 *Agricultural implements in Prehistoric and Roman Britain*, BAR, **69**

Rigby, V, 1980 The coarse pottery, in *Rudston Roman Villa* (I M Stead), Yorks Arch Soc Monogr, Leeds

Robertson, A, 1975 Coarseware, in *Bar Hill: A Roman fort and its finds*, BAR, **16**, 138–68

Rogers, G B, 1974 *Poteries sigillées de la Gaule centrale, I: les motifs non figurés*, Gallia supplement **28**

Rye, O S, 1976 Keeping your temper under control; material and the manufacture of Papuan pottery, *Archaeology and Physical Anthropology in Oceania*, **11**(2), 106–37

Sanders, J, 1973 *Late Roman shell-gritted ware in Southern Britain*, unpublished undergraduate dissertation, London Institute of Archaeology

— 1979 The Roman pottery, in *Iron Age and Roman settlements at Farmoor, Oxfordshire* (G Lambrick and M Robinson), CBA Res Rep, **32**, 46–54, London

Saville, G E, 1986 *Alcester – a history*, Alcester and District Local History Society

Savory, H N, 1971 *Excavations at Dinorben 1965–9*, Cardiff

Schofield, J, and Leech, R, 1987 *Urban archaeology in Britain*, CBA Res Rep, **61**

Sealey, P R, and Tyres, P A, 1989 Olives from Roman Spain: a unique amphora find in British waters *Antiq J* **69**, 53–72

Sherlock, R J, 1957 Excavations at Deritend, *Trans Birmingham Warwickshire Archaeol Soc*, **73**, 109–14

Shotton, F W, 1978 Archaeological inferences from the study of alluvium, in the lower Severn-Avon valleys, in *The effect of man on the landscape, the lowland zone* (eds S Limbrey and J G Evans), CBA Res Rep, **21**, 27–32

Silver, I A, 1969 The ageing of domestic animals, in *Science in Archaeology*, 2 ed, (eds D Brothwell and E Higgs), 283–302

Stanfield, J A, 1935 A samian bowl from Bewcastle, with a note on the potters Casurius and Apolauster, *Trans Cumberland Westmoreland Antiq Archaeol Soc n ser*, **35**, 182–205

Stanfield, J A, and Simpson, G, 1958 *Central Gaulish potters*

Stead, I M, and Rigby, V, 1986 *Baldock: the excavation of a Roman and pre-Roman settlement, 1968–1972*, Britannia Monogr Ser, **7**

Strong, D E, 1966 *Greek and Roman gold and silver plate*

Stuiver, M, and Pearson, G, 1986 *Radiocarbon*, **28**, 805–38

Swan, V G, 1984 *The pottery kilns of Roman Britain*, RCHM Suppl series 5, London

Tatton-Brown, T, 1978 Canterbury, *Current Archaeol*, **62**, 78–82

Taylor, S, 1969 Nos 27–33 Bleachfield Street, *West Midlands Archaeol News Sheet*, 12, 16 and 21–22 and 33

— 1969 [Interim report on] Roman Alcester, *W Midlands Archaeol News Sheet*, **12**, 33

— 1972 [Interim report on] Birch Abbey, Alcester, *West Midlands Archaeol News Sheet*, **15**, 14

— 1973 [Summary report on excavations at Alcester], *W Midlands Archaeol News Sheet*, **16**, 22

Theophrastus, *Enquiry into plants* Sir Arthur Hort (ed), 1916, Loeb Classical Library

Trotter, M, and Glaser, G C, 1952 Estimation of stature from longbones of American whites and negroes, *American Journal of Physical Anthropology*, **10**, 463–514

— 1958 A re-evaluation of estimation of stature based on measurements of stature taken during life and of longbones after death, *American Journal of Physical Anthropology*, **16**, 79–123.

Vanderhoeven, M, 1962 *De Romeinse Glasverzameling in het Provinciaal Gallo-Romeis Museum te Tongeren* (Tongeren)

— 1975 *De terra sigillata de Tongeren*, Tongeren

Vertet, H, and Hartley, B R, 1968 Fouilles de Lezoux 1967, *Revue Archéologique du Centre*, **7**, 213–23

Vince, A, 1977 The medieval ceramic industry of the Malvern region, in *Pottery and early commerce* (D P S Peacock), Academic Press

Wacher, J S, 1962 A survey of Romano-British town defences of the early and middle 2nd century, *Archaeol J*, **119**, 103–13

Walden, H W, 1976 A nomenclatural list of the land mollusca of the British Isles, *Journal of Conchology*, **29**, 21–5

Wallace, C, and Webster, P V, 1989 Jugs and lids in black burnished ware, *J Roman Pottery Stud*, **2**, 88–91

Walters, H B, 1908 *Catalogue of the Roman pottery in the Department of Antiquities, British Museum*

Ward, G K, and Wilson, S R, 1986 Procedures for comparing and combining radiocarbon age determinations: a critique, *Archaeometry*, **20**, 19–31

Ward, M, 1989 The samian ware, in *Prestatyn 1984–5, an Iron Age farmstead and Romano-British industrial settlement in North Wales* (K Blockley), BAR, **210**, 139–54

Ward, M, 1993 A summary of the samian ware from excavations at Piercebridge, *J Roman Pottery Stud*, **6**, 15–22.

Ward, M, forthcoming (a) The samian ware, in *Excavations at Piercebridge* (S Large and P R Scott)

Ward, M, forthcoming (b) The samian ware, in *Roman Alcester: northern extramural area* (ed P Booth, J Chadderton, and J Evans) CBA Res Rep

Ward, M, and Carrington, P, 1981 A quantitative study of the pottery from a Roman extra-mural building at Chester, in *Roman pottery research in Britain and north-west Europe* (eds A C Anderson and A S Anderson), BAR Int Ser, **123**, 25–38

Waters, P L, 1976 Romano-British pottery at Great Buckmans Farm, *Trans Worcs Archaeol Soc*, ser 3, **15**, 63–72

Webster, G, 1982 The coarse pottery, in The excavation of a Romano-British rural establishment at Barnsley Park, Gloucestershire, 1961–1979, Part II, *c* AD 360–400+ (G Webster and L Smith), *Trans Bristol and Gloucs Archaeol Soc*, **101**, 1982 (1983), 146–74

— 1983 The function and organisation of late Roman civil defences in Britain, in Maloney and Hobley 1983, 118–20

Webster, P V, 1969 Excavations at Melandra Castle, Derbyshire 1969, *Derbys Archaeol J*, **89**

— 1976 Severn Valley Ware; a preliminary study, *Trans Bristol and Gloucestershire Archaeol Soc*, **94**, 1976 (1977) 18–46

— forthcoming The Segontium pottery, in *Excavations at Segontium 1975–79* (P J Casey, J L Davies, and J Evans)

Webster, W J, 1986 Roman Bronzes from Maryport in the Netherall Collection, *Trans Cumberland Westmoreland Antiq Archaeol Soc*, **86**, 49–70

Wedlake, W J, 1982 *The excavation of the shrine of Apollo at Nettleton, Wiltshire 1956–1971*, Rep Res Comm Soc Antiq London, **40**

Wells, A K, and Kirkaldy, J F, 1966 *Outline of historical geology*. Thomas Murby: London, 5ed

Wheeler, R E M, 1930 *London in Roman times* London Museum Catalogue, no 3 (reprinted 1946)

— 1936 *Verulamium: A Belgic and two Roman cities*, Rep Res Comm Soc Antiq London, **11**

Williams, D F, 1977 The Romano-British Black Burnished industry: an essay on characterization by heavy mineral analysis in *Pottery and early commerce* London (D P S Peacock)

Bibliography

Williams, D, 1978 Plant macrofossil contents of Medieval pits at Sewer Lane, Hull, in Excavations at Sewer Lane, Hull (D Armstrong), *East Riding Archaeology*, **3**, 18–32

Wilson, D M, 1963 A Saxon penannular bracelet from Alcester, *Transactions*, **81**, 142–3

Woodfield, C, 1983 The pottery in Brown, A E, and Woodfield, C, Excavations at Towcester, Northamptonshire: The Alchester Road suburb, *Northants Arch*, **18**, 74–100

Woods, A, 1983 The old pot boiler, *Bulletin of the Experimental Firing Group*, **2**, 25–31

Woodwards, L, and Greig, J R A, 1985 Landscape changes over the last two thousand years deduced from remains in Alcester, Coulters Garage, in Booth 1985, 91–5

Wright, R P, and Hassall, M W C, 1971 Roman Britain in 1970 II: Inscriptions, *Britannia*, **2**, 289–304

Young, C R, 1977 *The Oxfordshire Roman pottery industry*, BAR **43**, Oxford

— 1980 The late Roman finewares in The Romano-British site at Wycomb, Andoversford, excavations 1969–70 (B Rawes) *Transactions of the British and Gloucestershire Archaeological Society,* **98**, 11–55

Zienkiewicz, J D, 1986 *The legionary fortress baths at Caerleon II: the finds*

Index

Notes

1. Gateway supermarket site is abbreviated to GSS, Gas House Lane to GHL.
2. Main page references are in **bold**. Page references in *italics* indicate pages where illustrations/tables/plates can be found. There may also be textual references on these pages.
3. Bibliographical references are not indexed, and there are no separate entries for Roman or Romano-British references.

Acorn House, Evesham Street, pottery *23*
age structure
  cattle 111
  sheep 127
agriculture
  animal husbandry 111, 115, 127
  evidence for 139
  GHL xv, 87, 120, 121
  iron implements 104, 105, 106, *107, 108*, 122
  ploughmarks 43, 120, 135
  see also crop plants; horticulture
alder *18*
  as piling: bastion 11, 33, 40, 131, 133
  seeds 115
alluviation, GSS 1, 4, 36–7
Alne, River 1, 129
amber glass 115
angle bracket, iron *33*
animal husbandry 111, 115, 127
antefix *58*, 100, *101*
antler working xv, *58*, 110, 111, 112, 122, 138
Antoninus Pius
  coin 137
  Hadrianic-Antonine period pottery 19, 68, 75, 76, *86*
  pottery 19, 72, 75, 76, 77, 126, 130
aquatic plants 114–15
archaeological background **1–3**
Arden Sandstone 1
areas of excavation, GSS
  A 4, 6, 17
    bone 34
    iron *33*
    pottery 20–2, *22, 23*, 24–7, *26, 27*, **29–31**
    Phase I *6*, 11, 20, *22*, 23, 24, 29–30, 35, 36, **37–8**, 39
    Phase IIa *6*, 20, *22*, 23, 24, 29–30, **38–9**
    Phase IIb *6*, 20, *22*, 23, 24, 29–30, 39, **40**, 70
    Phase III *6*, 17, 20, *22*, 23, 24, 31, **40–1**
    Phase IV *6*, 20, *22*, 23, 24, 31, **40–1**
  area 7 (Coulters Garage) 4, *12*
  B 4, 6, 10–11, *33*, 39, 129
    bone 34

clay deposits 37
  iron *33*
  pottery 19, 20, *21*, 22–4, *23, 25, 27*, **27–9**, *28*, 30, 40, 58
  Phase A *6*, 38
    bank (earthworks) 4, *8–10*, 35, 36, **37**
  Phase B *6*, 19, 20, 35, 36
  Phase C *6*, 17, 19, 20, *21*, 23, 24, 27–9, **40–1**
C 17, *33*
  bone 34
  iron *33*
  pottery 19, 20–2, *22, 23*, 24–7, *26, 27*, **29–31**
  structures 4–6
  Phase I *6*, 11, *12*, 19, 20, *22*, 23, 24, 29–30, 35, 36, **37–8**, 39
  Phase IIa *6*, *14*, 19, 20, *22*, 23, 24, 29–30, **38–9**
  Phase IIb *6*, *14*, 19, 20, *22*, 23, 24, 29–30, 39, **40**, 70
  Phase III *6*, 17, 19, 20, *22*, 23, 24, 31, **40–1**
  Phase IV *6*, 19, 20, *22*, 23, 24, 31, **40–1**
D 6, 17, *33*
  bone 34
  clay deposits 37
  iron *33*
  pottery 19, 20–2, *22, 23*, 24–7, *26, 27*, **29–31**
  Phase I *6*, *11, 12, 13*, 19, 20, *22*, 23, 24, 29–30, 35, 36, **37–8**, 39
  Phase IIa *6, 11, 13, 14, 15, 16*, 19, 20, *22*, 23, 24, 29–30, **38–9**
  Phase IIb *6, 11, 14*, 19, 20, *22*, 23, 24, 29–30, 39, **40**, 70
  Phase III *6, 11*, 17, 19, 20, *22*, 23, 24, 31, **40–1**
  Phase IV *6*, 17, 19, 20, *22*, 23, 24, 31, **40–1**
E 6, *16*, 17, *33*
  bone 34
  iron *33*
  pottery 19, 20–2, *22, 23*, 24–7, *26, 27*, **29–31**
  Phase I *6*, 11, *12*, 19, 20, *22*, 23, 24, 29–30, 35, 36, **37–8**, 39
  Phase IIa *6, 14*, 19, 20, *22*, 23, 24, 29–30, **38–9**
  Phase IIb *6, 14, 16*, 19, 20, *22*, 23, 24, 29–30, 39, **40**, 70
  Phase III *6*, 17, 19, 20, *22*, 23, 24, 31, **40–1**
  Phase IV *6*, 19, 20, *22*, 23, 24, 31, **40–1**
Arrow, River 36, 137
arrowhead, iron *32, 33*, 34
Ashville 111
asparagus xv, *58*, 112, 114, 122, 135, 136

bag beakers *see under* pottery
Bainesse Farm, Catterick 89
Baptist Chapel, Alcester *2, 3, 135*, 136, 138
Bar Hill: BB1 pottery forms 72, *73*
Bard's Walk, Stratford 98
barley 112

Barnsley Park, Gloucestershire: pottery 74, 83, 88, 89, *90*, 97
Baromix site: samian ware 75, 76–7, *123*
Barton Court Farm 111
bastion (external tower), GSS xv, 1, *6*, 11–17, *14*, *16*, **40**, 130, **133–4**
  bone finds 34
  construction xvi, 6, 39, 132, 133, 138
  wood piling 6, 11–16, 33, 36, 40, 131, 133
Bath: pottery 79, *80*, 81, 88, 89, *91*
Baynard's Castle, London: defensive wall 130, 132
Beadlam, North Yorkshire: pottery *80*
beads, glass 115, 116, *118*
beakers
  glass 116, *118*
  see also under pottery
beam slots
  external tower (bastion) 11–16
  GHL 47, *51*, *56*, 121
  Lloyd's Bank 139
  town wall, GSS 11
beans 112, 136
Bear Inn, The *2*, 3, *128*, *135*, 136, 138
Bedfordshire: pottery supplies 89
beetroot, charred, GSS xv, *18*, 35, 38, 136
berms
  GHL earthworks 45, 120, 128
  Lincoln 92
Binchester, Co Durham *80*, 92
Birch Abbey
  iron objects 104
  market area 134
  pottery 41, 75, 79, 95
  No. 6
    animal bone 126, 127
    pottery *23*, *27*, 77, *123*
bird bones 111–12
Birmingham 1, 81
Bishopstone, Sussex: pottery 88, 89, *91*
Bitterne, Hampshire: defensive wall 133
blades, iron *33*, 105, *107*, 108
Bleachfield Street
  fort 139
  occupation 40
  pottery 78
  silver bracelet 41, 98
  Nos 1–5
    agricultural evidence 139
    animal bone 126, 127
    dating/chronology 139
    pottery 23, 24, 69–70, 71, 78, 81, 82, 83, 96, 97
    worked bone 110
  No. 21: pottery 40
  No. 64: pottery *23*, *27*
  see also Baromix site
bodkins, bone 109, *110*
bone, animal **126–7**, 139
  GHL *58*, *92*, **111–12**, 122, 123, 126, 127
  GSS *18*, **34**, 39, 126
bone, human
  GHL *58*, **111**, 122
  GSS 11, *18*, **34**, 38

bone, worked
  GHL *58*, 106, **109–11**, *110*
  GSS *18*
boreholes, GSS 4, *5*, 6, 10, 17, *18*, 35, 36, 37
bottles, glass 115–16, *117–18*, 124
bowls
  glass 116, *118*
  see also under pottery
bracelets *18*
  bone 109, 110–11, *110*
  shale 36
  silver 41, 98
Bradley Hill, Somerset: pottery 89, *91*, 97
bramble seeds 123
brass 40
Bridge End, Warwick 98
Brill, Oxfordshire: pottery 98
British Standard 1377 36
brooches
  copper alloy 102–3, *103*, 104, 123, 124, 139
  Polden Hill, GSS *18*, 33, 38
Brougham cemetery, Cumbria 77
bucket handle mount, iron 105, 106, *107*
Buckinghamshire: pottery manufacture 24
Builder's Yard site, High Street *125*, *126*, *135*, 137
building materials 138
  GHL *58*, **100–2**, *121*
  GSS *18*, **33**, 41
  see also structural ironwork
buildings **138**
  cill beam 45, 47, 48, 121, 126, 138
  function and status 127
  hypocausted 92, 100, *121*, 138
  timber/stone progression in 138
  GHL 120–1, *121*
    lack of complete 43
    A 45, *46*, *50*, *55*, 121, 137
      ironwork 105
    B 45, *46*, *50*, *55*, 121, 137
      ironwork 105
      tiles *101*
    C 45, *46*, 48, *50*, *51*, *56*, 121, 137
      ironwork 105
    D 45–7, *46*, 48, 119, 121, 137
      ironwork 105
      tiles 100
    E *46*, 47, *49*, *56*, 102, 121, 137, 138
      tiles 100
    F *46*, 48, *51*, *56*, 121, 137
      ironwork 105
  GSS 11, 37–8
    wooden shed, GSS 17
  Tibbet's Close 136, 137, 138
  see also granary buildings; structures; timber
Bulls Head Yard *2*, 3, 4, *5*
  earthworks *128*, 129
  radiocarbon dating 36, 134
  town wall 132
Bunting, John: collection 137
Burgh Castle, Norfolk
  shore fort 134
  wall defences 131

burials
    GHL
        pig *56*
        town wall rampart 49, *58*, 106, 111, 122
    GSS 4, *18*, 34, 38
    Tongres, Belgium 116
    York 116
burnt daub *58*, *102*, **102**
Burton Dassett, Warwickshire 98
butchery 34, 39, 111, 122, 127, 139
Butter Street
    coin hoard *135*, 137, 139
    site layout 137

Caerleon: fortress baths 116
Caerwent: defensive walls 134
Caistor-on-the-Wolds: town defences 134
Canterbury, wall at 132
Cape Taenarum, Greece 100
car parks 4, 6, 128, 129, 132
Carausius: coin 137
Carpow, Tayside 95
cat bones 111
Catsgore, Somerset, pottery 88, 89, 95
Catterick
    Bainesse Farm 89
    pottery 83, 89, 95
cattle bones 34, 92, 111, 112, 122, 127, 139
cemeteries
    Alcester xvi, 98, 140
    Brougham 77
    Lankhills, Winchester 116
    see also burials
ceramics *see* pottery
cereal pollen 35
cereals *18*, 35, 40, 112, 134
chalk: packing on defensive walls 130
charcoal
    concentrations 135
    copper alloy working *18*, 40
    wall construction 130
charred plant remains *see under* plant remains
Chelmsford: pottery 88, *90*
Chester 71–2
    Castle Street 76, 77
Chesterton: pottery 78
Chichester 87, *88*
Chilvers Coton, Warwickshire: pottery 98
chisel, iron 105, *107*, 108
cill beams
    building evidence 126
    GHL buildings 45, 47, 48, 121, 138
Cirencester (*Corinium*)
    bastions 133
    civitas capital 1
    pottery 70, *71*, 74, 79, *80*, 83, *86*, 87, 88, *91*
    villas 139
civitas xvi, 1, 139
    defence needs of 134
Claudius II Gothicus: coin 137
clay
    dump: GSS 11, 38

floors, GHL buildings 45, *51*, 121
    loam 43, 47
    and peat deposits 1
    town wall construction 11, 39
coffins 49, 106, 111, 122
coins 87, 136
    and dating 39, 40, 133, 134, 137
    GHL *58*, *109*, **109**, 124, 133
    GSS **34**, 38, 137
    hoards
        Butter Street *135*, 137, 139
        GHL xv, 40, 49, *58*, 68, 69, 109, 122, 137, 139
        GSS xv, *18*, 40, 109, 122, 139
    Iron Age 136
Colchester
    defences 135
    rosso antico 100
Cologne: pottery products 78
comb-making 111, 112, 122
cooking pots *see* frying pans *and under* pottery
copper alloy objects
    GHL *58*, **102–4**, *103*, 106, 123, 124, 139
    GSS 17, *18*, *32*, **33**
copper alloy working
    GHL 121
    GSS xv, *18*, **34**, 40
Corbridge: ironwork hoard 106
Corinium see Cirencester
Cornwall: pottery trade 72
Cotswold sites 111
Coulters Garage *2*, 3, *5*, 30, 39
    area 7 4, *12*
    coins and dating 39, 40, 133
    finds 40
    organic deposits 1, 36, 37, 135
    plant remains 35, 115
    structures 4–6, 37, 38
    town wall 132
    see also granary buildings
counters
    bone 110
    ceramic 77, 92–3, 95
craft tools, iron 104, 106, *107*, *108*
Crambeck pottery industry, East Yorkshire 95, 133
crop plants *18*, 35, 40, 112, *113*, 115, 134
crozier heads 41, 98
crucibles, copper alloy 34
cups
    glass 116, *118*
    see also under pottery

dairy products 111
dating/chronology
    and coins 39, 40, 133, 134, 137
    earthwork defences 130
    GHL **123–4**, 126
    occupation: NE of town **136–7**
    pottery 136–7
    of towers 134
    town wall 39, 42, 133

dating/chronology (*cont.*)
  see also dendrochronology; Gas House Lane site
    (periods/phases); Gateway supermarket site
    (phases); radiocarbon dating
daub 138
  burnt *58*, *102*, **102**
Davis, Bernard 1, *135*, 136, 138
  Collection **125–6**, 137
deer bones 34, 111, 112
defences and defended area **xv–xvi**, **125–40**
  see also bastion; earthwork defences; wall, town
dendrochronology
  bastion xv, 40, 133
  timber piling
    Roman walls 130
    town wall
      GHL 42, 49, *58*, 122
      GSS 11, 39
Devensian gravels 36
discs, ceramic, GHL 77, 92–3
dishes *see under* pottery
ditches 29
  lack of 129, 134
Dobunni xvi, 1, 139
dog bones 34, 111
domestic equipment, iron 104, 105, 106, *107*, *108*, 122
Dorchester: pottery 70
Dorset: BB1 pottery 69, 70
dress fittings, iron 105
drinking vessels
  glass 116, *118*
  see also under pottery
Droitwich (*Salinae*) 1, 96
drying/malting kilns 40, 98
  GHL xv, 49, *57*, 106, 112, 114, 122
Dukes Place, London: defensive wall 131, 132

earthwork defences 1, **127–30**, *128*
  circuit 129–30
  construction 138
    GHL 43–5, **120**
  dating/chronology 130, 134
    GHL 126
  decay, GSS 10–11
  Fosse: Colchester 135
  GHL xv, 37, *53*, *55*, 120, *128*
  GSS 4, *6*, *128*
  ironwork finds, GHL 106
  occupation 136
  Phase A bank (area B), GSS 4, *8–10*, 35, 36, **37**
  ramparts 128, 129
    GHL 59, 136
  revetment 128
  structure 127–9
ecological remains
  GHL *58*, **112–15**
  GSS *18*, **35–6**
  see also plant remains; snails; timber
elder 35, 114, 115, 123
elm 115
emmer 35, 112
English Heritage 4, 42

Ettington 1
Evesham Street
  Acorn House: pottery *23*
  No. 34
    animal bone 126, 127
    pottery *23*, *27*
Exeter 72, 111

faeces, human 114, 123
fair, annual 41
Farmoor, Oxfordshire 111
Faustina II: coin 137
fences 45, 47, 128
figs 114, 123
file, iron 105, 106, *107*
filings, iron 106
finger rings, copper alloy 103–4, *103*
fish remains 111, 112, 122, 123, 127, 139
flagons *see under* pottery
flasks, glass 116–17, *118*
flint: packing (defensive walls) 130
flood barriers: pottery *123*
floors
  clay, GHL buildings 45, 121
  opus signinum 136, 138
  tiles, GHL 100
  traces, GSS 38
flue tiles 100
food remains
  GHL 127
  GSS 34
footrings 77
Fosse earthworks, Colchester 135
fowl, domestic 111
Frocester, Gloucestershire 111
frying pans, iron/copper alloy 106, *107*, 108

Gallienus: coin 137
gaming counters *see* counters
garden crops xv, *58*, 112, 114, 120, 122, 135
Gas House Lane site (GHL) **xv**, 1, *2*, 3, 36, 37, 39,
    40, **42–124**
  periods
    dating/chronology *44*
    A 43, *47*, 59, **120**
      plant remains 114
    B 43–5, *55*, **120**
      earthworks 128
      pottery 59
    C 43, 45–8, *55*, 120, **120–2**
      animal bone 111, 127
      ironwork 105, 106, *108*
      material comparisons by phases *92*
      plant remains 112
      pottery 59–68, 69, *72*, *73*, 78, *79*, 80, 81, 82,
        83, 87, 88, 95
      Phase C11 45, 68
        pottery 59, 68, 70, 78
      Phase C12 45, *46*, *50*, *55*, 83
        buildings 137
        ironwork 106
        pottery 68, 71, 72, 77, 82, *84–5*, *89*, 91

Gas House Lane site (GHL); Period C (*cont.*)
    Phase C13 45, *46, 50, 55*, 83
      buildings 137
      ironwork 106
      pottery 68, 72, 73, 78, 82, 83, *84–5*, 88, *89,*
        91, *97*
      tiles 101
    Phase C14 45, *46, 50, 51*, 83
      buildings 137
      ironwork 106
      pottery 59, 68, 72, 75, 81, 82, 83, *84–5, 89,*
        91
      tiles 101
    Phase C15 45, *46, 50*, 83
      buildings 138
      ironwork 106
      pottery 68, 81, 82, 83, *84–5, 89*, 91
    Phase C21 45, *47*, 68
      ironwork 106
      pottery 59, 70, 77, *78*, 81, *89*
      tiles 101
    Phase C22 45, *46, 48*
      buildings 137
      ironwork 106–7
      pottery 59, 71, 72, 73, 77, *78, 84–5, 89*, 91
      tiles 100
    Phase C23 *46, 47, 49, 56*
      buildings 138
      mortar 102
      pottery 59, 68, 77, *78*, 81, 83, *84–5, 89*, 91
      tiles 100, 101
    Phase C24 *46, 49*
      pottery 68, *78*, 91, 92
      tiles 100, 101
    Phase C31 45, 48
      pottery 59, 68, 70, 81, 82
    Phase C32 *46*, 48, *51, 56*
      buildings 121, 137
      pottery 68, 71, 75, 77, *78*, 82, 83, *84–5, 89*, 91
      tiles 102
    Phase C33 45, *46*, 48, *51, 56*
      buildings 121, 137
      ironwork 108
      pottery 59, 68, 72, 73, 77, 78, 81, 82, 83,
        84–5, 88, *89*, 91, 92
      tiles 102
      worked bone 109
  D 43, 48–9, *56*, **122**
    animal bone 111, 127
    antlers 110
    bone working 112
    coin hoard 109
    ironwork 105–6, *108*
    material comparisons by phases *92*
    plant remains 112
    pottery 68, 69, 70, 71, 73, 78, 79, 80, 81, 82,
      83, *84–5*, 87, 88, *89*, 95, *96*
    tiles 101
    Phase D1 48
      human burial 111
    Phase D2 49, 122
      flue tile 100

      pottery 68, 69, 71, 78, 81, 82
      tiles 102
  E 43, 49, *57*, **122–3**
    ironwork 106, *108*
    pottery 69, *78*, 82, 83, 91
    stone finds 120
  see also earthwork defences; pottery; wall, town
    and GHL references within entries
Gatcombe, Gloucestershire, defences 37, 129
Gateway supermarket site (GSS) **xv**, 1, *2*, 3, **4–41**,
  120
  Phases (area B)
    A *6, 33*, 38
      bank (earthworks) 4, *8–10*, 35, 36, **37**
    B *6*, 19, 20, *33*
    C *6*, 17, 19, 20, *21*, 23, 24, 27–9, *33*, **40–1**
  Phases (areas A, C, D, E)
    I *6, 11, 12, 13*, 19, 20, *22*, 23, 24, 29–30, *33*, 35,
      36, **37–8**, 39
    IIa *6, 11, 13, 14, 15, 16, 17*, 19, 20, *22*, 23, 24,
      29–30, *33*, **38–9**
    IIb *6, 11, 14, 16*, 17, 19, 20, *22*, 23, 24, 29–30,
      33, 39, **40**, 70
    III *6, 11*, 17, 19, 20, *22*, 23, 24, 31, *33*, **40–1**
    IV *6*, 17, 19, 20, *22*, 23, 24, 31, *33*, **40–1**
  see also areas of excavation; bastion; earthwork
    defences; pottery; wall, town *and* GSS
    references within entries
geology, GSS **1**
glass objects
  GHL *58*, **115–18**, *117–18*, 124
  GSS *18*, **36**
glassware, GHL 87, 88
Gloucester: town defences 130, 134
glume 112, 115
goads, iron 105
goat remains 34, 111
gold coins 137
gorse 114
grain: collection/storage 134
granary buildings, GSS
  large stone building xv, xvi, 1, 4, *6, 11, 12–13*,
    33, 37–8, 132, 139
    construction 35, 134
    dating 133
    demolished *17*, 39
    mortar *18*
    pottery 30
    timber (possible second) 4, 37, 38, 134
grassland plants 35, 115
gravel: town wall packing, GSS 11
gravel 'island', GSS *6–10, 7*, 36
Great Casterton, Leicestershire: defensive walls
  134
Great Dunmow, Essex: pottery 88, *90*

Hadrian, Emperor
  coin 137
  pottery
    Hadrianic-Antonine period 19, 68, 75, 76, *86*
    Trajanic-Hadrianic period 77
hare bones 111, 112

hawthorn 35, 115
hazel 112
hedgerow plants 115
hemlock, charred, GSS xv, *18*, 35, 38, 136
Henley Street
    No. 38 *2*, 3, *135*, 136
    Old Police Station 2, 3, *135*, 136–7, 138
hides, cattle 111
High Street, Alcester 130, 133, 137
    Builder's Yard site *125*, *126*, *135*, 137
    No. 27 1, *2*, 3, *135*, 137
        pottery 126
        structures 136, 138
hillfort: Oversley Castle (Iron Age) 139
hobnails, iron *33*, 105, 106
horn cores 111, 127
horse bones 34, 111
horticulture xv, 121, 136
    see also agriculture; garden crops
hypocausts 92, 100, *121*, 138

Ilchester
    pottery *86*, 87
    timber revetment: defences 128
imbrices 100, *101*
Iron Age
    coins 136
    hillfort: Oversley Castle 139
    marsh: Coulters Garage 1
    pottery 82, 130, 135, 136
        GHL 43, 59, 120
    Tibbet's Close activity 126
    timber availability 40
    woodland 35
iron objects
    GHL *58*, **104–8**, *107*, *108*, 122
    GSS *18*, *32*, **33–4**
iron slag
    GHL *58*, **109**
    GSS *18*
ivory crozier head 98
ivy 115

jars *see under* pottery
Jepchott, E W 137
joiner's dog, iron 105
Jones, Martin 42
jugs
    glass 116–17, *118*
    see also under pottery
Jurassic Lower Lias 33

keys, iron 105, 106, *107*, *108*
kilns
    drying/malting 40, 98
        GHL xv, 49, *57*, 106, 112, 114, 122
    see also under pottery
Kingscote 111
kitchen debris, GSS 34, 39
knives
    bone-handled *18*, 106
    iron 105

Langton Down brooch 102, *103*
Lankhills Cemetery, Winchester 116
lead: in samian ware, GHL 76
lead objects
    GHL *58*, **104**
    GSS *18*, **33**
Leintwardine: rampart timber lacing 128
Les Martres-de-Veyre: samian ware 59, 75, 76
Lezoux: samian ware 76
lids *see under* pottery
limes frontier (Germany) 104
limescale/sooting deposits: pottery *87*
limestone
    outcrops 98
    packing: town wall 11
    in pottery 81
    tiles 100
linchpin, iron 105, *107*, 108
Lincoln
    early defences 128
    town wall 92
Lloyd's Bank site 41, 98, 139
London
    Angel Court: pottery *90*
    bastions 133, 134
    defensive wall 133
        Baynard's Castle 130, 132
        Dukes Place 131, 132
    pottery 78, 88, 89
    Riverside wall *90*, 130, 131

macrofossils, plant 114, 115
Mahany's
    site D 139
    site F 139
    site G 139
    site K 2, 3, *128*, *129*
    site M xv, 2, 3, *135*
        earthworks 127, *128*, 129, 130
        occupation 136
        pottery *123*, 126, 133
        structures 136
        town wall 39, 131, 132
Malt Mill Lane site 2, 3, 98, 122, *135*
    earthworks *128*, 129
    occupation 136
    pottery 125, 126
    town wall 132
    watching brief 1
malting/drying kilns 40, 98
    GHL xv, 49, *57*, 106, 112, 114, 122
Malverns: pottery 98
Manpower Services Commission 4
marble 100, *121*, 139
market charter, granting of 41
Market site, Alcester 2, 3, 4, *5*, 36
    earthworks *128*, 129
marsh deposits 4
medicinal plants 35, 136
medieval period
    drying kiln *see* drying/malting kilns (GHL)
    late: stone-lined pit, GHL 49, *57*, 98, 106

medieval period (*cont.*)
  town establishment 4
  see also under Gas House Lane site (Period E);
    Gateway supermarket site (Phases C/III/IV)
    and under pottery
Meeting Lane
  No. 1 *2*, *3*, *135*, 136, 138
  No. 9 *2*, *3*
    earthworks *128*, 129
    town wall 132
  No. 11 *2*, *3*
    earthworks *128*, 129
    town wall 132
  see also Baptist Chapel
Melandra Castle: first defences 128
Mercian Mudstone 1, 36, 120
metalwork 98
  GHL *58*, **102–9**, 121, 122, 138
  GSS xv, 17, *18*, *32*, **33–4**, 38, 40, 41, 138
    in hollow 30
  pottery repairs 76, 77
  see also coins
method of investigation
  GHL **42–3**
  GSS **4–6**
mice bones 112
Midland Bank *2*, *3*, 4, *5*
Mildenhall: defences 133, 134, 135
Moorfield area 1, 36
Moorfield Marsh 4, *5*, 129, 138
Moorfield Road 36, 37, 120, 133
mortar
  GHL *58*, **102**
  layers, in defensive walls 131, 132
  Malt Mill Lane 136
  packing: external tower, GSS 16
  surfaces/floors, GSS 6, 17, *18*, 30, 38
  town wall foundation, GSS 11, *18*
mosaics, patterned 138
mount, bucket handle (iron) 105, 106, *107*
Much Hadham pottery 97

nail puller, iron 105, 106, *107*
nails
  copper alloy 106
  iron *32*, *33*, *58*, 104, 105–6
Neatham, Hampshire: pottery 87, *88*, 89, *90*, 96
necklace 116
needles
  bone 109, *110*
  iron 105
Nene Valley pottery 122
New Fresh Wharf: pottery 76

oak
  piles: town wall 11, 33, 39, 40, 130, 131, 133
  remains
    GHL 114, 123
    GSS *18*
oats 112
oil, trade 95
Old Penrith, Cumbria 72

Old Police Station, Henley Street *2*, 3, *135*, 136–7,
  138
olive 130
opus signinum floors 136, 138
organic deposits, GSS 1, 36
ovens, drying *see* kilns
Oversley Castle: Iron Age hillfort 139
oxgoads, iron 105, 106, *107*
oxshoe, iron 106
oysters 122, 127, 139

palette 100, 138
peat deposits, GSS 6, 7, 36
Pevensey: Saxon Shore fort 130, 131
Piddington: villa excavation 97
Piercebridge, Co Durham: samian ware 75, 76, 77
pig bones 34, 111, 112, 122, 123
pig burial *56*
pilae *58*, 92, 100, *121*, 138
piling, timber *see under* timber
pins
  bone 109, *110*
  iron 105
pitchers *see under* pottery
pits
  earthworks 129
  GHL 43, 48, 59, 98, 100
    stone-lined, late medieval 49, *57*, 98, 106
  GSS 17
    127 (area B): pottery 27–9
    areas A/D 6
  pottery 130
  see also tanning pit
plant remains
  charred 135
  GHL 122–3
    charred xv, *58*, **112–14**, *113–14*, 120, 122
    from trench A **114–15**
  GSS 6, 40
    charred xv, *18*, **35**, 38, 136
    waterlogged *18*, **35**, 115
plaster 47, **102**, 136, 138
plate brooches, copper alloy *103*, 104
ploughmarks 43, 120, 135
Polden Hill brooch, GSS *18*, 33, 38
pollen analysis
  Coulters Garage 40
  GHL *58*, 114, 115
  GSS *35*, 36
Pompei: ironwork 105
Portchester
  Castle 77
  pottery 88, *91*
  Saxon Shore fort 133, 134
  wall defences 40, 131
post pads: GHL buildings 45
post-and-slot construction, GSS 6, 38
postholes
  earthworks 129
  GHL 43, 45, *46*, 47, 48, *51*, 120, 121, 138
  pottery 130
  town wall 131

Index

pottery
    amphorae 27
        comparative functional analysis *86*
        GHL **69**, 95
            functional analysis *84–5*
        GSS *21*, *22*, *27*, 29
    Antonine period 19, 72, 75, 76, 77, 126, 130
    bag beakers
        GHL
            barbotine-decorated *61*, 78
            Nene Valley ware 68
    Banbury-Brackley type ware, GHL 98
    beakers 27
        1st-century carinated 130
        comparative functional analysis *80*, *86*
        Nene Valley ware 78
        GHL 96
            BB1 72, *73*, 83
            cornice rimmed *61*, 78
            functional analysis 83, *84–5*
            indented 78
            necked *61*, 78
            Nene Valley ware *79*
            Oxfordshire colour-coated *79*
            Oxfordshire red colour-coated 80
            'Rhenish' type *61*, 78
            rouletted *61*, 78
            samian ware 76
            sub-cornice rimmed 78
        GSS 24–7, *25*, *26*, *27*
            Nene Valley colour-coated 21, 29, *30*
            Nene Valley ware 27–9, *28*
            Oxfordshire colour-coated 27, *28*
            Oxfordshire pentice-moulded 29
    Black ware, GHL 98, *99*, 100
    Black-Burnished ware (BB1) 60, 72, *125*, 126,
        133, 136
        at Catsgore 89
        at Cirencester 70, *71*
        obtuse-lattice 130, 136
        GHL 59, *60*, 68, **69–73**, *73*, 89, 95, 123
            copies 83
            East Gaulish 68
            frequencies of forms (period C) 72
            repairs 89
            sooting *60*, 87
        GSS 20, *21*, *22*, *23*, 24, *25*, *26*, 27, *28*, 29, 31,
            37, 38, 70, 130
    bowls 27, 125, *126*
        BB1 136
        BB1 flange-rimmed 126
        carinated 27
        comparative functional analysis *86*
        flanged 83
        functional analysis: various groups *80*
        Rheinzabern 77
        GHL
            BB1 *73*
            BB1 flange-rimmed 72, 73
            BB1 flanged 68
            fine ware 96
            flanged *66*, *67*, 79, 82, 83
                functional analysis 83, *84–5*
                grooved-rimmed flanged 95
                Malvernian ware, late 98, *99*
                moulded (samian ware) 76
                Nene Valley ware *79*, 80
                Oxfordshire colour-coated ware *79*
                Oxfordshire ware 80
                samian ware 76
                Severn Valley ware *63–5*, 82
                Severn Valley ware flanged *64*, 68
                shell-tempered *74*
                South-Western brown slip ware 79
                wide-mouthed 83, *84–5*
        GSS 24, *25*, *26*, *27*
            BB1 27, *28*, 29, 37
            BB1 with dropped flange 130
            carinated *25*, *26*, *27*
            flanged 24
                Nene Valley colour-coated 21
            mortaria 24
            Nene Valley colour-coated ware 21, *28*, 29
            Nene Valley grey-coated ware *30*, 31
            Oxfordshire colour-coated miniature 29, *30*
            Oxfordshire colour-coated ware 24, 27, *28*, 29
    burnished grey wares 97
    Cistercian ware, GHL 98, *99*, 100
    coarse buff storage jar, GSS *21*, *22*, *25*, *26*
    coarse reduced sandy cooking pot ware 98
    coarse wares 89, 130
        Cirencester *71*
        GHL 59, 69, 73, 96–7, 100, 123
            repairs 89
        GSS 20, 22, **23–4**, 30
    colour-coated *mortaria*, GHL *62*, 68
    colour-coated wares *61*, 69, 81, 97
        GHL *61*, 68, 69, 78–9, *79*, 80, 95
        GSS 20, *21*, *22*, 23, 24, *25*, *26*, 27, *28*, 29, *30*
    cooking pots
        coarse reduced sandy ware 98
        GHL 73, 87, 89, 96, *99*, 100
        GSS 24, 40
            BB1 27, *28*, 29
    counters, GHL 77, 92–3, 95
    cross-joins, GHL 89–92
    cups 27
        'Tudor Green' 98
        GHL
            Cistercian ware 98, *99*, 100
            hunt *61*, 78
            samian ware 76
            stamped samian 77
        GSS 24
    dating 136–7
    Davis Collection **125–6**
    decoration
        barbotine-decorated bag beaker, GHL *61*,
            78
        BB1 126
            GHL 59, 69, 73, 95, 123
            obtuse-lattice 130, 136
        on jars 126
        Nene Valley, GHL 59, 68

156

pottery; decoration (*cont.*)
  samian ware 75
    GHL 76
  Devonshire granite-tempered ware 70
  discs, GHL 92–3
  dishes 27, 125, *126*
    BB1 133, 136
    comparative functional analysis *86*
    functional analysis: various groups *80*
    GHL
      BB1 *73*
      BB1 flange-rimmed 72, 73
      BB1 grooved rim 72
      flange-rimmed 95
      functional analysis 83, *84–5*
      Nene Valley ware *79*, 80
      oxidized *66*, 82
      samian ware *66*, 76
      Severn Valley ware *63–5*, 82
      shell-tempered *60*, 73, *74*
      straight-walled *66*, 83
    GSS *25*, *26*, *27*
      Nene Valley colour-coated ware 21
      Oxfordshire colour-coated ware *28*, 29
  Dorset Black-Burnished ware, GSS *21*, *22*
  drinking vessels 27
    GHL 83
    GSS 24, *27*
  English stoneware, GHL 98
  fine wares 97
    GHL *61*, 69, **77–80**, **87–9**, *89*, 95, 96,
      121–2
    GSS 20, **20–3**, *23*, 24, 30, 40
    various sites *80*, *90–1*
  flagons 27, *126*
    comparative functional analysis *86*
    functional analysis: various groups *80*
    GHL
      functional analysis 83
      Nene Valley ware *79*
      Oxfordshire colour-coated ware *79*
      oxidized *66*, 81, *82*
      Severn Valley ware *63–5*, 82
      white-slipped ware *66*, **82**
    GSS 25
      Oxfordshire colour-coated ware 27, *28*,
        29
      white slipped oxidized *21*, *22*
      white-slip *25*
  Flavian period *86*
    GHL 75, 82
  Flavian-Trajanic period 19
  functional analysis **83–92**, *84–6*, *88*
  GHL xv, 41, **58–97**, *60–7*, *94*, 126, 133, 139
    taphonomy **89–92**
  glassware, GHL *89*
  graffiti, GHL 76, *94*, 95
  grey-coated ware, GSS *21*, *22*, *25*, *26*, *30*, 31
  greywares 70, *71*, 89, *96*, *97*, 125, 126
    GHL 59, *66*, 73, 83, 96, 98
      sooting *66*, 87
  gritted wares, GHL **80**

GSS **19–33**, 40, 126, 133
Hadrianic-Antonine period 19, 68, 75, 76,
  86
handmade wares, GHL **82**
Harrold shell-tempered wares, GHL *60*, 96
Iron Age 82, 130, 135, 136
  GHL 43, 59, 120
jars 27, 125, *126*
  3rd-century fragment 130
  BB1 126
  comparative functional analysis *86*, 87
  constricted-necked *86*, *126*
  functional analysis: various groups *80*
  obtuse lattice decoration 126
  wide-mouthed *126*
  GHL *66*, *67*, 68, 83, 87
    BB1 *60*, 68, 69, 72, *73*, 83
    constricted-necked 59, *65*, *82*, 83, *84–5*
    everted-rimmed storage *60*, 73
    functional analysis 83, *84–5*
    greyware *66*, 83
    Malvernian ware 80, *81*, 95–6
    Nene Valley ware *79*
    oxidized *66*, 82
    Severn Valley ware 59, *63–5*, 82, 87
    shell-tempered *74*
    storage: Malvernian ware 80, *81*
    wide-mouthed 83, *84–5*
  GSS 24, *25*, *26*, *27*, *28*, *29*, *30*
    coarse buff storage *21*, *22*, *25*, *26*
    large storage 27, *28*, 29
    Nene Valley Grey ware 27, *28*, 29
    Severn Valley ware 27, *28*, 29
    shell-gritted 27, *28*
    storage *25*, *26*, *27*
jugs *27*
  GHL
    BB1 *60*, 72, *73*
    functional analysis 83, *84–5*
    limescale 87
  GSS *25*
kilns/industries
  Alice Holt 89, 96–7
  Crambeck 95, 133
  Gloucestershire 79
  Great Buckmans Farm 81
  Harrold, Bedfordshire 73, 96, 97
  Malvern Link 81, 95
  Mancetter 81
  Nene Valley 89
  Newlands 81
  Northamptonshire 24, 73
  Oxfordshire 20
  Perry Barr, Birmingham 81
  Rheinzabern: samian ware 19, 59, 76, 77
  School Road, Alcester 32, 40
  Severn Valley 97
  Trent Valley 89, 97
  Trier 19, 76, 78
lids 27, 125, *126*
  comparative functional analysis *86*
  functional analysis: various groups *80*

pottery; lids (*cont.*)
    GHL
        BB1 *60*, 72, *73*
        functional analysis *84–5*
        Malvernian ware 80, *81*, 95–6
        Severn Valley ware *63–5*, 82
    GSS: Nene Valley colour-coated 21, *28*, 29
  local reduced, GSS 20, *21*, *22*, *23*, *25*, *26*, 31
  Malvernian Metamorphic ware, GSS *21*, *22*, 24,
    25, *26*, 31
  Malvernian Metamorphic-tempered ware, GHL
    61, 80, *81*
  Malvernian Severn Valley wares, GHL 96
  Malvernian ware
    GHL 95, 98, *99*
      sooting/limescale *61*, 87
  Mancetter *mortaria*, GHL 59, *62*, 68
  Mancetter whiteware, GHL *67*, 83
  Mancetter whiteware (brown slip), GHL 83
  Mancetter-Hartshill, GHL 81
  Mancetter-Hartshill hammer-headed *mortaria*,
    GSS *30*, 31
  Mancetter-Hartshill *mortaria*
    GHL 95, 121
    GSS *28*, 29
  Mancetter-Hartshill white *mortaria*, GSS *21*, *22*
  Mancetter-Hartshill white ware, GSS *25*, *26*
  material comparisons by phases, GHL *92*
  medieval
    GHL 58, 59, 68, 87, **97–100**, *99*, 122
    GSS 17, *18*, 20, 27, 29, 30, *31*, **31–3**, 40, 97
  mica dusted ware, GHL *61*, 77, 78
  mortaria 27
    comparative functional analysis *86*
    GHL 59, *62*, 68, **81**, 95, 121
      functional analysis 83, *84–5*
    GSS 20, *21*, *22*, 24, *25*, *26*, 27, *28*, 29, *30*, 31
    samian ware 77
      GHL 76, 77
  Much Hadham 97
  Nene Valley colour-coated ware *61*, 69, 97
    GHL 81, 95
    GSS *21*, *22*, 24, *25*, *26*, 27, *28*, 29, *30*
  Nene Valley Grey ware, GSS 27, *28*, 29
  Nene Valley grey-coated ware, GSS *21*, *22*, *25*,
    26, *30*, 31
  Nene Valley *mortaria*, GHL 81
  Nene Valley oxidized, GHL 79
  Nene Valley ware 78, *80*, 96
    GHL 59, *61*, 68, 78, *79*, *80*
    GSS 27–9, *28*
  New Forest ware *80*
  Northamptonshire shell-gritted ware, GSS *21*, *22*
  Oxfordshire colour-coated wall-sided *mortaria*,
    GSS *29*, *30*
  Oxfordshire colour-coated ware 97
    GHL *61*, 78–9, *79*
    GSS 20, *21*, *22*, 23, 24, *25*, *26*, 27, *28*, 29, *30*
  Oxfordshire *mortaria*
    GHL *62*, 68, 81, 95, 121
    GSS *25*, *26*
  Oxfordshire parchment ware, GHL *67*, 83

Oxfordshire red colour-coated *mortaria*, GHL *62*,
  68
Oxfordshire red colour-coated ware, GHL *61*, 68,
  69, 80
Oxfordshire red ware, GHL 80
Oxfordshire red-slipped ware, GHL 96
Oxfordshire rim-sherds 125
Oxfordshire ware 89
  GSS 20, *21*, 23, 40
Oxfordshire white *mortaria*, GSS 20, *21*, *22*
Oxfordshire white ware, GSS 20, *21*, *22*
Oxfordshire white ware *mortaria*, GSS 29, *30*, 31
Oxfordshire white-coated *mortaria* 27, *28*, 29
  GSS *21*, *22*
Oxfordshire white-coated ware, GSS 24, *25*, *26*
Oxfordshire white-slip *mortaria*, GHL *81*
oxidized wares
  GHL *66*, 79, **81–2**, *82*, 95
  GSS *21*, *22*, 24
pink-grogged ware 97
  GHL 80
pitchers, GHL *99*, 100
post-medieval
  GHL 59, **97–100**
  GSS 17, 20, 27, 29
quantification, GHL 59
red-slip *mortaria*, GHL 81
reduced wares 82, *125*
  GHL **82–3**, 95, 96
  GSS 23, 24
repairs, GHL **89**
residual, GHL 58
Rheinzabern bowl 77
Rheinzabern ware, GHL 59
'Rhenish' type ware, GHL *61*, 78
rims *31*, 32–3
  GHL: samian 59
  GSS 21–2
rough laminated buff ware, GHL 98
samian ware *23*, 125, 130
  Central Gaulish (CG) *123*, 126
  East Gaulish (EG) *123*
  South Gaulish (SG) *123*
  GHL *58*, 59, *66*, 68, **74–5**, **74–7**, 78, 89
    Central Gaulish (CG) 75, 76, 77, *78*, 95, 96,
      121–2, 123–4, *123*
    East Gaulish (EG) 75–6, 77, 122, 124
    repairs 76–7, 89
    small finds 92–3, 95
    South Gaulish (SG) 75
  GSS *18*, *19*, **19**, 20, *21*, *22*, 23, *25*, *26*, 29, 31,
    37, 75, 130
    Central Gaulish (CG) 19
    East Gaulish (EG) 19
    South Gaulish (SG) 19
sand-tempered greyware, GHL: sooting *66*, 87
sandy buff ware, GHL 98
sandy greywares, GHL 73
sandy orange ware, GHL 98
Saxon 139
  GHL 49, *58*, 97, 98, 100, 122
  GSS 41

pottery (*cont.*)
Severn Valley oxidized ware, GSS *21*, *22*
Severn Valley wares *23*, 27, 80, *97*, *125*, 126, 136
  ending of 89
  limescale 87
  GHL 59, *63–6*, 68, 71, **81–2**, *82*, 95, 96
    small finds 93–5, *94*
  GSS 20, *23*, 24, *25*, *26*, 27, *28*, 29, 31, 37, 130
shell-gritted wares *23*
  GSS 20, *21*, *22*, 23–4, *23*, *25*, *26*, 27, *28*, 31
shell-tempered wares *71*
  GHL *60*, 68, 71, **73–4**, 96
    sooting *60*, 87
shell/limestone-tempered ware 32
shelly wares 97
sooting and limescale deposits 87
South-Western Brown Slipped ware *61*, 78, *79*, *80*, *96*
  GHL *61*, 68, 69, *80*
Southern Shell-Tempered ware 70
  GHL *60*, 71, 73
Spanish amphora, GSS *21*
spindle whorls 77, 92, *94*
stamps
  potters/potters' stamps
    Advocisus 76
    Banuus 76
    Casurius 76
    Cinnamus 76
    Do(v)eccus i (I) 76
    Iullinus 76
    Iustus 76
    Mercator iv (II) 76
    Paternus v (II) 76
    Pugnus group 76
    Pugnus-Secundus group 76
    Regullus 76
  samian ware 74, 75
strainers *27*
tablewares 87
tankards *27*
  GHL
    functional analysis 83, *84–5*
    oxidized *66*, *82*
    Severn Valley ware 59, *63–5*, *82*, 87
  GSS *24*
  Severn Valley ware 80, *125*, 136
Trajanic-Hadrianic period 77
'Tudor Green' ware, GHL 98, 100
vessel types
  GSS 20, **24–31**
    miniature, GSS *27*
Warwickshire grey ware, GHL 100
white *mortaria*, GSS *21*, *22*
White Slip Decorated ware, GHL 98, 100
white wares 81
  GHL *67*, **83**
  GSS *21*, *22*, *25*, *26*
white-coated *mortaria*, GSS 20, *21*, *22*, 27, *28*
white-coated ware, GSS *24*, *25*, *26*
white-slip flagon, GSS *25*
white-slipped, oxidized flagon, GSS *21*, *22*

white-slipped ware, GHL *66*, **82**
Yellow ware, GHL 100
see also tiles
Prestatyn, North Wales: samian ware 76

Quaternary alluvium 1
quernstones 119–20

radiocarbon dating
  defensive area 134, 135
  GHL 36, 114, **120**
    plants 115
    trench A 120
  GSS **36**
rake tooth, iron 105
ramparts
  earthworks
    GHL 43–5, *55*, 128, 129, 136
      pottery 59
    GSS 43, 128, 129
      area B 6, 37
      timber-revetted xv
  town wall 49, 132
    GHL *56*, *58*, 122, 132
    GSS 6, *11*, *13*, 30, 39, 132
Ratae (Leicester): *civitas* capital 1
Rectory Gardens *2*, 3, 36, 133
  crozier head 41
  earthworks *128*, 129
  medieval ox-bow lake 135
red deer bones 34, 111, 112
revetments
  of earthworks 128
    GHL 43, 120
    GSS xv, 10, 37
  stone: of drying kiln, GHL 49
  of town wall 130, 132
    GSS 11, 39, 132
  turf, GHL 43
Rhine, River 130
Richborough: wall defences 131
rims *see under* pottery
river terrace gravel, GSS 6–10, *7*, 36
roads, Roman 130, 137
roe deer bones 111, 112
rosso antico *58*, 100
Royal Oak Passage *2*, 3, 120, 135
rubbish deposits 138
  GHL 109, 111, 122, 127
    town wall 49
  GSS 27, 34, 39, 41
  Segontium 69, 92
Rudston, Humberside 87
rye 112
Ryknild Street 1

St Albans
  town defences 134
  see also Verulamium
Salinae (Droitwich) 1, 96
salt, containers for 96
'Salt Way' 1

sandstone 1, 11, 33, 39
Saxon period
  Shore forts 133, 134
    Pevensey 130, 131
    Portchester 133, 134
  West Stow 77
  see also under pottery
scrub
  vegetation 115
  woodland 35
Segontium, North Wales
  BB1 deposits 69
  common finds *93*
  fort 92
Septimus Severus: coins 137
Severn, River 71
Severn Valley: trade xvi, 122, 139
sex structure: cattle 111
Shakenoak: pottery *80*
shale, GSS *18*, **36**
sheep bones 34, 111, 112, 122, 127
sheet
  iron *32, 33*
  metal clippings 40
  nailed 106
Shore forts, Saxon period 130, 131, 133, 134
Silchester
  defences 128, 135
  pottery *86, 87, 88, 91*
silver
  bracelet 41, 98
  coins 137
sloe 112, 115
slots, GHL 45, *46*, 47, *55*, 121
smiths 105
snaffle bit, iron 105, 106, *107*
snails *18*, **35**, 36, 115
soil analysis, GSS 6, **35–6**
Somerset, north: BB1 pottery 69, 70
sooting/limescale deposits: pottery *87*
spelt 35, 112
spindle-whorls, ceramic 77, 92, *94*
Spittle Brook 1
spoon, copper alloy 104
stone
  building materials
    GHL 45, 100
    GSS 41
  buildings 138
    GHL 45, 121
    GSS 4–6
    Tibbet's Close 138
  drying oven: Bleachfield Street 40
  finds, GHL *58*
  lined-pit, late medieval, GHL 49, *57*, 98, 106
  objects, GHL *58*, *119*, **119–20**
  packing: external tower (bastion), GSS 16
  pads, GHL 47
  samples, GSS *18*
  walls (of structures) 136
  see also buildings; granary buildings; tiles; wall, town

strainers *27*
strap *33*, 105
Stratford: Bard's Walk 98
Stratford House, pottery *23, 27*
Stratford Road, Alcester: No. 52 120
Stratford-on-Avon District Council 42
stratigraphy
  GHL **43–57**
  GSS **6–17**
Stretton-on-Fosse: pottery 83
structural ironwork 104, 105, *108*
  GHL 122
structures
  GHL: post-built 48
  High Street, Alcester: No. 27 136
  Mahany's site M 136
  stone: area C, GSS 4–6
  see also buildings; granary buildings
studs, copper alloy 106
styli, iron 105, 106, *107*, 108
sword mount 98

tankards *see under* pottery
tanning pit (possible): GHL xv, 49, 112–14, 123
tegulae 100, *101*, 102
tessellated pavements 136, 138
tesserae 121, 136, 138
  limestone 100
Tetricus I 38
textile working, domestic 105
Thames Valley sites 111
Thorpe-by-Newark: defences 135
Tibbet's Close xv, 1, *2*, 3, 120, 132, *135*
  animal bone 126
  coins 137
  earthworks *128*
  malting kiln/drying oven 40
  occupation 136, 138
  pottery *23, 24, 27*, 77, *123*, 126
  stone/timber building 137, 138
  town wall 132
Tiddington, Warwickshire 29, *97*
  occupation 138
  Wellstood collection 72
tiles
  ceramic 138
    GHL *58*, **100–2**, *101*
    GSS *18*, 33
  flue, GHL *58*
  GHL *92*, 121
  limestone, GSS 33
  roof 100, 101
  sandstone, GSS 33
  stone 138
    GHL *58*, **100–2**, *101*
    GSS *18*
timber
  buildings 138
    GHL 121
      E: wall 102
      timber/timber-and-stone xv

timber; buildings (*cont.*)
    granary (Coulters Garage site) 4, 37, 38, 134
    medieval shed, GSS 17
    timber/stone: Tibbet's Close 137
  cill beams, GHL 45, 121
  earthworks
    foundations, GSS 1
    revetments
      GHL 43, 128
      GSS xv, 10, 37, 128
  fragments, GHL 106, 114
  lacing: construction of defences 131
  malting process, GHL 122
  piling
    external tower (bastion), GSS 6, 11–16, 33, 36,
      40, 131, 133
    town wall 130–1, 132, 133
      GHL 42, 43, 49, *56*, 122
      GSS xv, 6, 11, *15–16*, 33, 36, 39, 40
  preserved
    GHL *58*
    GSS *18*
  radiocarbon dating, GHL 120
  remains, GHL 123
  see also alder; elder; elm; oak; willow
tines, iron *33*, 106, *107*, 108
Tom Pettifer (Contractors) Ltd 42
Tomlinson, R A: excavations *2*, 3, *128*, 129, 132
Tongres, Belgium
  defensive wall 130
  glass bottles 116
Towcester
  Alchester Road: pottery *90*, 97
  Grammar School: pottery *90*, 97
  pottery 88
tower, external *see* bastion
town wall *see* wall, town
trade
  oil 95
  in pottery 71–2, 76, 89, 122
  Severn Valley xvi, 139
  and town wall 134
Trajanic period
  coinage 124, 137
  pottery 19, 77
trenches
  GHL
    1 48, 122
      ironwork 104, 105
      pottery 68
    2 45, 49, *121*, 122
      coin hoard 109
      ironwork 104, 105
      pottery 68, 69, 70, 71, 73, 78, *79*, 82, 83,
        84–5, 88, *89*
      tiles 101
    3 49, 121
      little ironwork 104
      pottery 68, 71
    4 45, 120
    5 49, 122
      little ironwork 104

    pottery 68, 71, 78, *79*, 82, 83, *84–5*, 88, *89*, *96*
    tiles 101
  7(n) 43, *46*, 47, 48, *50*, *51*, *54*, *55*, 120, 138
    buildings *121*
    ironwork 105, 122
    pottery 59, 68, *70*, 71, *78*, *79*, 81, 82, 83,
      84–5, 88, *89*, 91, 95
    Phase C11 45
    Phase C12 45
    Phase C13 45
    Phase C14 45
    Phase C15 45
  7(s) *53*, *55*, 120
    earthworks 43, 45, *46*, 120
    ironwork 105, 106
    pottery 49, 68, 89, 91, 97, 100
  A 43, 49, *52*, *56*, 122, 138
    flue tile 100
    human burial 111
    ironwork 104, 105, 106
    Period B earthworks 45
    Phase D1 48
    plant remains 112, **114–15**
    pottery 68, 69, 71, 73, 78, *79*, 82, 100
    radiocarbon dating 120
  B 43, 45–7, *46*, *53*, *56*, *121*, 135
    buildings 137–8
    ironwork 105
    ploughmarks 120
    pottery 59–68, *69*, 70, 71, *78*, *79*, 81, 83,
      84–5, *89*, 91, 95
    tiles 100, 101
    Period A 43, *47*
    Phase C21 45, *47*
    Phase C22 *48*
    Phase C23 *49*
  C 43, 45, *46*, 47, 48, 49, *51*, *54*, *56*, *57*, 120, 122
    buildings *121*
    ironwork 105, 106, 122
    plants 112
    pottery 59, 68, *70*, 71, *78*, *79*, 81, 82, 83,
      84–5, 88, *89*, 91, 92, 95, **98–100**, *99*, 120,
      136
    worked bone 109
    Period A 43
    Phase C31 45
    Phase C33 45
  D 43
  E 43
  F 43
  GSS
    area A 4
    area B 4
    area C 4–6
    B 136, 138
    external tower (bastion) 11, 40
    I: area D 6
    II: area D 6
    T2N 38
    town wall foundation *11*, 39
Triassic sandstone 33
Tripontium 78

tufa 100, *121*, 138
turf: earthwork revetment 43, 128

urine storage 87

Valentinian I: coins 39, 137
Verulamium 87
  defences 132, 135
  glass remains 116
  pottery *88*
  see also St Albans
vessels
  glass 116–18, *117*, *118*
  iron 106, *107*, 108
  see also under pottery
villas, evidence for 139
Vindolanda, Northumberland 72, 95
Viriconium (Wroxeter): *civitas* capital 1
Vitruvius: on wall construction 130, 131

wall, town 1, **130–3**
  circuit 132–3
  construction 139
  dating 133
  and early earthworks 129
  function of 134
  occupation 136
  ramparts *see under* ramparts
  significance 127
  structure 130–2
  GHL xv, 43, *52*, 111
    construction 43, 48–9, **122**, 131, 132
    finds *58*
    human burial 49, *58*, 106, 111, 122
    ironwork 105
    pottery 58
    stone finds 120
    timber piles 42, 43, 49, *56*, 122
  GSS xv, 4, 6, *13–17*, **38–9**, 122
    bone finds 34
    construction xvi, *6*, *11*, 30, 37, 38, 131, 132
    destruction 31, 38, 41
    foundations 33
    mortar 11, *18*
    occupation 136

  pottery 40
  timber piling xv, 6, 11, *15–16*, 33, 36, 39, 40
  see also bastion
wallhooks, iron 105
walls
  post-and-slot, area C structure, GSS 6
  traces of, GSS 38
Warwick: Bridge End 98
Warwickshire County Council 4
Warwickshire Museum 4, 42, 58, 59, 73, 136, 137
Wasperton, Warwickshire 98
waterlogged plant remains *see* plant remains
waterlogged timber piles
  external tower (bastion) 6
  town wall 11, 49
wattle: fencing 128
wattle and daub, GHL 45, 121
weeds 35, 112, 115, 136
wells
  Castle Street, Chester 77
  GHL 100
  possible, GSS (area B) 17, 29
  pottery deposits 87
West Stow: Saxon village 77
wetland plants 115
wheat *18*, 35, 40, 112
whetstones 119
Whitehall Farm, Wiltshire: pottery 82
wild plants *113–14*
willow 114, 123, 130
Winchester 137
  Lankhills Cemetery 116
window glass 115, 116, *118*
wire, copper alloy 104
wood *see* timber
woodland 35, 114, 115
wool 111
writing equipment, iron 104, 105, 106, *107*, *108*, 122
Wycomb, Gloucestershire 79, *80*, *96*

Xanten, Germany: defensive wall 130

York: inhumation burial 116